The Dönme

*Jewish Converts, Muslim Revolutionaries,
and Secular Turks*

Marc David Baer

Stanford University Press

Stanford, California

Stanford University Press
Stanford, California

Printed in the United States of America

Library of Congress Cataloging-in-Publication Data

Baer, Marc David, 1970-
  The Dönme : Jewish converts, Muslim revolutionaries, and
secular Turks / Marc David Baer.
    p. cm.
  Includes bibliographical references and index.
  ISBN 978-0-8047-6867-2 (cloth : alk. paper)--
ISBN 978-0-8047-6868-9 (pbk. :   )
  1. Dönmeh--History. 2. Jews--Turkey--History. 3. Muslim
converts from Judaism--Turkey--History. 4. Turkey--Ethnic
relations. 5. Turkey--History--Ottoman Empire, 1288-1918.
I. Title.
  DS135.T8B33 2010
  956'.004924--dc22   2009024653

Typeset by Bruce Lundquist in 10.9/13 Adobe Garamond

For Firuze and Azize, every day a miracle

Contents

Preface

Over the past few years, hundreds of thousands of copies of two books by Soner Yalçın entitled *Efendi: Beyaz Türklerin büyük sırrı* (Master: The White Turks' Big Secret) and *Efendi 2: Beyaz Müslümanların büyük sırrı* (Master 2: The White Muslims' Big Secret) have been sold in Turkey.[1] The first purports to uncover the secret Jewish identity of the secular elite that has guided the nation for over a century; the sequel claims to unmask the hidden Jews within leading religious Muslim families. The cover of *Musanın çocukları Tayyip ve Emine* (Moses' Children Tayyip and Emine) by Ergün Poyraz, the second best-selling book in Turkey in 2007, is a photomontage of Turkish religious Prime Minister Tayyip Erdoğan and his headscarf-wearing wife Emine—both of Jewish origin, it contends—trapped within a Star of David.[2] Everyone important in Turkey, it seems, has Jewish ancestry. Ghost Jews haunt the Turkish popular imagination.[3] Many Turkish secularists believe that Prime Minister Erdoğan is a crypto-Jew working to undermine Turkey's secular order. Islamists and, increasingly, large segments of the Turkish reading public think atheist Jews overthrew the Ottoman sultan, dissolved his Islamic empire, replaced it with an anti-Muslim secular republic led by the "secret Jew" Mustafa Kemal Atatürk, and still today control the country.[4]

The Republic of Turkey has in fact never been led by a secret Jew. Nevertheless, the popularity of sensational accounts about secret Jewish plotters scheming to undermine Turkey has shed light on a group that would otherwise have remained lost to history. A group of people who seem to have acted as crypto-Jews did exist for over two centuries in Ottoman Salonika and later, after the First Balkan War, when the city surrendered to the Greeks in 1912, in Greek Thessaloníki, and then after the Greek-Turkish Population Exchange of 1923–24, in Turkish Istanbul. Whether we call them *Ma'aminim* (Hebrew, Believers), as they called themselves, or *Dönmeler* (Turkish, Converts; hereafter Dönme), as others called them, either way, both terms refer to the descendants of Jews who converted to Islam along with their messiah Rabbi Shabbatai Tzevi three centuries ago. Shabbatai Tzevi's story, and that of the first generation of his followers, has been told by Gershom Scholem and others,[5] but the ethno-religious identity, history, and experience of the descendants of the original Dönme in the modern period remains unexplored. Although many believe conspiracy theories about the Dönme, very few know the real character and history of the group. The aim of this book is to answer a number of questions. To what extent is it appropriate to refer to these descendants of Jewish converts simply as Jews? If their beliefs and practices placed them outside the Jewish fold, by what means did they maintain their distinction from Jews and Muslims, and why? How did they view themselves, how did others view them, and how did these perceptions change over time? What role did the group play in late Ottoman and early Turkish republican history? Whether describing conversion from one religious tradition to another, or from a religious way of being to a secular one, how do we know when conversion has occurred? What are the limits to being a Jew, a Muslim, a Turk, or a Greek?

After their initial conversion, the Dönme were accepted as Muslims for two centuries, and by the end of the nineteenth century, they had risen to the top of Salonikan society. From that vantage point, they were able to help bring about new ways of thinking, and of being in the world, in the Ottoman Empire. However, they fervently maintained a separate ethno-religious identity and firm social boundaries, preserved by detailed genealogies, endogamous marriage practices, and separate schools and cemeteries. The Dönme helped transform Ottoman Salonika into a cosmopolitan city by promoting the newest innovations in trade and finance, urban reform, and modern education, combining morality and science, literature, architecture, and local politics. Their greatest and most controversial contribution was in serving as a driving force behind the Committee of Union and Progress (hereafter CUP), the secret society of Young Turks that dethroned the last powerful sultan, Abdülhamid II, following the 1908 revolution.

Soon after the revolution, the Dönme faced a double-pronged attack. In Istanbul, they were castigated for their membership in what many perceived to be the atheist and immoral CUP and the decision to remove the sultan from power. For the first time their Islamic faith and practice were also doubted. They were not only targeted for what they believed, but for what they did, namely, engage in foreign economic networks and local politics. After Salonika fell to Greece in 1912, there was no room in the city for pluralism. In what became Greek Thessaloníki, some Dönme managed to hold on to their political and financial capital, but after the establishment of the Republic of Turkey just over a decade later they were expelled from Greece, which could not tolerate "non-Greek" elements with substantial financial connections beyond the nation-state. In their new homeland, Turkey, which had seen a decade of anti-Dönme rhetoric, the Dönme faced opponents who used ethnicized religion (conflating being Turkish with being Muslim) and racialized nationalism (only accepting those with "Turkish blood") to deny them a secure place in the secular Turkish nation-state. Relating to this external pressure was a turn away from endogamy, which brought about the real end of Dönme distinctness. The greatest irony is that although they had contributed to the major transformations replacing the empire with the nation-state, the Dönme dissolved as a group during the process.

A further irony is the way the Dönme have been remembered. To their admirers, they were enlightened secularists and Turkish nationalists who fought against the dark forces of superstition and religious obscurantism. But to their opponents, they were atheists, or simply Jews who had engaged in a secret Jewish plot to dissolve the Islamic empire and replace it with an anti-Muslim secular republic led by a crypto-Jew. Both points of view, whether complimentary or critical, assumed that the Dönme were anti-religious. However, the historical record shows that the Dönme created a new form of ethno-religious belief, practice, and identity, which made them distinct, while promoting a morality, ethics, and spirituality that reflected their origins at the intersection of Jewish Kabbalah and Islamic Sufism. Their syncretistic religion, along with a rigorously maintained, distinct ethnic identity, meant that they were neither Jews nor orthodox Muslims.

The three-centuries-long history of the Dönme in the Ottoman Empire, Greece, and the Republic of Turkey has not been the subject of a major academic study. There are many reasons for this. One is the idea that serious scholars should avoid controversial matters, especially the stuff of conspiracy theories. Another is the ethical minefield of writing about a secret community whose descendants neither want nor deserve to be exposed. But the biggest roadblock to writing about the Dönme is simply that discovering with certainty who members of this group were and locating them in Ottoman and Turkish historical sources is nearly impossible for an outsider. The Dönme were officially considered Muslim, had common Muslim names such as Ahmet and Mehmet, and are thus indistinguishable from other Muslims in the Ottoman archival records available in Thessaloníki and Istanbul and in published Turkish sources. In order to compensate for the difficulty of studying this group, whose identity was an open, if not openly recorded, secret, a historian has to draw from a number of architectural, epigraphic, oral, archival, literary, and official sources, which do not explicitly state that the people in question are descendants of the followers of Shabbatai Tzevi. Only by combining sources can one determine who belonged to the group. In order to investigate those invisible in the nineteenth century, one must first find them in the twentieth century, when major shifts in historical processes made them visible, and then work backward. To the best of my ability as a historian, I have written a narrative moving forward, correlating information contained in written and oral sources. We know the most about the Dönme in the early twentieth century, second most about the group in the late nineteenth century. After 1950 and before 1850, the picture is much less clear, because we have fewer and less reliable sources for these periods. This book thus chiefly deals with the period about which I am most confident in my sources. Short vignettes dramatizing some of the key events and illustrating the lives and sentiments of participants in them, based on historical documents, are embedded in the narrative.

I do not come from a Dönme family, nor did I marry into one. Because I am an outsider to the group, the difficult process of sleuthing together the narrative of this book would not have been possible without the help of many people. It has not been an easy or transparent process and has required much labor, imagination, chance encounter, and good fortune. First, I had to locate and make contact with descendants of Dönme in Turkey, the United States, and western Europe who were willing to discuss their family histories. Along with the very few who allow themselves to be publicly identified as descendants of the group, I discovered three types of interviewees. One consists of those who told me a great deal, but made me promise never to publish anything about the group, because it would only be taken the wrong way. I have honored their concerns and refrained from publishing significant material I collected from them. Another group of interviewees were those who told me everything they knew and provided ample documentation, but would not permit me to use their real names. The final group were those who allowed me to use the names of their ancestors but not their own.

There are many challenges to conducting research within a culture of secrecy. Some Dönme came to me desperate to learn about their religion and history. Many demanded anonymity. Some wanted publicity. Others sought to persuade me not to research the subject, thus exposing their secrets, whereas others wanted to use me to promote their intragroup interests and prove their claims. Some professed not to know that well-known relatives of theirs (who publicly acknowledged their identity) had spoken on the subject. One day people greeted me with warm receptions and a willingness to be interviewed for hours, to discuss family lore, to show me photographs, postcards, and genealogies, and ask me to decipher Ottoman documents (since the 1928 language reform, Turkish has been written in Latin script). They would offer to introduce me to all of their relatives. But the next day or the next time I called, or the next few times I called, they were either unreachable, or said their relatives were ill or busy, or out of town.

At first, I thought these people feared exposure of their names. Yet why, in that case, had they agreed to the initial meeting and been so willing to provide so much family history and document it? Were they afraid of being recognized for who they were? Then I realized I was playing an important function for many individuals and families: I served as both a release and accomplice. I would listen to all of their pent-up stories and jumbled histories and, they hoped, sort them out or make sense of them. I was in on the secret, yet not part of the secretive group. Coming from abroad, with the stamp of the academy, I could confirm the history underlying their strange stories, the odd instances of discrimination, the bizarre things their grandmothers had told them. And then, freed of the photographs, and the genealogies, and the stories, they could go back to blending in, and being unmarked secular, nationalist Turks, obscuring their grandparents' strange practices with a heavy dose of secular Turkish historical narrative.

Despite challenges such as these, information culled from the oral histories I conducted, supplemented with genealogies, provided names that allowed me to trace a number of families back several generations. Next, I surveyed inscriptions written in Ottoman Turkish script and modern Turkish on tombstones at the main Dönme cemeteries in Istanbul (in modern Thessaloníki, these no longer exist), which contain the graves of thousands of people who were mainly born in Salonika around 1880 and buried in Istanbul in the 1930s. This allowed me to learn their names prior to the adoption of surnames in 1937. Once I compiled information on their social and economic positions and family links in Salonika from the tombstones, I then turned to the Ottoman archives. At the Atatürk Library in Istanbul, I examined the official *Selânik Vilâyeti Salnamesi* (Yearbook of the Province of Salonika), published between 1885 and 1908. I used this source to gather more information on the economic, cultural, and political role of leading Dönme families in Salonika, and their social and financial links and networks. Additional interviews with descendants informed me of the neighborhoods in which Dönme had lived in Salonika, allowing me to then systematically search two additional Ottoman-language sources. The first is the 1906 Arazi ve Emlaki Esasi Defteri (Register of Lands and Properties), a neighborhood-by-neighborhood property register preserved at the Historical Archive of Macedonia in Thessaloníki. The second is the Muhtelit Mübadele Komisyonu Tasfiye Talepnameleri, the 1923–25 Records of the Mixed Commission, which list the wealth and property of Dönme who were part of the population exchange between Greece and Turkey. These files are today kept at the Archive of the Republic in Ankara. From these two sources, I learned about the web of relations Dönme once had in Salonika, enabling me to locate their co-owned family residences and family businesses, and to map their spatial presence and impact in the city. Other sources in Ottoman and Turkish from the Dönme perspective include the literary journal *Gonca-i Edeb*, histories of the two Dönme schools, and memoirs published in Turkey. I also learned much from the Ottoman and Turkish newspapers and journals *Akbaba, Akşam, Büyük Doğu, Cumhuriyet, Mihrab, Resimli Dünya, Resimli Gazete, Resimli Şark, Sebîlürreşat, Son Saat, Ulus, Vatan, Vakit, Volkan,* and *Yedi Gün.*

Several visits to Thessaloníki afforded me an opportunity to investigate the few traces of the Dönme that remain, namely, the design and layout of buildings such as the New Mosque and seaside villas, and enabled me to interview the people who currently work in these buildings. I also found useful Greek memoirs, the Jewish *Journal de Salonique* and the Greek *Efēmeris tōn Balkaniōn, Faros tēs Makedonias,* and *Makedonia* newspapers, turn-of-the-century Greek tourist guidebooks, commercial guidebooks, archives of the chamber of commerce and industry, the file of associations and clubs, and voting registers. Finally, I utilized American, Austrian, British, and French diplomatic and commercial reports from Ottoman Salonika.

The Introduction, "Following the Jewish Messiah Turned Muslim, 1666–1862," is mainly concerned with the development of the unique ethno-religious identity of the Dönme as they and others perceived it. It explains the complicated religion, culture of secrecy, and history of the Dönme from their origins in the wake of the messianic movement of Rabbi Shabbatai Tzevi to when the Ottoman state first recognized their distinctness from other Muslims. It explores Shabbatai Tzevi's conversion to Islam, the ensuing conversion of one group of his followers, the co-alescing of the group in Salonika, and its splitting into three sects (Yakubi, Karakaş, and Kapancı). Arguing against how the Dönme are portrayed today and how they have been depicted in Greek, Jewish, and Turkish historiography, which consider the Dönme to have been Jews, it describes what made Dönme religion distinct from Judaism and Islam. The chapter considers not only Dönme religion and ethnic identity, but also what Jews thought of the Dönme, and seeks to discover in what ways a comparison with "crypto-Jews" is accurate.

After the Introduction, the book is divided into three sections. Part I concerns the Dönme in Ottoman Salonika. Chapter 1, "Keeping It Within the Family, 1862–1908," focuses on Dönme belief, practice, and boundary maintaining mechanisms. Chapter 2, "Religious and Moral Education: Schools and Their Effects," concerns their schools. Chapter 3, "Traveling and Trading," explores the social and economic networks of the Dönme. Together, the chapters have as their main purpose illustrating the inter-relation between the worldview of the Dönme and their impact in Salonika between 1862 and the Constitutional Revolution. The Dönme way of being is illustrated by successful turn-of-the-twentieth-century Saloni-kan Dönme merchant families that maintained a particularistic religious core and firm social boundaries—especially evident in detailed genealo-gies, endogamous marriage practices, segregated residential patterns, and distinct mosque and cemeteries. An excellent example is also presented by the two Dönme schools, which reflected the role religion and morality played in Dönme life and influenced both Salonika's literary scene and Dönme architecture.

Part II concerns the period between the end of empire and rise of the nation-state. Chapter 4, "Making a Revolution, 1908," concerns the history and experience of the Dönme during the Ottoman Constitutional Revolution and in the context of racism and nationalism, when other Muslims began to take notice and attack them. The chapter explores how many leading Dönme entered first local politics, especially seeking the office of the mayor, and then turned to Freemasonry and revolutionary organizations, including the CUP. The chapter in particular addresses the role of the Dönme in the 1908 revolution, as well as in the "Action Army" sent to Istanbul to crush a counterrevolution a year later. A main question the chapter addresses is why the Dönme began to attract so much attention after the revolution, particularly in Dervish Vahdeti's journal *Volkan* (Volcano). Responding to conspiracy theories of secret Jews and world revolution, the chapter compares the Dönme and Soviet Jews, who played a disproportionate role in the Bolshevik Revolution.

Four short years after the Constitutional Revolution, following Ottoman losses in the two Balkan Wars, Salonika was conquered by Greece. Chapter 5, "Choosing Between Greek Thessaloníki and Ottoman Istanbul, 1912–1923," analyzes how the Dönme responded to the new political circumstances. The chapter explores how the new Greek administration of Thessaloníki viewed the Dönme, especially those in local politics, the economic and political situation of the Dönme who remained in the city during this period, the fate of Dönme institutions such as schools, and the careers of leaders, including the last Ottoman mayor, a Dönme. After discussing how some Dönme chose to leave Greek Thessaloníki and reestablish their lives in Istanbul, the chapter discusses the racist written attacks they faced in their new homeland. These included a vicious anonymous caricature linking the group and their international ties to moral and physical corruption, claiming that the Dönme were the main force spreading immorality, charges rebutted by the army veteran Major Sadık, son of Suleiman, who emphasized Dönme moral piety in a secular age.

Part III concerns the Dönme in Turkish Istanbul. Chapter 6, "Losing a Homeland, 1923–1924," explores the population exchange between Greece and Turkey, which involved the expulsion of all Salonikan Dönme from their ancestral home to Turkey, and how they managed this unwelcome transition, establishing themselves in a nation-state whose population was loathe to receive them. Chapter 7, "Loyal Turks or Fake Muslims? Debating Dönme in Istanbul, 1923–1939," interprets controversies in Turkey about Dönme race and religion. It concerns the new challenges Dönme faced after arriving in Istanbul, how they met them, and how the challenges in turn changed them, and how others viewed them then. This era witnessed the creation of a homogeneous, secular, Turkish national identity from a plural, religious Ottoman identity, debates about who was a Turk, the Turkification of Istanbul, and the change from Ottoman indifference to Turkish debate with and fierce opposition to the Dönme. Dönme also played a major role in the public debate over the history, religion, and identity of the group and its ability to integrate into the nation. While Mehmet Karakaşzade Rüştü took a racialized nationalist line, arguing that the Dönme were racially and religiously Jews and foreigners and not Muslims and Turks, Ahmet Emin Yalman contended that they had always been loyal servants of the nation and were as a group in the process of total dissolution within it. Yalman was countered by many who saw evidence of the continued practice of Dönme religion and perpetuation of their identity. One such was İbrahim Alâettin Gövsa, principal of a Dönme girls' school in Istanbul.

Chapter 8, "Reinscribing the Dönme in the Secular Nation-State," and Chapter 9, "Forgetting to Forget, 1923–1944," focus on how Dönme and others failed to allow the group to assimilate into Turkish and Greek society. Chapter 8 answers the question of how the Dönme maintained their social and religious distinctness and institutions in their new homeland by focusing on self-segregation and separate schools and cemeteries in Istanbul. A change is noticeable. Whereas the Dönme schools in Salonika had produced religious youth comfortable in international contexts, in Istanbul, they were charged with producing secular nationalists. Chapter 9 begins by exploring how those who remained in Greek Thessaloníki faced charges of disloyalty and foreignness similar to those brought against the Dönme in Istanbul. In Istanbul, the wealth tax episode during World War II—which when implemented marked Dönme as distinct from Muslims—showed the failure of both Dönme attempts to assimilate and the secular Turkish nation-state's promise to treat them as equals.

The Conclusion traces how the transition from cosmopolitanism to nationalism and racism to antisemitism affected the Dönme and memory of the Dönme. It asks what impact knowledge of the Holocaust had on the Dönme and narrates the Dönme experience in the era immediately following World War II. Finally, the Postscript discusses the impact of the return after 1950 of articulations of crude anti-Dönme rhetoric, culminating in attacks on descendants of Dönme, including an attempt in 1952 to assassinate Ahmet Emin Yalman.

Acknowledgments

My greatest thanks are due the Dönme interviewees who agreed to share so much of their hidden or misunderstood past with me. Because of the sensitivity of this book's topic in Turkey, I do not refer to my interviewees by name or even location unless their identity as Dönme is already publicly known.

Many people provided expertise that led me to, assisted me with, or analyzed the oral and written sources upon which this study is based. In Istanbul, Rıfat Bali shared with me his endless knowledge of Jewish and Dönme history, as well as hard-to-reach sources. He also introduced me to Ilgaz Zorlu, with whom I first began to conduct research. Paul Bessemer and I had many discussions about Mehmet Cavid and the Dönme. A descendant of the Kapancı family who goes by the pseudonym Barry Kapandji provided indefatigable energy and original sources including family genealogies, postcards, and photographs. A Turkish student bravely accompanied me to the main Dönme cemetery, giving me courage in the face of stray dogs and ghosts. Thomas Berchtold helped with the deciphering of Ottoman-language tombstones. Faruk Birtek and Çağlar Keyder discussed the socioeconomic dimensions of the subject with me. Erdem Kabadayı assisted me in deciphering Ottoman postcards. The staff of the Atatürk Library provided published sources. The official historian of the Jewish community, Naim Güleryüz, graciously agreed to an interview. In Ankara, Director Ahmet Ceylan and the helpful and earnest staff of the Archive of the Republic enabled me to successfully conduct my research in a very short period of time. Mustafa Özyürek facilitated matters in Turkey in general. Without his opening of doors, my research in that country would not have been very fruitful.

In Thessaloníki, I was assisted by my energetic research assistants Paris Papamichos Chronakis and Sotiris Dimitriadis. Eleni Karanastassi, Konstantinos Giantsis, and Virginia Mavridou provided much-needed sweetened iced coffees and assistance at the Historical Archive of Macedonia. Eleni Limpaki narrated to me the history of the Ahmet Kapancı villa. John C. Alexander and Vassilis Demetriadis shared with me their long experience working with sources in Thessaloníki. Alberto Nar, the official historian of the Jewish community, acceded to my request for an interview. I was honored by an invitation to present my research before the Group for the Study of the History of the Jews of Greece at the University of Macedonia. Nicholas Stavroulakis, Rena Molho, and Tony Molho gave important feedback. Penelope Papailias again facilitated matters in Greece in general. Without her, everything Greek would be a mystery to me.

In the United States, Engin Akarlı and Heath Lowry first introduced me to the topic and to Dönme contacts in the United States and Turkey. Fatma Müge Göçek first discussed the socioeconomic dimensions of the Dönme experience with me. Timothy Baldwin introduced me to studying the Dönme in Greece. Aron Rodrigue and Julia Phillips Cohen filled in gaps in my knowledge of Sephardic Jewish history. Shaul Magid shared his knowledge of rabbinic debates about conversion. Robert Dankoff helped translating Ottoman literature. Sonja Hamilton and Adam Guerin assisted me with questions about French material, Richard Wittman and Laurel Plapp with German.

Many audiences and fellow participants in workshops and seminars in the United States and Europe gave much crucial feedback, which shaped the book as it developed. This includes the Leslie Humanities Center at Dartmouth College, where a fellowship for the semester-long seminar "Converting Cultures: Religion, Ideology, and Transformations of Modernity" enabled me to think about conversion from religious to secular identity. The seminar was convened by Kevin Reinhart and Dennis Washburn, and I benefited enormously from conversations with Fellows Ertan Aydın, Laura Jenkins, Barbara Reeves-Ellington, Nancy Stalker, and Alan Tansman. Serving as a commentator on a panel at the conference with which the seminar culminated allowed me to realize the global context of what the Dönme experienced in Turkey. Several of us—Laura, Barbara, Nancy, and I—convened a panel at the annual meeting of the American

Historical Association, where we benefited from the keen comments of Eliza Kent.

My understanding of the place of the Dönme and minorities in modern nation-states and ethno-religious identity of the Dönme was developed in several workshops. These include "Armenians and the End of the Ottoman Empire" at the University of Chicago and "Contextualizing the Armenian Experience in the Ottoman Empire" at the University of Michigan organized by Ron Suny and Müge Göçek, "Borderlands: Ethnicity, Identity, and Violence in the Shatter-zone of Empires Since 1848," convened by Omer Bartov at Brown University, the SIAS summer institute on "Hierarchy, Marginality, and Ethnicity in Muslim Societies (7th Century to Second World War)," held in Berlin at the Wissenschaftskolleg zu Berlin and in Princeton at Princeton University and organized by Mark Cohen and Gudrun Kraemer, the workshop entitled "After Antiquity What? Jews and Greeks in Byzantium and Modern Greece: Symbiosis, Tensions, Cultural Transfer," organized in Berlin, Germany, by Saskia Dönitz and Joannis Niehoff-Panagiotidis at the Freie Universität Berlin and the Wissenschaftskolleg zu Berlin; "Jewish Religion in Ottoman Lands," organized by Matthias Lehmann and Kemal Sılay at Indiana University, Bloomington; and "Diaspora and Return: Sephardic Jews Beyond Spain," Sephardic Culture and History Conference, University of California, Irvine, organized by Michelle Hamilton. Aron Rodrigue and Alexander Orlov invited me to present the Dönme to Jewish Studies audiences at an early stage of my research at Stanford University and the University of Pittsburgh, respectively. Aron Rodrigue invited me to return to Stanford and present the Dönme to the Mediterranean Studies Forum just before I sent the book to the Press.

My thinking on cosmopolitanism was shaped by fellow participants in a number of conferences. These include "Global Cities / World Histories," at the 22nd Annual History & Theory Conference, University of California, Irvine, "The Late Ottoman Port Cities and Their Inhabitants: Subjectivity, Urbanity, and Conflicting Orders," convened by Malthe Fuhrmann and Vangelis Kechriotis, organized by the Mediterranean Programme of the Robert Schuman Centre for Advanced Studies at the European University Institute, Florence, Italy, and "Thinking Through Turkey, Theorizing the Political," at the Center for Research in the Arts Humanities and Social Sciences (CRASSH), University of Cambridge, United Kingdom, organized by Yael Navarro-Yashin and Meltem Ahıska.

My approach was also shaped by commentators and audiences at invited lectures in U.S. and European departments of history including those at the University of Southern California, Williams College, Tulane University, the University of California, Irvine, the University of California, Santa Cruz, and the Albert-Ludwigs-Universität, Freiburg, Germany. Research institutes in Canada and Europe, including the American Research Institute in Turkey, Istanbul, the Wissenschaftskolleg zu Berlin's The Middle East in Europe / Europe in the Middle East lecture series, and Centre canadien d'études allemandes et européennes, Université de Montréal, Montréal, Canada, were other locales where I discussed the Dönme with engaged audiences. I thank Tony Greenwood, Nora Lafi, Gudrun Kraemer, Georges Khalil, and Till van Rahden for these latter three opportunities to receive valuable feedback on the Dönme.

Martha Fuller's "Autobiography, Memoir, and Fiction" course at the University of California, Irvine greatly improved my ability to tell and, more important, show the history of the Dönme. Matt Goldish and Hasan Kayalı read the book in parts. The graduate students in my "Transgressing Boundaries: Race, Religion, Gender" course at the University of California, Irvine, two anonymous readers for the Press, and Esra Özyürek read it in full. Peter Dreyer's meticulous editing increased the clarity of the narrative.

Esra Özyürek has helped make this project bloom from a dissertation proposal (for a dissertation never written) thirteen years ago into the book it is today. She even gave it its title. For all of this time she has been my intellectual partner and role model, as well as beloved partner, for which I am deeply thankful. We were doubly blessed by the births of Firuze and Azize shortly after I completed the manuscript. Their arrival has confirmed that miracles do happen. Twice.

In the end, the book's faults are entirely my responsibility, and whatever strengths it has are largely thanks to others.

The core of the book's argument was first presented in two articles: "The Double Bind of Race and Religion: The Conversion of the Dönme to Turkish Secular Nationalism," *Comparative Studies in Society and History* 46, no. 4 (October 2004): 678–712, and "Globalization, Cosmopolitanism, and the Dönme in Ottoman Salonica and Turkish Istanbul," *Journal of World History* 18, no. 2 (June 2007): 141–69.

A Note on Transcription

Official modern Turkish orthography has been used in transcribing Ottoman and Turkish words in the Latin script. Readers unacquainted with Turkish should note the following: *c* = *j* as in John, *ç* = *ch* as in church, *ğ* = soft *g* lengthens the preceding vowel, *ı* = similar to the *u* in radium, *ö* = French *eu* as in *deux*, *ü* = French *u* as in *durée*, and *ş* = *sh* as in ship. Diacritical marks have been minimized. For some terms, modern anglicized versions have been used.

The city known to modern Greeks as Thessaloníki was called Selânik by the Ottomans. In this book, "Salonika" refers to the city during the Ottoman era, while "Thessaloníki" is employed for the Greek period, after 1912–13. The ancient Greek name of the city is transliterated as Thessalonikē, however, and this form appears in book and article titles that have been transliterated from Greek. The name of Constantinople was not officially changed to Istanbul until after the founding of the Turkish Republic in 1923. Nevertheless, "Istanbul" is used here to refer to the city in both Ottoman and Turkish periods. The use of the names "Salonika," "Thessaloníki," and "Istanbul" does not imply support of any nationalist view.

Only in 1934 did citizens of the Turkish Republic adopt surnames. Thus, in that year Mustafa Kemal became Atatürk, Ahmet Emin became Ahmet Emin Yalman, and Mehmet Zekeriya and his wife Sabiha became Mehmet and Sabiha Sertel. In order to avoid confusion, I have used surnames throughout the text, even for periods before the historical actors went by these names.

The Dönme

Introduction

Following the Jewish Messiah Turned Muslim,
1666–1862

The Conversion of Rabbi Shabbatai Tzevi

We can trace the origins of the Dönme to a single event on a single day. On October 16, 1666, Rabbi Shabbatai Tzevi, who numerous Jews from northern Europe to southern Yemen believed was the messiah, converted to Islam before the presence of Ottoman Sultan Mehmet IV in the New Pavilion of the Royal Palace in Edirne in eastern Thrace. Ottoman chronicles from that time allow us to reconstruct what occurred before the gaze of the sultan:

§ The twenty-five-year-old with hazel eyes outlined with kohl gazes down unobserved from a latticed window upon the meeting of his ministers in his palace in the frontier capital.[1] Sultan Mehmet IV is immaculately dressed, although no one can see him. On top of an embroidered gold inner garment, he wears a spotted violet and gold embroidered cloak, on his head a simple cylinder wrapped in fine white cloth, with a green emerald the size of half an egg as an aigrette. He prefers to be out hunting in the forest, not sitting in this tower. But the extraordinary situation deserves his attention.

Under his gaze, are several men sitting around a very large red velvet divan. The black-bearded, short-sighted, and overweight grand vizier Fazıl Ahmet Pasha is on campaign against the infidels in the west.[2] In his place is the deputy grand vizier, Mustafa Pasha, dressed in a white satin coat covered in sable fur and a two-foot high turban composed of a cylinder-shaped base, around which he has wrapped a white muslin cloth, ornamented by a red cloth at the tip. Sitting next to him is the leading Muslim religious authority in the empire, Sheikhulislam Minkarizade

Yahya Efendi, who is recognizable by his more simple white fur. The Kurdish Imperial Preacher Vani Mehmet Efendi sits farthest away from the others, at the edge of the divan. In his captivating voice, he interrogates a thick bearded, owl-faced, humble, turban-wearing forty-year old rabbi from Izmir.

"The Jewish traitors believe you are a prophet!"[3]

God forbid! The sultan can not believe this. It's preposterous! While his brave and pious warriors are struggling to conquer the last infidel holdout on Crete, the Venetian fortress of Candia (now Heraklion), Jews have ceased work and flocked to the side of this rebel, who has declared that he and not his eminence should rule the imperial dominions. How could he dare contradict the fact that Muhammad was the seal of the prophets? The rabbi had been banished to a fortress, but the Jews also gathered there. Since according to their false beliefs, their saying "This is our prophet" had begun to disturb the peace, his eminence had been compelled to summon the rabbi.

Knowing that his execution is certain, the rabbi, who alternated between ecstatic bouts of enthusiasm and devastating fits of anguish and suffering,[4] seems to be in the latter mood. With dull eyes, he declares in a monotone, through barely parted lips, "all the nonsense said about me is not true."

Quickly, the Imperial Preacher interjects, "In that case, why don't you become a Muslim? After this council there is no possibility of escape: either come to the faith, or you will be immediately put to death. Become a Muslim at last, and we shall intercede for you with our gracious sultan."

The sultan observes that "the rabbi, with the guidance of God, the King who forgives, at that time became shown the right path, ennobled with the light of faith and a believer responsible to God. He deemed that from his exalted graciousness, a salaried position at the Middle Gate valued at 150 silver coins was proper for him." Having made the fake prophet accept the true prophet, the sultan slips out of the tower, changes into his riding clothes, mounts his horse, and pursues the chase. Mehmet IV thinks that he has converted the messianic claimant into a proselytizing force for Islam. But the aims of the converter and the converted are not always the same.

Faced with the stark choice of converting to Islam or martyrdom, Shabbatai Tzevi chose to change his religion. Since most Ottoman Jews traced their origins to Spanish and Portuguese Jews who had either converted or faced the choice of converting, his decision was not that shocking. Nonetheless, it split his followers into three groups. Most lost faith in him and returned, alienated, to normative Judaism. The German Jewish writer Glückel of Hameln, mother of twelve children, compared the letdown to suffering through nine months of pregnancy and birth pains only to break wind.[5] A second group, the Shabbateans, remained Jews, but furtively maintained their faith in Shabbatai Tzevi's messiahship. They placed special emphasis on Purim, mentioned in two of his commandments, for this Jewish festival celebrates Esther, the queen whose passing as a non-Jew allowed her to be in a position to save all the Jews of the Persian Empire. As late as the eighteenth century, their descendants continued to believe that Shabbatai Tzevi was a prophet and to practice the rituals he had taught. What polemical literature exists between followers of Shabbatai Tzevi and Jews were composed by this group and their opponents as they both sought to come to terms with what the messiahship of Shabbatai Tzevi meant for Jewish theology and Judaism.[6] Many important rabbis in Salonika, Edirne, Amsterdam, London, and Ancona were secret Shabbateans,[7] but the sect had disappeared by the beginning of the nineteenth century.

For one group, however, the radical failure of their messiah ironically led, not to disappointment and despair, but confirmation, renewed confidence, and the ecstasy of knowing that one cannot know the mysteries of God's chosen.[8] After all, "if his followers could believe him when he moved the Sabbath from Friday to Monday, abolished holidays, and emancipated women and let them be called to read from the Torah, then why not believe him when he said 'there is no God, but God'"[9] and Muhammad is God's messenger. Since the forced conversions of Jews in inquisitory Spain and Portugal normalized cryptofaith performance among Jews and promoted the inverse construction of reality, Jewish messiahs had arisen who elevated their intentions over their acts, including conversion to another religion.[10] Many prophets of and later followers of Shabbatai Tzevi were conversos, involuntary Iberian converts, for whom messianism, and above all, the appearance of a converso messiah was so important.[11] What is unique in this case is how this group of Jews set off on a new historical path, forging an ethno-religious identity outside the boundaries of Judaism and Jewishness.

Because he was a converso messiah, one might wish to argue that Shabbatai Tzevi's conversion was not profound, in the sense that it was not based on profound belief in Islam, and that rather, it was quite superficial, because he had been compelled to change religion. However, the profundity of his conversion lay rather in the way he explained what he had done: conversion was a temporary punishment for Jews for failing to recognize the true God that Shabbatai Tzevi had discovered. This third group of followers redoubled their messianic belief by also converting to Islam. They found ample justification in Judaism for this double play. Moses, after all, with whom Shabbatai Tzevi compared himself, remained for a long time in disguise in Egypt.[12] Shabbatai Tzevi's order not to intermarry with Muslims is a near-literal rendering of a passage from the corpus of Jewish law, the Talmud.[13] As Meir Benayahu concluded after having studied the treatises of the first Dönme and their opponents, "But their religion was not the religion of Islam. . . . They became Muslim, but not in order to fulfill its commandments and believe in its faith, rather . . . to effect divine restoration."[14] This was a case of apostasy for the sake of redemption. One had to become a Muslim to initiate the process of repairing the order of the universe to the way it had been prior to Creation and the breaking of the vessels that had contained the sparks of God's emanation.

The followers of Shabbatai Tzevi who believed it necessary to appear to become Muslims, consisting of two to three hundred families (i.e., 1,000 to 1,500 people), converted to Islam in the first few decades after his conversion, but they continued to believe in his messianic calling and his religious beliefs and practices, which emerged at the intersection of Kabbalah and Sufism. They coalesced first in Edirne and then, by 1683, in Salonika, where the major mosques had originally been churches, converted after the conquest of the city by the Ottomans in 1430. By the time of Shabbatai Tzevi's messianic calling, the city was renowned for its Sufis, who followed the path of Mevlana, Jalal ad-Din Rumi;[15] as a haven for conversos; and as a center of Kabbalah and rabbinic scholarship. Since the early sixteenth century, it had had a Jewish majority.[16] Ottoman Salonika was considered by some to be neither Turkish nor Greek, but Jewish; it was, said one writer, "the only Jewish city in Europe (aside from Warsaw)."[17] It is not surprising that it became known as the place where many of the Muslims had originally been Jews.

Shabbatai Tzevi was not the first messiah about whose arrival word was first spread openly and then maintained in secret by his devoted followers in Salonika.[18] Most famously, Paul of Tarsus preached in ancient Thessalonikē spreading the word of Jesus' life and death, and making many converts. The city had then witnessed the spread of Christianity among a secret brotherhood of fervent adherents who prayed in secrecy, recognizing other believers with secret signs and passwords.[19] Shabbatai Tzevi's movement was the second greatest millenarian movement among the Jews after Christianity. Without taking the comparison too far, one can suggest that Shabbatai Tzevi was like Jesus the Messiah to his followers. Like Jesus, Shabbatai Tzevi was a Jew whose Jewish followers established a breakaway movement that emphasized divine renewal, which derived from Judaism but radically diverged from it, abrogating the original laws and becoming something quite different, even if like the first Christians, they too claimed to have discovered the true understanding of the religion and the means of fulfilling divine purpose.[20] The early antinomianism of Shabbatai Tzevi was based on his personal knowledge of God, who directly affirmed or negated the laws Jews lived by and revoked the Torah. Shabbatai Tzevi's followers awaited the messiah's second coming, second advent, or reincarnation, like the first Christians.[21] Like the followers of Jesus after his death, the followers of Shabbatai Tzevi decided to continue a movement "launched with the expectation of a speedy end to the present age."[22] And like the first people who accepted that Muhammad was revealing the word of God, this group of followers also at first called themselves "the Believers," using the Hebrew form of the common Semitic word for belief (Hebrew: *Ma'aminim*; Arabic: *Mu'minun*).[23]

The Establishment of a Group of Converted Followers in Salonika

The nucleus of the Believer community was established in Salonika following the death of Shabbatai Tzevi in 1676 by his Salonikan survivors— his last wife Jochebed, who had converted with the rabbi and had been renamed Aisha, and brother-in-law Yakub Çelebi (Querido), to whom the soul of Shabbatai Tzevi was believed to have transmigrated.[24] Transmigration of souls, or reincarnation, was an important element in the Kabbalah and Sufism, inherited from the earlier cultural milieu in which Jewish and Muslim mystics shared beliefs and practices. In Kabbalah, for example, ever since the twelfth-century *Sefer ha-Bahir* (Book of Brightness), reincarnation had been a favorite topic of Jewish mystics. In Sufism, transmigration and reincarnation were central elements of Bektaşi theosophy prevalent in the regions in which the Dönme religion took hold.[25] The Dönme remained open to outside religious influence, particularly Sufism. Shabbatai Tzevi incorporated both Jewish tradition and Sufism

in his theosophy. Thus one group of his followers, the Karakaş, believed
that he had gathered the seventy souls that Moses had gathered on Mount
Sinai and then redirected them into the Karakaş' bodies. When they married out, they lost those souls; they married each other so as not to lose
the connection to that source, and ultimately, redemption. Theirs was an
otherworldly mission. Thus we see a mixing of Kabbalistic interpretation
of Moses' real duties on Mount Sinai, Sufi understandings of transmigration, and Jewish family values.[26]

Converting Shabbatai Tzevi's antinomianism into ritualized charisma,
Yakub Çelebi established the structures according to which Dönme belief
and practice were organized, so that a self-sustaining and distinct community emerged. Within a century, the size of the community grew to
around six hundred families (perhaps 3,000 people).

A crucial factor in the consolidation and perpetuation of this growing Dönme community was its adherence to the "eighteen commandments" (eighteen being a significant number with life-giving properties
for Jews, as well as for Mevlevi Sufis) laid down by Shabbatai Tzevi during
his lifetime. The oldest extant copy of these dates from roughly a century
after his death.[27] The commandments, which assert that God is one and
that Shabbatai Tzevi is the redeemer and messiah, order Dönme to "be
scrupulous in their observance of some of the precepts of the Muslims,"
and to observe "those things which are exposed to the Muslims' view."[28]
Dönme were to perform all public Muslim customs and rituals so that
other Muslims saw them carrying them out, especially the thirty-day fast
of Ramadan and sacrifice of animals at the time of the Hajj. Seeing them
fulfill the duties of Islam, Muslims would consider them pious Muslims.
Dönme were commanded to not worry or be concerned about whether
engaging in them would have a deleterious effect on their pursuit of the
Dönme path to God. The commandments also admonished Dönme
not to have any relations with other Muslims and to marry only among
themselves.

In practice, Dönme also avoided relations with Jews. The Dönme actively maintained their separate identity, keeping detailed genealogies,
and burying their dead in distinct cemeteries, walled off from others.[29]
To signal their divergence from Jews and Muslims, Dönme developed
their own rituals of burial.[30] Unlike the gravestones in Jewish Ottoman
cemeteries, Dönme tombstones comprised both head- and footstones
and were inscribed in Ottoman script, and their cemeteries were thickly

planted with cypresses, as Muslim cemeteries were. Yet unlike Muslim tombstones, Dönme headstones were rarely topped with turbans.

The symbolism of Dönme tombstones was explained only to members of the group. Dönme existence and persistence was based on secrecy and dissimulation, a radical rupture between public and private practice. As Georg Simmel has written, "The secret offers, so to speak, the possibility of a second world alongside the manifest world; and the latter is decisively influenced by the former."[31] The "second world" created by secrecy protects those who act in secret by making their actions and behavior invisible, thus allowing it to persist. Unlike the people described in Simmel's account, however, the Dönme, at the time of their conversion, had no plans for altering the society in which they lived. From the beginning, however, they engaged in what the anthropologist Michael Taussig calls "public secrecy": applying "the labor of the negative"—or knowing what not to know.[32] It is an act of dissimulation. For the Dönme, public secrecy or dissimulation was knowing when to talk and not to talk in public, knowing what to say and what not to say, knowing the right balance between revealing and concealing so as to not destroy the power of the secret by exposing it. As Elliot Wolfson writes, "the secret, therefore, retains its secretive character if it is hidden in its exposure, but it may be hidden in its exposure only if it is exposed in its hiddenness."[33] As among Freemasons, "secrecy and discretion, accompanied by rules for behavior," keeping one another's identities private, and meeting behind closed doors fostered communal bonds.[34]

The survival of the Dönme was in part owing to the fact that despite their differences from Jews and Muslims, they did not attract the attention of the Ottoman authorities after their initial conversion in the late seventeenth century. The sincerity of the Dönme's religious beliefs was not questioned until the modern era. Once they had converted, it was assumed that they were Muslims, and this was affirmed by their public religious practices. In the premodern empire, there were no policing or inquisitorial agents that attempted to regulate the beliefs and practices of converts to Islam. It was not a question of lacking the power to discipline converts, but of a lack of desire to do so. Religion was manifested primarily in communal belonging, rather than private belief. Yitzhak Ben-Tzevi, who compared the situation of Dönme he encountered in Salonika before 1912 with that under the Turkish Republic during World War II, observes that the Ottoman era was a "period of tranquility" for them.[35]

The Dönme did not develop a culture of secrecy because it was a key to survival, or because they needed to avoid violent persecution by the Ottoman authorities. Even their messiah did not in the end really have to fear for his life: although given the choice of conversion or death, his change of religion saved him. He was not only the first Jewish messiah to convert, but also one of the few neither killed in battle nor executed—crucified, beheaded, or burned at the stake.[36] But centuries later, the Dönme still maintained this hidden culture, one of the reasons being simply that the way to be a Dönme, the proper mentality, and way of acting, was to be secret.[37] Duplicity, or less pejoratively, the simultaneous play between simulation (acting like the majority) and dissimulation (hiding secret beliefs and customs), or *taqiyya*, which Sufis and Shabbatai Tzevi alike had practiced, was a fundamental rule of behavior and means enabling them to not attract attention to themselves while remaining distinct and segregating themselves from others.[38] Moreover, secrecy and sacredness go together. Secrecy helps create sacredness and maintains it. Secret initiation, rites, and rituals preserve it.

Despite a shared commitment to secrecy and the common desire for maintaining the unity of the group, several new leaders and splits quickly arose. Dönme religion was not static, and developments were swift and transformative in the early years. Mustafa Çelebi / Baruch Kunio opposed Yakub Çelebi's leadership of the group and implementation of Shabbatai Tzevi's principles. In addition, while he himself was considered to have the soul of Rabbi Najara, a disciple of the sixteenth-century Kabbalist Rabbi Isaac Luria, he claimed that Shabbatai Tzevi's soul had not transmigrated into Yakub Çelebi, but into the body of a baby named Osman or Baruchia, born to the son of one of Shabbatai Tzevi's most devoted followers nine months after the messiah passed away. This baby grew up to be Osman Baba (1677–1720), who was proclaimed messiah either in 1690 or around 1715 (it should be noted that Baba is a typical Sufi title).

By the 1690s, Mustafa Çelebi and his followers caused the first splintering in the movement. Yakub Çelebi's group became known as the Yakubi, and Mustafa Çelebi's group as the Karakaş (Blackbrowed). The former were marked by closer integration into the Muslim way of life and attention to the performance of Sunni Muslim religious obligations. Yakub Çelebi passed away while journeying to or returning from the Hajj, probably in 1690 in Alexandria.[39] The Yakubi group was much smaller than the Karakaş, whose members claimed that they adhered more closely to

Shabbatai Tzevi's principles. The Karakaş became the most antinomian, eclectic sect, with the greatest investment in the concept of reincarnation, and had links to the Bektaşi Sufi order.[40] The Bektaşi order was significant, for Shabbatai Tzevi reportedly participated in prayers and public recitations of God's names (*dhikr*) in their lodge in Edirne.[41] Karakaş informers told late-nineteenth-century German scholars that Shabbatai Tzevi had relations with antinomian Sufis, including Halveti Sheikh Niyazi Mısri.[42] As Gershom Scholem notes, because Mısri's followers established a Sufi lodge in Salonika, it may be that Karakaş and Halvetis actually were in contact, but that they transformed their real connections into a mythical encounter between the founders of their respective "orders." Regardless of what occurred, what is important is that the Karakaş accepted the link between their path to God and Sufism.

After his proclamation as messiah, the Karakaş Osman Baba attracted followers in central as well as in Ottoman Europe. One outcome was a movement in Poland, led by Jacob Frank (1726–91), an Ashkenazi Jew from Podolia (in what is now Ukraine) who traded in Ottoman territory, where he came into contact with Dönme. Frank was educated by Karakaş leaders in Salonika and converted to Islam. He set out from the Ottoman Empire to Poland, where he was recognized as a Dönme authority, the reincarnation of Shabbatai Tzevi and successor to Osman Baba. In the end, however, this resulted in the conversion of his followers, not to Islam, but to Catholicism. Frank himself converted to Catholicism in L'viv and was renamed Baron Jakob Jozef Frank in 1759. He and his followers established themselves in a royal fortress adjacent to the shrine of the Black Virgin in Częstochowa, then moved to Brno (in Moravia, today part of the Czech Republic), finally ending up in Offenbach on the Rhine in Germany, where he was close to the founders of a Masonic lodge.

The formation of the third Ottoman Empire–based group of Dönme, the Kapancı, was the other outcome of Osman Baba being declared the messiah. The Kapancı can be seen as representing a pietistic or revivalist streak among the Dönme, the outcome of Osman Baba's split. They sought to return Dönme religion to its first state, excising all accretions, and they developed ties to the Mevlevi Sufi order. A group of Karakaş denied that Shabbatai Tzevi had been reincarnated in Yakub Çelebi or Osman Baba, and that the latter was the messiah, preferring to believe that only Shabbatai Tzevi had been the messiah. They formed this final group after Osman Baba died around 1720. Osman Baba's grave, which

Scholem claims, incorrectly, but meaningfully, was located near a Bektaşi lodge,[43] became a major pilgrimage site for the Karakaş, who tended to reside in the neighborhood of Salonika, where it was located.

Through such pilgrimage sites and other means, leaders of the Yakubi, Karakaş, and Kapancı routinized the messiah's charisma, replacing simple belief in Shabbatai Tzevi's messianism with codified and disseminated rite, doctrine, and authority and institutional structures.[44] By the early eighteenth century, the Dönme had become Dönme, following a distinct path to God that gave them a new self-identity and moral authority, with a belief system and social structure to which one could adhere.[45] In order to create and maintain community, Dönme leaders established places of communal worship and imposed conformity to common religious and social criteria, adjudicating disputes and seeking to ensure the financial well-being of members. As Yıldız Sertel, a descendant of Karakaş Dönme, writes, "Like all other groups, the Dönme possessed their own schools, places of prayer (Friday mosque, small mosques, and Sufi lodges), hospitals, social clubs, and centers for social assistance."[46] The houses of sect leaders served as places of communal worship.[47] The "Saadethane" (Abode of Felicity) where Shabbatai Tzevi had once lived, located on Sabri Pasha [now Eleuthérios Venizélos] Avenue near the government building (*konak*) in the Yılan Mermeri neighborhood in the northwest of Salonika, served this function for the Yakubi from the beginning.[48] Yakub Çelebi's successor, Hajji Mustafa Efendi, lived in the Saadethane.[49] It is possible that the seaside villa of Mehmet Kapancı served this function for the Kapancı.

By the nineteenth century, when the Dönme numbered perhaps 5,000, it appears that at least one sect had an administrative council serving under its leader. For the Yakubi, male consultants took care of the day-to-day affairs and women aides were responsible for women, arranging crucial life-cycle events such as weddings and funerals and taking care of matters such as care for the elderly.[50] In order to adjudicate disputes among believers and ensure conformity, communal courts presided over by judges and served by policing agents and jails unrecognized by the Ottoman authorities were also established.[51] When excommunication or banning was deemed insufficient punishment, brutal methods, including torture, could be used. According to a matter-of-fact Ottoman archival document, in 1862, Ottoman authorities, searching for a missing person, entered the Yakubi Saadethane. Other than an elderly woman,[52] an ancient Persian sword (a symbol of the Sufis),[53] a long knife hanging on a wall, and a whip in a cellar room, possibly relics of Shabbatai Tzevi,[54] the house was empty.[55] What they found were implements of torture:

> One of the houses belonging to the *Avdeti* was raided and a bloody knife and flagellation set [bastinado rods] were found. . . . It was understood that the blood did not belong to [the missing person] but to someone who was a member of the Avdeti, those who appear in public as Muslim yet actually follow a Jewish sect. They follow this sect to such an extent that just as they had been punishing men and women who violated their rules and regulations by flagellation with the bastinado, so, too do they also secretly execute those who incline toward Islam. The aforementioned house is used as a place for the meeting of their council and a house of punishment where male elders meet at night and women elders by day to adjudicate cases and imprison offenders.[56]

This document provides an unexpected glimpse into the central house of worship and administration of one of the three Dönme sects and is the first hint that the Dönme would be considered a problem in the future. Evidence of a court, prison, and torture implements could be seen as a challenge to state authority and to the organization of society. Ottoman society normatively recognized four religious categories: Muslims, Jews, and Armenian Orthodox and Orthodox Christians. Each community was allowed a single judicial apparatus (judges, law courts, policing agents, and jails, the latter two implying the use of force and violence) for handling issues of personal law: marriage, divorce, inheritance, fulfillment of religious obligations, and paying community taxes. Along with the use of excommunication—causing one so sentenced to be boycotted and shunned by the community, economically, socially, and religiously until repentance—one could be deprived of canonically allowed food and rites in the house of worship of the group, and one's business might be boycotted.

Although each group was diverse, there were no separate courts, for example, for Ashkenazi (central European), Sephardic (Iberian), Arab, Greek, or Karaite (those who do not accept the Talmud of Rabbanite Jews) Jews. Communities that had adherents, such as Catholics and the Alevi (a syncretistic offshoot of Shi'ism), but no legal recognition, were not permitted their own courts. The Dönme, as descendants of converts to Islam, were officially considered Muslims. As Muslims, they had no need for separate law courts.[57] This unexpected revelation of an unrecognized, alternate, autonomous space was a shock. Why would these Muslims have a separate court and jail? At a time marked by centralization and reform, how could another disciplining power be allowed to challenge that of the state?

Dönme Religion and Identity: Not Simply Jews, Not Merely Muslims

By the late nineteenth century, Ottoman officials and others were beginning to recognize that the Dönme were not quite like other Muslims. They were labeled "Avdeti," "one who returns to his origins," that is, "one who apostatizes." In the 1820s, Benjamin Barker and other missionaries asserted that these "Jewish Turks" continued to maintain Jewish rituals and customs and wanted to obtain the missionaries' publications and a Turkish-language Bible.[58] For Christian missionaries, it was important to depict the Dönme as secret Jews, for it allowed them to proselytize to them; spreading the Gospel among Muslims was illegal. To German-Jewish scholars beginning in the 1860s, and culminating in the opinion of a turn-of-the-twentieth-century encyclopaedia entry synthesizing current scholarship, the Dönme were simply a "sect of crypto-Jews."[59] The "Maaminim [Believers] are Jews by birth, but not by religion," a Jewish social scientist explained in 1891. "They live in sets of houses which are contiguous, or which are secretly connected; and for each block of houses there is a secret meeting-place," where the leader conducted prayers.[60]

Writing in 1923, the Yakubi Dönme Ahmet Emin Yalman also discusses the iron discipline of the Yakubi and the functioning of their communal life, saying that the leader of the Yakubi ruled as a tyrant. Any Yakubi traveling, circumcising a son, marrying, choosing a profession, or even undergoing a medical procedure had to consult with him and get his permission. The leader collected alms from everyone, which were used to assist those who were needy or ill. There were several types of alms, one of which was mandatory, like a tax collected either by the leader or by the male and female keepers of the purse. Along with conducting circumcision, marriages, and funerals according to the rules of Islam, the leader would also read a prayer according to the Yakubi customs. Since they were so assimilated into Islam, Yakubi women "were fanatics in the matter of veiling" and would not be seen with any male other than their children, father, and brother. Veiling was required even around a husband's brothers, a brother's children. According to Yalman, an outspoken critic of the persistence of Dönme tradition, the leader's basic duty was to hinder innovation and see to it that there was no deviation from the norm. Men had to shave their heads, women had to separate their hair into thin braids. Any sign of turning away from these requirements or any deviating from the group's required clothing or footwear or way of life would be investigated. One of the leader's wives would serve as an inspector and the leader acted as a judge, offering admonitions and warnings. In the event that the offense was repeated, the wrongdoer would be called in person before the judge and face ostracism, which was the foundation of their entire penal system. The threat was sufficient to preserve "an iron discipline within the tribe. Discipline was such that no one even considered acting against what was commanded."[61] In this way, the Dönme were not unlike other religious communities, such as Jewish congregations, whose life centered in a building where they ran their charity funds, burial societies, and study groups, organized the allocation and collection of taxes and agreed salaries for their cantor, ritual slaughterers, the mohel (responsible for circumcisions), and rabbi.[62]

By the turn of the twentieth century, when they numbered ten to fifteen thousand, the Dönme had developed not only a radical theology, but all the apparatuses of what was understood to be a religion. Although unrecognized, they possessed their own lay and religious leaders, communal courts and jails, and places of prayer, like recognized religious groups in the Ottoman Empire; they had their own cemeteries and tombs, resided together in the same neighborhoods, collected a tax to take care of their needy, maintained detailed genealogies, and developed a unique religious calendar, liturgy, prayers, prayer books, and beliefs, which were shared by neither Muslims nor Jews.[63] Although they had originated in their own practices, neither Sufis nor Kabbalists claimed the feasts, fasts, and festivals of the Dönme. In Christianity and Islam, believers mark the passage of time by reliving events in the founding of the religion and the life of the messiah or messenger. We only need to think of Christmas and a similar Muslim celebration, the Maulid observance of the birthday of the Prophet Muhammad. Likewise, the rhythms of Dönme religious life were based upon events in the life of Shabbatai Tzevi. These included his conception, birth, and circumcision, and his messianic calling—its beginning, the first receiving of revelations, the coronation as messiah—and subsequent conversion. The yearly cycle was also rooted in the holidays he instituted, such as making the ninth day of the Hebrew month of Av a day of celebration of the messiah's birthday, rather than mourning the destruction of the first and second temples in Jerusalem. In addition, each Dönme sect added events to the yearly religious calendar and pilgrimage sites that celebrated its leaders.

Religious syncretism is not permanent. Beginning at the end of the nineteenth century, there was an increasing trend among Dönme to abandon Dönme religion for the paramount values of Islam. Some Dönme became sincere, upstanding Muslims, and some even advanced to high levels in the hierarchy of Ottoman Sufi orders in Salonika, especially the Mevlevi. None, however, were faithful Jews.

While Dönme religion was constantly developing in new directions, what remained constant was public Jewish denunciation of the group, although it should not be discounted how in the first two centuries, some of this was partly done for show by rabbis who were secret followers of Shabbatai Tzevi. From the time of their apostasy in the seventeenth century to the end of the Ottoman Empire in the twentieth century, the Dönme were not considered Jews by Jewish leaders nor did Jews believe that the followers of Shabbatai Tzevi practiced Judaism. From the beginning, rabbis declared that those who followed Shabbatai Tzevi into apostasy were not Jews but voluntary converts, defectors from Judaism, who unlike forced converts could not easily accepted back into the community; thus psychologically and juristically, the Dönme were not Jews, no longer Jews, former Jews whose heretical practices outraged real Jews.

Concerning rabbinic debates about conversion and apostasy, the majority view held that a Jew cannot become a non-Jew. It was the minority view that a Jew could fully convert to another religion. Even on the question of voluntary conversion, legal authorities considered the heretics still to be Jews—for example, allowing conversos back into the fold without converting. This meant that they had never legally ceased being Jews. Suffice it to say that the Dönme were not the converts of the usual type. The upheaval they caused among Jews was considered so damaging to Judaism and Jews that rabbis adopted harsh views of them and were unwilling to overlook their consuming unclean foods, eating on fast days, celebrating holidays not in the Jewish calendar, and rejecting the commandments of the Torah.

According to the rabbis, the Dönme were deviants, engaging in all categories of what was considered religious perversion in the early modern period, including criminal acts, sexual deviance, transgression of Jewish ritual law, offenses against communal ordinances, transgression against rabbinic law and authority, and, of course, apostasy.[64] A Salonikan rabbi opined in 1765 that the Dönme were apostates who persisted in their heresy, desecrated the Sabbath, posed as if they had embraced another religion, acting like Muslims: they were "the converts among us, who rebelled against the words of God in distant times and continue to hold to their impurity until today"; accordingly, "there is no difference between them and the Gentiles at all, transgressing against all that is written in the Torah, certainly taken for Gentiles in every matter." Therefore, "for all intents and purposes they must be considered non-Jews."[65] In the late nineteenth century, Sephardic Jews simply ignored the subject of the Dönme in their writings, because they considered them well outside the Jewish fold.[66] At times of crisis, the Dönme drew the ire of Jews. A circular published by the chief rabbi in Istanbul in 1914 blasted the Dönme for their alleged frightening immorality, sexual perversity, infidelity, lack of honor, dishonesty, religious blasphemy, trickery and charlatanism, financial impropriety, and lack of ethics.[67] The circular blamed the corruption of Salonikan Jews on the Dönme. The Dönme possessed beliefs and maintained traditions that Jews regarded as heresy. If they observed Judaism, it was a version of Judaism that Jews condemned, like the religion of the first Christians.

The feelings were mutual. The Dönme did not consider themselves Jews, nor that they were secretly practicing Judaism in an atmosphere of persecution either. They were not crypto-Jews, privately engaging in the dogged practice of Judaism, to which they remained inwardly true, always nourishing a hope that at some time in the future when the political conditions were favorable, they would be able to return to Judaism openly again.[68] For Janet Liebman Jacobs, crypto-Judaism is "the clandestine observance of Judaism among individuals and families who had undergone conversion but who secretly remained faithful to Jewish beliefs and traditions."[69] For Maurus Reinkowski, a crypto-Jew "continues to secretly adhere to his original religion, whether in a rather unconscious continuation of religious practices or in the form of a conscious loyalty to the former religion."[70] These definitions cannot be applied to Dönme practices. In fact, when the Dönme "reverted to form" in the twentieth century, they became Muslims. Expelled from Thessaloníki in 1923 as part of the population exchange between Greece and Turkey, the Dönme were compelled to abandon their ethno-religious identity and live in accordance with their ancestors' affirmation that God is one and Muhammad is God's messenger, not Shabbatai Tzevi.

Jean-Paul Sartre wrote: "The Jew is the one whom other men consider a Jew."[71] Sartre was not saying that those called Jews are Jews, rather, he was focusing on the mentality of those who see Jews everywhere. Despite the history I have just narrated, it is remarkable how, along with their Ottoman and Turkish Muslim detractors, modern scholars writing within the divergent paradigms of Greek, Jewish, and Turkish historiography often tend to be unwilling to accept that the Dönme were not simply Jews. In Greek historiography, making these people into Jews allows scholars to claim that the only progressive elements of the Muslim Ottoman community were really Jews. Alternatively, the Dönme are depicted as the allies of the Muslims, legitimizing their being deported from Greece in 1923 and subsequently written out of the Hellenic past. In Jewish historiography, despite the fact that the Shabbatean movement emerged in the Ottoman Empire and Shabbatai Tzevi's followers lived as a distinct group with a corporate identity and unique beliefs and practices after his death, accounts of Shabbatai Tzevi and his movement, which especially focus on its origins and earliest stage, and are mainly based on Hebrew and European-language sources, consider his followers "secret" Jews, and analyze their religious practices and history within the framework of Jewish history and Jewish thought alone.[72] "For over 250 years, the Sabbateans existed as a secret Jewish sect garbed in a Muslim cloak,"[73] according to this conventional wisdom; they attempted "to maintain secretly within Islam as much as possible of Judaism, its lore and rites," although modified by Shabbatean messianism.[74]

Turkish historiography wears similar blinders. Although until the late nineteenth century, the Ottoman state did not acknowledge Dönme difference and until the end of empire, the Dönme were considered Muslim by both religious and secular Ottoman law, attention has always been paid to their ancestral Jewishness. According to the influential study by Abdurrahman Küçük, even after converting to Islam, intractable Jews were zealous in guarding their unchanging Jewish core. Thus even if a Jew appears in another guise, he can never escape his essential Jewishness.[75] In this sense, like medieval inquisitors, modern historians and Muslim enemies of the Dönme hold that any trace of an apparently Jewish practice is proof of their being secret Jews. Jewish historians in Turkey share this assumption. Thus Avram Galanté, the author of the first monograph on the group, published in 1935, would not concede that they could have maintained a unique ethno-religious identity, nor some of them have been pious Muslims, instead arguing that they had a tendency to be reconciled with Judaism, an approach that has continued to prevail among work that explores their religious tenets and practices in the context of Jewish history and does not allow for the complexity of their history, experience, or dynamic expression of religion to emerge.

Turkish historians have been bewildered by the Dönme in part because on the surface, Dönme practice appeared to be hybrid. While ostensibly following the requirements of Islam, including fasting at Ramadan and praying in mosques, one of which they built, the Dönme at the same time practiced kabbalistic rituals, and recited prayers in Hebrew and Ladino, the language of most Jews in the Ottoman Empire.[76] It would seem as if the distinct paramount values of Judaism and Islam were given equal consideration, and that the Dönme maintained both religions.[77] Yet rather than being a hybrid of Judaism and Islam, in which the two religions coexisted side by side, the Dönme religion syncretized elements of the two, merging or combining them to form new ritual and paramount values in the process. Their religion was a spiritual synthesis based on two religions, which incorporated elements of Kabbalah Judaism and Sufi Islam—Bektaşi for the Karakaş and Mevlevi for the Kapancı—into a new construction that neither Jews nor Muslims recognized. As Benayahu argues, "Islam was the outward garment" of their religion, "but its inward spirit was not founded upon the bases of the Torah, as the situation demanded, but, on the contrary, impaired the root principles of Judaism."[78] For the Dönme, unlike Jews or Muslims, Shabbatai Tzevi's (and his successors') messiahship and rituals based upon it were the central elements in their religion.

Yet being Dönme was not limited to maintaining unique rituals and a distinct creed. Attached to their religious core was an ethnic identity. The Dönme chose to distinguish themselves from Jews and Muslims. They managed to maintain cultural difference through social segregation while assimilating into Ottoman society.[79] They assimilated while remaining a devout religious community, forming both a closed caste protecting a unique religion and a fully acculturated group fitting in with their surrounding culture. They thus created and maintained an ethnic social group. In the Ottoman Empire, they were able to be fully Dönme among other Dönme and fully Ottoman Muslim in public, at ease inhabiting two worlds, fully insiders in both.[80] They did not have to abandon their religion to be full members of society, to choose between them in order to play their political, cultural, and economic role. The heritage of a convert was not something to be examined. Conversion was at the heart of being Ottoman. For much of Ottoman history, the elite members of the military, administration, and even royalty—the mothers of sultans—all were converted Christians. Sir Paul Ricaut, an astute English observer of late-seventeenth-century Ottoman society, argued that the Ottomans were open to receive every type of person as a Muslim, whatever his or her language, or nation, whether a slave, commoner, or a member of the elite.[81] Ricaut wrote "no people in the World have ever been more open to receive all sorts of Nations to them, than they."[82] He added, "the Turks call it Becoming a Believer."[83]

Before race, before religion as faith, the Dönme did not possess such an anomalous position in Ottoman society. There were many other descendants of converts to Islam who maintained exceptional ethnic and religious characteristics, such as the Hemshin, seventeenth-century Armenian converts to Islam who preserved the Armenian language and customs long after converting.[84] Moreover, there were Christians who carried Christian and Muslim names, attended church and mosque, had their children baptized and circumcised, observed Lent and Ramadan, and shared pilgrimage sites, spiritual guides and their tombs, with Muslims on Cyprus and Crete, in Albania and Kosovo, Macedonia and northeastern Anatolia. Many Muslim groups, such as Bosnians, Chechens, Circassians, Crimeans, Pomaks in western Thrace, and the descendants of converts to Islam on Crete, practiced endogamy and maintained their pre-conversion languages.

The problem lies not in the premodern behavior of such groups, but in how modern contemporaries and historians have interpreted it. That people of different religions shared saints, tombs, pilgrimage sites, rituals and practices, sacred springs, feasts, fasts, and festivals, as well as holy men, without converting to the other religion casts doubt on the "crypto-religion" ascription, especially when given by European Orientalists and colonialists searching for protégés and allies. The label is also suspect when posited by nationalists seeking to redeem their convert ancestors, who they assert were coerced or forced to convert and accepted it as a necessary evil, pining for the moment when they would be able to revert to the prior religion.[85] They largely fail to comprehend the fluidity of boundaries between practices and beliefs of different groups. Despite popular opinion at the end of the Ottoman Empire, the early years of the Turkish Republic, and especially today, never were those who converted in the name of Shabbatai Tzevi or their descendants simply Jewish.

If not simply Jews, were they at all similar to crypto-Jews? At first glance, the Dönme present a similar case to the *Jadid al-Islam*, "New Muslims," Jews forced to become Muslim in nineteenth-century Mashhad, Iran, or the conversos, "New Christians," Jews compelled to convert to Catholicism in medieval Iberia and their descendants, on the question of their "Jewishness" and "crypto-Jewishness." According to their origins, the Dönme were Jewish converts to Islam and their descendants. Thus from a genealogical or ethnic point of view, one can consider them Jews until they began intermarrying at the turn of the twentieth century. Scholem argued that although the Dönme had "voluntarily left Judaism—or rather the religious framework of the social and religious organization of the Jews," they "remained Jews at heart despite becoming Muslims formally," like conversos. That is to say that although Shabbatai Tzevi had contacts with Sufism and Sufis, and he and his followers then converted to Islam, they remained Jews, "the Jewish character of the Dönme was preserved in all matters of consequence,"[86] and that one who leaves Judaism is still a Jew. In labeling someone a crypto-Jew, one assumes that Jewish converts to other religions wish to remain Jews. By masking their true identity, the crypto-Jews attempt to protect themselves against annihilation. But this framework for understanding crypto-religion derives from the particular historical experience of "antisemitism, religious persecution, and the dangers associated with Jewish identity,"[87] such as the conversos and Mashhadis experienced, since forced conversion can lead to the practice of crypto-religion. But the followers of Shabbatai Tzevi who voluntarily converted faced none of this when they emerged as an identifiable group. Whereas in Iran, the animosity of Muslims ensured the persistence of the crypto-Jews, because neighbors kept them under close surveillance and threatened them with death if their observing Jewish law and customs was discovered,[88] in the Ottoman Empire, the opposite was true: the Ottoman religious and administrative authorities allowed the Dönme to live as Dönme without harassment. The Jews were not a persecuted minority in the Ottoman Empire. As a corollary, neither were the Dönme.

Scholarship also assumes that crypto-Jews engage in accommodation and resistance to cultural hegemony and assimilation by engaging in religious persistence to ensure the survival of Judaism after they are forced to convert.[89] Such a paradigm may fit other groups who aimed to maintain Judaism and a Jewish identity, but does not describe the Dönme. Unlike many conversos, the Dönme neither participated in Ottoman Jewish life nor fled the empire to become Jews in exile elsewhere. The Dönme were not only allowed full membership, but also were able to rise in Ottoman society despite their origins. Unlike most Mashhadis who openly became Jews in Israel and the United States after emigrating from a Muslim society where reversion to Judaism was punishable by death, only one Dönme has become Jewish since freedom of religion was declared in the Ottoman Empire in 1856. This occurred less than a decade ago and was not met with enthusiasm by Turkish Jews.[90] There is no evidence of a mass desire on the part of the Dönme to become Jews.

One might argue that the existence of distinct Dönme institutions at the end of the nineteenth century means we are witnessing the moment of creation of the Dönme religious community. Instead, we are witnessing the moment of creation of the Muslim community in the Ottoman Empire, in the sense that the term "Muslim" was debated, defined, and normalized during the reign of Abdülhamid II, a period when Ottoman Muslims looked closely at the religion they practiced. This is not to say that there were not self-recognized Muslims before, that believers in what Muhammad revealed had not been debating since the seventh century what it meant to be a Muslim, and had not formed communities of Muslims. Rather, it is to point out that Islam, like Christianity and Hinduism in the late nineteenth century, became a religion inasmuch as the category of "religion" was invented and its beliefs and practices were understood as comprising a faith, a belief system.[91] As Talal Asad has pointed out, what was new was "the emphasis on belief," which meant "that henceforth religion could be conceived as a set of propositions to which believers gave assent, and which therefore could be judged."[92]

Once religion moved from primary emphasis upon communal belonging to a belief system, an individual's faith could be tested for the first time. Religion was conceived as being private, interior, and exclusive. The state, or the community, could look inside one's mind and test to see if what was there was correct, and acceptable. As an eighteenth-century British observer notes, in Ottoman Salonika the Dönme were not questioned about their religious belief, faith, or sincerity as Muslims. Sir James Porter writes: "It is difficult to conceive how they remain unnoticed by the Turks; or rather, it shows with how easy a composition the Turks are content in these matters. An outward profession of their own religion compensates for private exercise of the other."[93]

In great contrast, in the late nineteenth century, the Ottoman state engaged in Islamization campaigns by sending pious religious teachers as missionaries throughout the empire to correct the beliefs of both mainstream and marginal Muslims, converting Muslim heretics (Alevi, bedouin, and Shi'a), especially in the eastern half of the empire, to what was considered an acceptable version of Islam, disseminating official, standardized versions of the Qur'an and publishing other texts approved by the state, patronizing and employing religious scholars in its new schools and other administrative institutions, and building mosques and supporting religious endowments and infrastructure including building a railroad to facilitate pilgrimage.[94] Thus by the final years of the Ottoman Empire, largely for the first time, one's beliefs and ethnic identity could be examined by others. Those found wanting in both categories could be especially targeted for reprobation or, worse, exclusion from the body of the nation. It was only then that the Dönme began to be considered Jews: not by themselves, not by Jews, but by Muslims.

I
Ottoman Salonika

§1 Keeping It Within the Family, 1862–1908

The marriage of the Muslim Mehmet Zekeriya and the Kapancı Dönme Sabiha, daughter of Nazmi Efendi (later Sertel), in 1912 was a revolutionary act, breaking down walls of distinction. It is believed in Turkey to have been the first between a Dönme woman and a Muslim Turkish man. As we see in the biography of Sabiha and in Mehmet Zekeriya's autobiography, Dönme greeted the decision with a mixture of shock and celebration:

§ Sabiha's Salonikan home was turned into a battlefield by the strong-willed teenager's decision to marry a Muslim man.

"Dönme do not marry outsiders," her sister warned her. "It would only bring disaster."

"Dönme are narrow-minded," Sabiha replied. Look how they say, 'We are all one, religion, language, nationality make no difference among us.' . . . Will they then still refuse to intermarry?"[1]

"Are you crazy? You are a Dönme. How can you marry a Turk [i.e., a Muslim]?"

"I do not know whether I am a Turk. We are all humans. We match, he wants me, and I am pleased to accept."[2]

Her older brother, Hidayet, was outraged: "What? Our sister, a Dönme, marry a Turk? Choose her own husband? This one is crazy. Mother, she will ruin the honor of the entire family. She will humiliate us in the eyes of all Dönme!" He advises his mother to keep the seventeen-year-old at home so that she cannot humiliate the family any further.[3]

Meanwhile, her prospective groom was being congratulated.

"Dönme have collected information about me," Mehmet Zekeriya thinks to himself, "and have decided to meet with me once and see me

up close, because the decision they are going to make about me is very
important, even bearing historic import."[4] The bride is a member of a
Dönme family, "and the Dönme do not allow their daughters to marry
outsiders. If her family approves, it will be the first time a Dönme girl
has married a Turk." Word got out that "I was about to marry a Dönme
girl."[5] One day, Dr. Nâzım of the Central Committee of the Committee
of Union and Progress [CUP—the formerly secret society of Young Turks,
which since the 1908 revolution had been transformed into a political
party and at the time of this marriage was running the empire] called me
to appear before him. He congratulated me, saying: "Do you know the
significance of what you have done? You may not be aware of it, but you
are opening the gates to the unification and mixing of two societies that
have looked askance at each other for centuries. You are delivering the
fatal blow to the Dönme caste. We must analyze this event as it deserves
and must celebrate the union of Turks and Dönme now enabled by your
action. This should be regarded as a national and historic event."

Mehmet Zekeriya was surprised and asked Dr. Nâzım what he
should do.

"We'll conduct your marriage ceremony," Dr. Nâzım replied. "We'll
pay all the expenses. We'll announce it to the press. In this way, we'll turn
it from being merely a marriage between two families into a national and
historic event.'"

"The marriage of Sabiha and myself did indeed become an example
to the Dönme," Mehmet Zekeriya wrote later. "After us, the number of
Dönme men and women marrying outsiders increased greatly. And in this
way, the Dönme caste was destroyed and became a thing of the past."[6]

At this point, around the beginning of World War I, at least in this circle, Dönme were not seen as a racial group, and their mixing with other
Muslims was seen as a positive action. The wedding was announced and
hosted by the CUP, whose secretary-general at the time the influential
Mehmet Talat Pasha, minister of the interior during World War I, and
Dr. Tevfik Rüştü (Aras), a future foreign minister (1925–38), who married Dr. Nâzım's sister, gave away the bride and groom, respectively,
during the ceremony.[7]

Mehmet Alkan argues this marriage reflected ongoing attempts
by Dönme at that time to resolve conflicts between the three Dönme
sects—in part, through committees set up to try to unite them—and,
concomitantly, to improve their relations with Muslims. Neither effort
was successful. The marriage of Sabiha and Mehmet Zekeriya was an im-

portant development, a first serious step in establishing closer relations with Muslims, but it caused major disputes among the Dönme, and even a crisis, because it went against prevailing marriage customs.[8]

Endogamy and Genealogies

One of the main ways in which the Dönme preserved their distinct ethno-religious identity was by marrying only members of the same Dönme sect. Endogamy and genealogy are important features of many crypto-faith communities, whether conversos, Huguenots, or Moriscos, Muslims compelled to convert to Catholicism in Iberia. For all of these groups, as for the Dönme, marrying insiders allowed them furtively to continue their religious practices, protect a separate way of being, and maintain close economic networks. Marrying outsiders would expose their secrets and could be considered a betrayal of the ancestors.[9] Closed communities remained loyal to their origins. Genealogy and religious meaning were interwoven: "Preserving the memory of one's ancestors is therefore part and parcel of remaining faithful to the covert religion."[10] Being Dönme meant both engaging in certain ritual practices and belonging to a group related by blood. Religion and community were intertwined. Groups such as the Dönme compile genealogies, not only to preserve a religion, but also as part of a social practice aiming to perpetuate a people. Keeping alive the memory of ancestors entailed repeating names: as was common among Mediterranean Jewish and Indian Ocean Muslim diasporic groups, newborn sons were named after grandfathers.[11]

Such naming practices are "akin to leapfrogging backward to eponymous ancestors tied to places. Like climbers roped together on a rock face, the generations together maintain a tenacious grip, despite their precarious individual hold on the surface."[12] This process of "positional succession" serves to confer "the blessings inherent in an ancestral name" on a descendant.[13] Like the conversos, who considered themselves "The Nation," and the Jews, who were a people with a religion, not merely members of a religion, the Dönme kept genealogies, because Dönme identity was part religion, part peoplehood, part diasporic belonging. The memory of the ancestors recorded in genealogies allowed them to know whom they could marry. Using genealogies hindered intermarriage, because it maintained corporate identity, a key constituent of the Dönme way.

I was able to trace the Dönme in part through genealogies provided me by descendants of the Yakubi, Karakaş, and Kapancı, which like genealogies of other diaspora groups, have both open and closed aspects.[14] When compiling a genealogy, a family has to decide what and whom to include, and what and whom to exclude, in order to stake claims, which are often of a religious nature. What gets left out? Is the genealogy to be patriarchal, or matrilateral? Are men or women or both included? Is the importance of women emphasized? A balance is established between exclusion of the elements that do not fit the ideology of the narrative, which itself is a claim to history, argued by the genealogy, and inclusion of the elements that strengthen that narrative. Genealogies are important for groups that live on the frontier, which is the limit of their geographical space, and the boundary between insiders and outsiders, and for diaspora groups who are beyond the range of the homeland and need to police membership in the group when there is a great potential for mixing with others. They complement means of daily contact, such as marriage, trade, news, and postcards, with a more historical, authoritative record.

While other diasporic groups' genealogies express connections to new societies, the Dönme genealogies were used to preserve group boundaries, not expand them. Dönme kept genealogies in part to ensure proper Levirate marriages, in which a widow was required to marry one of her deceased husband's brothers. One does not find (except in the most recent genealogies) Dönme wives in western and central Europe, for example, until after the Dönme began to deteriorate as a social group. Dönme genealogies begin with male progenitors, but include daughters and wives, spelling out the choice of partners, who can marry whom. Unlike other diasporic Muslim groups, among whom patrilineal descent was crucial, making intermarriage normal, the Dönme, who had both Islamic and Jewish roots, not only preserved patrilinealism, but added the matrilocal, thus combining Jewish and Muslim definitions of descent. Hence the importance of both one's father *and* one's mother being Dönme. Individuals who do not fit the image the family is trying to present of itself, individuals who break the chain of continuity going back to illustrious forebears, are excluded. One does not expect to find prostitutes, concubines, and bastards in family genealogies. But what is remarkable about the Dönme, and another reason they did not later fit into the bourgeois framework of the nation-state, was how the Dönme included second and even third wives in their genealogies, women who were very close family members, as well as children who would be considered bastards by other groups, such as Jews.

Conflicts could arise in diaspora among such a group, and genealogies could serve as very important mediating contracts. As Esra Özyürek has pointed out, since the 1990s, many Turks have sought to recover and remember their diverse past, including the trauma of dramatic, sudden change suppressed or erased by the homogenizing early republic.[15] Swept up in this nostalgic wave, one also finds a new effort by descendants of Dönme to record their family histories, in so doing interviewing the elderly to figure out the webs of family relationships. These genealogies are different from the earlier ones in that they are produced with a sense of nostalgia, and with the aim of writing popular books on the topic—family histories recorded desperately before the last relatives who know something pass away. They are thus unlike genealogies written before World War II, which were recorded to ensure distinctions between Dönme sects and Dönme and the rest of the world, which is to say, with a religious and not merely documentary intent. The aims of the compiler today, especially when married to an outsider, are far from those of the original compilers.

Genealogies also have a legal nature. Kinship and marriage offer rights to inheritance. In a group as closely knit (yet divided into three sharply delineated sects) as the Dönme, it was crucial to keep relationships well ordered, not only to keep marriages in line with the aims of the group, but also to keep wealth and property in the proper hands as well. Marriage and family alliances were mapped onto trade alliances. Genealogies can function as legal wills. Inheritance claims can be substantial.[16]

The Dönme primarily practiced endogamous marriage in Salonika in part in order to keep their wealth and businesses within the family. Nothing illustrated communal belonging better. Breaking this marriage pattern, marrying outsiders, was a way of leaving the community. Dönme opposition to exogamy was so strong that Dönme leaders imposed the death penalty on those who strayed, according to the Ottoman archival document dating from 1862 cited in the Introduction, and those who wanted to marry outsiders had to take extreme measures. The marriage between Mehmet Zekeriya and Sabiha, daughter of Nazmi Efendi, is well known. Less well known is its precedent. According to an Ottoman document from 1891,[17] the eighteen-to-twenty-year-old Rabia, daughter of a Dönme (referred to as an Avdeti) named Ali Efendi, fell in love with a Muslim named Hajji Feyzullah Efendi of Monastir, who told her to leave home and to appear before a deputy judge, where she could publicly convert to Islam. Ali Efendi understood that his daughter's conversion was a pretext to marry the Muslim, and he was as dead set both against her marriage to the Muslim and to her conversion. He refused to approve either. The governor of Salonika referred the case to the meeting of Ottoman ministers in Istanbul, where it was noted that Rabia was of legal age to decide whether to marry or not, with or without her father's approval. Thus they supported Rabia's conversion and marriage to Hajji Feyzullah. But in order not to create a scene in Salonika, the couple was secretly brought to Istanbul on the first available ferry, because it was deemed better for them to marry far from the city where the Dönme were so prominent and might try to hinder the marriage.

Several features strike the reader of the 1891 document. First, members of the group are referred to as having long resided in Salonika. This draws our attention to the fact that Muslims had been aware that the Dönme had made the city their home—it was an open secret—for as long as anyone could remember. Thus it appears that memory worked for others the same way it worked for the Dönme: for others had always known that the Dönme were there, that they existed in Salonika. And at the end of the nineteenth century, others began to point them out, call upon them, sowing the seeds for discriminating against them both in Greece and in the Turkish Republic. Second, although Dönme should have been considered Muslims, by this point at the end of the nineteenth century, they were regarded as different from other Muslims. There is no other way to explain how the term for conversion (*ihtida*) could be used in this case, as if Rabia had been a Christian or Jew changing her religion. The document even notes how the Dönme had not practiced intermarriage with Muslims *until now*. Moreover, the Avdeti are referred to as living under the cover of Islam. A distinction between Dönme and other Muslims had thus by this point been made, which would have serious consequences for the next generation of Dönme.

The Dönme practiced both Levirate and first-cousin marriage. Among the Kapancı, according to the genealogy extending to the eighteenth century provided by the descendant of Yusuf Kapancı, this practice goes at least as far back as İbrahim Kapancı (b. 1820). With his first wife, Hasibe, İbrahim had two daughters and two sons, Ahmet and Mehmet. With his second wife, Fatma, he had three daughters and a son, Yusuf. Ahmet, Mehmet, and Yusuf are discussed at length in this book. Yusuf Kapancı (1858–1910) also had two wives. With his first wife, Aisha, he had three children, including İbrahim, discussed here. With his second wife, Emine, he had five additional children, including Osman (1880–1932). Osman is also discussed at length in this book. The year Yusuf died, Osman was widowed when his wife Sabite died in labor. Three years later, in 1913, İbrahim, who served as a journalist and correspondent of Austrian newspapers, was accidentally killed the same day King George I of Greece was assassinated in Salonika. Osman then married his brother İbrahim's wife Aisha (1881–1960), his first cousin, since she was the daughter of Mehmet.[18] They lived in a wooden house next to the Church of the Ascension (Ekklisia Analipseos) opposite Mehmet's seaside mansion. Osman's first daughter, Nevber, became Yusuf's cousin and stepsister, because Yusuf's mother Aisha married her father. Osman and Aisha then had a daughter, whom they named Wonder (Harika). Osman followed in his father's and grandfather's footsteps.

A descendant of the Kapancı Osman Ehat provided me with a family genealogy.[19] The family traces its origins to Sarrafzade [Son of the Money Changer] Halil Efendi, who was born in Salonika between 1835 and 1840 and passed away there by 1899. His son Sarrafzade Osman Ehat was a merchant and money changer. Mustafa Fazıl and Sarrafzade Osman Ehat came from different branches of a larger family. Osman Ehat's son Sarrafzade Ahmet Tevfik Ehat, a tobacco merchant, married Nasibe Emine Fazıl, the daughter of Mustafa Fazıl. Sarrafzade Ahmet Tevfik Ehat's brother, Sarrafzade Kudret Ehat married Acile Akif, daughter of the important tobacco merchant Duhani Hasan Akif. The Akifs also formed another branch of the same Sarrafzade family. Another branch of the family, named Ata, was well known for its role in textile production and distribution. Mustafa Fazıl's youngest daughter, Nefise Mukbile Fazıl, married Ahmet Feyzi Ata in Istanbul in 1919.

In another Kapancı family, first-cousin marriage was practiced as late as the early twentieth century. Hasan Akif's oldest daughter Fatma Akif's son Ali Rıza married Nuriye, the daughter of another of Hasan Akif's daughters, Emine Akif. The two sisters may have been five years or so apart. There is a photo of Fatma Akif and Emine Akif when the two were young, wearing identical dresses. These two sisters married their children to each other. The two first cousins married in 1920.

Detailed genealogies compiled to ensure endogamy, including Levirate and first-cousin marriages, enabled the Dönme to maintain strict separation from other people, and most often also from members of other Dönme sects. This served to maintain their cohesiveness in the imperial period, but as will be discussed in Part III, it would haunt them in the nation-state, where those of "Jewish blood" were not welcome. Since they chose to marry one another, it is not surprising that the Dönme also preferred to reside together as neighbors in family groups.

Self-Segregation

Where did the great interrelated merchant families live and conduct their business? How does the spatial distribution of the Dönme within Salonika provide evidence of their way of being? Did members of the three different sects live together as neighbors, or did they reside in different neighborhoods? Why did they live in the neighborhoods in which they lived? Did they live among Jews, or Muslims? Did the Dönme form self-chosen ghettoes? Where did they build their schools and mosque? What does their spatial location in the city say about them?

It is inappropriate to speak of ghettos in the Ottoman Empire, because in most Ottoman cities, although there were neighborhoods that were referred to as Christian or Jewish, and despite a great deal of self-segregation, no neighborhood was exclusive to any one group. No group was forced by law to reside in a particular district. This was also the case in Salonika. According to the first Greek census of the city in 1913, fewer than one-third of the city's inhabitants lived in neighborhoods where 80 percent belonged to a single religion.[20] While different groups predominated in different districts of the city—Christians in the east, Jews in the south, Muslims in the north—one could still find Jews in Muslim neighborhoods and vice versa. The term "ghetto" is troublesome, moreover, because it is too loaded to use objectively.

Since they were officially Muslim and lived ostensibly as Muslims, the Dönme established themselves in predominantly Muslim neighborhoods of the city, not in Jewish ones, inasmuch as neither they nor Jews considered themselves to belong to that people or to their religion. In the process, they converted apparently Muslim neighborhoods into Dönme ones. The Dönme tended to own businesses in the neighborhoods where they resided, as well as in the central business district, like members of all other groups. Thus Karakaş primarily owned businesses in predominantly Karakaş areas. Again, this fits the depiction of the Dönme as a closed group, not only marrying only other members of the same Dönme sect, and residing together, but also doing business with partners from the same sect and establishing economic concerns in the same neighborhoods.

Similarly, they built their schools where they resided. This ensured that a Dönme could be born, schooled, married, and initiated into business life in the same neighborhood, which here seems like a ghetto, although self-imposed or enforced by communal leaders.

Owing to their international business, religious, familial, and administrative positions compelling temporary or longer-term dispersal throughout the Ottoman Empire and western and central Europe, Dönme lives were not limited to the neighborhood in which they were raised. Nevertheless, their spatial distribution in Salonika allows us to make some generalizations about the different Dönme sects.

The Dönme were not only open to the new and the international, but perpetuated that which marked them as separate. For example, the Karakaş appear more conservative, choosing to remain together in the closed streets of the city's medieval core, its predominantly Muslim north-central district, especially in the six contiguous neighborhoods of Balat, Katip Musliheddin, Kadı Abdullah, Hacı Hasan, Sinancık, and Hacı İsmail. These neighborhoods were marked by Karakaş residences, businesses that Karakaş owned and operated with their extended families, schools (Hacı İsmail, Sinancık, Katip Musliheddin),[21] and their main pilgrimage site (Kadı Abdullah), the tomb of Osman Baba, the founder of the group,[22] which the Karakaş visited before the most important life-cycle events, including circumcision and marriage.[23] Descendants of Karakaş Dönme told me that even as late as the 1970s, there had been elderly people who made pilgrimages to the still-remembered site and collected small amounts of its holy earth in jars to take back with them to their home countries. An interviewee told me that when she tried to take some soil, Greek residents in apartments overlooking it yelled at her not to disturb a holy site.[24] Apparently, Orthodox Christians had appropriated the memory of the sanctity of the space. This had been the main Karakaş quarter, she said, and Baruchia (Osman Baba) had his "home" there. The plot of land where the house had stood was considered a holy spot, and until a few years ago, it was roped off, with a tree in the middle, but no trace of this remains today. The famed educator Şemsi Efendi, who is discussed in Chapter 2, owned property on Eski Zindan street near the tomb.[25] We can speculate that street was the heart of Karakaş settlement in the city and the location of a secret house of worship and communal gathering.[26]

Karakaş choice of these neighborhoods may reflect close affiliation with the Bektaşi Sufi order, known for its esotericism and antinomianism and underground nature, especially after the order was banned throughout the empire in 1826. It also reflects their desire to live near its main pilgrimage site, the tomb of Osman Baba, the group's messianic incarnation of Shabbatai Tzevi. Yet on the other hand, their location next to the new seat of local government also positioned them to participate in all of the local changes occurring in the late nineteenth century, particularly serving as civil servants and in local administration.

That the Karakaş resided in neighborhoods contiguous to two predominantly occupied by Kapancı, who preferred to remain in the core of the city, reflects the origins of the Kapancı as an offshoot of the Karakaş.[27] One of these Kapancı neighborhoods contained the converted St. Demetrius Church (renamed Kasımiye Mosque), whose shrine was administered by Mevlevi Sufis, the order Kapancı frequented. Kasimiye was the site of the Kapancı Terraki school on Pazar Tekkesi street (after 1912 renamed Odos Kassandrou), where Sabiha Sertel's father, Nazmi Efendi, had his two-story timbered home and Duhani Hasan Akif's son and daughters lived.[28] Thus in the core of the city, Karakaş and Kapancı resided in adjacent neighborhoods containing major tombs in the main officially Muslim district in the city's north-central area.

The Yakubi mainly lived near their meeting house in Yılan Mermeri, a Muslim district several neighborhoods west of the main Karakaş cluster, on the other side of the seat of government, befitting their assimilation into Islam and local government role. On the eve of the Dönme departure from the city in 1923, Safiye, the wife of Osman Said, the mayor of the city and son of former mayor Hamdi Bey, resided in neighboring Şehabeddin neighborhood on Saatli Cami street.[29] That the Yakubi are harder to locate, and were the only group to endow a mosque in the city, its main benefactors being men who had made the pilgrimage to Mecca, illustrates Yakubi assimilation into the Muslim community.

The Yakubi mosque was built, and Yakubi Dönme Mayor Hamdi Bey resided, in Hamidiye (named for Sultan Abdülhamid II), the first suburb of the city to be built outside the Byzantine walls.[30] It was a religiously diverse neighborhood, and the Dönme elite from all three sects lived there. By 1906, it had one church (Holy Trinity), one mosque (the New Mosque built by Yakubi Dönme), and one synagogue (Beyt Şaul).[31] The neighborhood contained wide boulevards, parks, ornate mansions, and cafés and was built as a planned district, connected to the old city by tramway.[32] Its main boulevard, likewise called Hamidiye, was also referred to as Seaside

Villas (Yalılar) because it boasted over fifty of them.[33] Wealthy Dönme naturally chose to live in this new suburb, beyond the crowded urban core, where they could use their fortunes to build themselves spacious, sumptuous seaside villas. Most Kapancı resided in Hamidiye, where they tended to live next door to one another, or at least as close as possible. According to a descendant of the tobacco merchant Duhani Hasan Akif, "All of the adjacent houses were occupied by relatives and so it was really a family neighborhood."[34]

Like other wealthy Kapancı, the family of Hasan Akif owned a mansion in Hamidiye, only a few houses down from Mehmet Kapancı's villa, I was told.[35] The latter's address was Hamidiye Boulevard 108, and that of the former, 120.[36] The 1906 Register of Land and Properties confirms that Kapancı Dönme resided next to one another or in close proximity in the district. Mehmet, Ahmet, and Yusuf Kapancı owned villas near one another on Hamidiye Boulevard (today named Odos Basilissis Olgas), the younger brothers' residences being separated by the villa of Osman İnayet Efendi. I counted only three hundred steps separating Mehmet Kapancı's villa (built in 1898) and Ahmet's (built in 1900).[37] Ahmet Kapancı's villa was next door to that of Osman İnayet Efendi, and neighbored those of Emin Receb Efendi, also listed in the provincial yearbook as a great merchant, in the same trade as other Kapancı,[38] and Osman Dervish Efendi, listed as a famous banker and owner of cashmere concerns.[39] All four men were board members of the Kapancı Terakki school; Ahmet Kapancı was selected the head of the administrative council of the school in 1910 and ran the boys' school; Dervish Efendi ran the girls' school.[40] If we consider that Yusuf and Mehmet Kapancı lived nearby, and if the Fazıl Efendi who resided next to Ahmet Kapancı as mentioned in the 1906 Register was Mustafa Fazıl, meaning that four members lived next door to one another (Mustafa Fazıl, Ahmet Kapancı, Osman İnayet, and Yusuf Kapancı), two of whom were brothers, then half of the founders and early board members of the school were part of a very close and closed social community. This was not an ordinary school set up just for any students. As in the central Karakaş districts, a street in Hamidiye was also named for Şemsi Efendi.[41]

Because of their choice of Hamidiye, and the buildings they constructed there, the Kapancı appear to be the most dynamic, forward-looking, and experimental of the sects. This may be related to their close association with the Mevlevi order of Sufis, which counted among its members much of the Ottoman urban elite. That so many Kapancı were able to build seaside villas in the poshest district of the city also attests to their ability to take advantage of nineteenth-century economic developments. Like other Ottoman cities' new outlying suburbs, the quarter "attracted wealthy merchants to move out of the old city" and build mansions where they could display and stage their social status.[42] Their choice of residential segregation, however, confirms their continued closed nature. The two impulses competed in them.

The Kapancı's other reasons for choosing Hamidiye are less apparent. Among these were the absence there of mosques, and the opportunity for family and sect members to live side by side. In his autobiography, the Karakaş Reşat Tesal, son of a parliamentarian in Salonika, relates how his father had wanted to move after he married from a densely crowded predominantly Muslim quarter of the city, most likely one of the six mentioned above, to Hamidiye, but his parents refused to let him do so, in part because they didn't want him to move out, but more because they did not want him living so far from a mosque.[43]

Most Dönme lived in neighborhoods in the center of Salonika, between the predominantly Muslim and Jewish sections of the city (Karakaş and Yakubi). This reflects the fact that they were seen as in between Jews and Muslims in both a religious sense and a social sense (an understanding manifested in the 1942 wealth tax in Turkey, discussed in Chapter 9). And while living in between does not always mean having a mediating or in-between role, we know that residential patterns in Salonika at the turn of the twentieth century mapped onto and symbolized identities.

The Dönme Mosque

The Dönme lived apart, but did their buildings look like those built by others? How does their distinct architecture illustrate the Dönme way? Syncretistic Dönme tastes were inscribed in the visual language of their buildings.[44] Dönme architecture displayed an experimental boldness and synthesis of western European and Ottoman forms. As we have seen, the Dönme chose to build their seaside mansions, mosque, and schools in the new suburb of Hamidiye. Ahmet Kapancı's 1900 villa contains Corinthian capitals, Moorish arches, bands of multicolored Spanish tile, and baroque touches, as I observed on several visits (see fig. 1.1). The monogram "AK" is prominently etched in Latin letters on the front of the building. The architect, Pierro Arigoni, was influenced by the Danish

FIGURE 1.1 Ahmet Kapancı villa, Thessaloníki. Photo by author.

Hansen and Austrian baroque styles; this building could be referred to as having a Turkish baroque style. Mehmet Kapancı had hired Arigoni to design his art nouveau villa, Château Mon Bonheur (My Happiness), with its neo-Gothic and neo-Moorish elements, two years earlier (fig. 1.2). The two villas rival each other in splendor.[45]

A photograph taken in the first decade of the twentieth century on the steps of Ahmet Kapancı's villa shows the Kapancı clan wearing the latest western European fashions. Ahmet Kapancı stands at the top of the stairs, left hand in the trouser pocket of his three-piece suit, pulling his suit jacket back and showing the gold chain of his pocket watch. He is bareheaded, and his Panama hat, doubtless meant to be out of view of the camera, sits on the railing in the corner of the photo. Next to him stands a young man in a fez and a three-piece suit, and next to him is a man in a bowler (derby) hat, which signified membership in the professional class. The three men stand above four elegantly dressed women, including an impressive matriarch, some wearing ornate hats, and a young boy.

FIGURE 1.2   Mehmet Kapancı villa, Thessaloníki. Photo by author.

In the same years, another Italian architect, Vitaliano Poselli (1838–1918), Yakubi Dönme Mayor Hamdi Bey's municipal builder, was hired to build the New Mosque (fig. 1.3), fifteen to twenty minutes' walk from the Kapancı villas. It was to be a Muslim house of worship like no other. Poselli had the masons add a plaque of white marble inscribed "Mimar Vitaliano Poselli" in the modified Ottoman Arabic script, with "Architetto" in Italian beneath it, reflecting the New Mosque's mix of western European and Ottoman styles. In a photograph of the New Mosque's 1904 inauguration, a large crowd of men look on in approval, among them Third Army Field Marshall Hajji Mehmet Hayri Pasha, who owned a mansion across the street and had endowed the mosque. Major Ali Salhi, director of the Imperial Military Preparatory School, and Hajji Agha of Serres, a former director general of the Post and Telegraph Department, who had both also made contributions to the work, are there as well. The architecture of the New Mosque is strikingly innovative.[46] The design was the peak of daring architectural eclecticism in the city, bringing together baroque and Ottoman mosque styles, Moorish flourishes and the modern decorative

FIGURE 1.3   The New Mosque, Thessaloníki. Photo by author.

arts, even Habsburg Orientalism, picked up in Vienna.[47] Its Corinthian columns, paying homage to the Greco-Byzantine history of the place and to neoclassicism, hold up Alhambra-style Andalusian arches, referencing Islam as well as the origin of many of the Spanish Jewish Dönme ancestors, above which prominent bands of six-pointed stars in marble wrapping are inscribed on the building's interior and exterior, conjuring up comparisons with Italian synagogues. Above the entrance, a large six-pointed star is embedded within an ornate arabesque. Among the arabesques on the ceiling is a star and crescent. Finally, clocks positioned near the top of two turrets on the front of the building remind one of the era's accelerated pace, whereas a sundial on the south side represents older local ways of telling time.[48]

We can interpret the construction of this mosque in at least three ways. First, we might assume that the Yakubi Dönme who endowed it were sincere Muslims, and that the building was a manifestation of their faith. Second, we might imagine that the Dönme prayed in the mosque like other Muslims, but added extra Dönme prayers and rituals. Thus they were "Muslims plus." Or we might believe that although they built a mosque, and prayed in it, they either did not do so sincerely, or never actually engaged in Muslim rituals there. From all the evidence I have gathered, what strikes me as most convincing is the second, that the Dönme, even in their own mosque, or especially in their own mosque, practiced both Muslim and Dönme rituals, in keeping with Dönme character.

The question remains: when did they start attending mosque? Prior to the building of the New Mosque, they must have prayed in their neighborhood mosques, in addition to their central Dönme prayer houses. It is hard to imagine the Dönme completely feigning Islam, praying five times a day, at home before dawn, and with the community on Friday afternoon, and remaining unaffected. It is hard to imagine the mind of the individual being completely absent when he went through the motions. It is more logical to assume that the Dönme prayed like other Muslims, but added additional Dönme prayers and rituals, just as they did at their exclusive burial services.

The question then emerges, with whom did they pray? It is also hard to imagine that individual Dönme would pray at mosques shoulder to shoulder with Muslims who might notice a difference in their prayers. If the New Mosque was the main mosque used by Dönme for funeral prayers before burials, then it may have served a function similar to that of the Teşvikiye mosque, which all sects of the Dönme began to use for funeral prayers before burials in the 1920s, many attended by Sabiha Sertel,[49] when they arrived in large numbers in Istanbul.

An answer to questions about Dönme mosques may come from the architecture of Dönme schools, explored in the next chapter. Dönme schools looked like the state school buildings of the Hamidiye era. They were symmetrical, neoclassical, built of dressed stone masonry, and had arched windows and ornamental staircases and entrances. Unlike state schools, however, as we learn from the board meeting notes of the Terakki in 1900, by which time non-Dönme were also allowed to matriculate there, Dönme schools did not contain mosques.[50] For had they done so, Muslim students might have noticed something was different about the prayers conducted there. It is more credible that Dönme who still practiced their religion in the early twentieth century prayed together along with other Dönme in neighborhood mosques where they predominated, before finally building their own, exclusive mosque.

The Dönme New Mosque is not only architecturally diverse, but illustrates how Dönme buildings were adorned with meanings, temporal as well as ritualistic, only they could create, making what was Jewish or Islamic into their own. The first is the Ottoman inscription on the sundial, "Turn your clocks back ten minutes." This may be a reference to the Dönme custom of publicly fulfilling all of the requirements of Sunni Islam, but with slight alterations. Thus, for example, Dönme ended their Ramadan fast each day five minutes prior to its official end, invalidating it. The second is the Arabic inscription in gold letters within the white marble of the mosque's prayer niche (*qiblah*), which states, "Turn your face in the direction of the Noble Sanctuary." This Qur'anic verse (2:142–44) is a logical one for a qiblah of a mosque, for it tells the believers to cease praying toward Jerusalem like Jews and to turn toward Mecca, since they are a distinct community of God that has replaced the Jews as God's covenanted people. One can find other Ottoman mosques with the same inscription over the qiblah. However, in choosing this particular verse, the Dönme expressed *their* turning away from the practices of their Jewish ancestors, distinguishing themselves from Jews, just like the first believers in seventh-century Arabia, who had also turned away from Jewish practices. Yet another reading of the same verse allows the Dönme to express their distinction from Muslims, for the Dönme did not act as other Muslims. The verse tells the Dönme to face the right direction when they pray; according to the eighteen commandments of Shabbatai Tzevi, Dönme observance of Ramadan and public prayers was meant for public viewing, in order to deceive Muslims about their true beliefs and rituals.[51] Thus, publicly praying like Muslims, or even building a mosque, did not necessarily mean that all Dönme were like other Muslims.

I see the Dönme mosque as an extension of the Dönme time zone into the public realm. In his discussion of the complicated nature of converso identity in Argentina, José Faur highlights the inside/outside dichotomy, noting how the public world allows the private to exist, and connects the converso to another time and space. "*Outside,* we shared the culture and values of the Europeanized Sephardim intertwined with those of the old Buenos Aires," Faur writes. "*But upon entering into the house* and speaking to our grandparents, the outer world vanished, and we joined a *time zone* inhabited by people and places *belonging to a different epoch* and a different realm."[52]

Exploring Dönme architecture, in particular the mosque, allows me to answer the question where precisely the Dönme acted as Dönme, and where as Muslims. Consider the Yakubi, who appear to have had their council meetings and prayer services in the home of their leader, which was surrounded by thick walls, indistinguishable from other homes from the outside, and, as seen in the case of a police raid on it, must have had guards who kept a watch for such raids. Yalman mentions how his house in the heart of the city was "kept safe and private behind high walls and without any outside windows on the first floor."[53] On the other hand, think of the Dönme mosque, which superseded it. Imagining the architecture, inscriptions, and iconography, I surmise that Dönme meaning was built into the physical structure and that, as at their funerals, additional Dönme prayers or rituals were added. The question of interiors and exteriors is an important one for the dense, crowded city center where Karakaş lived. As seen in late Ottoman treatises, Muslim neighbors would peer into windows of Dönme homes and check on what they were doing, whether they were fulfilling the requirements of Islam, whether, for example, the Dönme awoke before dawn and took the predawn meal during Ramadan.

At the same time, there is a turn away from inward-looking, unremarkable private architecture (homes in the medieval city center) to ostentatious public displays of newly acquired wealth (seaside villas in the new suburb). The Dönme moved from conclaves in hidden meeting houses behind walls, which were thus invisible from the street, to a public house of worship, the city's newest and last Ottoman mosque, in the new suburb beyond the city center in a period of literal and figurative smashing of old barriers. Yet, as always, they erected boundaries between themselves and others, such as by inscribing meaning into their mosque that only they were meant to understand and by segregating their dead.

Separate Cemeteries

Death is part of life. Death, like marriage and birth, is one of the times in one's life when community affiliations are most clearly articulated. In death, as in life, Dönme tended to cluster together according to sect. A crucial practice that maintained their distinct identity was burying their dead in their own cemeteries. In an empire where groups were divided from one another by religion, this was another clear sign that the Dönme were neither simply Jewish nor merely Muslim. In Salonika, there were separate Dönme cemeteries for each sect. Each sect also tended the tombs of its leaders, for example, that of Osman Baba in the center of Salonika, cared for by the Karakaş. Although hardly a trace (only a couple of photographs) remains of these cemeteries, we can piece together information about them.

Salonika did not have secular municipal cemeteries. Each individual had to be buried by the burial society of a religious community in a plot of land set aside for its members. If the Dönme had been Jews, or had been considered Jews by Jews, they would have been buried in the vast Jewish cemetery in the city, with its estimated 300,000 tombstones, the largest Jewish cemetery in the world,[54] but this was not the case. What is peculiar is that the Kapancı cemetery was built adjacent to the Jewish cemetery, forming part of its northwestern boundary, to the east of the Byzantine core of the city.[55] The Kapancı began interring their dead next to the Jewish cemetery in the early eighteenth century. The oldest tombstone discovered by archaeologists dates from 1737. Their cemetery was walled off, forming an enclosed space restricted to Dönme graves, abutting yet separated from the neighboring Jewish graves. The Karakaş maintained two cemeteries northwest of the Byzantine core of the city near the Mevlevi Sufi lodge.[56] Their cemeteries are referred to in the *Journal l'Indépendant*'s turn-of-the-twentieth-century city map as "Cimetières turcs." The two cemeteries faced each other across a street.

§2   Religious and Moral Education
Schools and Their Effects

The voluminous writings of Ahmet Emin Yalman, a member of the Yakubi Dönme sect born and raised in Ottoman Salonika, provide great insight into the changing circumstances of Dönme life. In his Turkish-language autobiography, Yalman discusses the pivotal role that education at Dönme schools played in transforming the city in the late Ottoman era. The founder of the Turkish Republic and its first president, Mustafa Kemal, known as Atatürk after 1934, attended the exclusive school of the Dönme educator Şemsi Efendi in 1886–87 (not the Terakki school or the Feyziye school, as is popularly believed in Turkey). Yalman tells of an interview he had with Atatürk at Çankaya Kiosk, the latter's office and residence in Ankara, in the winter of 1922:

§ The horse tram stops in front of the garden home in Çankaya, which has a view of countless minarets, the city of Ankara, overlooked by the ruins of the ancient citadel, and beyond, a sunny, calm, wide plain.[1] The kiosk is a very simple building. Once inside, Yalman passes along a wide, long hall, with a tiled fountain in the middle. From the hall, he enters Atatürk's office. It is filled with books and gifts that have been given to him, among them the famous sword of the North African Sufi leader and warrior Sheikh Sanusi in recognition of Atatürk's help organizing Libyan resistance against invading Italians just before World War I, other weapons presented to him, an ode in ornamental gilded Arabic script, books in French, and two Qur'ans given by Sheikh Sanusi, which sit on a small table. The eye fills with all the gifts on the desk that foreign admirers have sent Atatürk.

The general arrives just as the clocks strike eleven. He wears an outfit made of coarse cloth, which suits Ankara's wartime fashion. The first question Atatürk answers concerns his earliest memories:

"The first thing I remember from my childhood is the problem of entering school. There was a severe clash between my mother and father over this. My mother wanted me to begin my education by enrolling in the neighborhood's religious school, with chanting of the appropriate religious hymns. But my father, who was a clerk at the customs office, was in favor of sending me to Şemsi Efendi's newly opened school and of my getting the new type of education. In the end, my father artfully found a solution. First, with the usual ceremony, I entered the religious school. Thus, my mother was satisfied. After a few days I left the religious school and enrolled in the school of Şemsi Efendi. Soon afterward, my father died."[2]

This passage has been interpreted to mean that Atatürk depicted the late Ottoman period in Salonika as a time of struggle between the forces of the traditional (Islam) and the new or modern (secularism). The Dönme leader Şemsi Efendi (fig. 2.1), whose name means "The Illuminator," is

FIGURE 2.1   Şemsi Efendi. Tombstone portrait, Istanbul. Photo by author.

placed in the latter category. Although not stated, it is assumed that Şemsi Efendi's school was not religious, although it was. But what happens to Atatürk's narrative when we realize that what was at stake was not a struggle between Islam and an implied secularism, but between two interpretations of how to live ostensibly as Muslims?

Şemsi Efendi and the First Dönme Schools

The key features of all Dönme schools established in Salonika at the end of the nineteenth century—morals and ethics, foreign languages, progressive values—are succinctly stated in a 1904 graduation speech by the Feyziye school's founder, Mustafa Tevfik, who said that "next year more attention will be paid to students' moral development. Classes in morals and ethics are being added and increased in primary and middle school. Moreover, in implementing the decision of the Primary and Middle School Teachers Congress in Paris, a classroom teacher has been added to every class, which is very important for discipline and morals." The classroom teacher, who always stayed with the students, unlike the usual "roaming" teachers, was to "explain moral and ethical subjects and always observe the students closely." Although they focused on the mind and morals, "it would be a mistake to forget about the body: we plan to hire a teacher of gymnastics. While in the past we thought it was essential to focus only on teaching French to the best of our abilities, without other foreign languages detracting from it, now we have decided to add German, an important language of commerce. We also plan to develop our girls school."[3]

The outlook of the Dönme merchant families was especially evident in their schools, where foreign and local languages, modern sciences, and business skills were taught together with religion, ethics, morals, and Dönme social bonds and boundaries. All were purposely combined in meaningful ways allowing Dönme youth to perpetuate the local and international networks of which the Dönme were a part. Prior to the late nineteenth century, Dönme schooling occurred behind closed doors, mainly in the central buildings of the head of the group's compound. Religious leaders were trained by their predecessors and studied the precepts of Shabbatai Tzevi and his successors, whether Yakubi, Karakaş, or Kapancı. In the late nineteenth century, at the outset of a wave of educational reform and change in the empire that affected all religious communities, Dönme educators began to emerge into the open, adding modern conceptions of religion, including ethics and morality, yet still at first only teaching members of the group.[4]

Inasmuch as private Dönme schools predated the establishment of state schools under Sultan Abdülhamid II, Dönme educational efforts were in advance of the state, as well as of the initiatives of local Muslims in promoting new curriculums, teaching methods, and moral character building.[5] Both state and Dönme schools aimed to satisfy "the demands of the present," or modern age. For the state, this meant fostering a loyal, honest civil service.[6] But for the Dönme, it entailed ensuring that Dönme were able to be educated in Dönme religion and values, in addition to being well placed financially and politically. Dönme schools not only emphasized Islamic morality but taught French, which served to further their international business relations. Another aim of the Dönme schools was to ensure that Dönme youth only befriended and socialized with other Dönme: after being dismissed at the end of the day from school, students were to not stop in the street or play, but go home, and they were never to befriend any but children from the school.[7] Even on Friday, when the first Dönme school had no class, students were to come to school and play with classmates until evening. Whether they needed this extra incentive was unclear: in Sabiha Sertel's biography, we read that "her friends were wealthy Dönme girls" including the daughter of Etem Efendi, one of the wealthiest timber merchants.[8]

The Yakubi Dönme mayor Hamdi Bey erected modern public buildings and also opened a school called Selimiye for educating Dönme youth.[9] Hamdi Bey's school did not last long, however, and the most enduring Dönme educational efforts trace their origins to Şemsi Efendi.[10] In 1873, at the early age of twenty-one, he opened the Şemsi Efendi school in the tiny mosque of the predominantly Karakaş neighborhood of Sinancık, with the assistance and support of the director of education and donations from others. The school was just one block from the seat of the governor and across the street from the Rüşdiye for girls and the Ministry of Justice.[11] This was a year before French Jews established the first secular Alliance israélite universelle school for boys in the city, where students learned Turkish, French, and trades.[12] When Governor Midhat Pasha toured local schools, he visited Şemsi Efendi's and was pleased to find that it used the latest pedagogical methods. When he asked why they did not have a better building, the administrators and teachers responded that they feared attack by gangs of bigots. They

were all invited to the governor's mansion and given gold watches. Galip
Pasha, later governor, helped finance and construct a new building.[13]
Ahmet Kapancı, en route to western Europe, helped the school obtain
a teacher from Istanbul.[14] The school taught French, Ottoman Turkish,
and Islam. Turkish historians writing to promote the image of the school
claim that it was the first private Muslim school to open a preschool
for girls and to allow girls to continue their education, and established
close relations with administrators and teachers from French schools,
using the example of French textbooks to establish lesson plans and
curriculums.[15]

Soon afterward, Şemsi Efendi moved the school to where it appears
on post-1880 maps, behind Sufi Lodge street and across the street from
İpekçi street, named for another leading Karakaş family. The school was
both popular and famous for teaching critical thinking, rather than rote
memorization, and for inventing a new type of blackboard. There were
attacks and pressure on it, however, and the number of students declined.
Finally, Şemsi Efendi was forced to close it in 1891.

The Karakaş Dönme Galip Pasha (Pasiner) (not to be confused with
Governor Galip Pasha) also began his education under Şemsi Efendi.
In his memoirs, he recalls how at the age of six, he was in a traditional
school, where learning was by rote and students sat on the floor.[16] But like
Atatürk's, his father decided one day to send him to a new school. When
he entered its courtyard, he noted twenty to thirty children at play and a
young teacher, perhaps twenty or twenty-one years old, in their midst, who
turned his attention to him. This was Şemsi Efendi. After he had played
for a while with the others, they were told to enter the classroom. They
formed two lines and fell in behind the teacher. As soon as Galip entered
the classroom, he was struck by the fragrant scent of two rows of brand-
new pine desks, a beautiful raised chair for the teacher, reached by two
steps, and the blackboard, chalk, and eraser. He recalls how the windows
were open, allowing in (symbolically charged) fresh air. The same windows
would also serve as an escape route for Şemsi Efendi after he was accused of
teaching the children according to "infidel" methods and letting them play
games and do gymnastics. Galip Pasha describes the last days of the school:
while they were in the classroom, a mob of forty or fifty men gathered
outside, cursing loudly, broke down the door, and entered. Şemsi Efendi
dived out of a window to escape, and the men threw the students out of
the classroom and then destroyed it, breaking the teacher's chair, chalk-

board, windows, and doors. Only twenty students—the children of police and bureaucrats—remained at the school after that. Şemsi Efendi opened a new school in his own home, but it was also attacked. This time he saved himself by hiding. Although they didn't touch his home, they again destroyed his blackboard, symbol of infidelity. Years later, Şemsi Efendi told Galip Pasha how they had caught him, beaten him, and threatened him at knifepoint, ordering him to leave Salonika or stop teaching. But he paid no heed and taught students at their homes at night.[17]

Şemsi Efendi's innovation was based on new pedagogical methods, such as using Ottoman texts with vowels to make learning to read easier.[18] His school became a model for others, notably, the Terakki and Feyziye schools, founded by Dönme inspired by his example.[19]

The Kapancı Terakki and Karakaş Feyziye Schools

Galip Pasha (Pasiner) and Atatürk use the example of Şemsi Efendi to illustrate the turn from old ways to the new. This idea was reflected in the name of the next Dönme school to be founded. In 1879, the founders of the first new Dönme school after Şemsi Efendi's school opted to use the term *terakki* (progress, renewal) in naming it, expressing their belief in the Enlightenment concept that humans could influence the process of natural human progression and improvement. In accordance with this positivist view, largely influenced by the work of August Comte, the only way to progress was through a solid education in the arts and sciences. Education, seen as the basic means of societal improvement, thus became the most important field of reform and experimentation in the late Ottoman period.[20]

Leading Kapancı Dönme financiers, who had connections especially in western Europe (France and Belgium), including Mehmet, Yusuf, and Ahmet Kapancı and Duhani Hasan Akif, funded the construction of a school that shows how the Dönme adopted a modern view equating religion with morals and using education to effect social and cultural change. The sixteen Kapancı Dönme who made up the committee that established the Terraki school included leading members of the business and professional classes and civil service: textile and tobacco merchants, directors of tobacco factories, lawyers, teachers, bankers, and Abdi Bey, Ottoman consul in Iran.[21] Among the members of the first Terakki school board were Ahmet Kapancı (chairman), Consul Abdi Efendi, tobacco merchant Duhani Hasan Akif, Mustafa Fazıl, and Osman Ahad / Ehat.[22] For the next few decades, its board of directors would include prominent merchants (Ahmet Kapancı, Duhani Hasan Akif), bankers (Mehmet Kapancı, Yusuf Kapancı, Namık Kapancı, İbrahim Kapancı), professionals (attorneys, doctors, pharmacists), and civil servants (directors of the state monopoly tobacco factories, railway officials).[23] The Terakki school was across the street from the Pinti Hasan Mosque and the Rüşdiye school for boys, in a neighborhood in which Kapancı predominated.[24] It grew rapidly; by 1907, it had three new buildings: a boys' school, a girls' school, and a boarding school in the new Hamidiye suburb.

One of the founding board members was Duhani Hasan Akif, whose life I learned about through interviews with a descendant.[25] Hasan Akif was related to another board member, Abdurrahman Telci, a dealer in silver wire. Osman Telci (Telci Osman Efendi), a merchant dealing in silk and gold wire and thread,[26] and his wife Emine Dudu, who are buried in the Kapancı section of the main Dönme cemetery in Istanbul,[27] paid for the construction of a new Terakki school building in Hamidiye.[28] A street there was named after Osman Telci.[29] The family was evidently devoted to the school, and Hasan Akif's six daughters were educated there. Emine Akif (d. 1935) and her brother Hüsnü were both teachers at the school, and Hasan Akif's granddaughter Nuriye (b. 1881) was also among its students. The family possesses a photograph of Nuriye and Şemsi Efendi on her graduation day.

Testifying to the role played by Kapancı merchants in establishing the school, in 1906, a plaque was hung on the wall of the principal's office thanking Mehmet Kapancı. It read: "This school building came into existence with the laudable, knowledge-promoting assistance and support of his honor the fortunate Mehmet Kapancı Efendi."[30] This man, who made a name for himself in international commerce, saw to it that Dönme youth were educated in Dönme principles.

Following the Kapancı Terakki, the Karakaş established a school in 1883–84, named Feyz-i Sıbyân (The Excellence of Youth, later shortened to simply Feyziye, Excellence). Its first location was in an old Qur'an school in the Katip Musliheddin neighborhood, the second in Hacı İsmail, both heavily populated by Karakaş and, like the Terakki school, near the seat of government. The person who first conceived of the idea for the Feyziye was Karakaş Dönme Mısırlızade Abdurrahman Zeki, a translator at the French consulate, a man educated in foreign schools, who understood the connection between knowledge of foreign languages and international commerce.[31] The Mısırlı family, who like the other main Karakaş families were heavily involved in the textile trade, were descendants of Jewish cloth merchants in Spain.[32] After Abdurrahman Zeki's death, his son Mustafa Tevfik, clerk in the office of the governor, established the school. Among the members of the first council or board were the international traders Mustafa Cezar, Karakaş Mehmet, and İpekçi İsmail.[33] İpekçi İsmail (b. 1853) served on the board from 1885 to 1932 and was head of the board until his death in 1936.[34] Without neglecting their international and imperial connections, these Dönme businessmen and government officials found time to help run a private school to educate members of their own ethno-religious group.

Both schools chose names that suited their similar aims. Just as the revolutionary Committee of Union and Progress (İttihad ve Terakki Cemiyeti) chose the word *terakki*, pregnant with meaning, to represent its aims and principles, claiming in its program that the CUP came together "in order to warn our Muslim and Christian countrymen against the system of government of the present regime, which violates such human rights as justice, equality, and freedom, which holds all Ottomans back from progress,"[35] so the founders of the Kapancı Terakki school intended to promote a new type of school that would foster a new type of Ottoman citizen. In these new schools, teachers as well as students were trained to be modern individuals. Teachers were not only responsible for their lessons but had to discipline students and administer the school as well. The mind and the body were both educated: from the beginning, Swedish-style gymnastics were part of the curriculum.[36] Sports were promoted as a means of disciplining and managing the students. According to a 1909 regulation, one hour each day was set aside for the "education of the body." The school also employed a doctor to monitor the health of the students. Timetables and schedules were produced and adhered to, and teachers kept registers of student names and detailed lists of student performance and attendance. Photographs of students show them wearing fezzes, frock coats, trousers, and ties.[37] In order to raise a new generation of Dönme youth able to expand the group's international economic links, the Terraki school emphasized commerce, bookkeeping, accounting, and French, in addition to Turkish. The school fed students to the best schools in Istanbul and placed its graduates in positions in commerce, finance, and the railway in Salonika.[38]

The Feyziye school aimed to fulfill the promise of its name, "Excellence," by creating a perfect religious and moral person. Its curriculum was calibrated to instill linguistic, spiritual, scientific, and vocational knowledge and skills through eight years of education. The student was both taught ostensibly Islamic virtues and prepared body, mind, and soul for the new society of the turn of the century.[39] He could clearly and fluently express his thoughts in Turkish, Ottoman, and French, regarded as the leading European language and language of commerce; he was disciplined, organized, and well prepared for a profession. His body was fit: "gymnastics taught by special teachers will increase and perfect the physical and spiritual progress of the students, and will urge the students to be morally virtuous and make serious efforts."[40] Foreigners taught gymnastics. Physicians instructed students in hygiene.[41] A graduate both possessed local knowledge and was prepared to function in an international environment, guided by the morals and ethics of his people. The latter aim was ensured by having Şemsi Efendi serve in the administration of the school and teach religious precepts from 1900 to 1912, when he migrated to Istanbul.[42] Thus although the curricula of Dönme schools by this point were matched by those of other schools, especially the state schools, Şemsi Efendi's teaching religion points to the difference: he was the leading Dönme religious thinker of his day, and he did not teach in any but Dönme schools in Salonika.

In keeping with Şemsi Efendi's aims, the education of girls was not neglected. In the 1890s, the Feyziye and the Terakki opened girls' schools; the Feyziye's eventually expanded into a middle school for girls.[43] The Terakki Girls Commerce School was founded around 1908.[44] In 1911, when Sultan Mehmet V Reşat visited Salonika, he was greeted by Terakki schoolgirls, viewed an exhibit of their handiwork, and even donated money to the school.[45]

Students in Dönme schools were well prepared to engage in international commerce and serve the empire. In 1904, new courses were added that would aid future civil servants, including official-style writing, political economy, commercial law, physical geography, chemistry, economics, and economic geography.[46] There was such a strong emphasis on commerce that the Feyziye board considered making it the Ottoman Commerce School, and around same time, offered to establish a commerce school jointly with Terakki school, which also had a strong emphasis on commerce.[47] The most important Ottoman merchants were former students of the Terakki school, because of its stress on foreign language and commerce, according to *Mütalâa* (Contemplation), a periodical founded by Osman Tevfik,[48] Atatürk's teacher of calligraphy and penmanship at the military preparatory school in Salonika.[49] The Feyziye school also produced many important people in the world of commerce, as well as many people who would be of importance in the capital. Mehmet Rüştü Karakaşzade (b. 1880) graduated in 1892 and became a merchant.[50] Eight years his junior, Osman Tevfik's son Ahmet Emin Yalman, who like Atatürk also attended the military preparatory school in Salonika, studied under Şemsi Efendi at the Feyziye in the 1890s. Both Karakaşzade and Yalman would play prominent roles in public debates over the Dönme in Turkey in the 1920s.

The Feyziye school had good relations with the state, which saw it as a helpful asset. Şemsi Efendi in particular was on excellent terms with all the sultans who ruled between the time he opened his first school and the year Salonika was lost to Greece. He received many sultanic honors for his efforts, from Sultan Murad V in 1876 to Sultan Abdülhamid II thirty years later. After having brought his Feyziye students to Istanbul in 1909 to visit the sultan, the next year he was rewarded with the Education 3rd degree mark of distinction. In 1911, he received the Mecidi 2nd degree from Sultan Mehmet V Reşat during the latter's visit to Salonika.[51] One of the reasons he was repeatedly honored was that students he taught served the empire. Because the school emphasized commerce in the last few years of the curriculum, most who graduated from the Feyziye secondary school went into business.[52] But all graduates were prepared to matriculate at the preparatory school for civil servants (Mülkiye), and many enlisted in government service.[53] Mehmet Tevfik Bey, governor of Salonika in 1901, notes in his memoirs that the Feyziye was superior to all other schools and produced successful civil servants.[54] The *Journal de Salonique*, established in 1895, when Dönme were most influential, had a very positive attitude toward their contributions to urban life, particularly the establishment of progressive schools, and calls the school the most beneficial and well administered.[55]

Graduates at turn-of-the-twentieth century Feyziye ceremonies were applauded by the leaders of the city, including its administrators, leading financiers and merchants, and military men, illustrating the importance of the school and the Dönme connection with, and membership, in the bureaucratic, commercial, and military elite of the city. Foreign consuls also attended, illustrating the school's international connections.[56] At the same time, the Dönme schools, like Dönme businesses, continued to be based on an ethno-religious model. The *Journal de Salonique* compared the Feyziye graduation ceremony of 1899 to a family gathering.[57] The newspaper was not far from the mark. In 1902, the members of the board were largely related: the thirteen members were headed by Mustafa Tevfik and included his older brothers Suleiman Şevket and Osman Vasıf and his brother İbrahim Ziver. Osman Fettan, Mehmet Sarım, and Mehmet Rıza, who owned Kibar Ali Brothers and Sons, which was recognized both at home and abroad for its role in the hardware and metal goods businesses, and for selling American goods, were also on the board.[58]

The schools emphasized Dönme morals and ethics as one of their core purposes. In a 1903 announcement placed in the Dönme Fazlı Necip's *Asır* (Century / Age) newspaper soliciting student applicants, the Terakki school boasts of devoting particular attention to morals and ethics.[59] Unsurprisingly, considering the heavy emphasis Şemsi Efendi placed on morality, the founder of the Feyziye school, Mustafa Tevfik, emphasized morals in the 1904 graduation speech quoted earlier, which was reported in the Dönme-owned *Selânik* [Salonika] and *Asır* newspapers. Tevfik also stressed the need for graduates to be both local and international, looking to their own morals (mentioned five times), while participating in international commerce, aided by mastery of foreign languages.

Morals were also instilled through the exercise called "public assembly." Once a week, the principal would give several questions to a student, who had two days to prepare answers, which he delivered before an assembly. After the student's presentation, the principal would give a lesson on morality based on the questions the student had answered. The aim was to ensure that students would be able to express themselves, defend their thoughts in public, and be ethical.[60] The Dönme were creating a moral community. In 1897, the *Selânik Vilâyeti Salnamesi* (Yearbook of the Province of Salonika) noted approvingly that the Feyziye school attempted to ensure students' spiritual and material advancement by instructing them in Islamic virtues.[61] The yearbook also lauded the fact that the Terakki aimed to reform and improve the character of those who attended its schools, instituting courses devoted to improving students' morals.[62]

A textbook guide to morality issued under Abdülhamid II in 1900 promoted morals similar to those that had been emphasized for years in Dönme schools: sound morals were based on Islamic virtues, which included religiosity, faithfulness, cleanliness, effort, ascetic discipline, sound management, contentment, knowledge, patience, order, self-knowledge, self-control and restraint, obedience and respect, a sense of justice, sociability, benevolence, kindness and gentleness, sincerity, love and brotherhood, and duty.[63] These virtues are comparable to those extolled in Şemsi Efendi's Rules of Behavior for Students. Students were to be clean, hardworking, punctual, disciplined, organized, good-tempered, well-behaved, helpful, polite, brotherly, nonviolent, dutiful, and respectful of teachers, elders, and parents, control their tongues and be quiet, look out for others, never lie, steal, cheat, be hypocritical, or engage in double-dealing, and always be purposeful.[64] Already in 1877, teachers were also given a very long list of rules to follow, one of which demanded that they be good role models to the students in manners and morals.[65]

The Schools' Influence: Literature

In the 1880s, educated Dönme who made up the avant-garde in the Salonika literary scene produced *Gonca-i Edeb* (The Rosebud of Literature), a journal dedicated to internationalism, science, French literature, Sufi spirituality, religion, and ethics, reflecting their worldview, which attracted a wide and diverse audience of readers, mainly from among those also engaged in disseminating the new forms of culture.[66] Teachers and students from the Terraki and Feyziye schools and Dönme civil servants and intellectuals contributed to this extraordinary literary journal, published in Ottoman Turkish, which, like the curriculum in the Terakki and Feyziye, combined science and religion and displays a mastery of French and Ottoman language and literature.[67]

The name and contents of *Gonca-i Edeb* both express the interplay between what was outward and what was inward for the Dönme in turn-of-the-twentieth-century Salonika. *Edeb* is a classical Islamic term referring to education, learning, and proper morals and manners, as well as a genre of literature (*Edebiyat*), and the first piece in the first issue, by Fazlı Necip, was entitled "*Edeb veya* [or] *Edebiyat*."[68] By choosing this term, the creators of the journal were referring to over a millennium of Islamic cultural practice in Arabic, and by writing in Ottoman Turkish, to several centuries of Ottoman cultural practice, not yet rejected. Numerous pieces were written in the *qasida* or *ghazal* form, including a ghazal by a gendarme commander,[69] and a poem in the style of the sixteenth-century court poet Fuzûlî (1483?–1556) was composed by Cudi Efendi, a teacher at the Terakki school.[70] However, *Gonca-i Edeb* also displayed an openness to change, incorporating the latest western European technological developments, literary forms, and styles, including children's stories. In the first issue's opening statement, the editors proclaimed that the youth of Salonika aimed to advance the cause of education by publishing "original compositions, translations, and selections of rare works and current sciences."[71] The writers asserted that they would write in "plain language" so that youth would be able to understand the work without difficulty. Yet the language used in the journal includes French, Italian, and Sufi words and phrases in addition to more standard Ottoman vocabulary, and French literature and Ottoman and Persian poetry are discussed. *Gonca-i Edeb* might have "blossomed in a quiet corner of the rose garden of literature," but its founders hoped that this "plant newly sprouted" in Salonika, planted by "the youth of the city," would "perfume the area" of the "gardens" of the "region of literature."[72]

Most of the journal's writers and readers were drawn from among those who played a role in crafting the new culture of the late Ottoman Empire: intellectuals, male and female students, teachers, and school administrators, civil servants, professionals, military officers, and even the Karakaş Dönme general Galip Pasha. One important writer was the Dönme intellectual Fazlı Necip (1863–1932), who had graduated from the school for civil servants and worked in the office of the chief secretary of the provincial government. This office had many Dönme employees, including Yakubi Osman Tevfik and Abdi Fevzi, founders of *Gonca-i Edeb*, who when Fazlı Necip was head clerk served as treasurers and accountants. Like other Dönme and Jews who would join the Constitutional Revolution in 1908, he was also rewarded for his years of service with a sultanic honor, along with Mehmet Kapancı, Mustafa Cezar, Mehmet Karakaş (b. 1867), and Emmanuel Carasso.[73]

Displaying their links to the wider world, writers for *Gonca-i Edeb* translated French and European literature, philosophy, and writings on social science. In keeping with the needs of the age, the rapid transformation of Salonika, and the introduction of new technologies into everyday life, the journal was filled with scientific articles. Teachers of French wrote original pieces on subjects such as obtaining a pearl, carbonic acid, coal gas, dynamite, salt, and Christopher Columbus. They translated pieces from French, including wisdom literature, poetry, articles on bees, birds, death, the solar system, the transfer of heat, earthquakes, and the meaning of true help.

Gonca-i Edeb did not only include work that one might have found in many publications in that era. Contrary to what is asserted by the Turkish historian İlber Ortaylı, the authors did not refrain from writing about religion or using Muslim and Sufi approaches to life.[74] The articles are peppered with religious language. For example, Suleiman, a fourth-year student at the state Ottoman Secondary School of Salonika, wrote an essay praising the fact that students learned Islamic languages (Arabic and Persian), together with professional skills (accounting) and science (geography). He compares school to a garden adorned with the shoots of education. A page of every book taught in it "demonstrates God's greatness and divine nature." When a person enters the garden (i.e., the school), he cannot help saying that "it is as if it is a piece of paradise placed on earth."[75] In an article entitled "Ma'muriyet" (Prosperity), Abdi Fevzi explicitly links good morals to education and prosperity: "just as wasteful squandering causes prosperity's ruin, education brings it to life," and "education is a necessity for prosperity; the two are inseparable. In fact, education and prosperity are twins born of good morals."[76]

Reflecting educational values of the Terakki and Feyziye schools, *Gonca-i Edeb* also carried pieces on Sufi and Islamic themes. This displayed the continued interplay between being open and closed, distinguishing between who was a Dönme and who was not, while remaining open enough to cross the threshold into Mevlevi Sufism. Religious and Sufi expression in the journal include an essay discussing exertion on the ritual pilgrimage to Mecca (the Hajj), a poem by an official in the Ministry of Tithes based on a Sufi work, a piece by the head of the Sufi lodge located in Salonika's marketplace, and a poem written on the signboard at the Mevlevi lodge in Salonika.[77]

The Mevlevi connection is not surprising. Mevlevi Sufis appeared at ceremonies held at the two Dönme schools, such as at the opening of the Terakki Commerce School, and the children of Mevlevi sheikhs received free education at the Terakki.[78] Mustafa Fazıl (1854–1935) and Osman Ehat (1855 or 1859–1895 or 1899) were two of the founders of the Terakki school. I interviewed a descendant of Osman Ehat's.[79] In the genealogy he provided, Mustafa Fazıl (fig. 2.2) is referred to as "Dede Bey," a name with Mevlevi Sufi connotations; "Dede" is the title given to a Mevlevi master. Hasan Akif's descendant Esin Eden, a distant relative of this family, makes frequent allusions to Mevlevi Sufis. Her Dönme cookbook contains a photograph labeled "Family photograph of child in the habit of a Mevlevi murid [disciple]."[80] During one of our interviews prior to the publication of the cookbook, she had shown me this photograph, which stood out among many portraying people in typical western European dress. Yıldız Sertel, in her novelistic biography of her mother, Sabiha Sertel notes how Sabiha's father, and the author's grandfather, Nazmi Efendi, had enjoyed participating in Mevlevi rituals, and then sharing meals with the sheikh and his other disciples at the Mevlevi lodge in the city, ever since he was a boy. He had made sure that his son Mecdi, who attended the Terakki school and worked as a secretary for the Singer firm, also saw attending the lodge as a normal part of life. Yıldız Sertel depicts her grandfather as being glad to be the grandson of a Mevlevi Sufi (Dervish Ali), because with the Sufis, one felt part of a family.[81] His wife Atiye also speaks of "we Mevlevis" at one point, and she is well-versed in Sufi interpretations of creation; close relatives were disciples of Bektaşi sheikhs: "According to the Bektaşi, a human is part of God's beauty, a light that emanated from

FIGURE 2.2   Mustafa Fazıl. Tombstone portrait, Istanbul. Photo by author.

God. When God creates humans, he gives them His own light. Bektaşi see God in inanimate objects and in people, and say 'To look at an object is to look at God.' In fact, both Bektaşi and we Mevlevi say 'In order to reach God it is necessary to love Him.' This love of God unites a human with God. Study Sufism well, understand it well."[82] This was also a period when some Dönme became leading Mevlevis. Mehmet Esad Dede, for example, who was born into a Kapancı family in 1843, had a dream that caused him to become a proper Muslim, referred to in his biography as a conversion, and eventually, he became one of the leading turn-of-the-twentieth-century Mevlevi sheikhs in Istanbul.[83]

Sufi pieces such as "Vahdaniyet" (The Unity of God), by the gendarme commander Osman Agha, are prominent in *Gonca-i Edeb*, reflecting the Dönme-Sufi connection.[84] The article provides an ingenious numerological explanation of a couplet written by the author, which he uses to prove the singleness of God: "There is one God, yet His 1,001 names imply duality; / But remove the superfluous two [letters] from 'others' [i.e., than God] and what remains manifests the Beloved [God]."[85] The unity of God is a core principle of Judaism, Islam, and Dönme religion, as manifested in the first commandment of Shabbatai Tzevi.[86] The unity of God is also a common Sufi theme, according to which everything other than God is a manifestation of God's qualities, evident in God's names. "Being" is one, but "duality" arises, since God wishes to be known and therefore shows forth names in the manifold things of the world. In the Sufi interpretation, "others" refers to all things other than God, "beloved" to God. Remove the first two letters from the Ottoman word used in the couplet for "others" (*ağyar*) and "beloved" (*yâr*) remains. Hence, one should not focus on the manifestations of God, but on the Beloved (God) Himself. The head secretary of the Ministry of Tithes of Salonika wrote an essay in which he explains how he discovered that the numerical significance of the phrase *Gonca-i Edeb*, "rosebud of literature," is 1299 (1883), the year the journal first appeared.[87] For military officers and civil servants, religion was an integral component of being. Thus, the articles in *Gonca-i Edeb* display the writers' and readers' purposeful mixing of morality, spirituality, science, and technology in their lives. Being Muslim, Sufi, or Dönme, and having an ethical and moral core was not incompatible with being in tune with the latest western European trends.

Dönme literary journals not only had a religious side, but were also revolutionary. Ahmet Emin Yalman explains the founding of *Gonca-*

i Edeb, again promoting a traditional / modern binary, while adding its
political importance. He writes, "At the early age of seventeen [his fa-
ther], with a few friends of his age, had taken the initiative of establishing a literary weekly, *Gonce-i-Edeb*, which took a veiled stand against the
conservative world."[88] Ahmet Emin Yalman's father's progressive literary
weekly *Mütalâa* included poems such as "What Is the Use?" Because the
palace asked what the use of schools, books, science, hospitals and factories was, the author asked what the use was of having despotic rule, which
meant darkness, slavery, misery and humiliation. Yalman, who had been
a student at Terakki, which he called a "progressive school," boasts: "This
autographed poem soon disappeared. I hid it so that I, too, could have
a revolutionary secret. I rejoiced in being the possessor of a 'pernicious,
dangerous paper.' I soon gave up all sorts of games and concentrated my
whole interest on publishing a weekly paper of my own. I named it The
Intention and spent my holidays in writing it by hand. . . . I was carried away by the revolutionary undercurrents."[89] A cousin of his mother's
was sent into political exile for opposing the sultan.[90] Yalman's father was
forced to close *Mütalâa* that same year, and moved his family to Istanbul.[91] The Karakaş Feyziye school produced *Çocuk Bahçesi* (Kindergarten)
until 1908; thereafter, its name was changed to *Bahçe* (Garden), and it was
no longer for children. The pre-1908 version was intended to be used in
the classroom and included writing from students including Sabiha, the
daughter of Nazmi Efendi (Sertel).[92] Although a children's journal, it was
a mouthpiece for dissidents and included writing by famous adult writers
on political topics, including the negative effects of Abdülhamid II's rule
on the empire. It faced the censor.[93] The *Journal de Salonique* noted that
it was suspended for disregarding his warnings.[94]

Religious Actors and Societal Transformation

Because the Dönme schools were their only institutions to have survived (although transferred and transformed to suit other aims in the
Turkish Republic), Turkish public memory focuses on their legacy. It
is their depiction that represents much of what is remembered of the
Dönme. The public recollections of those who attended Şemsi Efendi's
first school and the histories written by those affiliated with the two
later schools established by Dönme emphasize the themes of modernity,
progress, and revolutionary thought. What they do not mention in their

analysis are the subjects of religion and morality, which are assumed to be anti-modern and reactionary. This is an important oversight, and it is even more surprising when the historical evidence shows that Dönme at the time emphasized morals in their schools and journals, illustrating how Dönme were both religious *and* progressive.

The relation between tradition and modernity was very complicated for the Dönme. They clung to some of their oldest beliefs and rituals, while engaging in entirely new ways of being. The struggle was not simply between the traditional and the new, as Atatürk and others later claimed; rather, it was an effort to maintain traditions in a new age, to be externally connected and internally isolated at the same time, using the traditional as a means of buttressing their identity, demonstrating that neither had to clash with religion and morality, which were central to the Dönme way of being in the world in turn-of-the-twentieth-century Salonika. It was only after the community faced insurmountable pressures to dissolve in the early Turkish Republic that they were eventually transformed into secularists. The Dönme were not proponents of cultural or political nationalism either. In an era in which the subject peoples of the Ottoman Empire began to imagine themselves as members of nations that had a right to rule themselves within bounded territories, the Dönme promoted a society that reflected their identity of a cultural multiplicity antithetical to nationalism, combining elements of western European and Ottoman culture instilled with Dönme religious meaning. Their schools, for example, transmitted, not only what was new and modern, but also their heritage and what was old.

Dönme religious meaning was imparted in the schools when religious precepts were taught by Şemsi Efendi. The second most important name after Şemsi Efendi in the history of Dönme education is Mehmet Cavid. He was one of the leaders of the Karakaş and belonged to the most important family of the group, descendants of Osman Baba.[95] This economist and Feyziye graduate was administrator of the Feyziye school from 1902 to 1908.[96] Among the changes he introduced were closely monitoring the morals and ethics of teachers and students, and opening a business school in 1904. He required frequent reports of student performance, successes, and morals, comparing them with others students, students in other classes, and students in previous years.[97]

Mert Sandalcı's 2005 official school history takes a very Kemalist approach, in which modernity and the West are contrasted with tradition, reactionaries, and Islam, and identifies the Feyziye founders, administrators, teachers, and students with everything progressive. Although never once using the term Dönme, the author aims to demonstrate that Dönme actions anticipated the republic. In interviews, Sandalcı also outlined the secular and nationalist credentials of his family, going back to his grandfather, who, he says, was entirely against the Dönme tradition, fighting against it and wanting it to dissolve as soon as possible. For this reason, Sandalcı says, he and others supported an education in the positive sciences, hoping that it would break the hold of superstition on youth. Unlike Sandalcı, Mehmet Alkan, the author of the history of the Terakki school, writes openly that its founders were Dönme and says one of the reasons they founded schools "was because members of Dönme communities wanted to educate their children in their own schools," the Karakaş at the Feyziye and the Kapancı at the Terakki.[98]

Adopting a different strategy from Alkan, Sandalcı told me he did not want to discuss the Dönme in his book, only to write about a modern educational establishment, to show what staunch Turkish nationalists and Kemalist secularists the graduates of the Feyziye school and its successor have been. This is not too different from the aim of Alkan, who writes that the Terakki school had been originally founded to "raise a generation of modern, enlightened people," exemplifying Ottoman modernization and the role education played in it.[99] But Sandalcı's book goes much further. It was written to serve as a counter to anti-Dönme conspiracy theories. He did not want to consider the distant past. To him, it is an ancient religious story that is unrelated to the school, and in fact, reviews of his history in the Turkish press did not write about the Dönme aspect.

Sandalcı says that the Dönme schools have neither taught about the Dönme religion nor raised their students as Dönme since relocating to Istanbul after Salonika fell to Greece in 1912. The operative part of this assertion is "since relocating to Istanbul." While morals play a large role in the examples of speeches quoted by Sandalcı and the lesson plans he includes in his book, he studiously avoids mentioning religion and morality in his analysis of his schools. To do so would upset the narrative of the schools' supporters, who engage in a nationalist rewriting of Dönme education to fit the aims of the secularist republic. Sandalcı follows a long line of Dönme writers who have made these arguments. Ahmet Emin Yalman published his (first) memoir in English in 1956, as a parable of the transformation from empire to nation-state. For Yalman, the Ottoman Empire represented all that was religious, corrupt, decadent, and sick, an empire that was in agonizing decline for four centuries, led by arbitrary rulers devoted to splendor and "exotic physical pleasures."[100] In contrast, he sees the Turkish Republic as representing all that is modern, democratic, and secular. Yalman uses the history of his family and himself to illustrate this transformation. When we overlook the important role that religion and morality played in Dönme life, however, we both misinterpret their experience and overlook the contributions of religious actors to Turkish history.

Ignoring Dönme religion, Turkish historiography claims that the Dönme paved the way to secular nationalism in Turkey. Many are convinced that the Dönme, educated in secular schools, became zealous secularists (or, to their detractors, atheists) who supported the CUP because it opposed the caliphate and wished to bring about the ruin of the Islamic Ottoman Empire, so that in its place a secular, nationalist republic could arise. The fact that its first president, the ardent secularist and nationalist Atatürk, although born in a Muslim quarter at the eastern edge of Salonika, far from the quarters marked by Dönme residence, was a student of the most important Dönme educator in the city allows people to assume a connection between allegedly secular education in Dönme schools and the aims of the early republic.

Many writers are troubled by or gloss over aspects of modern society, such as the continued significance of religious beliefs and practices that do not fit their sweeping teleological modernization and secularization theories.[101] Instead, they deploy a religion/traditional and secularism/modern binary, and downplay separate Dönme religious identity. This approach reflects conventional wisdom in Turkey, where it is claimed that there was an inevitable contradiction in seeking to combine scientific education with Islamic morality, which was ultimately unresolved, because one could not synthesize Islamism and modernism; the teaching of Islam thus hindered the evolution to modern (secular) education. Without making religion secondary and secularism primary, it is argued, one could not have modern schools or teach students to be modern.[102] "As a result of their education, Dönme girls [including her mother, Sabiha Sertel] in Salonika began to accept a positivist, even secular, point of view," Yıldız Sertel contends.[103] This approach was accepted without criticism most recently by Aslı Yurddaş, who makes the implausible argument that the Dönme adopted secular Turkish nationalism in the late Ottoman Empire in order to save themselves from religious oppression.[104]

The claim that Dönme schools made secularists out of their students is also found in influential works by foreign writers. In Vamik Volkan and Norman Itzkowitz's psychobiography of Atatürk, it is argued, for example, that his father, Ali Rıza, wanted him to attend Şemsi Efendi's school so that he could receive a secular education, against the wishes of his religious mother, Zübeyde.[105] And although Atatürk did not call that school "secular" in his interview with Ahmet Emin Yalman, Mark Mazower asserts in *Salonica, City of Ghosts* that "helped by his education . . . [he] became a pronounced secularist."[106]

In reality, religion and religious actors contributed to creating the new public sphere and proto-nation that became the Turkish Republic. Leading Muslims promoted a reformed religion, based on reason, that was scientific, modern, rational, explicitly anti-superstition, and opposed to ignorant customs.[107] The Nurcu (or Salafiyya) movement, for example, linked science, technology, and modernity with faith, religion, and monotheism, as well as placing a key emphasis on education. The Nurcu used modern forms of communication and technology to offer Muslims a way to reconnect to language, emotion, belief, familiar aesthetics, and ties of personal obligation in everyday life.[108] For Nurcu, Dönme, and much of the rest of Ottoman Muslim society, religion became "a major source of rational, moral subjects and a central organization aspect of the public spheres they created," which were marked by "political interaction[s] that are crucial to the formation of national identities."[109] The empire adopted this standardized rational religion to build loyalty, civic-mindedness, and civic nationalism, and to eliminate nonconformity and heterodoxy.

Finally, the nation-state that replaced the empire moved this rationalized religion to the private sphere, ethnicized it, and replaced it with racialized nationalism, which, rather than being neutral, still had religion as one of its constituent elements.[110] Yet this did not stop it from intolerantly coercing and suppressing religious actors. The irony was that the exclusion of religion was based on a false premise, its contributions in forming the modern nation-state were forgotten, or misremembered, and its leaders were deemed enemies of the nation and destroyed.

§3   Traveling and Trading

§ Café Europa, Vienna, autumn 1907. İsmail Kapancı examines a hand-colored postcard depicting street life near the Kaiser-Franz-Josef Bridge. Red electric tramway cars share the streets with sepia horse carriages, their image blurred by movement. Sharply dressed men, wearing hats and topcoats, and women in long black dresses, wearing hats and carrying umbrellas, pass one another. One man stands in the middle of the street between a horse carriage and a tramway car, hand on one hip, looking at the camera. An overweight man waits to cross the street. Another man hurries, taking long strides, briefcase in his right hand.

İsmail's family business, Yusuf Kapancı and Sons (Youssouf Kapandji et Fils), established in the 1880s, specializes in the textile trade and does business in most of Ottoman Europe.[1] By now the firm has branched out into insurance as well, with an agency in the European quarter of Salonika.[2] İsmail turns over the postcard and writes on it in Ottoman Turkish, with a smattering of French words, to his brother Osman in Salonika:

October 24, 1907
My dear brother Osman Kapancı Efendi,
Last night I arrived safely in Vienna, twenty minutes late. Today I shall inform father [Yusuf Kapancı] by telegram of my arrival. And I plan to set out for Berlin immediately, since I cannot make this decision on my own. I showed the man next to Café Berlin the print seal that you gave me. He said it would be ten crowns for a new one, so of course I offered three crowns. Finally, he said he would not be able to make it for less than seven crowns. Let me know right away if you are willing to pay six crowns and I'll have it made. Later, I asked at several other places. Every single

one said they would not be able to do it even for seven crowns. However, I think I'll be able to have it done for six crowns.

In conclusion İsmail notes that he is staying at Café Europa, which "although not beautiful, is very cozy. I gave ten crowns for the night, but I paid in two installments" (he wants Osman to know that he is a cagey businessman). The Kapancı brothers worked closely together and with their father, traveling from Salonika to Vienna and Berlin to further the family business, always keeping one another informed of every decision made along the way, particularly those that display an ability to get the best deal.

Salonika at the Turn of the Twentieth Century

In the late nineteenth century, Ottoman port cities were transformed physically and culturally almost beyond recognition. Financial capitalization by local, imperial, and international interests, connections to world trade centered in northwestern Europe, and the accompanying new modes of communication (the telegraph), international transportation (roads, railways, steamships), and local transportation (tramways) propelled their change.[3] In this context, Ottoman Salonika was converted from a sleepy borderland Macedonian town into a major cosmopolitan port.[4] The face of the city was dramatically altered: as in Istanbul at the same time, ancient walls were knocked down, suburbs emerged beyond the city's Byzantine core, and straight, wide, tree-lined paved avenues were built.[5] The harbor and port were expanded to handle steamships, and the city's port was linked to a railway grid connecting western Europe and the Ottoman Empire. After Istanbul (1 million), Izmir (350,000), and Beirut (170,000), Salonika became the fourth leading port city in the Ottoman Mediterranean, a terminus for steamships and railways, a significant manufacturing and commercial center, and the most industrialized city in the empire.[6] Salonika possessed "a strategic position that made it a node for continental transportation, a harbor that could be made to accommodate deep-sea vessels, a productive hinterland that could be exploited for its cash crops and markets, and a political and economic potential that attracted capital, exploiters, and workers."[7]

As a result of economic dynamism, immigration, and improvements in public health, Salonika experienced rapid population growth. The city was one of the largest in the Ottoman Empire: its population tripled in thirty-five years, from 54,000 people in 1878 to 150,000 in 1912.[8] One-third, 50,000, of the inhabitants were Muslim. By 1923, Dönme comprised as much as one-third of this Muslim population. Thus the city had the smallest Muslim population of all large Ottoman cities—in Istanbul it was nearly half—and a significant proportion of that population was not merely Muslim, but Dönme. Salonika also boasted a large foreign contingent because many consulates were located there. The city was undoubtedly oriented toward western and central Europe. The first rail service to Paris (1888) preceded rail connection to Istanbul by nearly a decade (1896).[9]

Late Ottoman Salonika was thus situated at the interstices of cultural, economic, and religious connections between western Europe (particularly France) and southeastern Europe (the Ottoman Empire). This contributed to new internal linkages and intersections for the city's people, who as in other great European cities "found themselves in situations with unprecedented possibilities for talking, card playing, drinking, clubbing, or just mixing with relative strangers."[10] The construction of the modern port stimulated the proliferation of new places of social exchange in offices, cafés, bars, hotels, and, later, cinemas along the waterfront promenade.[11] Men and women congregated day and night in spacious cafés or luxury hotel restaurants, where they sat on Viennese chairs at round marble tables, read Paris or Istanbul or local newspapers, smoked cigarettes, and consumed hors-d'oeuvres, cakes, cheese, and alcohol, while an orchestra played in the background and other patrons played pool.[12] In the European quarter, Salonikans shopped at branches of Paris, London, and Vienna department stores and boutiques, or at the American or Chinese bazaar.[13] They were not merely engaging in mimicry.[14] Salonika was not the Paris of the Ottoman Empire; it was a distinct city, where fountains gushed forth sour cherry juice, an Ottoman favorite, at opening ceremonies; passengers on the Belgian-made tramcars were segregated by sex;[15] and clocks had two faces, one with Arabic and one with Latin numerals, simultaneously telling Christian and Islamic time.[16]

The cityscape and public institutions of turn-of-the-twentieth-century Salonika reflected its cosmopolitan inhabitants. One found there a purposeful mixing of baroque, neoclassical, and Islamic architectural styles. The city boasted modern, hygienic public markets, with Islamic architectural features, a densely crowded city core, and broad-boulevarded suburbs with seaside villas that had diverse features taken from western

European and Ottoman tastes. The city's schools incorporated the latest in French pedagogy (critical thinking, lesson plans, strict disciplining of students and faculty, education of the body as well as the mind) and Ottoman religious education, an Islam suitable for the age.

Merchant Dönme Families

§ It is a spring day in 1902. Nazmi Efendi, Sabiha Sertel's father, puts on a black suit jacket over his starched white shirt. His polka-dotted bow tie matches his unruly salt-and-pepper mustache, and his tight red fez makes his large ears stand out. Leaving his two-story timbered home on Pazar Tekkesi street in the Kasımiye neighborhood—with its mosque that had once been the Church of St. Demetrius, the city's patron, whose tomb is now tended by Mevlevi Sufis—he walks toward the harbor. Approaching the quay, his penetrating eyes spy a kebab house, and he fills his empty stomach. Then he settles into a chair at his favorite café at the quay. Sipping his tiny cup of coffee, he watches the ships entering and exiting the harbor: "Most were merchant vessels. Horse-drawn carts carrying goods to the customs office rushed by him. This was his world. Since his appointment as head of the Customs Office, he had become familiar with the goods and people of this city. How lively Salonika's harbor was!"[17] How much it had changed. How open to the world Salonika had become.

The role the Dönme played in contributing to the development of Salonika into a cosmopolitan city in the nineteenth century had a precedent in the role conversos played in the New World economy in the fifteenth and sixteenth centuries. As Nathan Wachtel explains, New Christian merchants from Iberia contributed to the elaboration of new forms of exchange and to the great commercial networks, previously unknown on such a global scale, that were established in the context of the European discovery of the New World and overseas expansion.[18] This process of capitalist expansion and the conversos' role in it was predicated upon the understanding that if a Jew in Spain converted, he would be granted all the rights and privileges (above all commercial privileges) as a Catholic subject.[19] The forced migration of Jews from Spain and Portugal at the end of the fifteenth century had disrupted and caused the decline of the traditional commercial system.[20] The outlets for this forced migration were Portuguese colonial holdings, which helped produce new markets, and new Ottoman lands in the Balkans. The networks that connected these parts of the world were both familial and commercial, but revolved around a sense of the "nation" of conversos: "Planetary dispersion, transcontinental and transoceanic solidarities: this immense network that joined the *conversos* of Lisbon, Antwerp and Mexico, and the Jews of Livorno, Amsterdam and Constantinople introduced a new and remarkable character," which united "tens of thousands of persons who do not officially profess to the same religion, yet share a sentiment of belonging to the same collectivity, designated by one word: 'Nação' [nation]."[21] Moreover, the new configuration of long-distance commerce demanded knowledge and experience that the Old Christian merchant elites lacked. At the same time, the New Christians, emancipated from the restrictions that had marginalized them as Jews, could finally access all the charges and functions of the New World economy. The mastering of new techniques of credit and production allowed them to engage commercially through the routes that the discoveries of the New World and the colonial enterprises opened up to them, particularly in the sugarcane market.[22]

Both identity—who they were—and historical juncture—when they consolidated as a group—formed the context and contingency of the conversos' commercial rise. Freed of Jewish status, benefiting from new opportunities in world trade, and networking among an expanded "family" linked by a shared sense of identity, the conversos mirror the Dönme in the nineteenth century. Moreover, Jews in the Ottoman Empire did not face the same restrictions as Jews in Iberia and Iberian holdings abroad, and, as Muslims, the Dönme were more privileged than Jews. Like the fifteenth and sixteenth centuries, the nineteenth century witnessed a radical expansion in trade accompanying high colonialism, and Ottoman markets, including Salonika, were penetrated by western European capital. Goods and technologies moved between empires aided by a fully developed Dönme diaspora. As Yuri Slezkine notes of Jews in the neighboring Russian Empire, there was "a network of people with similar backgrounds and similar challenges who could, under certain circumstances, count on mutual acknowledgement and cooperation." Their "intragroup trust" assured "the relative reliability of business partners, loan clients, and subcontractors"; most of their businesses were family businesses.[23]

Salonika found itself "fully located within specialized global circuits of finance, labor, technology, and capital,"[24] and the main space of intermediation in the transactional encounter between western Europe and the Ottoman Empire.[25] Dönme bankers and textile and tobacco merchants, who financed their projects themselves and with the backing of western European capital, played a considerable role in the local economy and international trade and finance. Only the uppermost strata in society had both savings and liquid assets to put to work in their businesses and in banking.[26]

According to the official Ottoman *Selânik Vilâyeti Salnamesi* (Yearbook of the Province of Salonika), most Dönme businessmen were based in the European commercial, diplomatic, and residential district of the city. Dönme connections with foreign finance and Dönme in western Europe allowed them to engage in international trade. The progenitor of one of the most important Kapancı Dönme families was Kavaf [Cobbler] Yusuf Agha, born at the end of the eighteenth century. The title "Agha" indicates he was head of a group of merchants, or guild.[27] With its established economic niche, and control of one specialized market, this family was well placed for the shift to accelerated capitalism.

One of the most influential descendants of Kavaf Yusuf Agha was the prominent banker and merchant Mehmet Kapancı, who headed Salonika's Chamber of Commerce, its symbol of economic development, received state honors from the sultan, and served in the Assembly for the Administration of the Province, an elected position, from 1902 to 1905.[28] Mehmet Kapancı was primarily engaged in the textile trade.[29] By the turn of the twentieth century, this advocate of railway connections between Salonika and the rest of Europe, whose office was located across the street from the French consulate, was one of the ten richest men in Salonika.[30] According to the archives of the Banque d'Orient, he possessed extensive and valuable property worth 60,000 Turkish pounds, owning the Bezciler [Cloth-Seller] Han in the Istanbul Market on Sabri Pasha Boulevard, which he purchased from the Jewish Modiano family in 1900.[31] He also owned a large department store in the main market district near the harbor.[32] Mehmet Kapancı had two noteworthy younger brothers engaged in the same pursuits. Yusuf Kapancı, who became wealthy through the textile trade in Ottoman Europe, was a well-known merchant, and the *Selânik Vilâyeti Salnamesi* identifies him as one of the city's eight renowned bankers doing business in the European quarter.[33] The same source calls Ahmet Kapancı one of the city's best-known big merchants; like Yusuf Kapancı, he made his money in the textile trade in Ottoman Europe.[34] He became a member of the Chamber of Commerce, Industry, and Agriculture, serving as its head in 1907.[35]

The Karakaş Dönme also played a very significant role in the textile trade. In interviews I conducted, a descendant of Mehmet Karakaş informed me that textiles were most important to the group's economic strength.[36] He said that his family name, Sandalcı, does not refer to "oarsmen," as might be assumed, but to the sellers of a certain type of silk cloth. He also noted that most of the leading Karakaş families, including the Balcı, Dilber, İpekçi, Karakaş, and Mısırlı were all in the trade, and said that the Mısırlıs were descended from Jewish cloth merchants in Spain. The 1908 French-language report from the Salonika Chamber of Commerce lists Balcı and Karakaş as dealers in socks, stockings, and shawls.[37]

Tobacco was one of the most important staples in Salonika's new economy, and the tobacco trade was also an area where the Dönme, especially the Kapancı, played a leading role. One example is the family of Kapancı Tütüncü [Tobacco Merchant] Dr. Nâzım, who would later play a very significant political role. The Dönme preferred to own their own businesses, without partners, and to deal only with relatives.[38] Because of the global extent of the tobacco market, branches of Dönme families such as that of Kapancı Duhani [Smoke/Tobacco] Hasan Akif, recognized in the *Selânik Vilâyeti Salnamesi* as another of the great merchants of the city and included in the list of four prominent tobacco merchants,[39] started a tobacco business in Salonika and expanded it into a tobacco empire with branches in Austria, Belgium, Germany, and England, exporting tobacco as far as North America.[40] An early nineteenth-century Ottoman-French dictionary noted that the Dönme were so dominant in the manufacture and trade of tobacco products that the state referred to them as "the community of merchants of tobacco."[41] Foreigners had long commented that the Ottomans labeled the entire community of Dönme as "the group or social class of tobacco merchants" due to their long association, at least since the mid nineteenth century, with this product.[42] It is significant that the Dönme dominated the production, distribution, and sale of cigarettes, which suited the pace and lifestyle of the turn-of-the-century city better than the traditional pipe.[43] This was an era of accelerated communication: with the advent of steamboats, and then railroads, the time needed for a letter from Salonika to reach Paris decreased from a month in the early nineteenth century to two weeks in the 1860s and less than three days in the 1880s.[44]

All those people coming and going needed places to stay, to eat, and to be entertained. Dönme merchants also owned coffeehouses, hotel cafés, and hotels. Nazmi Efendi's favorite café at the quay may have been the Belle Vue, which, as we learn from ads placed to rent it in the Greek newspaper *Faros tēs Makedonias* (Beacon of Macedonia), was owned by a fellow Kapancı Dönme, Mehmet Kapancı.[45] According to the 1923–25 records of the Mixed Commission for the Exchange of the Greek and Turkish Populations, set up under the bilateral Treaty of Lausanne on January 30, 1923, which sought to establish the wealth and property of all Muslims in the city, Duhani Hasan Akif's family owned cafés and hotels: the café of the Olympos Palace Hotel (on what is today Plateia Eleutherias, the city's central square) and the Izmir Hotel.[46] Ownership was shared with Kapancı family members. Ahmet Kapancı's wife Nefise owned a share in the Olympos Hotel and Café and its attached stores, as well as in the Filikia Hotel and Café on Hayri Pasha boulevard on the quay.[47] Yusuf Kapancı's son İbrahim and his sister Emine owned the Alhambra Café,[48] its name an ironic product of the "Moorish" craze sweeping North America and Europe at the time, at the Wharf Station tramway stop.[49]

The Kapancı were internationally recognized for their economic role in the city, even in new industries. A 1908 cable to car manufacturers in Detroit from the U.S. consulate in Salonika called the local market for automobiles unfavorable, noting that very few people there could afford one, and that there were only two cars and no automobile agents or agencies in the city.[50] Nevertheless, since the American consul's aim was to assist American businesses in foreign markets, the cable mentioned eight individuals who might be interested in receiving car catalogues, among them Mehmet Kapancı. His being listed along with Jewish, Levantine, and Greek notables and members of the city's military and administrative elite is evidence of his wealth and high status. Another cable from the American consulate in Salonika, the following year, identified Mehmet Kapancı as owner of one of the most important banking houses in the city.[51] His wealth and broad worldview made it possible for him to consider adopting the new form of private transportation.[52]

Cables sent from the French consul in Salonika also note the significant role Kapancı families played in the city's trade and finance and their role in western European trade. The French consul played an important role in assisting his country's businessmen and in linking French and Salonika-based capital and interests. French businessmen wrote to him inquiring about local banks and businesses, and the consul responded with the most up-to-date information, enabling them to make financial decisions. A cable in 1910 from the French consul in Salonika to a businessman in Lille in northern France noted that an Ottoman Textile and Fez Company (Société anonyme Ottomane pour la fabrication des fez et tissus) had been established with a capitalization of 20,000 Turkish pounds by five men, including Ahmet Kapancı and Osman Telci, another Kapancı Dönme. Yusuf Kapancı was also involved, as was Osman Dervish. "The company inspires confidence," the consul added.[53] A 1914 Greek study also mentions the firm.[54]

Another cable from the French consul at Salonika a few weeks later, sent to the owner of a tanning and leather-softening business in south-central France, underlined the role of Kapancı merchant families, saying: "M. Youssouf Kapandji and his son(s) are established representatives in Salonika. They also conduct business with banks. Their presumed means range from 150,000 to 200,000 francs. They are considered honest and active."[55] On March 1, the French consul cabled a businessman concerning Faiz Kapancı, who was the son of Ahmet Kapancı, according to a family tree provided by a descendant of Yusuf Kapancı's. "In reply to your letter from the fourteenth of last month, I am pleased to inform you that M. Faïz Kapandji is established in Salonika as a sales representative," the consul wrote. "His presumed means are on the order of 70,000 francs. He enjoys a good reputation there."[56] Faiz Kapancı's position as sales representative and commission agent and as his good reputation are confirmed both by the French-language 1908 report of the Salonika Chamber of Commerce and a cable sent to the U.S. State Department in 1910.[57]

Until the end of Ottoman rule, the Dönme continued to play a dominant role in the city's economy. There were about forty large commercial houses, with assets between 10,000 to 80,000 Turkish pounds. In 1906, the Kapancı Ahmet Kapancı (a banker with a capital of 60,000 pounds), Mehmet Kapancı (merchant of industrial goods with a capital of 60,000 pounds), and Emin and Rasim Receb (20,000 pounds) were among the most important entrepreneurs.[58] The Ottoman Textile and Fez Company used the most sophisticated machines of the period, being equipped with thirty spinning looms and six fez-weaving machines, and employed one hundred workers. Its daily production reached six hundred meters of woolen textiles and six hundred fezzes.[59] This Dönme-headed venture exemplifies the Dönme's wealth and role in the industrialization of the city.

A Greek-language guide to Greece published in 1911 also notes the important role of Kapancı merchants and manufacturers in Salonika, listing

Yusuf Kapancı and Faiz Kapancı as factory owners, Ahmet Kapancı as
a manufacturer and fez and cloth merchant, and Mehmet Kapancı and
Namık Kapancı as the owners of banking houses.[60] Comparing these
names with a genealogy provided by the descendant of Yusuf Kapancı,
I found that Namık was Mehmet Kapancı's son. He had been earlier
listed in the French-language Salonika Chamber of Commerce guide as a
money changer.[61] In 1911, in celebration of Sultan Mehmet V Reşat's visit
to the city, the Ottoman Textile and Fez Company erected a large victory
arch on what later became Plateia Eleutherias, illustrating the company's
wealth, visibility, and importance to the city's economy.[62]

Dönme Networks in Central and Western Europe

Twelve turn-of-the-twentieth-century postcards written in Ottoman
Turkish or French, provided to me by a descendant of the Dönme Yusuf
Kapancı in Istanbul, offer evidence of the Dönme economic and social
networks across early twentieth-century western and central Europe and
show how the Dönme way of life was manifested in family bonds carried
with them on their travels.

A 1905 postcard in French from Yusuf Kapancı to a man in Paris who
was seeking information about a person known as "the one from Homs"
who lived in Aleppo in Syria, then a major Ottoman trading center, said
the name "Homsi" was not enough; Yusuf needed the man's first name to
locate him. Since the names "Mısırlı" (Cairene / Egyptian) and "Şamlı"
(Damascene / Syrian) were connected to well-known Karakaş Dönme
families, this may be evidence of another Karakaş Dönme family, the
"Homsli." It is noteworthy that the French businessman sought assistance
from one of the leading Kapancı families, which may suggest trade relations between Karakaş and Kapancı at the time (the rest of the postcards,
however, indicate the contrary). Another postcard, sent by Osman from
Berlin in 1909 to his brother İbrahim, provides evidence of the Kapancıs'
central European trading relations. "I'd be glad if you could send me the
address of one of your [Frankfurt] contacts," Osman wrote.

Other postcards, although written to spouses, also provide information
on Dönme trade in western and central Europe. Osman Kapancı, who
had spent three months in central Europe on business, dashed off a postcard to his pregnant wife Sabite in Salonika from Geneva on May 21, 1910,
for example, saying, "I've just arrived. . . . Since this morning we have

been visiting the workshops here. It was spectacular, but visiting these big factories and going on this long long trip have tired me. Most of the trip is finished and it is finally time to return home." Unlike his brother, Osman spared no expense when he traveled, and the front of the postcard depicts a very plush hotel salon in the Italian capital. Sabite would not survive this childbirth, and Osman was to marry his brother's widow; perhaps he should have taken Sabite with him to Rome. Eleven years later, Osman wrote a series of postcards in French to his and Sabite's daughter, Nevber. Father and daughter later spent much time in central Europe and western Europe, although not always together. Nevber remained in Vienna while Osman spent weeks at a time traveling. He sent her postcards from Brussels and Bad Gastein, Austria, an Alpine spa town—both Osman and Nevber suffered from poor health, and he was seeking a cure in the thermal springs. "My very beloved daughter," he wrote, "You have not told me in the letters that you sent whether you have practiced the piano—if you do not practice, I fear you will forget everything you have learned. I want to know right away of your practicing your previous lesson. Write about your practicing the piano in your next postcard." An undated postcard sent from Vienna by Nevber's cousin and stepbrother Yusuf, the son of her father's brother İbrahim and Osman's Levirate second wife, Aisha, also admonishes her to practice the piano.

Photographs provided by the descendant of another Kapancı family, that of the Sarrafzade or Ehatzade, also illustrate the mixed Ottoman and western European aspects of Dönme life. A photograph from 1910 depicts nineteen members of the Ehat family standing before an immense fountain in Baden-Baden, Germany, where they had gone to take the waters. Most of the women wear stylish white dresses and broad-brimmed hats. Some wear white gloves; others have bare arms and necks. The handlebar-mustachioed men in dark, three-piece western European suits and ties are either bareheaded or sport Panama hats or fezzes.

By the turn of the twentieth century, Duhani Hasan Akif, who had made his fortune in the tobacco business in Salonika and Kavala, was established in Germany, and in 1912 he moved with his family to Munich. A photograph shows a fez-wearing Hasan Akif with a German business partner and his wife and daughter in Munich. According to a descendant, Hasan Akif was the son of Ramadan Efendi of Izmir, who had three wives. The first was from Salonika; the second, from Izmir, site of one of the Christians' seven churches of the Apocalypse; the third, from Konya, "the city sacred to the memory of Mevlana Jelal ad-Din Rumi."[63] Hasan Akif was born to the second wife in Izmir. After his mother died, he was sent to Salonika to be raised by his aunt.[64] In 1917, Hasan Akif died in Munich and was buried there in a grand tomb at a ceremony attended by men in top hats. After his death, this international tobacco merchant's company continued to thrive. His grandson Ali Riza Hüsnü (d. 1964), who in his earlier years posed for a photo in full "Oriental" outfit, smoking a water pipe, became the manager of the Grathwohl cigarette factory in Munich, and there was also a branch of the business in Vienna. During World War I, Ali Riza served as the purveyor of German tobacco products to the sultan. The family boasted that their Istanbul tobacco warehouse was the most modern in the empire. Ali Riza married his cousin Nuriye (photographed as a child with Şemsi Efendi) in Salonika in 1920. By 1928, the family had moved to Brussels.

Dönme Morality Abroad

Although participating in international commerce and culture, the Dönme preserved their unique religious beliefs and practices. Hasan Akif's descendant—born and raised in Belgium—told of the remarkable piety of her family, reflecting Dönme, Kabbalah, normative Islamic, and Sufi elements. "There was a time in the early part of the year when lamb was not eaten, and then suddenly 'milk lamb' would appear, stewed with tomatoes and parsley," she recalled. This was the Dönme Festival of the Lamb. Preparing a family cookbook, the author relied in part on recipes passed down orally from Hasan Akif's wife. Culinary details provide additional insight into late Dönme religious practices.[65] As the multiple dishes of lamb cooked with butter demonstrate,[66] the Dönme had a complete disregard for kosher rules, which makes sense considering Shabbatai Tzevi's inverting of what was considered permitted and what was considered forbidden. The book includes a recipe for Peach Kebab, the dish eaten at the Festival of the Lamb at the end of the period when Dönme were forbidden to eat lamb. The dish contains the offal: the brain, liver, kidneys, testicles, spleen, and intestines of a very young lamb.[67] Moreover, "Not everyone fasted during Ramadan but at the time of *iftar*, the daily evening breaking of the fast, some sort of sweet would usually appear, sometimes made with dates. As with everyone else, Aşure ["Noah's Pudding," a mixture of grains, fruits, and nuts] appeared during Muharrem and was distributed to friends, relatives, and the poor in great quantities."[68] Nicholas Stavroulakis says Aşure was treasured by the Dönme because they saw Shabbatai Tzevi as the incarnation of the spirit of prophecy passed from Muhammad to Ali to his sons, Husayn and Hassan, the Prophet's grandsons. Ashura means "tenth" in Arabic and represents the 10th day of the Muslim month of Muharrem, in which Husayn and his brother Hassan were martyred at the battle of Karbala in 680 C.E. (61 A.H.).[69] Yıldız Sertel notes how the imam of the Dönme mosque presided over a family engagement ceremony prior to 1913 at which an animal was sacrificed and Aşure distributed.[70]

Dönme customs were also evident at home. Hasan Akif's descendant explains how she was taken out to see the new moon each month and to recite a prayer that her mother taught her: "O God, I see the Moon, O God I do believe. Let the Moon be blessed by God." It is likely that the custom of greeting the new moon stemmed from the eighteen commandments of Shabbatai Tzevi. Number fifteen states: "Each and every month they should look up and behold the birth of the moon and shall pray that the moon turn its face opposite the sun, face to face." Gershom Scholem explains: "This is the observance of the Sanctification of the (New) Moon according to the Zoharic interpretation [the Zohar is the most important medieval Spanish Kabbalist text] of it as an allusion to the hope for a 'holy union' between the sun and moon ('face to face')."[71]

This Kapancı woman related that even in Belgium, at Kandil, nights when Muslims celebrate events in Muhammad's life, including his conception, birth, ascent, and the revelation of the Qur'an, "we would gather together and have special sweets and sing: 'Butter money, candle money / This night, festive oil lamp money / Like skewers in a row come the dervishes / Lacking meat they ask for fish.'"[72] As the descendants of converts to Islam, Dönme thus also celebrated events in the life of Muhammad, the last (publicly sanctioned) prophet prior to Shabbatai Tzevi, according to them, and modeled their celebrations of the life of their prophet Shabbatai Tzevi on these (as well as on those of the Christians).

The Dönme Diaspora

Three overlapping Dönme groupings or networks can be distinguished: (a) traders dispersed throughout central and western and Ottoman Europe, functioning mainly in French; (b) imperial officials throughout

Ottoman southeastern Europe, whose language was Ottoman Turkish; and (c) a discrete ethnic and religious population that prayed in Hebrew, Judeo-Spanish, and Arabic. Their language of education was mixed (formal schools offering training in Islamic as well as western and central European languages, and informal education occurring in the family in Jewish languages), as was their familiar language, which included Spanish-language recipes. Their language of memory, as it was publicly visible inscribed on their tombstones and mosque, was Ottoman Turkish and Arabic. However, the Dönme simultaneously occupied parallel Dönme and Muslim universes, embodying different meanings. In each world, they took care to preserve their own distinct religious, moral, and ethical character. Dönme officials who very publicly kept the difficult thirty days' fast of Ramadan made sure to break their fast each day exactly five minutes before other Muslims, thus violating it.

The Dönme practiced strict social segregation throughout their lives. Assisted by detailed genealogies, they married their first cousins or their brothers' widows in Levirate marriages. They self-segregated, living together in Salonika according to sect, and established distinct schools for educating and socializing their children, and a unique mosque where they could pray together. They buried their dead in separate cemeteries, walled off from others' burial grounds. When they traveled and lived abroad, they made every effort to remain distinct. They jealously guarded their social exclusivity to maintain their culture and religion—for example, not allowing exogamous marriage—but were at the same time progressive, transgressive, and radical, operating in diverse environments. Dönme society was closed, traditional, and conservative, yet intellectually open to the world. They were mobile, yet committed to a particular place, Salonika, the central node in all of their relations, from religious pilgrimage to international business.

A map of the Dönme universe, the shape of the space they operated in, although centered on southeastern Europe, would have Manchester in England as its northern and western terminus and Izmir at its southern and eastern end. Between these points, descending north to south, we find Dönme connections in London, Berlin, Brussels, Paris, Frankfurt, Munich, Geneva, Vienna, Rome, Ulcinj in Montenegro, Serres, Monastir (Bitola, today in the Republic of Macedonia), and Istanbul. The Dönme functioned smoothly both in the Ottoman and Austro-Hungarian empires and throughout French, British, and German Europe.[73] The infusion of capital into Salonika in the late nineteenth and early twentieth centuries enabled them to carve out a niche in the expanding global economic system. This first wave of globalization allowed for overlapping economic inflows. Capital, labor, and commodities moved easily across frontiers.[74] The rise of the Dönme in economic, social, and political importance in their transregional world was facilitated by the shifting spectrum of commercial activities, actors, and dynamic alliances.[75]

Along with their location, the ethno-religious and legal status of the Dönme put them in a position to promote change. Being on the religious margins of society, yet also officially recognized as Muslims, they were able to advance in the administration and military. Legally, Dönme were Muslims in the eyes of the Ottoman bureaucracy. In the empire, once a person converted to Islam, he or she and his or her descendants were considered Muslims, and given all the rights of the group. Past affiliations did not mark the future life chances of converts.[76] Living ostensibly as Muslims, they were able to rise to top governmental and military positions at the turn of the twentieth century, positions that Armenians, Jews, and Orthodox Christians could not attain. Christians and Jews could become wealthy, but could not become mayors, generals, or governors. The Dönme counted among their ranks pashas as well as mayors, along with numerous customs agents and secretaries in government offices, and still later high officials in the Post and Telegraph Department and foreign missions. From this unique position, this group stood out from all others, transforming Salonika from a quiet town into a major node in the transregional economy and a center of revolution.

The Dönme way ultimately caused others to turn against them. The Dönme did not approach "those distinctly different from themselves hospitably, with a willingness to get to know them, even to like them."[77] They were not socially open to others. Although they crossed imperial and what later became national boundaries, they did not become creoles, crossing social boundaries by mixing with other groups, did not seek social interaction or contact, did not intermarry with local women wherever trade took the men; nor did they like to fraternize or enter into business partnerships with outsiders and strangers. They were not pursuing universal knowledge or a universal religion; nor did they allow outsiders to convert and join their religion. They promoted their own form of religious orthodoxy, morality, and ethics, and before 1923, they cannot be labeled secularists engaged in a struggle against the forces of intolerance, as one major trend in Turkish historiography sees them. They were intolerant in their own way. The Dönme were both an island unto themselves—even divided further into three islets—and among others. Such a mode of being served the Dönme well in late Ottoman Salonika. But racialized nationalism and ethnicized religion in Greek Thessaloníki and republican Turkish Istanbul would ensure that they and the ideas they promoted would be no longer welcome in the nation-states that replaced the empire, an ironic consequence of a revolution in which they had played a considerable role.

Between Empire and Nation-State

§4   Making a Revolution, 1908

A conversation between the sultan and the chief rabbi at Yıldız Kiosk in Istanbul in spring 1908 just before the Constitutional Revolution that summer alerts us to the role the Dönme played in progressive politics. It also points out that still by this late date, even a sultan intent on promoting an orthodox Sunni Islam to marginal Muslims in his empire considered the Dönme pious Muslims. Because he was convinced of Shabbatai Tzevi's genuine conversion, Abdülhamid II overlooked the political role Dönme played in the movement conspiring against him:

§ Sultan Murad V had been a Freemason, installed in the imperial seat by Freemasons, and he did not last long. They called him mad and deposed him just over three months after his enthronement in 1876. He was replaced by a sultan forever etched in the mind of the West with a hooked nose and red fez, Abdülhamid II. By now Abdülhamid has been in power for over three decades. A devout Muslim, Abdülhamid II seeks to preserve the leading position of Muslims in the state, not sell out to the Muslim liberals and Freemasons and their foreign masters. He sends spies throughout the empire and into western Europe and Egypt to keep an eye on those who stand in the way of forging a stronger, more Muslim empire. But despite his best efforts, the opposition is gaining momentum. He asks who is beyond the agitation against his rule. He expects to hear that it is Armenian and other Christian separatists backed by foreign missionaries, or even the covetous czar's Jews, buying land in Palestine. When he is informed instead that Salonika is the main center of the movement and that the Dönme make up a large segment of those working to topple him, he is surprised, and seeks information about Shabbatai Tzevi.[1]

He summons his longtime ally Moshe Halévi, who has been acting chief rabbi even longer than the sultan has been in power, to appear before him.

The sultan warmly welcomes the conservative rabbi, with whom he is on intimate terms. He regards the rabbi, who opposes the progressives in his own community, highly.[2]

"Tell me about the various Jewish sects."[3]

"There are two, your excellency, my emperor. One, the Rabbinite, maintains what is enjoined by the Torah and the Talmud. The other, the Karaite, only maintains what is prescribed by the Torah." The Dönme are noticeably absent from his presentation.

"And who is Shabbatai?"

"He was a false messiah. His followers had no relation with the two Jewish sects. May I beseech his excellency to allow me time to correspond with the chief rabbi of Salonika so that I may obtain more complete information on this subject?"

By order of the sultan, Halévi writes in Hebrew to Jacob Hanania Covo, chief rabbi of Salonika, asking for details on the life and machinations of Shabbatai Tzevi. Covo promptly carries out the order, responding to Halévi with a biography of Shabbatai Tzevi in Hebrew. Halévi's grandson translates the biography into Ottoman, and Halévi presents it to the sultan.

A few days later, the sultan again invites Moshe Halévi to the palace.

"I have read about the personality of Shabbatai Tzevi. That man was a saint, a person close to God [*veli*]."

He reimburses the rabbi for his expenses in gold and decides no longer to concern himself with the Dönme.

Perhaps he should have. Both he and Halévi would lose their positions following the 1908 revolution, in which Dönme played a significant role.

The Dönme Enter Local Politics

The first step in making the revolution was to enter local politics. The Dönme intellectual and bourgeois elites who contributed to the new schools and literary journals of Salonika entered municipal politics, where they had an even greater transformative role. One can explain the rise of the Dönme in local politics in the late nineteenth century in the context of the changes accompanying economic growth and urban reform. First, it is difficult to measure their place in the ancien régime or to find mention of Dönme prior to the sweeping reforms of the Tanzimat era (1839–76). This era was marked by the creation of a new class of bureaucrats who aimed to guide the empire through a period of administrative and legal reorganization, reforming and centralizing it and increasing the bureaucracy's control through newly developed technologies and specialization of office, including new provincial and urban administrations. This led to widened public control of administration, diffusion of authority, the bringing of new people into administration, new education and educational capital, open to all, irrespective of religion, secularization in law and education, demilitarization of officeholding, making all citizens equal and eligible to vote and serve in parliament, liberalizing the economy, and protecting a right to private property.[4] The Tanzimat reforms came fully to Salonika in 1868, when a municipality consisting of a mayor and municipal council (although more like an advisory body than a parliament) was created, which introduced local governance. As in other model Tanzimat cities, this coincided with the destruction of the city walls. Salonika's had guarded the coast; their opening was a symbolic act, representing the city's new openness, coming as it did at the time when the Suez Canal was opened (1869). Extramural urban expansion followed as the "countryside of previous centuries was connected through wide boulevards to the city centre."[5] This was happening throughout Europe: Amsterdam, Antwerp, Barcelona, and Vienna all saw their walls demolished in the 1860s and 1870s to allow urban renewal.[6]

The late nineteenth century in Salonika witnessed the emergence of new professional activities, white-collar and liberal professionals, private companies (banks, finance houses, insurance companies), new products, new consumerism, a new working class, and new municipal structures and civil administration. The city became an administrative metropole, a garrison city, an intellectual center, and an industrial pole, as well as continuing as an artisanal, merchant, and agricultural center as before. Demographic growth, economic prosperity, social and political diversification, and new contexts for social interaction such as cafés, bars, tramways, and promenades contributed to the creation in a relatively short time of a radically different place.[7]

Salonika was a laboratory of Ottoman urban political reform, becoming, a decade after Pera (Beyoğlu) in Istanbul, the second European city in the empire to be granted control over local governance. The new municipalities were established in part to rationalize the urban order to facilitate local and international commerce. They were charged with "urban planning, market control, health, public morality, and public welfare."[8] Turning away from the ancien régime of Ottoman urban order—notables, guilds, and confessional communities—the new municipality was to be based on new social classes, a liberalized economy, and equality between individuals of different religions. As Kemal Karpat argues, with the penetration of European capitalism, steps toward the legalization of private landownership, and the commercialization of agriculture, the old regime of wealthy landowners, especially foreigners, Christians, and Jews, and urban guilds and merchants had to face the fact of new rivals in the economy, a new Muslim middle class.[9] This was accompanied by laws passed in 1871 and 1878 for the equal participation of Christians, Jews, and Muslims in administrative councils and municipalities, further opening up local rule to new upwardly mobile elites.

The Salonika municipality, new seat of the governor, and new civil society committees and associations created a new structure, allocating power to locals, allowing them local autonomy and the ability to make changes.[10] Thus the creation of municipalities allowed broader and greater participation in politics and of the middle to upper classes, including the new rising merchants, literary elites, journalists, and professionals.[11] The bourgeoisie's new status and manipulation of new municipal structures enabled them to impact the city.[12] In Salonika, the new bourgeoisie included the Dönme.

The rise of the Dönme as a whole occurred in tandem with the reforms of the second half of the nineteenth century that introduced the locally selected mayorality, municipal council, and other local political bodies, as well as the introduction of the latest form of western European capitalism. A different politico-economic regime gave rise to a new elite. From the fifteenth century to the mid-seventeenth century, Salonika was the center of the Ottoman Empire's woolen cloth and textile industry, and Jews, who had founded the industry, predominated in it, both supplying the market and the elite Ottoman infantry Janissaries, receiving a monopoly to furnish their uniforms.[13] Leading sixteenth-century rabbis confirmed that "the main means of livelihood of the Jews of this city is the production of fabric."[14] The inflation in the ranks of the Janissary corps over the sixteenth century also benefited Salonikan Jews. In the seventeenth century, treaty clauses allowed western Europeans to export their textiles to the Ottoman Empire. Competition from English, Dutch, and French suppliers, rising prices for raw materials, and fiscal crises depressed the textile industry. One of those affected was Shabbatai Tzevi's father, Mordecai, who like many other Salonikan Jews, sought his fortunes instead in the boomtown of Izmir. As brokers and agents for English merchants, Mordecai and his two eldest sons made enough of a fortune to allow Shabbatai to study Jewish law instead with famous rabbis, also drawn to Izmir by its wealth.[15] As fortunes were being made and heresies hatched in Izmir, Salonika's woolen manufacture declined and became merely a military supply industry, continuing only due to the need to supply the Janissaries. By the eighteenth century, trade between Salonika and western Europe increased greatly, but Salonikan Jewish merchants and manufacturers had been largely replaced by other groups, including Italian Jews, protected by foreign consuls.[16] As Suraiya Faroqhi notes, the abolition of the Janissaries in 1826 "led to the final eclipse of woolen cloth manufacture by Jewish artisans."[17]

The decline of most Salonikan Jews afforded an opportunity to a minority of Jews and many Dönme, who stepped into their former role and became the leading textile merchants. Although we see the reemergence of wealthy Sephardic Jewish families such as the Allatini in Salonika by the end of the nineteenth century, new economic possibilities were also seized upon by Dönme, who soon became quite wealthy and significant economic players. This wealth, combined with being ostensibly Muslim, speaking both Turkish and French, and externally adopting Ottoman culture, allowed them to take advantage of their legal position and easily rise in a city in which Jews predominated, most of whom were still in many senses of the word part of the subordinate class. The Tanzimat reforms introduced new political positions, which Dönme could fill, thus expanding their power, wealth, and influence further in the city and its hinterland.

By the mid-1880s, Dönme served in many new governmental positions introduced by the Tanzimat. These included the *mutasarrıf* (governor of a subdivision of a province) of Üsküp, the commercial courts of Salonika and Serres, the director of finance of the province of Monastir, the imperial Ministry of Education, the new gendarme corps, the provincial education administration of Salonika, as well as Salonika's Chamber of Commerce, Industry, and Agriculture, and the Assembly for the Administration of the Province of Salonika. In a sense then, their prominent position in the late nineteenth century was owing in part to urban reform. The Greek newspaper *Faros tēs Makedonias* reported that the municipal elections of 1886 returned Duhani Hasan Akif Efendi (Kapancı) and Karakaş Efendi (Karakaş) to the council.[18] Mufti İbrahim Bey was the mayor, however, showing that the ancien régime had not yet been dislodged. Although

Yakubi Dönme had served in the office of the governor, no Dönme rose to be the governor, who was appointed from Istanbul. But in fact, since there was much turnover in this office—in the second half of the nineteenth century, the tenure averaged under six months—locally appointed or selected positions were more influential.[19] Although Salonika was one of the first Ottoman cities to receive a municipality, it took over two decades for a Dönme to rise to be mayor. But once that had happened, Dönme mayors continued to be appointed.

The mayors in the Tanzimat period were not financially independent, and were still controlled by the central government. Part of the reason why wealthy, powerful locals filled that office was that they could use their own finances and links to foreign capital to go beyond a restricted city budget and implement further city improvements. Dönme municipal officials who were part of international networks of finance and who profited from the introduction of new businesses in the city played a crucial role in the city's transformation. Yakubi Hamdi Bey, an urban reformist, local official, and businessman with western European connections, was the most visible Dönme in local politics. He was an entrepreneur, whose diverse interests included a hotel in the port area[20] and at least seven adjacent businesses in the main business district of the city (İştira),[21] where other Dönme concerns, such as Hasan Akif's tobacco business, were also located.[22]

Hamdi Bey became mayor in 1893 and served in that office until 1902. After he became mayor, he sought to create a better life in Salonika, like other progressive politicians of the day exploiting geography, demography, and hygiene for the welfare and productivity of the population.[23] Hamdi Bey "transferred his business acumen and experience to the affairs of the city, running it like a profitable enterprise: borrowing, building, selling, increasing revenue and investing it, advertising his product."[24] Like urban reformists in other Ottoman cities, Hamdi Bey aimed to make Salonika "a healthy city, which breathed freely, pulsated with life, and moved towards growth."[25] His municipality, allied with the private companies he established, which received some of their financing from western Europe, provided services such as public hospitals and a fire department, paving and sweeping streets, construction of public toilets to ameliorate public health, horse-drawn and later electric tramways to improve urban transportation, gas lighting for domestic and public spaces, and running water to homes to improve the quality of life.[26] He was granted an imperial concession to "construct, administer, and tap the water of Salonika," which allowed him to launch the Ottoman Water Company of Salonika with the backing of Belgian financiers. All of the companies that he founded or directed in the city were partly funded with Belgian capital or by Belgian companies. By 1900, his family was established in Brussels, where he later died and was buried. Hamdi Bey and his brother Ömer were granted a fifty-year imperial concession to make the Vardar River navigable for ships with small carrying capacities.[27] Hamdi Bey was also given a concession to establish and develop tramways, leading to his founding the Ottoman Tramway Company of Salonika; and he was granted authority to establish the Ottoman Gas Company.[28] After he became mayor, his municipality supported and controlled the horse-drawn tramway (the electric version arrived, along with electricity and the telephone, in 1907–8).[29]

Hamdi Bey considered paving all the streets in the city. He may not have been able to do so, but he altered the face of the city in other ways, hiring the Italian architect Vitaliano Poselli to plan and build most of the new public buildings in Salonika, including the neoclassical army barracks, government house, and municipal hospital.[30] Hamdi Bey was the mayor responsible for the fountain that delivered sour cherry juice, and he also built a public fish market on the waterfront, which was both Islamic and modern: customers entered the clean and hygienic market through the building's façade, which contained numerous Islamic architectural features.[31] It has already been mentioned that Poselli designed the eclectic Dönme New Mosque.

The fact that Hamdi Bey was a Dönme, and not a Jew, was the key to his mayoralty. No Christian or Jew, no matter how wealthy or influential, could have become mayor. Hamdi Bey was also the leader of the Yakubis—the Dönme group who most closely followed the public requirements of being Muslim—when he was mayor (which led to all Yakubis subsequently being referred to as "Hamdi Beys"). Being mayor allowed him to further the financial interests of the Yakubis, and to ensure that Yakubis could serve in local politics without suspicion or interference from governors sent from Istanbul, although the prevalence of Yakubi Dönme in municipal offices—recognizable by their shaved heads—had caused at least one governor, Midhat Pasha, to take notice less than a decade after the municipality was established.[32]

It may not be a coincidence that the Dönme schools in Salonika were very close to the seat of power in the city, the *konak*, where other Dönme presided. Şemsi Efendi's school was located just two blocks east of the governor's building. The Feyz-i Sıbyân was located one block southeast; the Feyziye built during Mehmet Cavid's time as director of school was one block northeast, and the dorm and girls' school were barely two blocks southeast, between the Feyz-i Sıbyân and Şemsi Efendi schools. The proximity of Dönme schools to the seat of the governor was symbolic of the heavy proportion of Dönme in government service in the city. As noted in the provincial yearbook, many graduates of these schools served in the administration of education in the province.[33] Ahmet Kapancı served as president of the Municipal Council. In 1908, Namık Kapancı, son of Mehmet Kapancı, was elected member of the municipal council.[34] At the end of February 1912, following municipal elections, and just before the end of Ottoman rule in the city, the governor appointed Hamdi Bey's son Osman Said, a municipal councilor, as the city's new mayor.

The Dönme Role in the Constitutional Revolution of 1908

The Dönme took on more importance when students and educators at Dönme schools, the writers and audience of Dönme literary journals, those who endowed Dönme buildings, and civil servants who shared in Dönme visions of the new Ottoman society turned from local to larger concerns and entered imperial politics with the aim of promoting wide-scale reform and progress. At a time when both local municipal and central administrative power were increasing, it is not surprising that what happened locally, such as in Salonika, mattered empirewide. Writing in *Gonca-i Edeb*, Fazlı Necip sent a veiled message to the sultan: "let us carry out justice, let us be free of oppression and we shall always be happy and fortunate."[35] Salonika was a site of great political fermentation, because it was the cradle of the Young Turk revolutionary movement and the center of the Committee of Union and Progress (CUP) and socialist organizations. It had the highest concentration of factory labor, particularly in the tobacco industry, in the empire, its Workers' Solidarity Federation, headed by a Bulgarian Jew, Avram Benaroya, was considered by the Second International to be the spearhead of the proletarian struggle in the East. It was a center of Masonic activity.[36] Salonika was one of the Ottoman cities best supplied with schools, including a Law Faculty, and army headquarters, both of which were open to new currents of thought. Professionals and civil servants who shared a progressive outlook, especially employees of the Post and Telegraph Department (such as Talat Pasha) and members of the Third Army (such as Enver Pasha), made up the bulk of the revolutionaries. The heart of the revolution of 1908 was Macedonia.

The revolution was spearheaded by the CUP, first organized in 1889 by students at the Royal Medical Academy in Istanbul, who were heavily influenced by biological materialist ideology, and later spread to Paris and Cairo, and then to cities throughout the Ottoman Empire, including Salonika. Until 1902, the CUP was an umbrella organization for most groups aiming to assassinate Sultan Abdülhamid II or dethrone him in a coup d'état.[37] One of the first to join was Dr. Nâzım, the director of the municipal hospital in Salonika (a building designed by Hamdi Bey's municipal architect Poselli) and scion of a leading Kapancı Dönme tobacco merchant family.[38] Dr. Nâzım was one of the few to continue in the CUP from its founding to the revolution of 1908, at which time he had become one of the organization's two main ideologues.

Although Dönme such as Dr. Nâzım would play a leading ideological role in the CUP, and there are echoes in Young Turk writings of the emphasis on progress and science and their harmony with Islam in Dönme school curriculums and journals, it is important to stress the differences between the original Young Turk ideology and the opinions expressed by most Dönme. Dr. Nâzım was about as representative of the Dönme as Leon Trotsky was of Russian Jews. Young Turk ideology was far more extreme, and the two diverged. Moreover, the ideology of the CUP leaders and its members, Dönme and others, were not necessarily the same. Different groups supported the overthrow of the sultan for diverse reasons. Yet this major difference is often overlooked, leading to gross mischaracterization of the Dönme and confusing them with Jews.

Unlike most Dönme, the Young Turks before 1908 were marked by a materialist, positivist (replacing religion with science), social Darwinist (survival of the fittest), and anti-religious political theory, which opened Young Turks to accusations of atheism. Reflecting positivist leanings, the CUP's Paris-based official publication, *Meşveret* (Consultation), was dated according to the positivist French revolutionary calendar, which began on January 1, 1789, and not according to the Muslim calendar.[39] At the same time, the CUP used Islamic rhetoric and references in their writing, calling Abdülhamid II an atheist.[40] Although they seemed to promote Islam in public, in private they disparaged it, and they hoped it would eventually play no public role. Şükrü Hanioğlu argues that they used Islam in order to persuade the public to follow their program, which was anything but Islamic. They saw themselves as a Muslim elite bringing scientific enlightenment to the masses in the guise of a liberal and progressive Islam, which had analogies to positivism: unlike the Dönme, the Young Turks "did not attempt to reconcile Islam with modern sciences and ideas, and they developed a positivist-materialist ideology by deliberately misinterpreting Islamic sources."[41] Indeed, "for the Young Turks religion was to be the stimulant and not the opiate of the masses."[42]

Along with diverging in regard to morals, ethics, and religiosity, another difference between most Dönme and CUP ideology was that the latter was elitist and racist. It promoted phrenology in the service of proving theories about the hierarchies of races.[43] As adherents of biological materialism, the Young Turks absorbed western European ideas about race, particularly the Frenchman Gustave Le Bon's obsession with protecting the superior race (in his case, white European) and Edmond Demolins's inquiry into the alleged superiority of the Anglo-Saxons.[44] After Japan's victory over Russia in 1904, leading thinkers such as Yusuf Akçura promoted Turkish nationalism based on race. In an influential piece entitled "Üç Tarz-ı Siyaset," (Three Political Systems), submitted to the extreme nationalist Young Turk journal *Türk,* based in Cairo, Akçura argued that the best choice among Ottomanism, Islamism, and Turkism, was the latter; it was best to "pursue a Turkish nationalism based on race [ırk]."[45] The term "Turk" replaced "Ottoman," and skepticism about the loyalty of "parasitical" Christians and non-Turkish Muslims was expressed in the main Young Turk publications. Young Turks wholeheartedly embraced theories of race, although they rearranged the hierarchies to place Turks on top.[46] By 1906, Turkish nationalism based on the pseudoscientific race theories of Europe had become the guiding ideology of the CUP.[47] These would be the traits of the official ideology of the early Turkish Republic, and carrying "Jewish" rather than "Turkish blood" would ultimately be used against the Dönme.

While the ideology and leading activists in the CUP are well identified, less known is the role that Sufi brotherhoods and Freemasons also played in oppositional politics in that era aiding the CUP and favoring the overthrow of Abdülhamid II. Chief among the radical Sufi brotherhoods are the Bektaşi and Mevlevi orders, to which Karakaş and Kapancı Dönme, respectively, adhered. As Hanioğlu notes, "some Sufi orders who were discriminated against by the sultan and his confidants in favor of other rival orders became ardent supporters of the Young Turks."[48] He mainly has the Bektaşi in mind. Although ruthlessly suppressed in 1826 along with the Janissaries, the Bektaşi made a comeback by the beginning of Abdülhamid II's reign and were the strongest Sufi order opposing the regime.[49] Irène Melikoff notes that Young Turks, precursors to the CUP, were sympathetic to the Bektaşi, because they considered the Sufi order to be liberal.[50] A letter from a revolutionary asserts that a number of Young Turks were Bektaşi.[51] The syncretistic tendencies of the Bektaşi matched the progressive ideas of the Young Turks, and Bektaşi were affiliated with Freemasons, who let the CUP use their lodges after 1906. After the revolution of 1908, revolutionary officers visited Bektaşi lodges to pay tribute; Bektaşi publications were again permitted; newspapers attacking the Bektaşi were closed; and new Bektaşi lodges were opened.[52] The CUP also had a relationship with the Mevlevi order. Mevlevi lodges distributed CUP propaganda, Mevlevi sheikhs hosted CUP meetings at their homes, and other sheikhs were exiled together with Young Turks for their activism.[53]

The Sufi role in revolutionary politics was significant, but it was the Freemasons who were more important in opposition politics than the CUP before 1895. Freemasons played such an active role between 1870 and 1918 that the assassins of an Ottoman statesman in 1913 claimed that "their aim was to recapture power that had too long been in the hands of the Freemasons."[54] After all, the Freemason Sultan Murad V, envisioned as an enlightened sultan who would unite Turks and Greeks, had come to power in a coup d'état facilitated by Freemasons in 1876.[55] The nucleus of the Young Turks sprang from the members of a Masonic lodge established by those who had brought that sultan to the throne. Until 1902, Ottoman Freemasons operated their own political organizations under other names and distributed political tracts on liberty and freedom across Europe.[56] Thereafter they supported the CUP, whose leader Ahmet Rıza's inner circle included many prominent Freemason leaders.[57] All the founding members, but one, of the Ottoman Freedom Society in Salonika (which became the internal headquarters when it merged with the Paris-based CUP, which served as external headquarters) were Freemasons or became Freemasons, and were members of either the Italian Obedience of Macedonia Risorta or the French Obedience of Véritas.[58] The CUP was based in Salonikan Masonic lodges, and Freemasons offered Young Turks safe houses. Freemasons declared themselves "the main force" behind the 1908 revolution, supported the CUP in power, and thrived after Abdülhamid II was deposed.[59]

Freemasonry played a key role in that revolutionary era. In a society not ready to abandon hierarchies of religion, and in which sectarianism had become a problem, leading to massacres in Anatolia and Syria, Christians, Jews, and Muslims could meet in Masonic lodges as equals, united in secrecy. Freemasons benefited from social egalitarianism, which allowed them to reconcile their religious differences and promote societal change.[60] At Masonic lodges, urban strangers were transformed into brothers seeking the same political goal.[61] Murad V's successor, Abdülhamid II, recognized the threat and repressed the Freemasons, his government labeling them "a habitual source of sedition."[62]

There were close links between secret societies of Freemasons and the diverse members of the CUP, a secret society imitating Masonic practices and meeting in Masonic lodges. Secrecy afforded political organization. The Jewish attorney Emmanuel Carasso, who received medals of honor from the very sultan he worked to overthrow, one of the leaders of the CUP in Salonika and in the hierarchy of the entire organization, headed the Italian rite Macedonia Risorta. Its lodge was the site of secret CUP meetings and the place where CUP archives and records were kept, and the order counted among its members the majority of the leaders of the Salonikan branch of the CUP.[63] Once the CUP came to power, it established its own exclusive Masonic lodge in 1909, Le Grand Orient Ottoman, in order to reduce the power of foreign-affiliated lodges.[64] Freemasonry was thus important for the CUP; Masonic lodges were not merely sites where they could hold their secret meetings prior to the revolution.

Many prominent Dönme were Freemasons as well as Sufis, which facilitated their entry into the CUP. Yıldız Sertel mentions Bektaşi, Mevlevi, and Masonic lodges in the same sentence in which she describes the Dönme New Mosque in Salonika.[65] The journalist Fazlı Necip, the future final Ottoman finance minister Faik Nüzhet (at the time the deputy inspector of public debt), and Osman Adil, the son of Mayor Hamdi Bey (at the time an assistant director in one of the offices of the Foreign Ministry), who was a regular contributor to *Gonca-i Edeb*,[66] were members of the Véritas [Truth] Obedience, established in 1904.[67] Osman Adil was among the founders of this order and sat on its supreme council.[68] Véritas's 150 members in 1908 included 129 Jews and 15 Muslims or Dönme, including one of the founders of the Terakki school, Tevfik Ehat.[69] It also counted at least four CUP members, two future grand viziers, Ali Rıza

Pasha and Hüseyin Hilmi Pasha becoming members after 1908. One-third of the members of another French-rite lodge, L'Avenir de l'Orient (The Future of the East) were Muslim or Dönme.[70] The names of 23 of its 60 members in 1911 were Turkish; the rest were Jewish. At least as early as 1908, members of the Terakki board and administration appear in the lists of members of Masonic lodges. These included Sabiha Sertel's brother, Celal Dervish, one of the founders and board members.[71]

Jews and Dönme were prominent in the clubs of Freemasons where the CUP met in Salonika.[72] Mason and dervish lodges, where many Dönme participated in Sufi rituals, sided with the CUP against the sultan in part because they promoted equality and brotherhood.[73] Conveniently, given Salonika's secret CUP cells and secret Masonic membership and revolutionary cells in the Third Army, ancient underground storage spaces located in the main Dönme neighborhoods allowed passage undetected from house to house and even from neighborhood to neighborhood. When police raided homes, people on the run and the secret documents they carried could easily disappear by this means.[74] The Dönme practice of secrecy and group solidarity and fraternal intimacy was a good model for the CUP. As it was for the Dönme, secrecy was inseparable from CUP membership. Here the sociologist Georg Simmel's understanding of the difference between the outer and inner worlds, and the protective function of secrecy, also based on Freemasonry, became a reality. By this point, many Dönme had turned from only having otherworldly concerns to trying to realize a political plan in the world. Dönme members of Véritas played a crucial role in the new CUP lodge.

The role of the Dönme in the CUP, like their role in Freemasonry, was significant.[75] They immediately responded when the CUP opened its first branch in Salonika in 1896 and began publishing news about its activities aimed specifically at the Dönme.[76] Already that year, Dr. Nâzım "openly commended their efforts for the Young Turk movement" in *Meşveret*.[77] This praise was seconded in Salonikan members' letters to the newspaper. When, after an internal split, a second CUP branch was opened in Salonika the following year, Dönme joined it "en masse."[78] They refused to pay dues, however, on grounds that they were already sending money to the CUP's Paris headquarters (further evidence of their international connections). Şükrü Hanioğlu writes that "in spite of the strong religious concerns of the ulema members [Muslim religious scholars] of the CUP, the Salonica branch worked under the auspices of the *dönmeler*."[79]

Dönme played a significant role in turn-of-the-century Ottoman politics and an important founding and supporting role in the revolutionary movement. In 1899, the Dönme Mazlum Hakkı and the Jew Albert Fua, an important early CUP ideologue, began to publish a political journal in Paris.[80] According to Nahum Slousch, writing in 1908, the Dönme religion and exceptional social position allowed them to become important intermediaries of the revolution.[81] Soon after the revolution, the *Journal de Salonique* published the names of renowned individuals and businesses in Salonika that had provided financial assistance to the CUP. Perhaps surprisingly, the banker, textile merchant, director of one of the largest banking and commercial houses in the city, and head of the Chamber of Commerce Mehmet Kapancı used his wealth to fund the organization.[82] We must not assume that wealth equals conservatism. Wealthy merchants such as Mehmet Kapancı supported the revolution because they were Freemasons and believed that the sultan was stifling society with his despotism. These were men who supported progressive schools that promoted critical thinking. In one recent writer's opinion, the Terakki school that Mehmet Kapancı and others founded "was one of the centers of the revolution. All secret journals and manifestos were secretly distributed at school."[83]

Some Dönme became so committed to political ideas discussed behind closed doors at the city's ubiquitous French, Italian, and Ottoman Masonic lodges in clandestine CUP meetings that they were considered the revolutionary vanguard.[84] *Meşveret* noted how crucial the Dönme role was when it proclaimed that the Dönme, whom it labeled one of the most "modern" groups in the empire, were "the only group working in the movement" in the city.[85] Slousch concurred with the view that Dönme intellectuals and civil servants were playing a crucial role. He noted that their history and religion caused them to evolve more and more into an association of freethinkers, separate from Muslims and Jews, placed in position to be an evolutionary and progressive factor in the city.[86] Slousch argued the youth had become liberals, a generation committed to physical and moral rejuvenation, free of former prejudices and constraints, ranking among the avant-garde of the army of civilization that propagated the ideas of justice and progress.

It is not coincidental that when the revolution went public, speeches were made at the outset in July 1908 on the first floor balcony of the Kapancı-owned Olympos Hotel on the freshly renamed Plateia Eleutherias (formerly Olympos Square). A black-and-white postcard depicts a massive crowd of men in white derby hats enthusiastically applauding the electric speeches of CUP leaders.[87] Among the speakers were Moiz Kohen (Tekinalp) and Sabiha Sertel's handlebar-mustachioed older brother Celal Dervish, who shouted: "We want brotherhood between all peoples. We are all one without regard to religion or sect. Long live the fatherland! Long live freedom! There are no Greeks, Jews, or Bulgarians, there are only Ottomans."[88]

Dönme journalists played an important role in the events of July 1908. Fazlı Necip, a member of the Véritas lodge, became a leading CUP activist and publicist and during the revolution was put in charge of organizing and coordinating all the movement's propaganda activities in Salonika.[89] Ahmet Emin Yalman, at the time employed by the daily *Sabah* (Morning) and the translation bureau of the Ministry of Foreign Affairs, wrote: "We journalists decided to take open action . . . to electrify the public. We staged a small revolution of our own in Istanbul. Famous writers in disfavor with the Sultan were all invited to write patriotic poems and articles welcoming the new liberty. We held the first street demonstrations, called a meeting of all sorts of writers, and organized a press association. Decisions were made immediately to communicate to the public excitement of the new era."[90] Yalman would become the news editor of the CUP's *Tanin* (a title roughly meaning "Echo") in 1914.[91] Yalman's alma mater, the Terakki, boasted that it raised freedom-loving, constitution-supporting youth, and that those who announced the second constitutional government were Terakki graduates.[92] In 1909, articles appeared in the *Journal de Salonique* celebrating the twenty-fifth anniversary of the founding of the Feyziye school. One article mentions the regrettable absence of the new finance minister Mehmet Cavid, formerly a Feyziye administrator, who could not attend the anniversary celebrations because important matters in Istanbul detained him, and then praises the revolution and the revival of "Young Turkey" by the heroes of independence through their struggle for liberty, equality, and the fatherland.[93] After 1908, the Feyziye's journal *Bahçe* (Garden), originally for children, became an enthusiastic supporter of the CUP, until it ceased publication two years later.[94]

Dönme had an excellent reputation among their allies in this revolutionary period. Their significance was corroborated by one of the first memoirs written by a CUP activist, the 1911 account of Leskovikli Mehmet Rauf. He had been arrested for working underground for the Committee in 1895, and exiled to Salonika. There he got to know Dönme, who helped him in the political cause, and he became a member of the executive committee of the CUP's first branch in the city. He argues that although the Dönme were accused of being greedy and mainly concerned about commerce, in fact, he found that among all those engaged in the struggle, the Dönme, who ran the best schools in the empire, were the most loyal and self-sacrificing proponents of liberty and supporters of the overthrow of despotism (i.e., the sultan), going "well beyond their Muslim brothers in struggling for freedom." He mentions how ignorant Muslims in Salonika cast doubt on their Islamic character and being true Muslims—which he argues was based on resentment that the Dönme were such a closed group that they did not intermarry—yet he asserts that they fulfilled all of their religious obligations like other Muslims, and that there was no reason to doubt their fidelity to Islam or to the Ottoman state. He concedes, however, that these descendants of Jewish converts did not marry other Muslims, "and in this way guarded the boundaries" of the group.[95]

Compelled to reinstate the constitution of 1876 in 1908 and to reconvene parliament, Abdülhamid II was left formally in power. But less than a year later, following an anti-revolutionary uprising, in 1909, he too ended up in Salonika. He was placed under house arrest in the architect Poselli's Allatini Villa.

Mehmet Cavid had had the duty of relaying to Abdülhamid II the news that a deputation had a communication to make to him. Emmanuel Carasso was a member of the delegation that conveyed to the sultan the news of his downfall.[96] That the first was a Dönme and the second a Jew would become pegs upon which Muslims and then Turks could hang their fears of Jewish conspiracy.

Foreign diplomats, who considered the Dönme Jews, noted the role of the Dönme in local politics following the revolution of 1908. "Ahmet Effendi Kapandji, a wealthy Deunme who has also acted for some time as President of the Municipality," is mentioned in a cable from the British consul general at Salonika to his ambassador in Istanbul in early 1909.[97] A fascinating cable from the French consul in Salonika to the French foreign minister, Stephen Pichon, in the spring of 1910 discusses the results of the election of the municipal council that March.[98] Six men were elected, half of them with Jewish names and half with Muslim names. Of those with Muslim names, two are identifiably Dönme: Osman Said (Yakubi), and Kibaroğlu Abdurrahman (Karakaş). The cable says that the election, to which the population had been looking forward, was marked by the defeat of the "Turks": among those who had obtained the majority of the vote, three were Jews and the three others "belong to the Dönme sect (Jews converted to Islam)." The CUP had put forward a common list with the Greeks, consisting of one Greek and five Turks, but the consul says that none of these were elected. Having been cheated by the Turks in a previous election, the Greeks did not want to be fooled again, so they gave their full support to the Jewish and Dönme candidates, preferring to not elect a Greek rather than elect Turks. According to this analysis, this was an example of Christians and Jews (here including the Dönme) uniting against the Turks, who are called their hereditary enemy.

The French cable reflects the biases of its western European writer, who bears in mind the interests of his audience in Paris. Yet one cannot dismiss entirely the sentiment it contains. It reflects a racialized understanding of identity. Although converts to Islam, the Dönme are not considered Turks (which is to say, Muslims). Instead, the author of the cable groups them with Christians and Jews and says that Dönme interests and political affiliations are not the same as those of the Turks. This was one thing when stated in a foreign ambassadorial cable, but quite another when it reflected Greek or Turkish governmental and public opinion.

The British and French diplomats were correct to point out the Dönme identity of one key actor. Of several Dönme government ministers who came to power after the sultan was deposed, and the so-called Action Army suppressed the counterrevolution, the most influential was the Freemason Mehmet Cavid, former Feyziye principal and instructor and director of a Dönme commerce school.[99] While serving as director of the Feyziye school, Mehmet Cavid became an active member in the same underground organization as Captain Mustafa Kemal (later Atatürk). The latter had founded the Fatherland and Freedom Society in Damascus in 1905 and had come to Salonika to open a branch in that city. He may or may not have founded a branch, but he was in contact with other opposition politicians. In the end, the Fatherland and Freedom Society became the Ottoman Freedom Society, all of whose members were Freemasons, and one of whom was a leading Sufi (Bursalı Mehmet Tahir, director of the Military School at Salonika and a member of the Melami order),[100] which merged with the CUP in 1907.[101] After the revolution, Mehmet Cavid served in the new parliament from 1908 to 1918, and he was one of the leaders of the CUP in 1916 and 1917. He was finance minister between

1909 and 1912, and again in 1917–18. Although influential, Mehmet Cavid was overshadowed by his fellow Salonikans Talat Pasha and Enver Pasha, who were pro-war. Mehmet Cavid's subsequent fall from grace in the early Republic has made his role both in the administration of Dönme schools and the Constitutional Revolution and World War I era particularly sensitive.

It is conventional for those writing today about Mehmet Cavid and the revolution to put a Turkish republican spin on the era. Mert Sandalcı writes that his grandfather, who was Mehmet Cavid's student, shared his anti-Abdülhamid and pro-freedom, liberal, and democratic thoughts with students.[102] Ahmet Emin Yalman and Sabiha Sertel, as well-known journalists in the Turkish Republic, did much to propagate the idea of Dönme contributions to the construction of the Turkish nation-state. In her biography of her mother, Yıldız Sertel emphasizes, not only the devout patriotism of the Dönme, as Yalman does in his autobiography, but also their fiery revolutionary conviction, both in 1908 and in 1923. Like Yalman, she also misleadingly narrates history through the Kemalist prism of the so-called struggle between the proponents of progress, who believed in the equality of men and women and in western European law, and the forces of reaction, who promoted the veiling of women and Shari'a (Islamic law), tracing a straight line from the 1908 revolution to secularism, Turkish nationalism, and the republic. She ignores the fact that Dönme progressiveness, religiosity, and worldliness were interrelated.

Elsewhere in their writings, however, Yalman and Sertel let slip comments that today are avoided by writers who have a favorable view of the Dönme. When Sabiha Sertel greeted her older brother Celal Dervish when the revolution started, she said: "It means you are also now a CUP supporter." "What do you think?" he replied. "We were raised as revolutionary youth in Salonika. We also became Masons."[103] "The prosperous, foreign Free Masonic Lodges afforded convenient opportunities for meeting" for secret organizations in Salonika, Ahmet Emin Yalman notes.[104] The "first spark of revolution" was ignited in him in the 1890s, when he was a student at the Terakki school.[105] He subsequently became a member of the CUP.[106]

The prominent role of Dönme in the revolutionary era made a major impression on the majority, the Muslims, which ushered in an era of racial and religious vilification of the Dönme, beginning in earnest immediately after the revolution.[107] Seeing a clump of "secret Jews" at the top, they assumed that people such as Mehmet Cavid, rather than being motivated by commitment to revolutionary ideals, which would later be devalued anyway by associating them with Dönme religion, acted out of a separate (Masonic-Bektaşi-Jewish) Dönme interest. It seems to have escaped their attention, and that of many of today's Turkish observers, that the fact that revolutionaries "formed themselves into secret societies and made use of Freemasonic ritual does not mean that they sold their souls to occult powers dabbling in world revolution."[108]

The Dönme played a role in modern transformation in part because their values are associated with bringing about new ways of thinking about and being in the world, not least political reforms. What Margaret Jacob explains for the second half of the eighteenth century is accurate for the nineteenth and twentieth as well: "The habit of border crossings, be they over lines of birth and breeding, or religion, or national groupings, created a predisposition to imagine reform and possibly embrace the revolutionary impulse," promoting progress and morality in the face of tyranny.[109] Such people find that revolution and democracy are more in their interests than monarchical absolutism. They find, unlike the majority, that the solution lies, not in nationalism, but in transcending it.[110] By 1908, the Dönme sense of political radicalism meant deposing the sultan and installing a liberal constitution and parliament. This made them a real and perceived danger to monarchs and those who defended them.[111] Not without substantiation, after the fall of the empire, such progressives, many of whom were members of Masonic orders, were accused of not identifying solely with their country, and thus were considered incapable of being good citizens.[112] Freemasons were viewed as sinister, secret political societies became suspect, and most prominent leaders were executed.

Muslims Take Notice of the Dönme after 1908

Sparked by their involvement in politics, the public identity and private beliefs of the Dönme began to concern Muslims after the revolution of 1908. Half a year after the Constitutional Revolution, members of the Committee of Muslim Unity were furious. Freemasons had just established a lodge in the imperial capital. Their opponents needed an organ to attack what they considered atheism and its fake Muslim proponents. They approached Dervish Vahdetî, a pious Muslim from Cyprus and muezzin (caller to prayer), who had been frequently exiled and jailed

for writing or supporting writers who opposed the rule of Sultan Abdülhamid II. Just before the Constitutional Revolution, he was imprisoned
far from Istanbul in remote Diyarbakir. After the revolution, he returned
to Istanbul and in December 1908, he began to publish *Volkan* (Volcano),
which he agreed to make the organ of the Committee of Muslim Unity.
Soon afterward, referring to Dönme, Vahdetî wrote: "There are many
Jews who came to Istanbul who, of course, are not really Muslim. Soon
afterward, some Muslims joined the Masonic lodges, also displaying their
Freemason nicknames, and no longer could be considered pious, and fell
into disgrace in the Muslim community."[113] He thus links the arrival of
the Salonikan Dönme with the spread of Freemasonry and immorality
among Muslims.

Vahdetî became most vocal of Muslims articulating opposition to politically active Dönme. He opposed the revolution of 1908 and helped
incite the countercoup the following year. Dervish Vahdetî and others opposed the "atheism" (secularism) of the CUP, its alleged attacks on Islam,
the fact that many of its members were influential Freemasons, and the
Jews and Dönme in its ranks.

Bernard Lewis blames the widespread circulation of conspiracy theories
about the CUP being part of an alleged Jewish Masonic plot, not on Ottoman Muslims like Dervish Vahdetî, but on British writers and its use
as Allied propaganda during World War I.[114] It is indeed striking how
British officials, especially ambassadors, in their official correspondence
between 1909 and 1916 explicitly referred to the CUP as a cabal of Jews
and Freemasons, calling it the "Jew Committee of Union and Progress,"
and to Mehmet Cavid as a "crypto-Jew" and "apex of Freemasonry" in
the empire, "one of the only members of the cabinet who really counts,"
who was working to have total Jewish influence over the Ottoman Empire.[115] Nevertheless, such arguments by Lewis and later Stanford Shaw
reflect these historians' aim of deflecting any charges of Turkish antisemitism onto Christians, foreign or Ottoman, and studied effort to avoid any
mention of such sentiment by Ottoman Muslims or Turks.[116]

Austrian and German antisemitism, French racial thinking, and Russian
antisemitism, especially political antisemitism, all influenced Ottoman
Muslim and later Turkish writers and thinkers. Many of these ideas were
transmitted to Ottoman cities such as Salonika and Istanbul by Ottoman
Muslim intellectuals who had spent considerable time in Paris, Berlin, or
who originated in the Russian Empire, such as Yusuf Akçura. In literature

from these sources, Jews are represented as physically and biologically different, with unique psychopathologies and abnormal sexual desires, leading to higher rates of sexually transmitted disease and insanity.[117]

Muslims such as the contributors to *Volkan* reflected such sentiment and engaged in vicious, polemical writings against the Dönme, whom they regarded as Jews. One was Fazlı Necip, who vociferously supported the CUP in the newspapers *Asır* (Century/Age) and *Zaman* (Time/Epoch). Others mentioned the supposedly arrogant speeches Şemsi Efendi had delivered in front of the government building (*konak*) during the 1909 campaign for the parliamentary election, which did not take the conservative Muslim point of view into consideration. Views of Dönme insincerity fueled the battles of the pen between religious Muslims and Dönme concerning the governing of the empire and society.

Another of the main magnets of anti-Dönme rhetoric was the most visible Dönme politician, Mehmet Cavid. Between 1909 and 1911, Mehmet Cavid's Muslim opponents in parliament called him a Salonikan Dönme in league with Jewish banks.[118] Articles published in 1908 and 1909 express disdain for the values that the Dönme allegedly supported and the institutions through which they apparently spread these values in society.[119] The values included Europeanization (adopting western European values, desiring western European goods), atheism, and the emancipation of women. The institutions through which these values were disseminated included Masonic lodges, which caused Muslims who joined to lose their religion, and the CUP. Contra these values and institutions, Vahdetî and his writers defended what they saw as true religion (Islam), Islamic law, Muslim unity, and the fatherland.

To understand the context of the attacks on the Dönme, it is important to analyze the criticism of Muslims in the pages of *Volkan*. Writers defined the limits to being a Muslim. To them, a nonbelieving Muslim was a threat to society. *Volkan's* greatest concern lay with irreligious or atheist Muslims. Vahdetî and other writers assumed that irreligion went hand in hand with corrupted morals, including the liberation of women, which harmed society. A. Şehabeddin wrote: "You can't expect the irreligious or atheists to have high morals like pious Muslims. The religious work for this world and the hereafter; atheists only care about this world." As a result, "in Europe many proudly declare their atheism. This goes together with many of their women practically going around naked in public. Men spend their time gambling, drinking, coveting each other's [wives] . . . it can't be denied how ever since we made contact with Europe, obscene European customs have caused more harm to us than cholera. In short, let's be religious!"[120]

Writers in *Volkan* argued that leaning toward western Europe had an impact on morals, piety, and belief itself. The problem with atheism was that atheists, by their nature, could not have any morals, since morals come from religion. Moreover, atheists could not be patriots. A link was made between loyalty and being Muslim. Accordingly, believing or trusting an atheist was out of the question, because atheists valued the material over the spiritual, and property over Islam. Muslims were urged to only fight for Islam and to become martyrs. Although Muslims were willing to be martyred for the empire, "The other elements of Ottoman society are never going to fight as we do for the fatherland. Religion is more important and valuable to us than the fatherland or, indeed, anything. Those who know the pleasure of religion are willing to sacrifice everything for it. Those raised on love of the fatherland, even if they implicitly protect the religion, do not really have an interest in it." Only someone devoted to the true religion could be truly loyal to the empire. Ottomanism without religious faith was meaningless, for "those raised to value religion first will, not implicitly, but publicly protect the fatherland as well and will obey the laws of their land . . . but those who only care about the fatherland will not do the same for the religion." Again, "religion is more sacred than the nation or fatherland and is their only protector; it is incumbent upon all Muslims to exert themselves as if it is."[121]

Loyalty to the empire was only conceivable for those who had true faith. In addition, religious piety would serve as an antidote to atheism. But it appeared that atheism had already taken root, causing irreversible damage. The religion of Muslims had been corrupted. Vahdetî argued that many Muslims even surpassed Europeans in their atheism. This Muslim atheism began after the Ottomans sent embassies to Europe. The ambassadors had taken Christian wives, had many children, and educated them in the mother's western European way. They learned European languages and were educated in Islamic beliefs and morals only by governesses and teachers of other religions. Many ostensibly Muslim men were raised in this fashion. For the author, "To expect these men who do not know their religion and did not receive an Islamic education to be religious is like trying to get oil from a cucumber. What good do you expect from the children of such cucumber men, who receive the same education as their fathers?" Muslims who surpassed Europeans in atheism might have Muslim names, but how can they be trusted with the fate of the empire? The fact that the minister of justice and many notables and members of parliament had attended the opening of a Masonic lodge in Istanbul should serve as a wake-up call for pious Muslims, Vahdetî felt, warning of the threat within.[122]

Masonic lodges were considered the centers of atheism in the empire, and Vahdetî was outraged that the government had given Freemasons permission to build them in the seat of the caliphate, even participated in their opening ceremonies, and was horrified that the ulema also became members. He was worried that this was a sign of the return of despotism and hoped it was not a big trick, and that the justice minister, a supporter of the Constitutional Revolution, was not being duped. Members of the elite and parliamentarians had hailed the opening of a lodge of Freemasons, who were allegedly diametrically opposed to Islam, and Vahdetî repeatedly called on the ulema not to fall for their ruse.[123]

One suspects that Vahdetî had the Dönme in mind in his description of Freemasons as secret followers of a mystic path who diverged from a major monotheist religion and had surreptitiously formed a new religion. According to Vahdetî, Freemasonry had emerged in the eighteenth century out of Christianity but, separating from Christianity, became like a Sufi order. He did not consider it to be a political movement; rather, uniting peoples of different nationalities, it had become an organization trying to establish freedom of religion—code for apostasy—and was subsequently banned as heretical. Freemasons had been trying to be accepted as a religious order, trying to establish freedom of religion for themselves, "but have not been successful and have never been spared attacks, have had to hide themselves, but developed signs and codes as a way of recognizing each other." In this way, Freemasons had become like "a Sufi order, a religious sect" "complete with their own holidays," although Dönme denied that they had gone from being a Sufi order within Islam to being a separate religion.[124]

Volkan also attacked the CUP, regarded as being in league with immoral atheists and Freemasons: "because Freemasonry spread in Salonika and acquired strength and power, as a result, the CUP was established easily and without being noticed."[125] The CUP was in fact an arm of the Freemasons, whose oaths and ceremonies it had adopted. Both Freemasons and CUP members, like the Dönme, came from Salonika. Furthermore, because it was an atheist, Masonic enterprise, the CUP refused to accept honorable members with good morals, but only brought in "men of disgusting morals."[126]

Dönme headed the list of men with repugnant morals. When he became the head of the Committee of Muslim Unity at the beginning of 1909, Vahdetî began to claim that the Salonikan Dönme were behind the spread of Freemasonry and thus of atheism in the empire and that this was a Jewish plot. In order to connect the dots in this argument, Vahdetî had to prove that the Dönme were secret Jews. He quickly found the evidence he sought. Vahdetî notes how in an article in a recent issue of the Salonikan newspaper *Zaman,* the term *gavur* (infidel) was misspelled as *yavur.* The author implies that the misspelling was neither a random mistake nor a slip of the typesetter, but was based on the fact that Jews mispronounced words that way. Since *Zaman* was a Dönme paper, the reader understands the connection made between Dönme and Jews. Vahdetî asks whether the author of the article with the telling misspelled word accepted or rejected hypocrisy and dissimulation and pretended to embrace Islam.[127] Later, he again discussed this Dönme gaffe using plays on the names of the Dönme newspapers. "This age, this epoch, how disagreeable! [Bu asır, bu zaman, ne yamandır!]," he writes. "Whatever day of this age [*asır*] or epoch [*zaman*] we look at is always full of carnal passions, sedition, and rebellion. This disgusting age [*asır*], this epoch [*zaman*] that we hate." He then goes on to more explicitly articulate his racist view of the Dönme, writing: "In our previous article, we criticized the author of the piece implying another cause for his beginning the word 'gavur' with a 'ya' instead of a 'kâf.' We later came to the conclusion that the reason the author of the piece, our brother Celal Dervish, spelled it that way is because that is precisely his predominant natural tendency in pronouncing the word."[128] Vahdetî had caught the slip, however, which revealed the true and unchanging Jewish essence of the Dönme.

Other writers in *Volkan* and their readers also attacked the Dönme. In a letter, Sheikh Abdurrahim, a member of the Council of the Committee of Muslim Unity, declared that "consenting to infidelity is infidelity." In his opinion, the editors of *Asır* and *Zaman* had made their infidelity manifest to all believers. A newspaper ridiculing Muslims and placing a sacred verse from the Qur'an on the same page was not acceptable to Muslims. Sheikh Abdurrahim insisted that if the editors had a conscience, they should remove the Qur'anic verse in the name of the religion. Otherwise, "we curse the newspaper" in the name of all Muslims: "You cannot put satire and religion together. As a consequence we do not have to think of that newspaper as an Islamic newspaper. May the one who does so repent and ask for pardon." Sheikh Abdurrahim identifies the origin of such infidelity as none other than the Dönme: "I think that the *Asır* and *Zaman* -newspapers published in Salonika belong to that well-known element in Salonika. If this is the case, then it is incumbent as a religious duty to ban them."[129]

Dönme writers, journalists, and newspaper publishers attempted to counter the harsh attacks. From *Volkan*, we learn that Dr. Nâzım thought that it was very shameful that people in Salonika wanted to read such newspapers: "If we cannot hinder people from reading them, then at least it should be known that in Europe, and even in the freest cities, such as Paris, honorable people feel restrained by shame and abstain from reading similar newspapers in public."[130] *Volkan* also claimed that the owner of *Yeni Asır* (New Century/Age), Fazlı Necip, and others had greeted this statement with enthusiastic applause. *Volkan* was boycotted in Monastir (Bitola), Kavala, and Salonika, and copies were sent back to distributors by newspaper sellers with threatening letters. In response, supporters of *Volkan* boycotted Dönme-affiliated or sympathetic newspapers elsewhere in the empire. An enthusiastic pious supporter of the newspaper, writing on behalf of "the zealous and patriotic people of Bursa" (in northwestern Anatolia), who was astonished at reports of boycotts of *Volkan*, announced the decision to begin a boycott of the CUP's organ *Tanin*, a journal for which Ahmet Emin Yalman later served as an editor, and its "evil accomplices" in Bursa.[131] Boycotts by Dönme of Islamist newspapers in Ottoman southeastern Europe and boycotts by Islamists of Dönme newspapers in Anatolia foreshadowed anti-Christian, anti-Jewish, and anti-Muslim boycotts in the following decades in Greece and Turkey.

In one of his final articles, which appeared the third week of March 1909, Vahdetî called on the army to remain neutral. Otherwise, "woe to the condition of the nation if soldiers engage in military service on behalf of four drunkards who were Westernized in Europe and then returned, believing in their claims of patriotism."[132] But the army did not heed his call. The government blamed *Volkan* for provoking counterrevolutionary actions, and Vahdetî was fingered as the inciter of the attempted countercoup of March 31, 1909. He fled Istanbul two weeks later as the "Action Army," organized in the CUP's Masonic lodge, and whose gendarmerie was headed by the

Karakaş Dönme Galip Pasha, Şemsi Efendi's former pupil, approached. A unit of Jewish volunteers also joined the march on Istanbul.[133] This included the labor leader Benaroya.[134] As Leon Sciaky notes, "Jews of the city who had never before handled a rifle joined with the warriors of the hinterland."[135] This fact, coupled with Mehmet Cavid's and Emmanuel Carasso's role in the sultan's deposition, helped drive rumors that the revolution was nothing less than an anti-Muslim plot serving Dönme and Jews.

Vahdetî was caught in Izmir and then hanged on July 19, 1909. In 1913, Hakkı Efendi, son of Hasan, one of the participants of an attempted countercoup against the CUP, claimed during his trial that its aim had been to regain power from the Jews and Freemasons.[136]

Secret Jews and World Revolution

The Dönme played a substantial role in Freemasonry, the CUP, the Constitutional Revolution of 1908, and Ottoman politics following the revolution. Many have noted that decisions by the CUP and actions taken by Mehmet Cavid and others set in motion a chain of events that led to the dissolution of the Ottoman Empire and its replacement by the Republic of Turkey. Because people have assumed that the Dönme were simply Jews, many conspiracy theories have been hatched about this role. Because the Dönme were not the same as Jews, did not consider themselves Jews, and did not have close relations with Jews, who did not consider them Jews, however, it seems obvious, yet necessary to assert, that they were not part of or behind a Jewish plot. Yet facts mean little to those who see a Jewish enemy everywhere and behind everything they oppose.

A useful comparison can be made with the real and imagined role of people of Jewish origin in a roughly contemporary event, the Bolshevik Revolution of 1917. Despite his atheism and apparent lack of any Jewish ancestry, Lenin (formerly Vladimir Ilyich Ulyanov) was dubbed "the Jew Lenin" by antisemites and the Bolshevik Revolution was labeled "the Jew Bolshevik Revolution."[137] The fact that Karl Marx (who identified capitalism with Judaism) and Lenin's collaborator Leon Trotsky (formerly Lev Davidovich Bronstein) were Jews contributed to this view. Jews did in fact participate in the Russian revolutionary movement in numbers proportionately greater than their share in the overall population, and their role in it was prominent. Jews, who were well represented among party leaders, theoreticians, and journalists, were considered "the most revolutionary national group in the Russian Empire," like the Dönme in the Ottoman Empire. Nearly two-thirds of those who returned from Switzerland through Germany with Lenin by sealed train in 1917 were Jews; a revolutionary millionaire of Jewish background named Alexander Parvus (Israel Lazarevich Gelfand, or Helphand), who resided for a period in Istanbul and had close relations with the Young Turks, arranged Lenin's return.[138] The Bolshevik leaders closest to Lenin in the beginning were Grigory Zinoviev, Lev Kamenev, and Yakov Sverdlov, all of Jewish origin. Among the men entrusted to carry out Lenin's order to murder the royal family were Sverdlov and two other men of Jewish origin, including the man who claimed to have shot the tsar.[139] The share of men and women of Jewish origin in leading army, party, soviet, and secret police positions during the Civil War following the revolution was greater than their proportion, not only in the population, but in the party itself.[140] What is important is that none of these prominent communists *wanted* to be Jewish; not considering themselves Jewish, they believed they had left their Jewishness—a thing of the past—behind them. Trotsky declared his nationality to be "Social Democratic."[141] Dr. Nâzım can in some respects be considered the CUP's Trotsky. If the other leading CUP ideologue, Bahaettin Şakir, had been Dönme, the comparison would have been even more fitting.

The prominent role of people of Jewish heritage in the former USSR masks other realities, namely, that most party members after the revolution were ethnic Russians, and that Latvians were the most overrepresented group. Nevertheless, as Yuri Slezkine points out, "Jewish participation in radical movements of the early twentieth century is similar to their participation in business and the professions: most radicals were not Jews and most Jews were not radicals, but the proportion of radicals among Jews was, on average, much higher than among their non-Jewish neighbors."[142] Without subscribing to paranoid plots, it can be asserted that the same can be said of the Dönme, who also converted commercial and educational networks "of people, books, money, and information," along with practices of mobility and secrecy, into revolutionary ones.[143] Moreover, scholars have argued that although Jews, the group Muslims confused with Dönme, played a part in the CUP before and after 1908, they could not have manipulated the CUP as a front for Jewish aims. Rather, Jews wholeheartedly supported the CUP because they were politically inclined toward Ottomanism.[144] Moreover, Macedonians, Bulgarians, Serbs, and

Albanians played a far larger role than Jews.[145] Just as Marxists praised the Jewish role in promoting progress culminating in the Bolshevik Revolution, CUP members praised the Dönme role in 1908.

The overrepresentation of Jews among Bolsheviks allowed people to assume that the Bolshevik revolution was the work of Jews and to equate Bolshevism and Judaism. Later, as Jews continued to fill prominent roles in the early Soviet state, their enemies considered the USSR to be run by a Jewish government, or to be a communist-Jewish regime.[146] The overrepresentation of Dönme in the CUP allowed people to believe the revolution of 1908 was a Dönme plot, and later to equate Kemalism with Dönme religion, even though most of the new Kemalist elite were not Dönme and most Dönme were not members of the Kemalist elite. Although there is no evidence that Mustafa Kemal Atatürk had any Jewish ancestors, he was considered to have launched a state on behalf of secret Jews. Both Lenin's and Atatürk's genealogies were suppressed. Revolutionaries who were assumed to have Jewish backgrounds but did not consider themselves Jewish played down their origins.

§5 Choosing Between Greek Thessaloníki and Ottoman Istanbul, 1912–1923

Greek Thessaloníki: The Beginning of the End for the Salonika Dönme

The end of the previous chapter explored how some vocal Muslims in Istanbul directed harsh rhetoric against Dönme based on their role in the political events of 1908. Only a few years after the Constitutional Revolution, Ottoman Salonika fell to Greece. Were similar concerns voiced there? How did the new Greek administration view the Dönme, especially those in local politics? What was the economic and political situation of the Dönme during this period, and the fate of Dönme institutions and leaders? As supporters of Ottomanism, how did the Dönme position themselves in the nation-state of Greece, which was diametrically opposed to a political philosophy of imperial inclusion?

The web site of the municipality of Thessaloníki displays a symbolic photograph from soon after the city became part of Greece.[1] The photograph, taken on the street before the government mansion (*konak*), was snapped on the date in the calendar reserved for the Orthodox Christian saint of the city, St. Demetrius, in 1913. It shows two men shaking hands. The stiff man in dress military uniform—striped pants, short coat, epaulets—on the left appears to be receiving the tall man on the right, wearing a fez, round glasses and a long black overcoat, who bends slightly as he offers his hand. The men are King Constantine of Greece and Mayor Osman Said, and the photograph captures the transfer of power from the Ottomans, represented by the mayor, who was the son of Yakubi Hamdi Bey, to the Greeks, represented by the king. During the first several years of Greek rule following the conquest of the city, Osman Said retained his post (1912–16). Thus he was both the last Ottoman mayor and also the first "Greek" one.

The Dönme entered a new phase in their history when Salonika fell to Greece, ending nearly five centuries of Ottoman rule.[2] Those Dönme who remained in the city faced new challenges. Despite all of the radical transformations spearheaded by Dönme since Salonika had obtained its municipal status, the city abruptly returned to being a more culturally and economically provincial town in 1912. Fearing that it would be cut off from its markets, some Jewish leaders proposed the city become an autonomous region protected by the major European powers. Dönme acted as intermediaries with Young Turks in Vienna, and a committee was formed in Istanbul to support the idea of internationalizing the city.[3] Dönme wrote to the Greek Prime Minister Eleuthérios Venizélos arguing that Salonika's independence, rather than incorporation into the Greek nation-state, would mean its continued economic prosperity.[4] Dönme leaders were not ready to throw in their lot with Greek nationalism and preferred a free state under the mandate of the Habsburgs of Austro-Hungary, an empire whose passports many Dönme carried.

Some Jews thought the future in Greek Thessaloníki looked bright. The socialist Avram Benaroya stayed on and became a very influential figure in Greece, at least through the Civil War (1946–49).[5] Other politically important Jews, such as Emmanuel Carasso, however, emigrated.[6]

The Jews and Dönme who did not leave Thessaloníki faced new circumstances. As Leon Sciaky and others relate, change was swift for those who remained in the city. "The wealthy Turkish [Muslim] families had, with the coming of the Greeks, left the city," Sciaky notes. One might add, many of the Dönme as well. Hurriedly, the Muslims "had packed what belongings they could and had gone to Constantinople or to Asia Minor." The cityscape was immediately transformed. Ottoman characters "vanished from shop fronts and from posters on the walls of corner houses, and Greek ones had taken their place. In ancient Byzantine churches which had been taken over by the Moslems at the time of their conquest, new altars had been raised and holy icons had displaced *suras* of the Koran proclaiming the oneness of God."[7] An Italian journalist wrote that the Dönme had "disappeared into their lanes and the cafés of the Upper Town."[8]

The Electoral Register of Thessaloníki of 1913, compiled following Greek conquest of the Ottoman city and published the following year, catalogues this apparent disappearance. According to this register, very few Dönme became Greek citizens. The electoral register lists only four Kapancı as eligible voters. Mehmet Kapancı, described as a 59-year-old banker (fifteen years younger than in his family tree), appears, as does Namık Kapancı, a 50-year-old banker, who had served on the board of the joint Feyziye Terakki Commerce School,[9] Firuz Kapancı, a 30-year-old secretary (listed ten years later by the Mixed Commission for the Exchange of the Greek and Turkish Populations as a commission agent), and the 44-year-old textile merchant, son of Ahmet Kapancı, Mehmet.[10] The appearance of these men provides evidence that leading Kapancı Dönme remained under Greek rule and some acquired Greek citizenship. They would not leave the city until forced to do so, and many would try to remain even when it was no longer legally possible.

It is surprising, however, that while the thorough register includes several Kapancı, it does not contain a single person with a Karakaş surname: Balcı, Dilber / Dilberzade, İpek / İpekçi, Karakaş / Karakaşzade, Kibar / Kibaroğlu, Mısırlı, or Şamlı. Several explanations for this fact are possible. One is that Karakaş Dönme left the city for Izmir and Istanbul. A second is that because they did not acquire Greek citizenship, none were eligible to vote. Most who remained may have chosen Albanian or Serbian citizenship. A third is that none wished to be registered to vote. The latter reason is supported by a 1915 Austrian commercial survey, which indicates that leading Karakaş families, including the İpekçi, Karakaş, Kibar, and Şamlı, continued to do business in the city.[11]

Some Kapancı also stuck it out as long as possible. In 1915, Ahmet Kapancı's son Mehmet is listed as a founding member and vice president of the Thessaloníki Landowners' Association.[12] Although he managed to remain in the city as an Albanian or Serbian citizen, his citizenship status, and thus his ability to own land in Thessaloníki, would be debated in the Greek press after 1923.[13] Following his uncle Mehmet Kapancı's passing, he initially retained one-third ownership of the Château Mon Bonheur.[14] Yet other family members—and by extension, all Dönme—had an especially difficult time holding on to their property. While signing over power of attorney to her home at 87 Basilissis Olgas (the former Hamidiye Boulevard), Nefise, wife of Ahmet Kapancı and mother of Mehmet, registered a complaint to the Mixed Commission about the Filikia Café, which had been damaged in the fire of 1917. It cost her great expense repairing it, particularly its doors and windows. Although she had a license to run it, and had to pay for the license every year, the government did not give her permission to use the property and confiscated it. She demanded 1,720 gold lira, the fee of the yearly license multiplied by seven (for the years from 1917 to 1924).[15] She signed this complaint and her power of attorney at her home before leaving for Turkey in 1924.

Attention had to be paid to the proper dividing up and turning over of Yusuf Kapancı's inheritance as well. After Yusuf and his son İbrahim had both died, Yusuf's wife Aisha was made the trustee and guardian of the shares entrusted to İbrahim's two minor sons, Yusuf and Mehmet.[16] The inheritance included shares in ownership of the Ahmet Kapancı villa at 79 Basilissis Olgas (Hamidiye Boulevard) and the Alhambra Café located at the Wharf Station on Nikas Boulevard, as well as a textile store and several properties in Hamidiye.

As noted earlier, some Dönme remained in political office. According to the memoirs of Periklis Argiropoulos, who was the prefect of Thessaloníki for the first three years following the conquest, the logic was simple: "After the occupation of the city, I, in accordance with Raktivan [Constantine Raktivan, minister of justice and new civilian governor-general of Macedonia], did not want to establish a new municipal authority, that is, to appoint a new mayor in the place of the existing one who was a Dönme (a Muslim and former Jew), and who was elected, and to disperse the municipal council and appoint a new one."[17] Not all Dönme public servants remained. Some changes ensued. According to the minutes of the Council of the Thessaloníki Chamber of Commerce for October 6, 1914, the Kapancı Osman Dervish announced his resignation from the council and left the city for Larissa.[18] Mehmet Kapancı is mentioned for the last time in these minutes in 1915.[19]

Along with their property and positions, Dönme also struggled to hold on to their schools. In 1912, the Terakki celebrated its thirty-second anniversary at a ball attended by Şemsi Efendi, Mehmet Kapancı, and board members Ahmet and Namık Kapancı.[20] But during World War I, all Terakki schools were closed and occupied by the Allies. Final classes were held in 1916. That same year witnessed the last board meeting, attended by Ahmet Kapancı, the merchant Faiz Kapancı and the banker Namık Kapancı.[21] In 1919, the Greek municipality appropriated the beautiful main building.[22] It was made into a hospital, and the Terakki schools also lost all their other buildings, except the girls' branch in the suburb, which closed in 1920.[23] Its director was a descendant of Hasan Akif, Ekrem Talat (Akev). In the autumn of

1924, Namık Kapancı and İbrahim Kapancı addressed the school's claim for compensation from the Greek government to the Mixed Commission.[24]

The Feyziye school remained open in Thessaloníki, but it is not clear where or how. Almost all of the Feyziye buildings burned down in the fire of 1917.[25] According to a complaint filed by Kibar Abdurrahman, among others, and recorded in the summer of 1924 in the Mixed Commission records, one of the buildings that had burned was confiscated in the winter of 1923 in order to be converted into a gendarme station.[26]

Despite the damage, the Feyziye school managed to continue to offer classes in Thessaloníki from 1917 to 1923, with the Mısırlı and Kibar families at its head. Some of the teachers were volunteers who were graduates of the school. By 1921, the school had to teach Greek. Yet still it maintained "communal" sense. Regulations for students from 1919–20 envision how: rule number four states that because the school is a family, all students are siblings. Rule number five states that students must love their teachers.[27] The Dönme schools still had a mission to bond youth together in an ethno-religious community. The rule list ends on a positive note, stating that rewards will be given to students who do the best and complete their lessons on time; likewise to the best behaved. Even in troubled times, morals remained a priority: a reward for virtue and good behavior and conduct was twice as esteemed as one for schoolwork.

The rules also spelled out a strict disciplinary regimen, which may have reflected a loss of authority, respect for Dönme leadership, and communal deterioration in troubled times, as well as the impoverishment of the Dönme in the wake of the cutting off of the city from its imperial networks. The administrator had not felt the need to articulate such rules before. According to rule number six, students must not speak without the teacher's permission. Rule number ten states that students' hair must be combed, their hands and faces clean, and their clothes and shoes not ripped or dirty. If they appeared dirty or unkempt, they would be sent home to wash. Number eleven demanded that as soon as the bell rang students must go to the assigned place in order without noise. The following rule declared students had to get in line and enter or exit the classroom when instructed. Rule thirteen required students to have their own supplies, and prohibited them from asking to borrow them from other students, which also reflected the fact that some Dönme families were hurt by the narrowed economic horizons of the nation-state in which they found themselves. All infractions to every rule resulted in punishments.

Number fifteen spelled out that notebooks and books must be clean and orderly and covered in paper; if there were stains, erasures, or doodles, the teacher would rip up the notebook. The remaining rules prohibited littering, drawing on walls, and spitting, which was "absolutely" forbidden. Other rules declared that there must be a very important reason not to come to school, for a lost day was as valuable as a lost year. Even play was a required task. According to rule twenty-one, while it was permissible for students to work in the morning and during lunch breaks, it was forbidden to do homework; at recess, it was necessary to stroll or play.

A memoir by the Karakaş Dönme Reşat Tesal summarizes the challenges the group faced. His family left Thessaloníki following the Greek conquest of the city, and resettled in Volos, a port city in central Greece. But life in Volos proved impossible, so they returned to Thessaloníki after the 1917 fire. By the time Reşat started school, there were hardly any "Turkish" (i.e., Muslim) schools left in the city, including the Karakaş' Feyziye. Despite the difficult conditions, his father, Ömer Dürrü Tesal, was elected to parliament representing Thessaloníki in 1913. He remained in office until 1924.[28] Nevertheless, life for the Tesals was challenging, because a mob of Greek refugees forcibly installed themselves in their home and remained there until the Tesal family left the city. Life for the Muslim minority in general was very difficult, for it faced constant verbal and physical attacks, sequestration of property, and the closure of its schools. The last director of the Feyziye school, İsmet Efendi, opened the "pitiful school" in a wooden shed in the yard of his home with a bent and crooked desk and a few worn-out benches and tiny blackboard. But it soon closed, because he was compelled to migrate to Istanbul.[29]

The 1917 fire had accelerated the Dönme loss of property. It affected the Dönme unequally; the worst hit were the Karakaş, because their six main neighborhoods were burned to the ground. The Dilber family especially lost many properties and buildings, including factories, first to the fire, and then to government seizure and appropriation in the subsequent years before the population exchange.[30] That the fire swept through Kadı Abdullah neighborhood was an especially bad omen for the Karakaş, for plans for reconstructing the city affected their main pilgrimage center, the tomb of Osman Baba. The fire allowed Greek, British, and French planners to expropriate land, demolish surviving Ottoman structures, and construct in their place a new Greek city shorn of its Jewish, Muslim, and Dönme past.[31]

The beautiful Kapancı villas, with their eclectic elements, were well suited to their owners when they were built at the turn of the twentieth century. After the Greek conquest of the city, however, Mehmet Kapancı's villa served as the home of the first Greek military governor of Thessaloníki, Prince Nikolaos and his wife, Princess Irene.[32] In 1917, it became home of Prime Minister Venizélos, then head of the anti-royalist Provisional Government based in Thessaloníki. Between 1922 and 1928, Orthodox Christian refugee families from Anatolia were accommodated in it. In 1928, the building was acquired by the National Bank of Greece. Ahmet Kapancı's villa was divided into three between 1924 and 1934: the ground floor belonged to Ahmet's son Mehmet, the first floor was occupied by the Spanish consul, and the second floor housed Orthodox Christian exchangees from Anatolia.[33] In 1926, the National Bank of Greece owned two-thirds of the building and Mehmet Kapancı, one-third. In 1934, he died, and four years later, his one-third share was sold by his remaining relatives, his mother and sister.

Şemsi Efendi's wife Makbule and daughters Yekta and Marufe stayed behind in Thessaloníki, where they faced difficulties, especially in holding on to their residences. The first portent of change came soon after Greek occupation. The name of the street on which they resided was changed from Army General Hasan Pasha to Army of Macedonia. The street named after their illustrious husband or father was also changed. Hamidiye Boulevard was in turn renamed Union, Prince Constantine, King Constantine, National Defense, Queen Sofia, and, finally, Queen Olga Avenue.[34] The fire of 1917 destroyed some of their properties. These were signs of worse to come. More significantly, according to the complaints they made to the Mixed Commission, in the five years following the fire, the Greek municipality seized and appropriated their homes, stores, and other properties in the city: numbers 58 and 60 on former Army General Hasan Pasha street, numbers 1, 2, 5, and 7 on former Şemsi Efendi street, a store located in the market in Tahtakale, and most crucial, a property in the heart of the Karakaş district of Abdullah Kadı on Eski Zindan street near the tomb of Osman Baba.[35] By 1923, Şemsi Efendi's wife Makbule and daughters Yekta and Marufe resided together in Hamidiye at number 80 Army of Macedonia (formerly General Hasan Pasha) street.[36] According to a Greek-language floor plan drawn with purple ink on transparent wax paper, one of their homes was a two-story, six-room building. They owned so much property in

Thessaloníki that they had to add additional paper affixed to the bottom of the form to cover it all and then described in detail the confiscation of their properties and their demands for compensation, underlining the monetary value in blue pen.

The Mixed Commission Records offer more evidence that the Kapancı and Hasan Akif families resided as close together as possible in the same district of Hamidiye until they were forced to depart the city. Ahmet Kapancı's wife Nefise resided in the four-story home at 87 Hamidiye Boulevard and owned other parcels of land and a factory on Teşvikiye street in the same district.[37] Yusuf Kapancı's son İbrahim, a commission agent, had resided at number 79.[38] After he passed away, İbrahim's sister Emine, his merchant brother İsmail, and the commission agent siblings Firuz and Osman, were still residing there.[39] Mehmet Kapancı's daughter Safinaz resided at number 102.[40] Hasan Akif's son Osman Nuri owned the homes at number 82 and 118;[41] his daughter Emine and the family had a connection to Burmalı Han at number 124, where some of them notarized their power of attorney letters after being ordered expelled in 1923;[42] and his daughter-in-law owned the three-story building at number 141.[43] Hasan Akif's daughter İnayet, who signed her property estimate form both in French and in Ottoman script, owned a two-story home in Hamidiye.[44]

Despite all of these challenges, as late as the eve of the establishment of the Turkish Republic and the ensuing population exchange, the Dönme maintained an economic role in the city. A Greek-language commercial guide of 1921 lists the firm "Yousouf Kapandji et Fils" as a representative of foreign and Greek commercial houses.[45] The following year the firm was included in the list of major importers-exporters.[46] Yet by 1922, local newspapers advertised Mehmet Kapancı's and Ahmet Kapancı's properties among vacant houses to be taken over by refugees.

In 1923, in accordance with the Treaty of Lausanne, the Feyziye and Terakki schools were not allowed to reopen, and in 1929, the Terakki school sold off the remaining land it owned in Thessaloníki.

A crudely cropped, spotted, and stained passport-size photo of Mehmet Kapancı shows him near the end of his life in Greek Thessaloníki. His face is thinner and longer, but he still sports a bushy mustache. Wearing a three-piece suit, with a lightly crumpled fez atop his thin gray hair, he sits slightly stooped forward. His eyes are slightly glassed over trying to focus on the photographer, and he looks shocked, stunned, perhaps ill or senile. He has forgotten to button one of the buttons on his shirt, and his bow tie is crooked.

This photo contrasts starkly with one taken when Mehmet Kapancı was at the height of his powers in Ottoman Salonika. The sepia photo shows a proud man looking over the left shoulder of the photographer. Mehmet Kapancı has dark thick hair beneath his fez and a perfectly waxed, dark, thick handlebar mustache. He has a large, broad head. His features were sharpened by whoever prepared him for the portrait—his cheeks are rouged, and his eyes are outlined with kohl. He is a good-looking man and wears a stunning black jacket with an ornate, floral motif gold filial in the center and two sultanic medallions pinned above his heart.

As symbolized by the aging Mehmet Kapancı, the situation for Dönme remaining in Greek Thessaloníki was challenging at best. Some continued to play an important political and economic role in the city, while others faced a loss of wealth and property and power. Osman Said was again mayor in the few years (1920–22) preceding the population exchange with the new Republic of Turkey in 1923, which signified the end of the Ottoman cultural milieu.[47] All Muslims were expelled from the city, and Orthodox Christian Greek expellees arrived from Asia Minor to replace them, marking the end of the long period of interreligious exchange in the city that produced such syncretistic groups as the Dönme.

Ottoman Istanbul: Beginning of a New Life

Once Salonika fell to Greece, many Dönme quickly packed their bags and moved to Istanbul. Şemsi Efendi left Salonika for Istanbul between 1912 and the end of World War I. The Yakubi Dönme Faik Nüzhet (d. 1945), a Freemason, had been a tax inspector, descended from a long line of doctors, lawyers, and pharmacists in Salonika, where he remained at least as late as the 1908 Constitutional Revolution, but by World War I, he had also moved with his family to Istanbul, where between 1920 and 1923, he served as the last Ottoman finance minister.[48] Kapancı Ahmet Tevfik Ehat, whose father had been a co-founder of the Terakki school, and who was one of the eight bankers (the others were Jews) who was a member of the Masonic lodge Véritas in 1906, according to its records,[49] evidently brought his entire family from Salonika to Istanbul in 1912.[50]

Şemsi Efendi, Faik Nüzhet, and Ahmet Tevfik Ehat were not alone. Up to 20,000 of the city's 50,000 Muslims and Dönme soon departed the city after the Greek takeover, among them the families of Mustafa Kemal Atatürk and Ahmet Emin Yalman. At the beginning of World War I, after returning from Columbia University, Yalman became assistant professor of philosophy and sociology at Istanbul University and news editor of *Tanin*, the CUP's organ and daily.[51] In 1917, on a return train trip to Istanbul from Germany where he was a war correspondent for *Tanin*, Yalman met Atatürk. He introduced himself as a journalist and son of one of Atatürk's teachers at the military preparatory school in Salonika. Atatürk knew of his teacher's son's writing and remembered his father, who had always paid special attention to him.[52] Yalman went on to become editor-in-chief of the daily *Sabah*, and then founded *Vakit* (Time) at the end of the war.

Between 1912 and 1919, the Kapancı Dönme who migrated from Salonika mainly settled in Istanbul in the newer, centrally located upper-middle-class and religiously and ethnically mixed districts of Nişantaşı and Şişli. These districts, which had significant numbers of Armenian, Greek, and Jewish inhabitants, lay at the frontier of the built and unbuilt areas uphill and north of the geographically and culturally cosmopolitan center at Taksim and Galata. Galata boasted the city's western European churches, embassies, schools, businesses, and residences. Dönme did not settle in the Asian half of the city. Yıldız Sertel offers a snapshot of a community in motion and in transformation, and the continuities between their Salonikan and Istanbul lives:

> The Dönme who migrated from Salonika settled in Nişantaşı. There Sabiha [Sertel] found her old friends and family members, and got caught up on the latest gossip. Emine became engaged to Aziz, the son of aunt Faize. Aziz went into the textile business with his brothers, and the business was going well. Seniye married Dr. Santur while they were still in Salonika. They had decided to open a hospital in Nişantaşı, called "House of Health." Seniye was happy, but the hospital kept her so busy that she did not even have time to blink. Teacher Atiye, together with the teachers and administrators from the Salonikan Terakki school, had begun to establish a new school. They were thinking of naming it "Şişli Terraki." Another group of Salonikans was about to establish a school named "Fevziye." Teacher Atiye was about to become engaged to a teacher from this school. Thus the community that migrated from Salonika had begun step by step to establish its own culture and health centers. For all, a new life was beginning in Istanbul. Most worked in these educational institutions, or in the professions as lawyers and doctors, or went into business. Older brother Mecdi began to work in the flour trade.[53]

With respect to the history of her family, Sertel observes that shortly after Greece took over the city, some wealthy Dönme sold their goods and property and migrated to Istanbul.[54] Sabiha Sertel's older brothers Celal Dervish and Mecdi Dervish made the move in 1912.[55] Then her older brother Hidayet decided that the entire family should move. As Ottoman bureaucrats—their father, Nazmi Efendi, was a retired head Customs inspector, and he himself worked for the Post and Telegraph Department—they should be well taken care of in Istanbul, he reasoned.[56] Celal became a lawyer in Istanbul, owned a beautiful apartment in Nişantaşı, and traveled to Vienna on holiday. Mecdi and another relative Avni also settled in Nişantaşı, in a nice home. Another relative, Neşet, was in Sofia, Bulgaria, but would also migrate to Istanbul. Sertel concludes: "In addition to the Dervish Ali family, many Dönme families also were part of this [1912–13] migration." Although they were able to make a smooth journey to a new life, it was a nevertheless sad departure from the city in which they had been born and raised.[57]

After his French-speaking Kapancı Dönme family had settled in the Osmanbey-Şişli area, in Istanbul, next to Teşvikiye and Nişantaşı, Osman Ehat Tevfik was enrolled, appropriately, in the Lycée de Galatasaray, where French was the main language of instruction. He later became a tobacco importer, moving to Izmir in 1920, where he bought tobacco from the Aegean region to send to the main factory in Vienna for processing. He was transferred to the headquarters of the family business in Vienna in 1922, and then sent to a branch office in Brussels in 1925–26. In the early 1930s, he moved back to Istanbul and left the tobacco trade in order to enter the textile business.

Racializing the Dönme

The arrival of so many Salonikan Dönme in the Ottoman capital caused alarm in some circles, and accusations were voiced that foreshadowed the attacks they would face in the early years of the Turkish Republic. In 1919, at a time of heightened insecurity for Muslims owing to the British and French occupation of Istanbul (1918–23), there burst upon the scene an anonymous treatise on the Dönme that significantly illustrates a new, racist attitude to them, entitled *Dönmeler: Hunyos, Kavayeros, Sazan.*[58] The most striking aspect of this publication is how it reflects an era in which having a "pure race" suddenly became important. Accordingly, groups that were seen as having mixed origins or as being rootless were despised. The anonymous author begins by including the Dönme among those "groups whose religion and nationality are unknown" (6). He defines the group as "a community that emerged in Salonika two and half centuries before, which since that time has been known as the 'Dönme'—neither Muslim, nor Jewish, or in other words, the Avdeti [those who return to their original religion]." They remain in a state of corruption between Islam and Judaism (9). Worse, Shabbatai Tzevi was a vagabond Jew who acted strangely and attracted Copts, Zoroastrians, and Jews to his side.

The problems with the Dönme cascaded from their being people without roots and of confused origins, the anonymous author of *Dönmeler* asserts. The Dönme had turned in on themselves, forming a new community, and endogamous marriage within a small group had endowed them with peculiar biological traits. Whereas the Hunyos [Karakaş] and Kavayeros [Kapancı] "resemble each other in type, the Sazan or Sazaniko [Yakubi] type is distinguished from the others by large, arched noses" (8). The author illustrated this with what purported to be the profile of a large-nosed Sazan male, wearing a tie and coat, who would seem to be a civil servant. A *sazan* is a type of carp, and when it turns in the water in sunlight, its scales reflect different colors. Similarly, the anonymous author claimed, the Dönme appeared different to outsiders depending on the circumstances. In addition, just as carp can live in both fresh and salt water, the Dönme, the author implies, could not be pinned down to being Jewish or being Muslim.[59]

Even worse, to the author, endogamy "has paved the way for some chronic and contagious diseases to spread and increase among them." Because of this, "in order to ameliorate the health of their offspring, since the Constitutional Revolution, some of them have begun to take Muslim girls in marriage, and even to marry vigorous, good-looking European girls." Muslims who give their daughters in marriage to "those among whom tuberculosis and neuralgia / neural disorders are widespread are committing murder, and Europeans who marry them are also endangering themselves" (10). Some Dönme girls, the author asserts, "speak like the crowing of roosters, and while speaking incessantly move their eyes, eyebrows, and even their entire bodies in strange and bizarre gestures, as though they were crazy," a manifestation of the nervous disorders prevalent among the group. An unflattering illustration appears immediately following this, labeled "the profile of a Dönme woman."

Unveiled, and teetering on high heels, she wears a dress that reveals her bare ankles and full figure.

It was not that the Dönme were only physically unhealthy. After a brief discussion of Dönme physiognomy, the anonymous author turns to Dönme morals. He attaches moral dimensions to imagined physical attributes. A weak moral character is displayed in physiological traits. A diseased body is a sign of moral weakness. The corruption of the one leads to the perversion of the other. The anonymous author of *Dönmeler*, like Dervish Vahdetî before him, was intent on linking the moral and physical corruption of the Dönme to much wider societal problems. "It must not be forgotten," he argues, "that the Salonikan Dönme are the main cause behind the spreading of immorality, irreligion, and various contagious diseases among Muslims" (10). The Dönme allegedly spread immorality, not only as an outside group, but especially through their position within Ottoman Muslim society; they are internal traitors, a Trojan Horse, whose actions cause the rot to spread from inside the unsuspecting body of the nation. The Yakubi type "always longs to possess government's gate. The Sazan are always the ones most addicted to government positions" (10). As for the Karakaş and Kapancı, "they are always occupied with commerce. Because they do not consider others to be human, they consider it among the laws and praiseworthy qualities of their religion to cheat other nations with various intrigues and schemes." Although "very few desire government positions, nevertheless, Cavid [Mehmet Cavid], who is from the Karakaş group, was able to become finance minister." In sum, while the Karakaş and Kapancı "dupe others in the world of commerce," the Yakubi "rob the government's treasury." The author argues that the Dönme are duplicitous (12). When they act honestly, it is not out of love of the fatherland or loyalty to the government, "but in order to guard their places and positions and protect their private interests and to ensure that their group's matters before the government are realized through legal and illegal means." In other words, "one should not expect that while they are in government service they will display good intentions and loyalty to the fatherland and nation."

The Dönme had spread, and with them the problem of atheism, disloyalty, and duplicity, the author warns. Previously, they "had never left Salonika. But lately, especially after the Balkan Wars, they have increased their miniscule presence in Istanbul. Although they settled in Izmir and many places in Anatolia, because they secretly maintained their old customs, and introduced themselves as migrants from Ottoman southeastern Europe or Salonika, no one knew they were Dönme." Acting in the guise of Muslims, the Dönme had a detrimental effect on good people, who did not realize the danger of the Dönme masked. They had an especially bad effect on Muslim women. The behavior "of their immodestly dressed women and indecent girls had a terrible influence on the pure-hearted people of Anatolia. The Dönme's irreligion and immorality made the people of Anatolia believe incorrectly that all people from Ottoman southeastern Europe were bad" (13). The author asserts that "the people of Anatolia should understand that all the immorality and irreligion blamed on Ottoman southeastern Europeans actually originate with the Salonikan Dönme, who pass as Muslims."

This last line causes the reader to suspect that this treatise was written by a fellow migrant from southeastern Europe who is not Dönme, perhaps someone who was from Salonika, where he had gained intimate knowledge of their religious and social practices. After arriving in Istanbul, the anonymous author may have written this treatise as a reaction to others linking him, because of his geographical origins, to the alleged corrupting influence of the Dönme.

At the end of his treatise, the anonymous author concludes by adding Dönme insincerity in religion to their alleged duplicity in public service and the economy. He ridicules Dönme piety, as well as their obligatory religious practices, including praying, fasting during Ramadan, and their alleged marriage and burial customs (13). He says the Dönme never attend mosque. If one attends, "of course one should know they are not praying to fulfill the requirements of Islam" (14). "Has anyone ever seen a Dönme who commits a wrong or breaks the laws of the group? They have a sort of law system among themselves. The most severe punishment is for the guilty to attend mosque for awhile. Rather than being to fulfill the requirements of Islam, the aim of this is nothing other than to display shameless insolence to Muslims."

Another form of shameless impudence apparently occurs during Ramadan. During this Muslim month of fasting, "in Dönme homes that are next to Muslim homes, at the time of the night prayer they act as if they are preparing to offer the extra night service, shouting, 'Daughter, have you done your ablutions? Hurry up and get ready [join the group assembled for prayer].'" But this is only a ruse. With other such sounds, "they make their Muslim neighbors think that are preparing to conduct their prayers. Before dawn, although they haven't actually set the table for the predawn meal, they make noises with forks, knives, and plates as though they were preparing the meal."

Concerning prayer and marriage, the anonymous author compares the Dönme to Jews. He writes that on Saturdays, Dönme pray according to Jewish rites in underground synagogues. Young Dönme only learn the secrets of Dönme religion the day they marry; until then, they have no idea whether they believe in Islam or Judaism, and know only that they are Dönme (14–15).

The most bizarre sections of the treatise concern Dönme burial customs (15). According to the anonymous author, just as they have separate imams, so too Dönme have their own cemeteries, located between the Muslim and Jewish cemeteries. The inscriptions on their tombstones do not include the Fatiha prayer (the first sura of the Qur'an) at the end. Furthermore, "because they implement the command 'do not come until your insides are clean,' they are buried only after funerary procedures during which the filth in their intestines is cleaned out."

Thus, for the anonymous author, the Dönme represent a threat stemming from their muddled, yet primarily Jewish, origins. Banding together and practicing endogamy, they became diseased. This affected not only the people whom they drew into their community, but society as a whole, for their physical breakdown was only matched by their immorality and duplicity in business, government service, and Islamic practice.

Defending the Dönme: Moral Piety in a Secular Age

Dönmeler's outrageous attacks on the Dönme incited a very lengthy rebuttal, *Dönmelerin Hakikati* (The Truth About the Dönme), written by pious and patriotic retired Major Sadık, son of Suleiman, who one suspects may have been a Dönme from the Yakubi group. This response was published only two months after *Dönmeler* appeared in 1919. Instead of race, those who defended the Dönme such as this veteran emphasized service to the fatherland. In addition, and for the last time this would be used in their defense, Major Sadık depicts Dönme fidelity to Islam:

§ Major Sadık, son of Suleiman, is feverishly at work on a major essay in Istanbul in the winter of 1919. The depressed veteran reflects glumly upon what had happened since that day he fell into enemy hands. Despite his depression, he is on a mission, and does not have much time. He writes as quickly as he can in Ottoman script, explaining how after he fell prisoner with his battalion at Yenice Vardar [Gianitsa, thirty miles west of Salonika] during the Balkan War, he could not stomach the newspapers that came into his hands, because they were full of disastrous and sorrowful news. Accordingly, he stopped reading them. After he was released and returned to Istanbul, he retired and withdrew from society, not unlike a Sufi withdrawing into seclusion. He had hoped to pass his time free of anxiety and care, "but in accordance with the saying of the Prophet Muhammad, peace and blessings be upon him, 'there is no peace on earth.' Even when a person retires and withdraws from the world, he is never spared from the sorrow, pain, and gloom which he carries within."[60] But all the anguish he and his fellow soldiers suffered was only part of the danger of his empire being destroyed. He explains how for someone like him, such a possibility was even more troubling. What had pained him most during his imprisonment "was seeing the enemy violate Islam's holiness by planting its flag on the dome of the tomb of the [fourteenth-century] Ottoman warrior Evrenos" in Gianitsa.

"I was overwhelmed thinking of the dagger of defeat that struck the breast of the mother of the fatherland and the chains of slavery that had been placed on the neck of her children. I was purposely not reading the newspapers and completely unaware of events" (5). But then a few days ago, "a careless treatise [*Dönmeler: Hunyos, Kavayeros, Sazan*] concerning the morals, customs, and piety of the Salonikan Dönme, written with a poison pen, came into my possession. I was very stunned and saddened by what I read. As is known, it is necessary that treatises presented to public opinion and other works serve the public interest and benefit the fatherland. But it is obvious that a work that hurtfully accuses others of atheism and immorality brings about harm instead of benefit."

Humbly, as a loyal officer, he stops and considers again whether it is appropriate to enter a political debate. He has never enjoyed mixing in affairs that are partisan or beyond his official duties, he says. Although he knows that it is not suitable for someone like him, who is only accustomed to military service, to be thrown into the position of writing to the public, he also knows that "love of the fatherland arises from faith." Without asking anyone's opinion on this topic, and in order to benefit all, he decides to write a "modest, measured treatise in order to defend this group. I hope that my treatise, which explains the group's devotion to Islam and excellent moral qualities, will help dispel and remove the baseless accusations directed at my wronged and injured brothers. With God's help."

Implicitly comparing himself with Evrenos Ghazi, Major Sadık launches into his fervent defense of the Dönme. The comparison seems apt. Evrenos Ghazi was a Christian who converted to Islam, made the hajj, and led numerous raids—"slaying the infidels and polytheists," as his tombstone reads—on behalf of the Ottoman dynasty in southeastern Europe. He was a man whose tomb was so holy it was visited by Christian and Muslim alike for divine intercession, and whose descendants led the Ottoman military in battle for two centuries and patronized the Bektaşi Sufi order.[61] The fact that the author's name Sadık means "loyal" also speaks in favor of his cause.

Faced with a sustained attack on Dönme racial origins and moral character, in his lightning response, which could be subtitled "The Dönme: Myths and Facts," Major Sadık chose to ignore the Jewish background of the Dönme, while emphasizing their Islamic piety and service to the empire. Major Sadık was quick to defend Dönme moral piety in an age of decreased religious observance. He frames his discussion within a critique of the secularization of Ottoman society following the Constitutional Revolution (3), which, he writes, made people throw old customs to the wind, lose ties of loyalty and obedience, and willfully violate the law (18). People lost their religious beliefs. Muslims were not fulfilling the obligations of the religion. During World War I, when the muezzin chanted the call to prayer, soldiers at the front slipped away and hid to avoid praying, whereas not so long ago, it had been considered shameful not to pray, and it had been rare for Jews not to grow beards and sidelocks, Christians not to fast, and Muslims not to fast at Ramadan. "Happy are those who in such a lax environment continue to pray, hoping to be close to God."

Closest to God are the Dönme. Major Sadık praises Shabbatai Tzevi for turning to Islam, not out of fear, but out of piety, referring to him by his Muslim name, Aziz Mehmet Efendi, and not by his original Jewish name. He never mentions that Shabbatai Tzevi and his followers were originally Jews. Shabbatai Tzevi became a great Muslim spiritual guide bringing many others to the faith (6). Major Sadık asserts that Aziz Mehmet Efendi converted not out of duress, but after studying sacred scripture. Aziz Mehmet Efendi was a sincere convert who "after perfectly being infused with the light of Islam brought many other people to the true faith" (7). If he acted strangely, it was not because he was trying to deceive anyone, but rather because he was "the subject of miracles manifest in him after being enlightened by Islam and nothing else." In short, there should be no doubt that he was a pious man shown the right path by God and everything said or written to the contrary was nonsense and lies (8). Major Sadık cannot understand how "when a noble saint [*evliya*] is zealous in being compassionate to others and leading people to the right path, he faces much antipathy from those around him, just like the thorns of a rosebush." In fact, all stems from a misunderstanding in 1666. If only the people at the sultan's court and the state religious scholars had been able to understand the Sufi language Aziz Mehmet Efendi used in Istanbul, or had had a council of Sufis look into his situation, they would have immediately understood that he was a spiritual guide to the right path and they would have shown him respect. Major Sadık compares Aziz Mehmet Efendi to Ibn al-Arabi and Hallaj and other saints, who faced opposition due to similar misinterpretation of their beliefs and aims.

Major Sadık thus places Shabbatai Tzevi in a long chain of Muslim mystics, a good illustration of how Dönme religion was understood to syncretize Sufism and Kabbalah (8). To Major Sadık, Aziz Mehmet Efendi "was a perfect spiritual guide [*mürşid-i kâmil*] . . . such that because of him, many people and their children and their children's children and descendants were honored by the glory of Islam and acted with the proper Muslim manner and became endowed with the good moral qualities of Islam." Sultan Mehmet IV had understood that he had become a Muslim and honored him with the name "Aziz," which was restricted to distinguished sheikhs and spiritual guides, and in accordance with his wishes, sent him to Salonika (9). His grave had subsequently become "a place of pilgrimage distinguished by its spirituality, which is more evidence of his high station." This was enough to prove that Aziz Mehmet Efendi had been a sincere believer and to cleanse his name of any bad imputations. The proof, moreover, lay in the spirituality of his followers, for this group produced many licensed religious scholars and others joined Sufi orders.

Major Sadık avoids discussing the racial or Jewish origins of the Dönme. He points out a simple error the anonymous author has made, and then a more fundamental one. How, he asks, could Copts be among the group's ancestors? (10). The Dönme's racial origins are in fact unknown, and it is inappropriate to research them. Although it is known that due to the quarrels between the leaders of the group, they ceased intermarrying and separated into three distinct groups, what is not clear is to which races they belong. Their geographically specific nicknames do not provide a clue, either. For if some are known by the name "Egyptian" (Mısırlı, a Karakaş family) or "Damascene" (Şamlı, also Karakaş), it is certain that they are not descended from people native to those places. Rather, these names stem from the fact that their ancestors traveled there on business. In the end, "it is not known to which races they belong" (11). Engaged as he is in an attempt to shift the discussion from race to religion, Major Sadık declares: "It is not humane or kind to search for people's roots or race."

Major Sadık launches into a lengthy defense of Dönme moral character especially during recent times. During World War I, when there were severe problems feeding people, this group, "out of pure selflessness and public spirit helped those families whose sons had been taken to the army and became an example to the rest of us" (12). He then gives an example of Dönme moral strengths from the nineteenth century. He narrates how when Midhat Pasha was governor of Salonika, one day, when chatting with a well-known local man, the latter began reproaching and disparaging the Dönme. The governor immediately ordered the commander of the gendarmes to bring before him a member of this group who was in jail. The commander responded, "Sir, there aren't any in jail." The governor responded, "How strange that despite their rather large numbers, there is not a single member of this group in jail. In that case bring me one of their beggars." The commander replied, "There aren't any beggars from this group." Major Sadık concludes: "The fact that no members of the group were imprisoned is proof they did not break the law and had no blameworthy people and always maintained their self-respect" (13). This also might reflect their adherence to the eighteen commandments of Shabbatai Tzevi, number seven of which reads: "There shall be among them no thieves."[62]

Major Sadık mentions the health problems related to endogamy to argue, not that the Dönme suffer from moral and physical deficiencies, but for their strengths (13). He first admits that although it may be true that the limited circle within which they marry causes physical problems for some, in fact, "they place great emphasis upon cleanliness and protecting their health; contrary to what has been claimed, they are not weakened by disease, but are quite healthy. The proof being that they can work and exert themselves nonstop. There are not a few among them who live to be 120 years old or more." The author salutes the Dönme disposition. In general, they are "cheerful, pleasant and agreeable, and courteous and friendly people. They do not mock or ridicule people. They do not curse anyone." Yet they do find it necessary to conceal their origins and do not enjoy speaking in public about their group. They even conceal the fact that they are Salonikan from those who do not know them, so as "to prevent some groundless and absurd rumors being spread about the group." Unfortunately because of the attacks upon them, however, the Dönme "forget how they have become honored by the glory of Islam, become distinguished living according to Islamic moral standards, and taken pride in the progress they have shown among all Muslim peoples." Nevertheless, "They do render their prayers at mosque at dawn" (14).

Major Sadık was spurred to rebut claims casting doubt on Dönme moral piety at length, attacking the anonymous author's logic (15). For, after all, if members of this community, who live separate and isolated, and, as much as they can, avoid relations with others, how can they be the only cause of contagious diseases, immorality, and atheism being spread in society? It is a great injustice to accuse these well-mannered people, who keep to themselves, of spreading disease and immorality. Major Sadık observes that "other than five to ten minutes at prayer times, when four or five people render their prayers, the doors of many big mosques in Istanbul are closed. There is not a drop of water in the ablution fountains for doing ablutions" (16). Is it the Dönme who are "the cause of houses of worship, which in our grandfathers' time were crowded and busy as beehives, being closed and deserted, and that people abandon their prayers? Do only their women go about dressed immodestly?" Far from Dönme women being immodest, until recently, they used to place great importance on veiling, not going out in the street unless they were wearing the old-fashioned cloak, and "this group knew nothing other than sticking to their own affairs, neither mixing in politics nor changing women's dress in any way" (15).

Major Sadık addresses the question of the influence of the Dönme on Anatolian society. Rather than spreading corruption, the Dönme, by spreading out throughout Anatolia brought good traits to the far reaches of the land. As for the people of Anatolia following the aforementioned group, "in fact what they tried to borrow [from the Dönme] were their habits of being in harmony, mutual friendship, and helping one another, their skill and proficiency in business matters" (23). In any case, the people of Anatolia know the proverb "Every sheep hangs itself by its own leg"— that is, "every person is judged by his own deeds." Major Sadık manages to turn around criticism: "Saying that [some Dönme] are in government service and the others play a role in the world of trade is actually to praise and appreciate them, which is what they deserve. In the end, this life is a struggle. Those who do not live according to the saying of Muhammad that 'the one who profits or the merchant is the beloved of God' will go hungry and become destitute." At a desperate time, when "other people turn to crime, becoming thieves and pickpockets, and the city is filled with greedy merchants who rob people, never has any complaint been made that merchants from among [the Dönme] rob others, because they are fair and well-intentioned, nor until now has anyone said that those [Dönme] who work for the government have done anything that is not marked by dignity, patriotism, sincerity or loyalty." Moreover, "the members of the Karakaş and Kapancı groups, as well as the Hamdi Bey (Yakubi) group, which is especially linked to the bureaucratic class, are gentle and good-tempered, virtuous, humble as Sufis, and overall clean [people]," who "always try to do what is right and good." And "no matter what is (24) said about them they hold even more fast to the Islam that they inherited from their forefathers." They are second to no one in having the greatest loyalty to the Ottomans. He concludes by rhetorically asking, "Shouldn't they be proud of their good qualities that distinguish them?"

Finally, Major Sadık addresses other questions relating to Dönme moral character. Oddly, undermining his earlier claims, he in passing confirms some of their most objectionable practices: "At the beginning of [their] Islamic history, they did not prohibit the old customs of the nations who converted to Islam. Celebrating the day of the vernal equinox, forty days after the vernal equinox, [and] the first day of summer, and candle snuffing [wife swapping] on the evening of March 21, and many more such customs openly continue, but no one considers them to take anything away from Islam" (25). This brief mention of extramarital sex during the Festival of the Lamb and downplaying its significance in a treatise devoted to defending Dönme morality cannot help but harm the group's reputation.

Muslims are the Dönme's brethren, and their friendships with them are sincere, faithful, and loyal, Major Sadık asserts. Why would Dönme be inclined toward Christians because of the independence Christians give to their women? (26). In order for women to move about freely or be independent there is no need for them to favor Christians. In fact, "Christian women walk about openly, which is considered to be their independence or free behavior, whereas Muslim women have the custom of veiling. It is known that when they are very little girls, Muslim women begin to veil bit by bit and cover their faces, so that it becomes so natural to them that when they grow up and a slight wind lifts their veil, they feel hurt, as if hot water had been poured on their heads." Moreover, "Christian women in Albania and non-Muslim women in the Arab world [also] wear the dust cloak and veil. This is not based on pressure or because it is imposed; when you think about it, you realize the veil is worn because it is suitable to women and looks good on them." This logic allows Major Sadık to then ask "what is so strange, outlandish, or foreign about the free movement / independence and social lives of some [Dönme] women? There are other reasons for the new veil and light cloak to be worn. Things go in cycles. Is it far-fetched to think that if today it is like this, a little later they will decide to return to the cloaks and veils their mothers used?" In conclusion, "When you compare what some of them do with foreign customs, you will see that it is more a question of wealth and natural disposition than anything else and will not consider it to be the sin of adopting foreign customs."

Concerning Dönme prayer, Major Sadık returns to his theme of secularization and also displays a return to the earlier prevailing Ottoman Muslim understanding of religion (27). He asserts that the proportion of Dönme who go to mosque is not lower than that of other Muslims. Major Sadık urges fellow Muslims to return to an earlier Ottoman mode of live and let live, saying: "We also should not have bad thoughts about a Muslim who is seen praying in a mosque, since we cannot know or understand what is in his heart." Among the Dönme "there are so many of excellent virtues and merits, pure moral qualities, conduct, and character that they perform their daily prayers and religious obligations without hypocrisy or dissimulation, for love of God, expecting nothing in return." Pious Dönme are pious Muslims, "Their eyes full of tears thinking of the End, they aim to maintain the same moral character until they die and avoid what is forbidden, keeping themselves pure, so that after they die, they may appear before God with a clean slate." Major Sadık is especially angered by claims of Dönme dissimulation. Just as "no one has the authority or right to say anything to other Muslims who pray, . . . no one could make such a great mistake as to believe that they render five prayers a day just as a show" (28). He ridicules the idea that Dönme pray in mosques only as a punishment for failing to live up to Dönme law, and actually warms to the idea for others. He asks whether it would not be a great idea if in order to mend his manners and morals after an offense the offender would have to pray with the community.

Concerning Dönme keeping of the Ramadan fast, Major Sadık inadvertently supports the dichotomy between Dönme public practice and private belief, confirming the existence and function of the central Yakubi meeting house (28). He says it is impossible to deny that they attend their neighborhood mosques during Ramadan and conduct the extra evening prayers in the homes of the upper class. For example, "the deceased Hamdi Bey and similar wealthy men brought imams from faraway places such as Serres to their mansions and offered[them] break-the-fast meals, after which they performed the extra evening prayers together. Would it make any sense to say that they were motivated, not by an intention to fulfill the duties and requirements of the religion, but out of fear of making sure they were seen performing them?" For such a night spent in prayer, "other than preparing for nighttime prayers or the predawn meal during the fast, what else could our learned brothers in religion endowed with such exalted Muslim qualities be doing? Concerning the latter, why else would they abandon the deepest and sweetest hour of rest and sleep if not to prepare the meal?" (29). Of course, among Dönme, just as among other Muslims, there are those who do not pray and do not fast. But "everyone knows that in the end everyone will have to account for all of their actions." Again and again, Major Sadık declares that it is not for us to judge others; private faith is a matter between humans and God.

In his rebuttal of *Dönmeler: Hunyos, Kavayeros, Sazan*, Major Sadık points out logical inconsistencies in its anonymous author's argument and again and again disassociates Dönme from Jews (29). The anonymous writer claimed Dönme liked Christians best, so Major Sadık asks whether it would be better if he said that the Dönme day of prayer was Sunday instead of Saturday, and that they build monasteries? To understand whether on their wedding day [Dönme] youth learn of their religion or not, we would need an eyewitness on the inside who could tell us. As far as having their own imams in order to fulfill their religious obligations, "like other Muslims, when . . . neighborhood imams . . . are busy, for example, being called to some government duty (30), they have to fill in with other teachers or sometimes from learned people from their own community. In Istanbul, they always have the neighborhood imam or Turkish teachers fill their needs." Finally, if they had clandestine, depraved non-Islamic beliefs, it would not be necessary for them to have recourse to Muslim religious scholars.

Major Sadık also rationalizes the location of Dönme cemeteries and their inscriptions (30). As for their cemeteries in Salonika being located between Muslim cemeteries on one side and Jewish cemeteries on the other, "when the Dönme arrived, these were the only empty lands where they could make cemeteries. One is found today outside of Yenikapı [labeled "Turkish Cemetery" on turn-of-the-century French maps, this is near the Mevlevi lodge just outside the western walls of the city], the other has no Jewish cemetery on any side. Do we not see the same writing on their tombstones as on the tombstones of other Muslims?" Major Sadık notes that inscribing the Fatiha sura on tombstones does not rest upon any Qur'anic verse or saying of Muhammad. He argues that in Anatolia and Istanbul, one does not always see the Fatiha on old tombstones, and one does not always find the name and date of death either. It seems (31) that only recently has the Fatiha begun to be inscribed upon tombstones. Moreover, he notes one does find the Fatiha on headstones in Dönme cemeteries in Salonika and in Istanbul. Concerning the claim of their cleansing the bowels of the dead, Major Sadık writes "the author mentions how Rabbi Ari [Isaac Luria] came from Poland to Jerusalem in 1573 and started the radical practice of purifying the dead, although it is not found in the Torah, nor in the writings of any prophets." However, the reader wonders, if this is not something that Dönme practice, why mention it? And how did Major Sadık know about Lurianic Kabbalah? Or is he referencing the Dönme belief that what matters in spirituality is not external Islamic practice, but internal belief, that the heart is clean and pure and loyal to Dönme religion? Again the author's rebuttal, because it contains a Dönme perspective and intimate knowledge of the group's boundary-maintaining mechanisms and religion has instead served to advance the cause of the treatise it is meant to refute.

In the end, the author returns to his claim that the Dönme are a very pious people (32). He argues it is a great error to question the sincerity of these good-mannered people, who need no one else, go about their business, and never harm others in order to profit. He asserts it is important to remember they are people who would never do anything with any fault or defect, especially when it comes to the afterlife, and who, unlike other Muslims, would not decorate their graves with pictures of animals. In sum, "They are such loyal and faithful people that paying attention to the life hereafter is to remember that they will pass from this base, material world to the everafter. Accordingly, they design a sign or mark to place at the head of every tombstone. They are such pure-hearted Muslims." For Major Sadık, "one can be sure that these brothers in religion of ours are sincere Muslims, and that any doubts on this subject are groundless" (14).

A Turn to Racialized Thinking

Reading the two treatises together, the anonymous attack on the Dönme and the rebuttal by Major Sadık, one concludes that both authors had inside information on the Dönme and their religion. One author was most likely a Salonikan Muslim who had recently migrated to Istanbul, and the other a retired army officer, a Muslim who knew Salonika well, or a Yakubi Dönme. Although one attacked the Dönme in toto, and the other primarily defended the Dönme as a group, the latter also noted the effects of individual Dönme actions. The authors had a great amount in common concerning their view of Ottoman society following World War I and the apparent influx of Dönme to Istanbul, or at least knowledge of the Dönme in Ottoman Thrace and Anatolia following the fall of Salonika to Greece. To both authors, Muslim society had been corrupted and secularized. They may have differed largely on the question of the piety of Shabbatai Tzevi and his descendants, who was primarily to blame in fomenting moral decadence, and in the importance of race, but both pointed to a general lack of piety and spread of Christian customs, particularly among Muslim women. Both mark 1908 as the pivotal year, which opened the floodgates of atheism and immorality, the anonymous author explicitly attacking the Dönme in general for causing corruption. What is surprising is how at so many points in his defense of the Dönme, Major Sadık makes arguments or references, such as their removing the bowels of the dead prior to burial, or claiming that there are as many irreligious Dönme as irreligious other Muslims, or even referring to their syncretistic practices, which contradict his ends, including defending their Muslim piety.

Major Sadık responded to a treatise that was part of a longer, yet ever-worsening trend for the Dönme. Sentiment expressed as early as the 1890s, and then in *Volkan* in 1908 and 1909, was reflected in anti-Christian and anti-Jewish writings published in the wake of the disastrous Balkan Wars of 1912–13 and the Ottoman loss of Salonika. The Balkan Wars concluded with military failure, disillusionment, a crushing of confidence, loss of great amounts of territory, and reports of Bulgarian and Greek atrocities committed against Muslim soldiers and civilians alike. Muslims, especially in the major Ottoman cities of Edirne, Istanbul, and Izmir, seething from these material and psychological losses, influenced by an influx of Balkan refugees, looking for traitors who had caused the defeat, searched for means to avert further disaster. They railed against the role of imperialists and their assumed comprador non-Muslim allies in the economy and promoted measures such as boycotts that would strip them of that role and create a Muslim business class and Muslim-controlled economy in their place.[63] For example, because they held Italian citizenship, wealthy Jewish industrialists, such as the Allatini family in Salonika, in whose villa Abdülhamid II had been kept under house arrest, were driven out of their hometown by a boycott of Italian goods following the 1911 Italian invasion of Tripoli (Libya).[64] Efforts to create a new Muslim economy occurred alongside efforts to assimilate non-Turkish Muslims into Turkish culture. Thus 1913 was a turning point in the history of Ottoman society, when many sectors of society explicitly turned away from the formerly prevailing plural Ottoman culture and politics of Ottomanism in favor of a more Turkish Islamic one.

This was only the beginning. Crisis, the end of World War I, the occupation of Istanbul by Allied forces, and the beginning of the Greco-Turkish or Christian-Muslim war, as after the Constitutional Revolution a decade earlier, caused writers to lump Dönme together with non-Muslims and foreigners and sparked renewed concern about the religion of the Dönme and their political loyalty. Syncretistic elements, especially the Dönme, were considered unworthy of acceptance. In 1919, along with the anonymous *Dönmeler: Hunyos, Kavayeros, Sazan*, other books attacking the Dönme and their apparent greed and disloyalty began to appear. The historian Ahmet Refik Altınay wrote that while the Turks suffered, Greeks, Armenians, and Salonikans (Dönme) became wealthy. Worse, the Salonikans deceived the Turks by hiding under a Muslim cloak.[65]

Defining who was a Turk became important when the possibility emerged that other peoples would try to pass as Turks. Opponents of integration searched for a new way to mark difference. Voices and body parts, such as noses and hands, were suddenly critical, as illustrated in *Dönmeler: Hunyos, Kavayeros, Sazan*. If the racial or inherent difference could be proven, if there were essential essences that biologically hindered people from integrating, then Dönme could not be made into citizens. Their difference meant they would not have to be given full rights, for they did not deserve them. Racism, which separated formerly commingled peoples into distinct racial categories, could be used to hinder the integration of minorities and exclude them from the body politic.

The debate in 1919 between the anonymous author of *Dönmeler* and the army veteran Major Sadık, with its ominous linkage of race and morality, served as a warm-up for the debate about the race, religion, and nationality of the Dönme that broke out immediately after the Turkish Republic was founded in 1923 and the rest of the Dönme of Salonika, the majority of whom had remained in that city after 1912, were sent en masse to Turkey. How did Dönme meet the challenges they faced after the empire fell, and how did the challenges in turn change them? How did others view them then? If their enemies emphasized their Jewish origins, who would consider the Dönme to be Muslims? But if, as their supporters argued, Dönme lived as pious Muslims, who would accept them in a secular state? Marked by unacceptable racial and religious attributes, how would the Dönme be defended?

III
Istanbul

§6   Losing a Homeland, 1923–1924

The Population Exchange of 1923

Stepping into the halls of the Université de Lausanne in Switzerland in the summer of 1923, we might overhear the following conversation:

§ "I represent Turkish Muslims in Macedonia" says the man to Rıza Nur, whose thick mustache sits like a brush above his upper lip. Nur is the second plenipotentiary, or representative of the Turkish delegation to the Lausanne conference, a native of the Black Sea town of Sinop who favors a fur cap. He is a medical doctor, Turkey's minister of health, and a former CUP member.

"Can you exclude Salonikan Muslims from the population exchange?"

Nur is not taken aback by the earnest request. Such a demand is not unusual at the time. Orthodox Christians of Antioch, for example, have petitioned the governor not to be subject to exchange.[1] But the Salonikan Muslim request disturbs Nur. He asks others to find out who he is.

He soon discovers he is actually a Dönme, a professor at the Darulfünun, the predecessor of Istanbul University.

Nur is an extreme nationalist who loves to insult other leading Turks by labeling them Kurds, Albanians, or Circassians. But he saves his best insults for Jews. He is no friend of Jews, especially not "secret Jews." He is already bothered by the presence on the Turkish delegation of Mehmet Cavid, and Haim Nahum, the CUP-supporting, former post-revolution chief rabbi of Istanbul. Nur knows the latter is there "only to stuff his pockets."[2] And hadn't that journalist Ahmet Emin Yalman been asked to be the personal interpreter at the conference of the head of the Turkish delegation, İsmet İnönü, but fortunately, had declined?[3]

"I don't like Jews at all," the outspoken politician later records thinking. "Jews are very contemptible and despicable things." They have a habit of deception, and one must be wary of falling for the Jew's trick. The CUP was in the palm of the hand of the Jews and Dönme.[4]

Suddenly the importance of the "Turkish Muslim of Macedonia"'s request dawns upon him: Although the man asked for the exemption, not because the Dönme were Jews, but because as Muslims they could serve "Turkish" interests in Salonika, Nur believes "This means the Dönme form a group in Turkey that thinks differently and has opposite interests than Turks. The disaster for us is that they appear as Turks. Greeks and Armenians are better than they, if for no other reason than we know they are Greeks and Armenians. This foreign element, this parasite, hides in our blood. They dye their faces and eyes with our blood so they can appear like us."[5] How many of them were there now among us? Nur was terrified of recognizing the Other, the Jew, in the self.

It was as if the Dönme were cross-dressers, or transvestites. They lived not only under a Muslim name, but appeared in Muslim dress.[6] The main reason for their being despised was their double life, which their outward profession of one creed and secret profession of another compelled them to lead.[7] The problem with the Dönme was that they were not what they appeared to be. It was time for them to come out of the closet, to be exposed for what they wore. The new male citizen could not be a cross-dresser. He would have to be stripped naked, revealing his true, inner, biological core. Then he could be disentangled, separated from true Turks.

Fears of the Dönme also reflected fears of being *taken* for a Dönme. Turks not only feared the Jew within, but feared being identified as Jews, or being like Jews without. The unsettled nature of Dönme identity—Jew or Muslim, foreigner or Turk?—rendered the relation between majority and minority, dominant and subordinate, uncertain, unstable, and unpredictable.[8] It made the dominant group—secular Turkish Muslims—doubt their own strength. They had a sense of self-disgust, and self-loathing, even a fear of the self, due in part to the knowledge of their actual history and complex mixed origins, which were whitewashed by an official or public discourse of purity, calling themselves Turks.

The Unmixing of Peoples

"Excellency! We have the honor to bring to your attention that the last convoy of exchangeable Muslims from this city left for Turkey on 26 December and that the evacuation of the city of Salonika of all Muslims may be considered as completely terminated from said date," the French official in charge of the population exchange at Thessaloníki told the governor-general of Macedonia.[9] The Treaty of Lausanne, signed on July 24, 1923 by Britain, France, Italy, Greece, and a Turkish delegation, was the final outcome of the civil war between Orthodox Christians (with foreign assistance from Greece and Britain) and Muslims (Turks and Kurds primarily).[10] After three years of warfare and political organizing, by 1922, the movement led by Atatürk had succeeded in its aim of winning political independence from occupation by Britain and France and their Greek allies. Atatürk had been one of the founders of a branch of the Ottoman Freedom Society—which played a key role in the revolution of 1908,[11] and which was closely related to Freemasonry, like the CUP being based in a Salonikan Masonic lodge.[12] Atatürk was a native of Ottoman Salonika. The future leader of Greece, Eleuthérios Venizélos, was a native of Ottoman Crete. The two leaders, despite being raised in cosmopolitan imperial environments, or because of it, sought to rule over homogeneous populations in their respective nation-states.

The treaty Greece and Turkey signed contained several key clauses that would serve this end. Non-Muslims in Turkey gave up the privileges of communal autonomy in order to be treated as equal citizens. As Clermont-Tonnerre proposed in revolutionary France in 1789, the principle was to the individual member of a religious community, everything, to the community, nothing.[13] Turkey became a secular republic, in which Islam was disestablished; soon afterward, the caliphate and sultanate were abolished. Most important, the Lausanne Treaty included the Lausanne Convention, signed January 30, 1923, which compelled an "exchange" of populations between Greece and Turkey. British Foreign Secretary Lord Curzon labeled the process "the unmixing of peoples."[14] New nations sought an imagined authenticity; cultural mixing was seen as negative and decadent, a threat to the purity of the nation. As a Greek staff officer wrote soon after his army took Salonika from the Ottomans, "How can one like a city with this cosmopolitan society, nine-tenths of it Jews. It has nothing Greek about it, nor European."[15] Sami Zubaida notes how "Cosmopolitanism is abhorred by nationalists," which was "echoed by Atatürk."[16] To Roel Meijer, analyzing trends in Alexandria, Beirut, and Istanbul, "The revolution that sounded the death knell of cosmopolitanism was proclaimed in the name of 'authentic' . . . indigenous values. After the fall of the cosmopolitan elite and the exodus of Greeks, Italians,

Syrians and Jews who were accused of collaborating with the Western colonial powers, the cosmopolitan-free havens were absorbed again into the hinterland. The new independent nation states retreated from the sea, seeking their identities in more solid terrains."[17]

The year 1923 saw the legalized ending of a decades-long process of expulsion and flight. The Ottoman Empire and Bulgaria had engaged in a population exchange in 1913. Following the loss of Salonika, in 1914 the Ottoman Empire proposed the "exchange" of 30,000 Balkan Muslims for 120,000 Anatolian Orthodox Christians, but it was hindered by the outbreak of World War I.[18] Cemal Pasha had plans to deport the Jews of Palestine, but foreign intervention prevented it.[19] Perhaps as many as one million Armenians were deported from Anatolia in 1915–17, which led to the deaths of most of them. Hundreds of thousands of Orthodox Christians were driven out of Western Anatolia under cover of war. Following the end of the Greek invasion and civil war in 1922, in which the Muslim (later labeled Turkish) side was victorious, within one month 650,000 Orthodox Christians left Anatolia; by the end of the year 1 million had emigrated to Greece.[20] It is ironic that a secular state approved the 1923 population exchange based on religion. Like the India-Pakistan population exchange two decades later, legalized expulsions in newly established secular nation-states made enemies of neighbors, divided people along religious lines, and alienated individuals from self-ascribed identities.[21]

At the same time as nation-states took upon themselves the ability to categorize people into religious groups, determining who belonged in which one, they also hindered movement between religions. Contrary to policy in the Ottoman Empire, where conversion had been the primary means of social integration and advancement, Christians and Jews were prohibited from converting to Islam at the inception of the Turkish Republic. To preclude their remaining in the new nation-state, the Turkish Grand National Assembly passed a measure in the summer of 1923 forbidding them to change their religion, evidence of the prevalence of ethnicizing religion.[22]

Populations subject to exchange are never consulted.[23] Worse, neither are they allowed to return to their native land. Moreover, once in their new country, they face the question of belonging, which is posed to them both by others and by themselves. Do they want to stay or leave? Do they want to go back? Do they regret the impossibility of returning? What does the impossibility of returning mean for the survival of their group?[24]

Answering several of these questions the wrong way would damage their ability to integrate into their new homelands.

The terminology of the agreements precluded their ability to answer several of these questions. According to the first article of the Lausanne Treaty, "As of May 1st, 1923, there shall take place a compulsory exchange of Turkish nationals of the Greek Orthodox religion settled in Turkish territories, and Greek nationals of the Muslim religion settled in Greek territories."[25] The use of the term "settled" alludes to an understanding of the transitoriness of minorities in the post-Ottoman states, as if these groups were merely passing through en route to their authentic domiciles. Despite the language of the treaty, the exchange was hardly a repatriation: Anatolia had been a Hellenic domicile and Christian heartland since antiquity; Muslims had made what is today modern Greece their home since medieval times.[26] Instead, it was more like "deportation into exile" for all parties concerned.[27] The use of the terms "Turkish territories" and "Greek territories" even homogenized the lands that were the common origins of diverse peoples. The compulsory exchange was irreversible. It offered no possibility of return; citizenship in the country of origin was immediately lost, and it was granted immediately in the country of migration.[28]

As a consequence, up to half a million Muslims in Greece, who mainly spoke Greek, were sent to Turkey, excluding those living in western Thrace. Up to 1.2 million Orthodox Christians of Turkey, many of whom spoke only Turkish, ended up in Greece. Most had fled following the defeat of the Greek army in Anatolia in 1922. The remainder, excluding those in Istanbul and the two islands remaining in Turkish possession, were "exchanged" in 1923. The Turkish delegation had attempted to get the Greek delegation to agree to the expulsion of all Orthodox Christians, including those of Istanbul, and to abolish the Orthodox Patriarchate; delegation members expressed how "it would have been better if none remained" in Turkey and hoped the rest would leave voluntarily.[29] Turkey promoted a quick, forced exchange. Contrary to the treaty, over ten thousand Orthodox Christians were also expelled from Istanbul.[30]

In some ways, the history of the Orthodox Christians of Istanbul paralleled that of the Dönme of Salonika. The former also had a phenomenal rise, especially in the economic sphere, between 1890 and 1914, just as the Dönme gained prominence between 1880 and 1912. Then, in the crucible of the Balkan Wars, just as some Dönme began to migrate to Istanbul and Izmir, some Greeks began to migrate to Salonika and

Athens. Perhaps if, like the Orthodox Christians, if the Dönme had been a religious community recognized by the Ottoman state, with a ceremonial religious leader at its head acting as a patriarch, they would have been allowed to remain in their home city. Yet the same economic logic that mitigated against the continued presence of the Dönme in Salonika was used against Istanbul Orthodox Christians. But at least temporarily, this much larger population was given reprieve. While there were ten to twenty thousand Dönme in Salonika in 1923, there were twelve times as many Orthodox Christians in Istanbul. That population had already declined by a third since just before 1908, to 120,000 from 180,000.[31]

The expulsion of Christians and Muslims so that they would not be able to be potential fifth columnists was an admission that religious minorities would not be considered a part of the social fabric of either Turkey or Greece; it was a final turn to xenophobia and away from accepting a plural society. This contributed to the ethno-religious homogenization of the population and economy of each country, the completion of a process begun in the deportations, migrations, and massacres of the Russian-Ottoman War of 1877–78, the Balkan Wars (1912–13), World War I (1914–18), Armenian deportation and massacres (1915–17), and the Greek-Turkish war of 1919–22.[32]

To understand much of this violent history, we have to return to examine CUP ideology and policy. Although after the revolution of 1908, the CUP was less ideological and more pragmatic, still, Darwinism, the supremacy of science and the struggle against superstitious religion, and antipathy to religion lurked in the background.[33] The leaders of the CUP had adopted Turkish racial nationalism and the dominant role of Turks in the remaining territories of the Ottoman Empire as their main ideology.[34] At the same time, they engaged in secularist policies, which paved the way to religion being a faith and a strictly personal matter in the Turkish Republic.[35]

The core of the CUP, which planned and implemented policies that promoted Turks and Muslims at the expense of Christians and other non-Turkish peoples adopted currents of thought that promoted new ways of thinking about religious and national difference. Interior Minister Talat Pasha, who was the architect of the deportation and massacres of Armenians and Assyrians, and Mehmet Reşid, a co-founder of the CUP and the governor in Diyarbakir in 1915-16 who implemented the deportations, were social Darwinists and positivists who believed there was a life-or-death battle of the fittest between Armenians and Greeks, on the one side, and Muslims and Turks, on the other. To Dr. Mehmet Raşid, who was honored by the young Turkish Republic for his services to the fatherland, in order to save the fatherland he had to kill the microbe or cut out the tumor (Christians) in the body of the nation (Turks), and this required violent measures in order to liberate the economy and people (Muslims).[36]

As a result of these policies and a devastating war, the populace faced cataclysmic mortality rates and ensuing homogenization. Anatolia was utterly devastated, facing proportionally greater population losses than even France. Two million Muslims, 800,000 Armenians, and 500,000 Orthodox Christians were killed between 1915 and 1922.[37] Half of the Jews fled during the 1920s.[38] Anatolia's population decreased by an estimated one-quarter between 1913 and 1923.[39] Whereas in 1913, one in five people (20%) within the borders of what would become Turkey were Christian or Jewish, by 1923 only one in forty (2.5%) were non-Muslim.[40] For example, whereas in 1900, the non-Muslim (i.e., primarily Christian) percentages of the population of the cities of Erzurum, Trabzon, and Sivas were 32, 43, and 33 percent, respectively, they had fallen to 0.1, 1, and 5 percent by 1927. Thus, "the success of the new nationalist republic in avenging itself on the Ottoman Armenians and Greeks who, as the victors saw it, had so treacherously turned against their Muslim compatriots was manifest."[41] Such demographic change, and the general feeling among Muslims that non-Muslims, particularly Armenians and Greeks, had acted as fifth columns, led to unprecedented anti-Christian sentiment. This was exacerbated when Greek forces occupied western Anatolia and committed atrocities during the Greek-Turkish War of 1919-22.

The Impact of the Population Exchange on the Dönme

In this time of great loss, suffering, and anxiety, as the Ottoman Empire was disintegrating, Turkish nationalism came to the fore among Muslim peoples in Anatolia. The new demographic and political situation allowed Muslims to imagine the creation of their own national state. And in this period, Muslims began to look more closely at the identity of the Dönme. They questioned the vanguard role that Dönme such as Mehmet Cavid, a member of parliament and of the cabinet, were playing in society. There was no parallel debate about Armenian or Jewish identity, since members of these groups openly identified themselves and did not claim to be Muslims. In addition, the numbers of Armenians and Jews had been radically reduced, as had Greeks, with the exception of those remaining in Istanbul, so they could no longer be considered a problem. The uncertainty surrounding the Dönme was due to the fact that they appeared to hide their true identity, although there was little if anything that would outwardly distinguish them from other Muslims.

Because they were considered Muslims by the Greek government, the Dönme of Salonika were subject to deportation to Turkey as part of the population exchange.[42] Avram Galanté says that relying on their Jewish origins, some Dönme asked the Greek government to excuse them from the expulsion, an odd request considering that the rabbis of Salonika refused to allow the Dönme to return to Judaism, since they opposed their customs and did not consider them Jews.[43] The government in Athens refused to allow the Dönme to remain, probably because it wanted to be rid of a significant non-Greek economic element in order to "nationalize" its economy.[44]

Other Dönme approached Turkish officials with the same aim although for different reasons. The response from Turkish Muslims illustrates how no one seemed to view them favorably. They had even lost the allies who had supported them only fifteen years earlier during the revolution period. Mehmet Cavid served as one of the advisors to the Turkish delegation to the Lausanne Conference. But there he had a falling out with İsmet İnönü and joined the faction against İnönü and Atatürk, which was a fateful decision.

Despite their protests and Turkish apprehension about their true identity and potential danger, the Dönme were thus compelled to abandon their native Salonika. The number of Dönme involved comes from the estimate proffered by Joseph Nehama, director of the Alliance universelle Israélite in Salonika, who obtained information from Dönme students. He says that in 1902, there were 4,000 Yakubi, 3,500 Karakaş, and 2,500 Kapancı.[45] Dönme from throughout Greece were subjected to the same treatment as those in Salonika, and all excepting those who left Greece for other countries were dispersed to numerous cities in Turkey, losing their concentration in one center. This was part of an attempt to cause them to lose their language and identity by the Turkish government, which was pursuing similar policies of diffusion and Turkification of (other) non-Turkish Muslim groups.[46]

Intended along with the population exchange was a wealth and property exchange. Although hardly a majority in the city's population, especially after 1912, Muslims and Dönme had owned the most property in Salonika. Seeing that most of the Dönme men, whether Karakaş or Kapancı, were listed as merchants or bankers by profession in the documentation of the Mixed Commission for the Exchange of the Greek and Turkish Populations, this would be a complicated affair of disentanglement. In theory, the population exchange appeared to offer a smooth transition for the migrants. They were free to transfer their moveable goods; those they could not transport, they were to leave where they were. Local authorities were charged with evaluating their worth and giving the migrants a form stating their estimate of the value. In addition, migrants' immovable goods were also to be evaluated. Each migrant family would arrive in Turkey with a copy of a document listing the amount and value of its property in Greece filled out by the family head, signed by the local committee, and approved by the Mixed Commission of Turks and Greeks as well.[47] The exchangee was to receive the equivalent in his or her new domicile.[48] Thus if a Dönme owned a home in Salonika valued at 10,000 gold Turkish lira, in theory, when he arrived in Istanbul, he was to receive an equivalent home of a deported Orthodox Christian, who one assumes would receive the Dönme's home in Salonika. Again, in theory, seen from the Turkish state's perspective, this process would kill two birds with one stone.[49] Anatolia had been devastated by over a decade of war and dislocation of the population. The reconstruction and repair of the country, and the replanting and tending of its land, was to be undertaken by the migrants who would settle in the ruined and abandoned homes and fields of the departed Orthodox Christians.[50] The Aegean and Black Sea regions were especially in ruins, and it was to these areas that the migrants were to be sent.[51] In the eyes of Mustafa Necati, head of the Turkish parliament's population exchange and settlement committee, the aim was to promote the national economy; the country would be rejuvenated by coreligionists, whose prosperity would make Turkey prosper.[52]

Despite the best-laid plans, however, problems immediately arose. Plans of settlement could not be implemented in part because the government did not have available sufficient formerly Orthodox Christian homes and fields, most of which had already been occupied by migrants or displaced locals.[53] According to a member of Necati's committee, even after the war had ended, even in the new national capital of Ankara, homes and gardens and fields had been destroyed or looted. Cessation of hostilities was in fact the beginning of a period of widespread looting, not a calm transfer of ownership of property.[54] It is not surprising that many Orthodox Christians did not want to leave; some were hidden by Turkish families, others became citizens of other countries and after leaving Turkey returned with foreign passports, or returned illegally, or with fake passports.[55] In all cases, they demanded their former properties. Moreover, even if there had been properties available, many migrants had left Greece without having any documents drawn up concerning the value of their property left behind; this made it extremely difficult in Turkey to determine how much they should receive.[56] Some of those who drew up documents in Greece exaggerated their wealth and snapped up more property in Turkey than they had owned in Greece. Some chose to emigrate outside government channels, without government or official help, since they did not want to settle where the state intended to settle them. Others, once in Istanbul, resisted being sent to the intended cities and even clashed with police.[57] Sometimes they were forced to board waiting ferries, but this did not stop some from jumping ship, or from returning to Istanbul after ostensibly being settled on the Black Sea coast.

The Turkish press featured heart-wrenching stories of the hardship migrants faced. Travel conditions were difficult, belongings were lost or stolen, guesthouses assigned to them were often overcrowded, rundown madrasas with broken windows, homes assigned to them were occupied by others, such as internal migrants also in need of homes in these cities or earlier migrants from southeastern Europe and the USSR.[58] Finally, they were sent from locale to locale in pursuit of sufficient housing. In fact, the main problem was where they would live. In short, the Turkish government had not done enough to prepare the ground for their proper reception.[59] Nor did it settle the migrants in a logical way: urban dwellers were sometimes sent to the countryside and farmers to the city. Many tobacco families were sent to the mountains, where they could not cultivate crops, professionals were sent to villages, farmers were sent to live in the centers of towns in the homes of departed Christian craftsmen and not given land on which to raise crops or livestock, olive growers were sent to regions without olives. Turkey's land and economy were in ruins. Not giving migrants the opportunity to work in their accustomed way did nothing to contribute to the hoped-for renaissance of Turkey's infrastructure, agriculture, commerce, and trade.[60]

Salonikan Muslims were quick to leave their hometown, but not exempt from such hardship in Turkey. Between mid-November and the end of December 1923, 50,000 left Salonika for Turkey.[61] By July 1924, 100,000 from Salonika and its environs had arrived.[62] After arriving on the ferry from Salonika, some refused to board ferries for Samsun and remained in Istanbul.[63] Guesthouses were set up to house the migrants in the Bayezid and Gülhane districts of Istanbul.[64] They were meant as temporary shelter while migrants were en route to the assigned place of settlement, but became more long-term homes for those who refused to continue their journey.

Reşat Tesal, whose own family were victims of the incompetence of the Turkish committee in Greece, says that from the point of view of the exchangees, both the preparatory work in Greece and subsequent resettlement in Turkey were badly bungled. Moreover, after they arrived in Turkey, the refugees were preyed upon by malefactors. Most Muslim exchangees were wronged and mistreated, Tesal claims.[65]

Businessmen in the various host cities came together to form committees to channel assistance to migrants, and in places where Salonikan Dönme were resettled, Dönme already in Turkey played a leading role in the effort to help their brethren. One example is Karakaş Kibar Tevfik who ran the Şark Tobacco Company in Samsun.[66] Samsun was the city where most Salonikans were supposed to be deported, because it was the center of the Turkish tobacco trade, and thus a place where Muslims from Salonika's hinterlands could grow tobacco and merchants from the city of Salonika could run the business end of the industry. In Istanbul, the assistance effort was undertaken by the Karakaş Balcı İbrahim, Kibar Saram, and Macit Mehmet Karakaş, the son of Mehmet Karakaş, who were members of the Chamber of Commerce.

These efforts were crucial in helping Dönme get back on their feet, because the Turkish government decided not to give migrants the equivalent of what they had left behind in Greece, but only one-fifth of what was recorded on the documents evaluating their property.[67] Nothing was to be given those who claimed over 50,000 gold lira in property. Those who left factories behind in Greece would not receive a factory in Turkey if none was available in the area to which they were sent. Such policies were especially harmful to the great textile, timber, and tobacco merchant Dönme families of Salonika and compelled them to buck government planning and settle where they could live as they had lived in Greece. The lack of government assistance made them rely more on their local relatives in Istanbul.

From records at the Archive of the Republic in Ankara, one learns that most Dönme arrived in Turkey self-divided into Yakubi, Karakaş, and Kapancı extended family groups, sometimes as many as over three dozen people together. They made the journey in the summer and fall of 1924, after most other Salonikan Muslims had already departed, and a full year after the migration process had begun. It seems the Dönme were in no hurry to leave Salonika; they quit the city in the last months before the terminal date set for Muslims to leave Greece. One can chart a Dönme migration calendar. The Karakaş came first. The Kibar family came in the third week of July; the Balcı, two months later, in the third week of September; the Karakaş (including Karakaş Mehmet's son Ali Macit),[68] Dilber (including Kibar Muhsin),[69] Şemsi Efendi (his wife Makbule and daughters Yekta and Marufe),[70] and Şamlı families (such as that of Dr. Ahmet Tevfik),[71] in the first week of October. After the Karakaş came the Hamdi Bey (Yakubi) group in the second week of October. Finally, the last to leave were the Kapancı, including the Kapancı family and the Akif clan, including the wives, sons, and daughters of Mehmet, Yusuf, and Ahmet Kapancı, and the son and daughters of Hasan Akif. They waited until the last day of October. Some important families, such as the İpekçi, are not documented, leading one to conclude they migrated either before or after the population exchange, or during the exchange but outside of governmental channels.

By 1924, Mehmet Kapancı and his two brothers, Ahmet and Yusuf, and other leading merchants, such as Hasan Akif, Karakaş Mehmet, and Mustafa Cezar, leading lights such as Şemsi Efendi, and local politicians such as Hamdi Bey had already died. Mehmet Kapancı must have passed away on the brink of being deported, because he was still listed as being alive in a document concerning the liquidation of the assets of his daughter Safinaz dated January 1924.[72] At the time of the population exchange, some of the children of leading Dönme resided in central and western Europe, such as Hasan Akif's tobacco merchant son Osman Nuri and his wife İkbal, who lived in Vienna.[73] In 1922, the Greek municipality confiscated Osman Nuri Akif's property in Hamidiye at number 141 Odos Basilissis Olgas (formerly Hamidiye Boulevard). Although he lived in Vienna, he pursued his claim with the Mixed Commission, even submitting a letter addressed to the municipality in Greek, and demanded monetary compensation.[74] The couple migrated to Turkey a decade later. Those who did migrate in 1924 included Dönme leaders' wives, children, and grandchildren, who would start a new life in the new homeland under radically different conditions from those in which these men had established their diasporic networks.

Dönme not only filled in the standardized forms estimating the value of their immovable and movable goods in Salonika and located proxies to liquidate their assets before they left, but added whatever documentation they thought would also substantiate their economic value. They filled out the forms in Ottoman and added documents in Greek, such as Greek floor plans of their homes, and added lengthy complaints in both languages concerning Greek appropriations of their property and taxation since 1912 for which they wanted to be compensated. Often the forms were not long enough. Some added numerous additional pages listing their extensive movable and immovable goods, such as the five Karakaş merchants of the Dilber family, including Mehmet Şevket, Mehmet Nazif, and Suleiman Sıtkı, who added six extra pages to include their nine properties and nine stores, hans, and factories, which were worth nearly 50,000 gold lira.[75]

The psychological state of the migrants comes through in the bureaucratic forms. The date on the documents illustrates how long it took the Dönme to wrap up their businesses and lives and decide how to proceed. They applied together to the Mixed Commission in Salonika as extended families, appearing on the same day to submit their claims and fully expecting to be compensated in Turkey. One wonders if they would have taken such care and effort filling in the forms if they had known how little, if anything, they would receive in exchange. Possibly knowing migrant claims of over 50,000 gold lira in wealth would disqualify them from compensation, few approached that amount; the largest was a claim of 48,000 gold lira. The archive in Ankara has no documentation of what the Salonikans received when they arrived, only list after list of what they lost. Perhaps they received nothing.[76]

After the Dönme arrived in Turkey, their ethno-religious identity sparked a furious debate over whether they belonged in the new nation-state. How was their religious and racial identity perceived by others? Was Rıza Nur's vicious distrust of Dönme a representative view? Were Dönme rejected as Jews and foreigners or accepted as Muslims and Turks? How did the Dönme attempt to come to terms with the conversion from an ethno-religious to a secular national identity in the first two decades of the Turkish nation-state? How did they attempt to explain the group's past in the Ottoman Empire and their future in the Turkish Republic? What solutions did they offer for their assimilation into Turkish society?

§7   Loyal Turks or Fake Muslims?

Debating Dönme in Istanbul, 1923–1939

Almost from the moment of their arrival in Turkey as part of the population exchange, the Dönme were greeted with suspicion about their true nature. At the beginning of 1924, a cartoon titled "One Word, Two Meanings" in one of the most popular humor magazines in Istanbul poked fun at the Dönme.[1] The caption plays on the double meaning of the word *dönme*. Two fez-wearing Dönme men, who appear puzzled, are talking. One says to the other, using *dönme* as a noun: "I don't know what we are doing wrong. They call us 'apostates from Judaism [*Yahudilikten dönme*],' and we call ourselves 'apostates [*dönmeyiz*].'" The noun *dönme* here signifies one who has genuinely adopted another faith, but if *dönme* is regarded as a verb, the same sentence denies the authenticity of Dönme conversion to Islam, becoming: "I don't know what we are doing wrong. They say to us, 'Don't apostatize from Judaism [*Yahudilikten dönme*],' and we say, 'We don't apostatize [*dönmeyiz*].'" Treating *dönme* as a verb would make the speaker say that they are not sincere Muslims, but in fact remain committed Jews. The Dönme were used to being declared defectors from Judaism. In the popular late Ottoman / early Turkish republican view of them as dissimulators of their true identity, they faced the charge that they were only pretended apostates.

It is conventional wisdom that the population exchange satisfied the aims of the two states, hastening their national project and utopian dream of building new homogeneous nations without ethnic or religious differences.[2] When we shift the focus from states to humans, however, we find another story. As this cartoon shows, it was not in fact an easy process. How could Greece and Turkey assimilate large populations that, to the increasing horror of the receiving states, did not in any way resemble the local population, but were stained by the marks of otherness?

As Kemal Arı has pointed out, forced migration, such as the population exchange, has lasting effects on the people compelled to abandon their homelands and the people who receive them.[3] Migrants lose social status, social and business connections. If wealthy, they can become poor, great economic losses obliging them to start over from scratch. These socio-economic problems contribute to psychological problems. Having lost social and political capital and wealth, forced to leave their home and hometown, established milieu, and land of their fathers, they then have to fit in and get along with a new society and neighbors in a new economy. The problem is made worse when it is assumed that they are blood brothers and thus carry the same habits and values of the new society, when in fact they do not. Forced migration leads to jealousy and suspicion and economic rivalry, which can result in clashes and murder, as occurred in Anatolia in disputes over the distribution of homes, land, and crops. In response, migrants settled in separate villages or separate parts of towns. Locals found them different, their customs strange, their foreign language or accents incomprehensible, their clothes and food odd, and their women's veils inappropriate. Not mixing, being foreign to each other, each group felt superior to the other and sought the upper hand.

When thousands of Muslims who were deported by Greece arrived in the new nation-state of Turkey in accordance with the population exchange, the Dönme deportees drew considerable public scrutiny. The group presented a puzzle to Muslims in Turkey. Were they really Muslims deserving of citizenship in the new republic, or were they secret Jews who had no place there? Were they Turks or foreigners? How could Turks or Muslims distinguish who exactly were Turks and Muslims, and who were Dönme? Public debates centered on questions concerning the fundamental nature of the new society being created: Should minorities that seemed to be a danger to the majority population be allowed to maintain their own identity within the society, or should they be forced to assimilate and renounce their belief in that which made them different? Could a parallel society be accepted? What should the society look like? What were its values?

Incited by the public pronouncements of Dönme, the identity of the group was debated in the Turkish press and parliament. Most crucial was the role that the Dönme played in defining the parameters of the discussion about who belonged to the Turkish nation and the Muslim community. Two Dönme, Mehmet Karakaşzade Rüştü and Ahmet Emin Yalman, presented to the anxious public radically different interpretations of their group's identity, the ability of the Dönme to integrate, and the boundaries of being Turkish, Muslim, and Jewish. An investigation of the debate about whether the Dönme belonged in Turkey provides insight into how the Dönme struggled to legitimize their existence in the new republic and come to terms with the radical new situation.

Karakaşzade Mehmet Rüştü: Organic National Identity

Ironically, in 1924 the public debate over the Dönme was incited by the proclamations of one of their own, Karakaşzade Mehmet Rüştü (hereafter Rüştü), a forty-five-year-old nationalist whose views primarily represented an organic understanding of national identity. To him, Dönme could not be considered members of the Turkish race, since Turks were Muslims by birth and not by conversion.

Befitting the group's international ties, Rüştü, a Karakaş Dönme graduate of the Feyziye school in Salonika, was a Dönme trader (of knitted goods—socks, stockings, blankets—and rainwear—galoshes and umbrellas) who owned stores and properties in Salonika as late as 1915 and in Berlin and Istanbul.[4] He had been married and divorced several times, and the reason for his public fulmination against the group may have had to do with marital discord, or he may have been paid to reveal the secrets of the group. Some questioned Rüştü's motivations. Were they financial? One newspaper asked whether he had secretly set up an anti-Dönme commercial organization to enable Turkish merchants to take control of Turkish commerce.[5] Was he simply trying to ruin his economic competitors, had he thrown in his lot with the Muslim Turks? He also apparently quarreled with some Dönme over loans and payments, and went to court in a dispute over alimony and ownership of properties with his Dönme ex-wife. He may have decided to take out his anger at these people by castigating all Dönme. Or did he have deep problems struggling among given, ascribed, and desired identity? Tiring of being referred to as a Jew, excommunicated from his community, did he go to Ankara to be awarded an envoy posting abroad where he could start a new life? In the Istanbul daily *Vakit* (Time), the Salonika correspondent Ahmet Arik wrote that Rüştü had been banished from the community at the age of fifteen, yet was still embarrassed when people referred to him as a Jew.[6] Claiming to have spent his whole life among Turks, and far from the Dönme (which did not explain how he had learned so much about them), he stated that he hated the Dönme because they did not conform to Turks' religion, morality, or nationality.

As large numbers of fellow Dönme began arriving in Turkey, Rüştü engaged in a campaign to alert the public to what he considered their true identity. He petitioned the Grand National Assembly, met with Atatürk, as Yalman repeatedly did, was interviewed by all the major newspapers in Ankara and Istanbul, and published an open letter to the Dönme. For Rüştü the problem was simple: the Dönme were Jews in origin and their disposition was absolutely alien to that of Muslims. His message to the Dönme was also clear: "O Dönme youth, who are still asleep! Wake up! The time for radical change has arrived!" His writings were a sensation. The Dönme reacted harshly: one young man warned that Rüştü would be killed by Dönme.[7]

Rüştü offered a simple answer to the complex question whether the Dönme had any relation to Turkishness and Islam. On January 4, 1924, *Vakit* carried a story on its second page entitled "Petition Concerning the Dönme—Petition Asks That the Salonikan Dönme Not be Subject to the Population Exchange."[8] Rüştü had petitioned the Turkish Grand National Assembly declaring that the group of which he was a member, the Salonikan Dönme, were neither Turks nor Muslims, and thus should not be accepted in Turkey in exchange for the Orthodox Christians or Greeks of Anatolia. "This is the age of nations," he claimed, and the very first principle of nationalism was that every member of a nation had to be the same in mind and body. But the Dönme "hid themselves under the name and cloak 'Muslim,' despite the fact that by origin and race they were Jews, and neither by soul nor conscience did they have any connection to Islam. Like other Jews, for three centuries they never mixed with Turks and Muslims and lived apart, preserving their own communal rites and particular conscience." Ever since they had accepted Islam they had been considered Muslims by the Ottoman authorities, but they always deceived Muslims by outwardly appearing and dressing like them: "With a thousand types of hypocrisy and false airs and costumes, they insinuated their way among the Turks. Masquerading as Turks they gained a great deal of wealth, acquiring the main commercial and economic positions, thus becoming an important and dangerous factor."

Rüştü continues by stating it was time for the Turkish Grand National Assembly to eliminate this problem definitively, saving the society and economy from this danger. He argues the population exchange had been established to bring in Turks. The government did not even accept Muslim Albanians, and the non-Turks were dispersed to the far corners of the country. The aim was to create a Turkish people. How could it then accept the Dönme, who were not Turks, never having intermarried with any other group, "not grafting themselves onto another root," nor accepted assimilation, and not Muslims, "as has been known for centuries by the Muslim Turks who lived near them," and as Rüştü can attest. This being the case, Rüştü asks rhetorically how the Turkish Grand National Assembly can allow this wealthy foreign group, which falsely hides behind Islamic and Turkish masks, to settle and gain fortunes in Istanbul, Izmir, and Bursa, the very economic gates of the country. He asks just because the military victory has been won, should they not continue the same vigilance of soldiers on the front? Life is a struggle, he argues, social, economic, moral, and political, and all require vigilance.

In the end of the article, Rüştü makes his request to the MPs, which allows for the probability that the Dönme will not be sent back to Greece. He petitions "that you either let these old refugees who are not of your blood or religion remain outside of the national boundaries, not accepting them as immigrants, or that you determine which ones are Salonikan Dönme, mark them, disperse them to every corner of the country, and pass a law ensuring that they mix with Turkish families and thus are assimilated." Doing so, he continues, will save the pure and moral Turkish people and Turkishness, and even himself, who works for the lofty aims of Turkishness, from being besmirched by the dirty name and stain of the Dönme. He signed the petition "in the name of the enlightened ones honestly desiring the Dönme mixing with the Turks." Rüştü holds out the possibility that the Dönme may mix with Turks, although this contradicts his understanding of being Turkish. He mentions intermarriage as a strategy of integration, which may have offered a way for the Dönme to belong while acknowledging their stark difference. One wonders whether Muslims would accept the Dönme into the heart of the nation if they were actually marked as Rüştü desired.

Rüştü's "Open Letter to All Salonikan Dönme," which appeared in *Vakit* three days after the first article appeared is a phenomenal statement of racialized nationalism.[9] Rüştü begins by claiming that the Dönme had deceived the Turkish nation for three centuries by "not revealing the extent to which we were separate and different in public and private in our social relations and actions, acting fanatically to continue our existence as Dönme." Because Ottoman society never compelled them to abandon their separate identity, they never mixed with other Muslims, retaining their foreignness. Rüştü avoids the subject of Dönme religious belief, but asserts that following Turkey's independence, "the hearts and conscience of people living in the lands that this honored Turkish nation rules from Edirne to Kars beat in unison and desire only to be composed of those bearing the ideal of Turkishness." He asks whether they think it is enough that five or ten Dönme "publicly mix with Turks, considering it a religious duty that is incumbent upon them; but as for the remaining ten to fifteen thousand of you, do you think Turks will endure and suffer a [one or two words censored by the newspaper] foreigner remaining in the body of the homeland?" To Rüştü, they are mistaken, for "truly only Turks have the right to live in this country, no other groups are included in the discussion." The reason is clear: "it is the Turks who defended this soil by irrigating and mixing it with their blood." Yet during recent events, when everyone's hopes were dashed, "sponging parasites like you were occupied with hoarding your wealth, not even sacrificing a tiny drop of your blood, nor an insignificant part of your wealth and fortune for the sake of the homeland and nation."

Unlike the parasitical Dönme, Rüştü argues, the Turks put their trust in God, resisting the attack against them from all sides, and defended the fatherland. Rüştü is outraged that faced with such a lofty scene, Dönme "are still indifferent, keeping your old traditions and just as in former eras living as a sponging parasite. But do you still imagine retaining your affluence and ease without being subjected to any objections being raised and voiced?" Rüştü then explains why he had traveled to Ankara, the new nation's capital. Ever since he arrived, he had realized that the representatives in the Grand National Assembly would be able to fulfill the wish he had nurtured since he was fifteen years old, namely, the dissolution of Dönme separateness. He notes how the Grand National Assembly even made a law concerning wild boars that damage cultivable lands. Consequently, "do you think that the leaders of the nation, who pay attention to such minute details, will be able to retain in its breast a mass of foreigners? No individual who is able to tolerate this any longer has been found or will be found." The phrase, "a mass of foreigners in its breast," is an image of a cancer or parasite. Rüştü uses the metaphor of comparing the Dönme to the filthiest animal imaginable to Muslims to refer to the damage these foreigners can cause to the nation's precious soil.

Rüştü concludes by offering the Dönme an ultimatum: either integrate or leave. He can see only these two alternatives: "either in accordance with a special law definitively mixing and intermarrying with Turks, working in common for the good of the entire fatherland and nation, or look for a way to solve our problem outside the boundary of the nation in whatever material and spiritual form it takes." Relieved of his burden, Rüştü then places responsibility on the shoulders of the government: "Our Grand National Assembly, which is successful in purifying and liquidating the filth accumulated for centuries, will, God willing, also soon take care of this inauspicious problem, and those who ascribe frivolity or other traits to me and attack me today will soon kiss my hand and appreciate and revere me. Guidance and success is from God."

Rüştü's furious attack reflected the view of many Muslim authors since 1906. Writing around 1907 against political decentralization, which would benefit Christian and non-Turkish peoples, the CUP leader Bahaettin Şakir argued that the Turks were "the real and legitimate owners of the fatherland that had been soaked with the blood of [their] martyred patriotic ancestors."[10] After 1913, an entire book and booklet series entitled "The Library of Awakening" published by Tüccarzâde İbrahim Hilmi was devoted to explaining the causes of Ottoman defeat in the Balkan Wars. Singled out in one book by Ahmet Cevat was parasitism. "Commercial parasites" were most harmful, because Ottoman economic interests were placed in the hands of foreigners / non-Muslims. Because Muslims were merely consumers, they were enslaved by foreign producers and merchants, who lived off their wealth. In this life-and-death struggle, the Muslims would have to expel foreigners and non-Muslims from their life source, the economy, symbolized by blood.[11] Moreover, some in the political elite, such as Talat Pasha, the minister of the interior until 1918, also utilized the parasite motif, proclaiming that Armenians, Greeks, and Jews shared all the benefits of the fatherland, yet bore none of its burden.[12] They "never participated in war" and "never spilled a drop of blood," but during times of war continued to make money through trade and lived well. Because Turks defended the fatherland, and the Dönme did not, Rüştü observes they should not be surprised that in 1924 people objected to their continuing their distinct traditions and living "as a parasite."[13]

Rüştü develops the host and parasite motif: the Turks are the unwitting host to a dangerous parasite that can destroy them.

Rüştü turned from the parasite motif to the metaphor of cross-dressing, asserting in *Akşam* (Evening*)*, that his "duty" was to "rip the [inner lining and surface of the] false cloak in which we have concealed ourselves for two and a half centuries."[14] He asks Dönme if they think that by putting up framed inscriptions such as "In the Name of God," or "The Merchant is the Beloved of God," in their stores they would either become Muslims, or trick Muslims into believing they shared the same faith. "The fashion," he argues, "of cheating people with names, words, and appearances has passed." He was on a mission to prove to all that Dönme were not Turks and not Muslims.

Interior Minister Ferid, when asked by a reporter from *Akşam* whether it was true that Rüştü had submitted a petition concerning the Dönme, responded that Rüştü had told him in Ankara that the Salonikans known as Dönme needed to identify themselves completely with Turkishness and Islam.[15] Although they appeared as Turks and Muslims, in fact, they maintained their special position, and Rüştü argued that they were hypocrites. There were some religious fanatics among them, but even the few "enlightened ones" who were not believers assisted each other and financially supported each other, thus displaying that they desired the group to continue to flourish. Rüştü urged him to take action, and the interior minister stated, "Without a doubt, the government will carefully examine this problem."[16]

Interviews of Rüştü were published in *Vakit* all through January 1924. The first, on January 9, carried the byline of the Ankara correspondent Hüseyin Necati. In this interview, Rüştü detailed the Dönme customs he learned from his mother and father and Dönme attitudes toward Turks.[17] His mother had explained to him the importance of abstaining from lamb for the entire year, except during the Festival of the Lamb, which he learned later allegedly was the day when four to fifteen couples gathered for ritualistic sex. She also emphasized not marrying outsiders and being wary of Turks. His mother compared Turks to onions, and asked rhetorically whether he had ever heard of an onion that was not bitter. Rüştü also describes the three separate Dönme communities, characterizing the first (Karakaş) as conservative and completely Jewish, even praying in "Jewish." The second group (Kapancı) was made up of enlightened ones, who gave little importance to the Dönme religion, yet did not mix with Turks, and mainly concerned themselves with their business interests. The third group (Yakubi) had so mixed with Turks that there were only a hundred of them left.

Rüştü tried to shock the Dönme and alarm the Muslim public and thereby cause the immediate flight or integration of the Dönme. Contradicting a widely accepted tenet of Ottoman Islamic law and custom, he proclaimed that even if the Dönme called themselves Muslims and acted like Muslims, because of their origins, they could not be considered Muslims. Rüştü may have been motivated by an aim to avenge his community, since he had been banished and had financial disputes. Yet his public declarations and frantic trips between Ankara and Istanbul to meet with press, parliament, and president speak of a man desperate to prove his own Turkishness, despite his lineage. He appears as a zealous convert to being Turkish who is more pious than those born into the religion he urged the Dönme to join. Ironically, Rüştü often vacillates between using the term "us" and "you" when discussing the Dönme. This pronoun-switching illustrates the difficulty he faced in defining his own place in the new nation. Yet did he imagine he could distance himself from being associated with the Dönme by expressing such loathing for them? Or was convincing Muslims that Dönme were Jews an elaborate ploy to have the exchange order rescinded so that Dönme could regain their businesses and properties in Salonika? Either way, his plan was contradictory, for by making Dönme identity a public scandal, and playing a key role in depicting Dönme distinctiveness to others, he may have hindered their smooth integration.

Dönme identity was difficult to resolve so long as the question of race surfaced and conceptions of race fed into understandings of the nation. People asked whether those of alien or non-Turkish or Jewish blood could be received as Turks if they pronounced a change in conscience to a belief in Turkishness. How could minority attempts at maintaining a distinct identity and embracing different beliefs and affiliations be feasible if belonging to the nation meant belonging to an imagined race? Faced with biological requirements for citizenship, how could Dönme defend and define their place in the nation?

Race, Class, and the Nation

Rüştü's public attacks on the Dönme gave fuel to others to vent their anti-Dönme hostility. *Vakit* and other newspapers took Rüştü's pronouncements very seriously and drew attention to the "flawed" population exchange. *Vakit* wrote that the question emerged of whether the Dönme of Salonika should be sent to Turkey or not as part of the population exchange, which was based only on the principle of religion.[18] The writer argued that even if a group such as the Dönme "were called by a Muslim name, in truth, if part of the population is not included in one of the existing, accepted branches of Islam, it is the right and duty of the government to ascertain who they are, and keep them from being transferred." *Vakit* published a report that like Rüştü, a parliamentarian in Athens named Mustafa Efendi had asked Greece to limit the exchange to Greeks [Orthodox Christians] and Turks [Muslims] alone, arguing that Dönme were Muslim in name but Jews in spirit, but that Greek authorities considered Dönme to be a thousand times more harmful to Greekness than Turks.[19] In a front-page article in *İleri* (Forward), Subhi Nuri wrote that "race is one thing, nationality another. In fact, they are not of our race."[20] He argued that those who were Turkified and had genuinely begun to be Turks could remain, but "otherwise, they have no right to live here." In any case, the Dönme wanted to remain in Greece, as they had openly stated, since their wealth was there. If they didn't want the Turks, he said, then the Turks didn't want them. In *Tanin*, the issue was taken up more politically as part of nationalist immigrant politics. Writers asserted that if the true Dönme aim was to flee Salonika, they must Turkify.[21]

Because people were declaring the Dönme to be Jews in race and religion, it was logical that daily newspapers next sought information from Jews. *Akşam* decided to interview the last Ottoman and first Turkish chief rabbi, Haim Becerano, former chief rabbi of Edirne, a close friend of Atatürk's.[22] The rabbi was asked whether there was a difference between Jewish and Dönme beliefs. "They followed a Sufi order whose beliefs are partly contrary to ours," he replied. When asked if they still observed distinct customs and prayers, he claimed that he did not know. As to whether they intermarried with Turks, he said "as far as I know, *you* [Turks] do not give your daughters in marriage to them." Finally, when asked whether "they can again become Jews," he responded: "If they want, they can . . . No . . . No . . . But I am not interested." A *Vakit* reporter then interviewed "a Jewish citizen" who, unsurprisingly, considering the nearly three centuries of separation dividing the two groups, was adamantly opposed to the Dönme, asserting that they were neither Jews, nor Muslims:

> The Dönme are not Jews. Judaism cannot accept them. Imagine, however, for the sake of argument, that we accepted their Judaism. Yet who can ensure that

shortly after that they would not say to us, "No, we are not Jews"? Judaism hates the Dönme religion. A Jew is the foe of a Dönme, because a Jew does not apostatize. Jews were slaughtered in Spain, but did not turn from their religion. In Russia, the tsar and Bolsheviks alike slaughtered them, but again, they did not apostatize, and do not apostatize. These Dönme form a wily group. To us Jews, everyone says, "You love money." But it is the Dönme who in fact worship it. Their worship does not resemble yours, nor does it resemble Jewish worship. To you Turks and Muslims, their special characteristics may make them appear like us, as Jews. However, in truth, they are far from both religions. They are a very different tribe and surely a strange family.[23]

İleri sent its reporters to the Bahçekapı and Sultan Hamam neighborhoods of Istanbul, which were associated with Jewish businesses in the popular mind, to find Jewish or Dönme (the author mixes the two) storeowners to help explain the issue.[24] The reporters made fun of the accents of those they found and criticized their knowledge of proper Turkish, using anti-Jewish stereotypes.

Jews disassociated themselves from Dönme, while Muslims expressed biological fears. A sociologist, who began by stating that the Dönme had played an important role in the Constitutional Revolution and the social advancement of Turkish society, nonetheless feared that if they integrated with Turks and adopted Muslim names, Turkish Muslims would not be able to tell the two groups apart.[25] A doctor interviewed in *Vakit* stated that with few exceptions, this generation of Dönme all had tuberculosis. He argued that "mixing our blood with theirs" would thus be detrimental to Turks. Such fears were based on the racial idea of hybridity popular in the late nineteenth and early twentieth centuries, which emerged from the biological and botanical sciences. Hybridity was defined as "the grafting or forcing of incompatible entities to grow together (or not)."[26] In biological terms, whereas a species is that which can reproduce, the hybrid is the infertile offspring of two different species.[27] From this the idea developed that since when different species of animals mated the offspring were infertile, when different races of humans had children together, their fertility would diminish over time and they would degenerate,[28] a sentiment voiced in the anonymous 1919 tract *Dönmeler: Hunyos, Kavayeros, Sazan*. The contamination of the pure race would lead to its decline and eventual extinction. The Dönme, of course, were neither hybrid nor creole; for centuries they had steadfastly guarded their biological separation from other groups. In fact, racialized Turkish nationalism shared the same principle with the Dönme way of being: the importance of maintaining purity and distinction between insiders and outsiders.

Nationalism is based on binary dualisms such as purity and impurity. But purity is an irreconcilable dualism. Mixedness is related to contamination, and nation-states such as the Turkish Republic denied the actual composite origins of its citizens and foreclosed a transcultural mestizo future out of fear for the health and perpetuity of the race. In the new Turkish Republic there was a desire to create a Turkish race by denying its actual mixed elements and precluding further mixing. Citizens of the new Turkish nation-state anxiously wondered what would happen if "true" Turks intermarried with Dönme, and whether this would harm the future of the Turkish race, causing it to degenerate. The roots of the Turkish plant were pure, it was believed, and would grow without grafting; neither hybridity nor cross-fertilization was desired. The Dönme could not be seen as a bridge to the future; rather, they represented the encircling vines of the Ottoman past, which needed to be uprooted, or the dead past, which was to be expunged.

As with matters of racial contamination, others voiced a general concern about a Dönme economic threat. An economist interviewed by the same newspaper worried that Dönme would "take the nation's economy completely in their hands." Yet some historians claim that a Dönme led the government-backed National Turkish Commercial Union (Milli Türk Ticaret Birliği), which aided the Muslim takeover of finance and banking and the purchase of Christian and Jewish businesses, and that many other members of it were also Dönme. Alexis Alexandris suggests that Ankara backed the Union as a ploy to win over the Dönme.[29] In the light of everything we know about opposition to the Dönme, and government knowledge of who was a Dönme, however, this does not appear to be a logical claim. It makes little sense when there was popular and official fear of Dönme and Jewish economic domination. In parliament, two MPs called for ridding the Turkish economy and government offices of Jews. They argued Jews posed a threat, and immediately should be kicked out of the Istanbul Stock Exchange, and that others should be aware that some so-called Turkish merchants were actually secret Jews.[30] Moreover, when one examines the list of the founding members, current officeholders, and members of the National Turkish Commercial Union, as reported in a British ambassadorial report, which contains no reference to them being Dönme, despite British attention to such details in other contemporary documents, one does not find any recognizable Dönme names.[31] There was firm opposition to the Dönme on racial, biological, and economic grounds.[32]

If their racial or inherent difference could be proven, Dönme in Turkey could not be assimilated and made into citizens. Racism could be used to hinder their integration and exclude them from the body politic. What strategies could a Dönme deploy to avoid the damning rhetoric of race? Would an argument presenting the Dönme as longtime loyal servants who were already secular be the more pragmatic path?

Ahmet Emin Yalman: Civic National Identity

People were thirsty for knowledge, and editors realized newspapers were selling briskly. At a time when foreign writers such as Wladimer Gordlevsky admitted that it was difficult for the researcher to rip away the veil of reserve and suspicion within which the Dönme were wrapped,[33] many Turkish newspapers persisted, seeking to uncover their secrets. To contribute to the discussion, the Islamist journal *Mihrab* (Prayer Niche) translated three pages devoted to the Dönme in Jean Brunhes and Camille Vallaux's *La géographie de l'histoire* that claimed that these anti-Muslim secret Jews had fomented the revolutions of 1908 and 1923.[34] Articles on the subject appeared in *Resimli Dünya* (The World in Pictures), *Resimli Gazete* (Photo News), and *Son Saat* (The Last Hour). The latter published a long series entitled "How Did Sabbateanism Appear, How Did it Develop?"[35] *Vakit*, determined to get to the bottom of the story, had its Ankara correspondent İhsan Arif write a report based on Dönme informers, including Rüştü, about Dönme beliefs, customs, prayers, and holidays.[36]

Many of the stories were sensationalist. Scholars and the public have long been interested in claims that the Dönme engaged in what is popularly known as "wife-swapping" in the West and "extinguishing (snuffing) the candle" in the East, a phrase Major Sadık unfortunately used in his treatise defending the Dönme.[37] Since ancient times, these phrases have historically been used, not to express the actual practices of religious or political dissenters, but to serve as metaphors emphasizing how antinomian or immoral they are, to strike fear into the hearts of other members of society about the alleged threat the group poses to society, especially if it should come to power. In Islamic history, allegations of "wife sharing" usually were automatically added at the end of a laundry list of claims of "communism" and property sharing, improper sexual behavior and moral laxity serving merely to illustrate how dishonorable these dissenters were. And in the Islamic world, claims throughout the centuries that widely differing groups have engaged in the same practice of "extinguishing the candle" makes one cautious about believing whether there can be even a kernel of truth in such attacks. Furthermore, claims of orgies, sexual rites, and swinging have interested sexually repressed bourgeois societies since Victorian times. Writing during the Victorian age, Lucy Garnett claimed about the Dönme, "As, however, little or nothing is positively known of their beliefs and practices, conjecture has full scope, and the imagination of their chief enemies, the Jews, runs riot in inventing crimes to lay at their door. They are accused of holding secret assemblies by night, at which they indulge in every kind of immorality, an accusation which has been brought against every peculiar sect which has made any secret of its doctrine."[38]

The Ottoman-language daily *Resimli Dünya* published one of the most lurid accounts of Dönme practice. A three-part account beginning in September 1925 concerned Meziyet Hanım, allegedly a Karakaş Dönme, who claimed that in 1923 her family, because they disapproved of her being in love with a man who was not a Dönme, and because she misled them by lying, saying it was too late not to marry him, for he had already impregnated her, dressed her up and sent her to a secret compound in Fatih, Istanbul, where she was forced to have sex with relatives. This must have reminded readers of charges of "extinguishing the candle."[39] In October, *Resimli Dünya* published an account by a young Kapancı who asserted: "I believe that the ceremony called 'the extinguishing of the candles' is still practiced by the Karakaş. I believe also that it was practiced by members of my group."[40] However, because he was single, and the ritualized sex was only practiced by married couples, he had had no opportunity to confirm its existence. This may have been a case of shifting the blame or having the public focus on the other still practicing Dönme group. Ottoman and then Turkish newspapers in this era were filled of such reports, and not only about the Dönme. Several years later, *Akşam* published a story about how "some individuals who were practicing the ceremony of the 'extinction of the candles' in a room were caught in *flagrant délit*."[41] The people in question were not Dönme, but Alevi, another group in the Ottoman Empire long subject to accusations of immorality.[42]

Those who spoke about the custom in the Turkish press were either outspoken enemies of the group or young people who had only heard about, not actually witnessed, the custom. Rüştü was one of the former. He confirms the existence of Dönme swinging at the spring festival.[43] An example of the latter was a young Dönme who claimed that the Karakaş still engaged in the practice (echoing Rüştü), but that the Kapancı no longer did, saying that "until recently Dönme were not allowed to consume lamb before celebrating the Festival of the Lamb. On that spring night, they boiled blessed lamb meat while performing prayer. A piece of cooked lamb was sent to every family; only after that were they allowed to buy lamb from the butcher." The reason he had not experienced the festival was that "Bachelors were not admitted. Only couples could participate. Bachelors were probably prohibited because they could not offer their own wife to share when the lights were extinguished. I tried to investigate the nature of this festival, but I only was told that I would learn about it after I married. But by now none of these practices remain among the Kapancı."[44]

Thus of two published accounts, both come from sources who had a reason to cast aspersions on the Karakaş, the Dönme group that still allegedly engaged in the practice. An outside observer, Gordlevsky, also mentions the ritual in his discussion of the debate in the press about the identity of the Dönme. But no internal evidence has emerged that the Dönme practiced it after they were compelled to migrate to Turkey; rather, the memory of such practices in Salonika was used as fuel for the fire by those who opposed the Dönme's inclusion in the new Turkish society being constructed.

Most articles about the Dönme in the 1920s were written in such inflammatory fashion. In great contrast to this trend, the most sympathetic, non-sensationalist study of Shabbatai Tzevi and the Dönme appeared in the daily newspaper *Vatan* (Fatherland). Following a week of front-page stories about the Dönme in other Istanbul dailies, including the persuasive petitions, writings, and interviews of Rüştü and others who asked why the Dönme, who differed in blood, race, and religion from Turks and Muslims (considered the same), had been allowed to immigrate to Turkey, it was not surprising that when readers purchased a copy of *Vatan* on Friday, January 11, 1924, they were met with a front-page article entitled "Tarihin Esrarengiz bir Sahifesi" (A Mysterious Page of History), written by an anonymous "investigator of history." This newspaper stood out from the rest. In a series of columns published on January 11–17 and 19–22, its readers were treated to the history of the Dönme, whom the author labels "Salonikans." It adopted a civic understanding of national identity, advocating an idea of the nation as a cultural identity to which people could choose to ascribe, and presents a historical and sociological narrative of the origins and history of the group. Ahmet Emin Yalman, the newspaper's founder and owner, was not only the editor-in-chief, but also a Yakubi Dönme who had received a Ph.D. in sociology from Columbia University. Most of the series—nine of the eleven articles—is devoted to a Yakubi narrative of Dönme history, the most assimilated and Muslim of the Dönme. The terminology, point of view, depth of knowledge, and methodology of the articles all suggest that the author was Yalman, a former student of Şemsi Efendi's at the Feyziye, like Rüştü.[45]

The author says he will seek to establish the truth from the material he has collected. This includes history books, namely, Naima's eighteenth century Ottoman-language history (which contains not a word about Shabbatai Tzevi and the Dönme) and a compilation of history (which I could not locate), and partly from oral history conducted with various men, clearly Dönme informers, most likely Karakaş, the only group he asserts is still thriving. The value of these articles thus lies less in their verifiable factual accuracy than in their being an articulation of Dönme history and the Dönme experience from a Dönme perspective in the crucial year 1924, containing information unavailable elsewhere.

The author makes his position clear in the first article. Like Rüştü, Yalman begins by anachronistically castigating Ottoman society and its plural nature. Since no unifying melting pot was to be found, a cultural mosaic prevailed. He asserts the problem of the Salonikans, the term he uses for the Dönme, who formed an insignificant part of the mosaic, "partly liquidated itself. It is necessary to liquidate its remaining debris." He attacks the Ottoman Empire's political system, which he considers strange. Rather than tolerance, it should be regarded as "indifference, ignorance, and the absence of the links of social solidarity." He bemoans what he sees as the fact that "while all over the world people engaged in a fusion movement with the weapon of nationalism, and naturally had recourse to every means of pressure in order to mold the distinct types of the country's people into one, the Ottoman sultan left everyone to his fate. In place of acts that would produce homogeneity, acts that would produce difference and variety prevailed." The Ottoman Empire lagged behind every other country in its zeal for assimilation and interest in producing a homogeneous population, breaking its medieval chains, and making progress. Yalman argues that the

Ottoman Empire remained the most "backward" and "primitive" because it did not unite its people in a single nationalism. Many Sufi orders, sects, particular group organizations, and local characteristics distinguish this country's people from one another. He demands that in order to develop Turkey, a true melting pot must be established, "asking everyone, 'Are you one of us or not?'; considering as one's own the parts that are assimilated or can be assimilated; and throwing out of Turkish society and framework the foreign parts that do not accept assimilation."

Having established this general historical and social framework, and critique of pluralism, Yalman is ready to focus on the Dönme as the example that proves his theory. Within the Ottoman Empire's mosaic framework "a number of mysterious groups that were formed in Salonika in the seventeenth century deserve our attention." Although numerically insignificant, "these mysterious groups displayed such unusual character-istics—having a secret existence, separating themselves from others—that that [Ottoman] society, which within a generation considered its own individuals who joined it, and did not find it necessary to inquire into the origin of a person who called himself a Turk and a Muslim, became slightly indignant." He again complains of Ottoman tolerance, arguing that in no other country would society faced with such a tendency have merely displayed mild indignation, for it certainly would have insisted that that group come out into the open, and either completely swallow and assimilate it or label it foreign.

Nevertheless, such groups are disappearing. Even without society's pres-sure, "time, knowledge, and wisdom have done their duty. Two of the Dönme groups no longer formed coherent, organized bodies. The third, and here he has the Karakaş in mind, still manifests some outdated be-liefs and practices. Linear progression is not enough. Yalman states baldly: "This problem must be decisively liquidated." He argues those who refuse to assimilate by saying that as members of a Muslim school of thought or Sufi order, they have unique characteristics, consider themselves separate, and intend to remain separate must be brought into the open. And in one of the most important lines in the article, Yalman asserts that in contrast, "Those who are truly Turkish and Muslim must be distinguished in public opinion and must be saved from the necessity of carrying on their back the social stain and mark that is only appropriate for those who are not."

Yalman's aim was "to render safe and sure the decisive dissolution and disappearance of this ridiculous situation," the continued existence of the

Dönme.[46] What bothered him, and compelled him to write the series, was that, unlike those of other premodern "charlatans," Shabbatai Tzevi's name had never been buried in the past and had become the issue of the day in the columns of newspapers such as his own *Vatan*.[47] In the new republic, identity would not be self-ascribed; the state would impose an identity on the population. In the past, difference always prevailed, an unfortunate legacy for the new nation-state of Turkey, where the populace was divided by many local identities. Like Rüştü, Yalman argues in favor of transparency, for the only action that would put the new Turkish nation on the path of development was the creation of a Turkish melting pot, to be accomplished by accepting individuals and groups that could be assimilated, and throwing out those that did not accept their Turkification. Yalman depicts the Ottomans the way secular Turkish nationalists saw the empire at the beginning of the republic. Tolerance and pluralism were the problem, homogeneity and nationalism the solution.

The Dönme is the group that most clearly signals for him the disturbing persistence of difference. He castigates Ottoman society since it did not investigate converts' backgrounds, a position Yalman would later interpret in a positive fashion. He also notes that whatever opposition they faced in society was in part their own fault, because they kept themselves as a group apart. He asserts that the Dönme call themselves Turks and Muslims, yet actually maintain a secret life. In sharp contrast to the assertions of Rüştü, the author says the Dönme are becoming "extinct" since they are dissolving as a community and abandoning a corporate identity. He speaks most favorably of the Yakubi, who he says are sincere, pious Muslims who fulfill the obligations of Sunni Islam and have produced many Muslim religious scholars and learned men capable of reciting Sufi poetry.[48] Indeed, one of Yalman's relatives told me that his ancestors were Muslims who included Sufi sheikhs in a Sufi lodge in Salonika, and Arabic calligraphers who decorated mosques.[49] Yet according to Yalman, writing in the 1920s, some still manifested "superstitions" and characteristics that "must be decisively eliminated." Unlike Rüştü, Yalman asserts that this is not an issue for the government; only social pressure can solve this societal problem. Surprisingly, he then declares that if some people still desire to be separate, it is their duty to openly proclaim their identity and their wish to remain apart. Was he offering the Dönme the autonomous status that non-Muslims were given in the Ottoman Empire but had recently publicly abandoned? According to Yalman, there is freedom of conscience in Turkey, and no one is to be subject to persecution on account of behaving differently. He then contradicts himself by asserting that the Dönme had to understand the true nature of the Turkish body politic and act accordingly by assimilating, for they had no other choice. One could no longer have a separate identity.

Yalman attributes the centuries-long coherence of the Dönme as a social group to the fact that the original families, faced hostile external pressure, turned inward and decided not to mix with others.[50] Their marriage pattern was the only reason they were able to maintain their separation from the society around them and did not disappear without a trace like other groups. Although the younger generation ceased following "tribal superstitions," the Dönme continued to exist in the 1920s, since they were slow to end endogamous marriage. Yet marrying out was "increasingly and definitively demolishing the old walls."[51]

As for their future, the author asserts that for the Yakubi, since the 1880s, the organization of the community and the marks that distinguished its members from others had disappeared; the new generation opposed the stultifying conditions of being members of the "tribe."[52] They knew nothing about their own customs. As governor of Salonika in 1874,[53] Midhat Pasha was astonished to find some of his employees with shaved heads, and he was informed that they were members of a Sufi order.[54] In fact, they were Yakubi Dönme, who wore beards as well.[55] He ordered that those who shaved their heads would be fired. Yakubis pledged to grow their hair, a great blow to the separateness of the group. Yet they opposed innovation, which was why they dressed the same way in the 1870s as they had the previous century. According to Yalman, "within this circle of black ignorance, carrying out Midhat Pasha's commands opened some eyes." The new generation raised between 1874 and 1883 began to feel a sense of rebellion and opposed the leader of the community's commands. He rained banishment punishments upon them for opposing his orders, but they were not moved. They only, it is said, respected those who were close to God (*veli*). This may be a reference to Shabbatai Tzevi. Yalman, who was born in 1888, was likely including his father, Osman Tevfik, in this group. They did not desire to be members of the "tribe" and hid the fact that they had been born into it. Yalman says in this series of articles in *Vatan* that writers in the literary magazine *Gonca-i Edeb*, founded in 1883 by Osman Tevfik and other young Yakubis, declared Shabbatai Tzevi to have been a charlatan. I have scoured the entire run of *Gonca-i Edeb*, however, and found no such assertion.[56] Yalman also argues that they wrote that it was ridiculous to remain a member of a secret order and not intermarry with the Turkish and Muslim community. The leaders began to accept some innovations, including the study of foreign languages, and the study of law and civil service, and later still, Yakubi youth were permitted to become pharmacists and veterinarians. Eventually, they could study medicine, and then be educated in Istanbul and Europe.

Yalman says that pronouncements against innovation did not matter much to the new generation. They opposed being members of the tribe and tried to forget the fact of their origins and have it be forgotten as fast as they could. Especially when serving as civil servants, they even hid the fact that they had been born in Salonika. Since the 1880s, the organization of the community and marks that distinguished them from others had disappeared; they had ceased to practice endogamous marriage and keep a separate cemetery. Yalman concludes by declaring: "The two-century existence of this strange society is completely a thing of the past. Today one can only find a feeling of attachment to the past in the minds of a few elderly people who are in their seventies and eighties." Because they view the past as completely extinct, the elderly "do not even dare mention it to the new generations, who view it as a ridiculous nightmare. People sent to the four corners of the nation as civil servants have completely become part of the general [Turkish and Muslim] society."[57]

In his penultimate column, Yalman turns to the new Karakaş and Kapancı schools established in Salonika. After the youth rebelled and demanded a serious education in the 1870s, the Feyziye primary school was opened, and for the first time, very well educated young Karakaş and Kapancı emerged. A five- or ten-year renaissance erased two centuries of poverty and ignorance. This was owing in part to the new schools, which were the finest in the empire.[58]

Whereas the Yakubis were primarily involved in government, the Karakaş were primarily engaged in crafts, trade, and commerce, Yalman says, although they produced many professionals and civil servants as well. The Kapancı were predominantly businessmen. This was important for Yalman, who sought to understand the reason for the Dönme's persistence and the perpetuation of their "tribal" organization. Like endogamous marriage, economic ties also hindered the breaking up of the community and its dissolution in the general population. He asserts that for the Karakaş, "had it not been for economic ties, there is no doubt that their breaking up would have been complete, as it was for the other two groups."[59] The Kapancı, "after managing to stay united for a while because of economic ties, later began to break up due to social reasons." The process of assimilation was not yet complete, however, he says in the final article. Some "debris" remained and needed "clearly to be swept away."[60]

Yalman argues that the discussion of Rüştü's pronouncements presented a good opportunity to compel the dissolution of the "tribe" and to "publicly rip off the veil of secrecy that has been covering them for centuries, and do away with it once and for all." He finds it astonishing that people were "kept captive for generations by a charlatan" named Shabbatai Tzevi, "engaged in ridiculous practices that anthropologists encounter only among the most simple and primitive tribes," or endogamy, and that they had existed for so long. Dönme had maintained their difference mainly through endogamy; even after they stopped believing in the practice, it continued due to their strict obedience to their parents. The Dönme had consolidated as a group because of the lack of acceptance by others, and had maintained their identity for centuries due to internal marriage. If only others would accept them, he implies, they would assimilate. He also places part of the responsibility on the shoulders of the Dönme. Marrying out was, however increasingly and definitively breaking down the barriers between Dönme and Muslims. Only a few traces remained among the elderly Karakaş, mainly, mutual assistance and the desire to maintain a separate cemetery. Yalman criticizes them for only wanting to aid those they knew; he urges them to tear down the old group barriers, help all Turks and Muslims, and give up the "ridiculous" idea of having a separate cemetery, since if they were Muslims, they could be buried with other Muslims. Rational men should scrap meaningless old beliefs. Nevertheless, although it was "ridiculous that for generations, three tribes had lived a life in Salonika as a Sufi order, bound by superstition, or as a secret society," the low incidence among the Dönme of murderers, criminals, and paupers was praiseworthy, and a modernized version of their system of social control and mutual assistance could usefully be employed in cities like Istanbul.

Overall, Yalman gives a rather positive assessment of the Dönme. Although he admits that they have distinct customs, he describes the Yakubis as living by the laws of Islam, not those of Judaism. The new generation of progressive youth identify with Turkey and the nation. Dönme identity should be considered a social and not a governmental problem.

No one should be persecuted. What is remarkable is how, contrary to all other accounts, he does not mention Dönme beliefs and race, or the role they had played in the revolution of 1908, the CUP, and the economy. On the heated question of whether Dönme were Jews or Muslims, foreigners or Turks, he says, primarily referring to the Yakubi, that they were just another "backward" Sufi order (*tarikat*), a unique sect within the Muslim community that was on the verge of dissolution. Using the term *tarikat* allows him to place the Dönme, or at least the Yakubi, within the Muslim community as a unique Sufi group. Moreover, he asserts that they are few in number. Unlike the figure of ten to fifteen thousand Dönme spoken of in the press, the only numbers Yalman mentions are the two hundred original families that followed Shabbatai Tzevi into conversion, the forty-three Yakubi families, and the original thirteen people that followed the anti-Yakubi split.

Yalman tried to calm the public by asserting that Dönme separateness was a thing of the past, and that members of the group had for generations been serving the nation and allying with its causes. His efforts to do so strike the reader as those of a person attempting to prevent his own future from being clouded by his background. "Those who are truly Turkish and Muslim must be distinguished in public opinion" and "saved from . . . the burden of the social stain . . . that is only fitting for those who are not," he writes in the *Vatan* series. His strategy was to promote nationality as a conscious political identity, using the metaphor of the melting pot to represent the process by which diverse individuals were to be recreated in "preexisting cultural and social molds," modeled on Turks and Muslims.[61] Non-Turkish and non-Muslim elements would, however, be incorporated into Turkish society. Dropping distinct religious identities, and emancipated from backward tradition, minorities would adopt the secular national identity and be rewarded by being treated as equals in the new nation.[62] They would convert to Turkishness. But what if they did not want to change? What if they resisted cultural conversion?

İbrahim Alâettin Gövsa: Beliefs and Customs Rather Than Race or Social Group

§ Allowed entry into the Office of the Principal at the Makriköy [Bakırköy] Girls' Boarding School in Istanbul in the winter of 1924, we would find a serious man whose pale white skin makes his thick black eyebrows seem even darker than they are. And when he furrows his brow, which he does often, the effect is even greater. The series published in *Vatan* makes him furrow his brow. He has read it with great interest. This native of Istanbul is the principal of a Karakaş Dönme school and knows that the author of "A Mysterious Page of History," a close friend, like him at the time in his mid-thirties, had attended the original Karakaş school in Salonika. But there is something deeply wrong with the argument. Yalman must have known better. In 1939, İbrahim Alâettin Gövsa (1889–1949) would write a book that offers a point-by-point rebuttal of Yalman's claims, saying:

> I am one who knows intimately that Shabbatai Tzevi's traditions are not merely superstitions that are a thing of the past. Although the series in *Vatan* entitled "A Mysterious Page of History" claims that other than mutual assistance among members of the group, nothing else remains to distinguish [the Dönme], and that their former traditions and superstitions are a thing of the past, I am the director of a school established by this group, and having been among them for a year and a half, I have personally witnessed how traditions and customs of Shabbatai Tzevi still predominate in their lives. In fact, I have found half-Hebrew, half-Spanish [Ladino] prayers in the notebooks of seven and eight-year-old Shabbatean [Dönme] children that their families had them memorize.[63]

Avram Galanté published his *Nouveaux documents sur Sabbetaï Sevi: Organisation et us et coutumes de ses adeptes* (New Documents on Shabbatai Tzevi: The Organization and Customs of His Followers) in French in 1935, reclaiming the Dönme for Judaism and the Jewish community, and Mustafa Kemal Atatürk died three years later, in 1938. Only then did Gövsa decide to add his personal knowledge to Galanté's account and present it in Turkish. The abandonment of Dönme belief—a fait accompli, according to Yalman's series in *Vatan*—would mean the conversion of the group. But Gövsa's observation of the Dönme provided evidence of the persistence of their unique beliefs, disproving his close friend Yalman.[64]

Gövsa first published *Sabatay Sevi: İzmirli meşhur sahte mesih hakkında tarihî ve içtimaî tetkik tecrübesi* (Sabbatai Sevi: A Historical and Sociological Study of the Famous False Messiah of Izmir), based on his experience with Dönme youth in the early 1920s,[65] as a series in the weekly *Yedi Gün* (Seven Days).[66] I find evidence suggesting that Gövsa was a member of the Karakaş. Rüştü and Yalman had both attended a Karakaş school in Salonika, and Gövsa was principal of a Karakaş school in Istanbul. The

debate over Dönme identity was thus among three men who had intimate knowledge of the Karakaş, the group most reluctant to give up its
customs. Whether Gövsa was a Dönme or not, Dönme disliked him for
publishing the first Turkish-language monograph explaining Dönme history and religion to the public.[67]

Gövsa argues that "the traces that Shabbatai Tzevi left behind are more
important than the movement during his lifetime" since the memory of
the messianic figure, "if only among a small group, is still kept fully alive"
(3). He notes how Rüştü had "revealed some of the secrets of the group
to which he belongs," and that the first analysis of Shabbatai Tzevi and
the Dönme in Turkish had appeared in *Vatan*, "which is published by this
group" (4). But he criticizes Yalman's series for "trying to convince everyone that the characteristics and customs of the group that Rüştü insists
are still alive and continuing are actually superstitions that have become a
thing of the past" (5).

According to Gövsa, only fifteen years before, in 1924, when Yalman's
series of articles appeared, Dönme children had begun their prayers with
the Judeo-Spanish words "In the blessed name of Shabbatai Tzevi, who
governs half the world. . . ." As evidence that their religion was alive and
developing, and that there was still a coherent community of Dönme,
Gövsa claimed that Karakaş prayers were also changing, as were their titles for their religious leaders. He notes the use of new titles in quoting a
1937 death announcement in *Cumhuriyet* (Republic) of a Salonikan (i.e.,
Dönme) man who resided in Şişli and was buried in his family's tomb
in Üsküdar, shorthand for the main Dönme cemetery (77). Moreover,
because Dönme cannot eat lamb before the "Month of the Lamb," the
school cook refused to cook lamb before that time (96).[68] Gövsa notes
that although there are Dönme who have begun to mix with the general
population and intermarry, "nevertheless, even if only for a small group, it
cannot be denied that the memory of Shabbatai Tzevi is still kept energet-
ically alive." Gövsa then defends freedom of religion in Turkey, and says
"there are intelligent and valuable members of Shabbatai's group who play
an important role in the nation's economic and intellectual life, including
some who are my friends," (6) most likely referring to Yalman.

Rather than arguing along the lines of race like Rüştü, Gövsa places
Dönme religion at the center of his analysis. Basing himself also on the
recently published monograph by Galanté, Gövsa notes that internal reasons had compelled the Dönme to maintain their distinctness. Unlike Yal-

man, who presented sociological reasons for their isolation, Gövsa argued Dönme did not intermarry and engaged in mutual assistance because they were following the commandments of Shabbatai Tzevi (71). Dönme acted as Muslims, yet actually celebrated religious festivals according to the traditions of Shabbatai Tzevi, some members of the group still enacting them (79–80). Gövsa attacks the series of articles written by Yalman for hiding the practice of Dönme religion, saying that *Vatan,* "which is published by the Shabbatean group," had published these articles as a response to the claims of Rüştü. The series "hides the special commandments of the Shabbatean group and takes every opportunity to claim that the group's traditions are either about to disappear, or have disappeared." What Gövsa found, however, was the contrary: "But even if what they claim may be true for some, it cannot be denied that some of Shabbatai's beliefs are still kept alive, his customs are enacted from birth to death, and there are Shabbateans who maintain their separateness by living in distinct neighborhoods and being buried in separate cemeteries" (81–82).

For Gövsa, the Dönme had established a distinct religion. He criticizes *Vatan* for not saying that the Shabbateans had their own belief system, distinct from Judaism, and that they and their community and life were organized around it (82). *Vatan* had claimed that the Dönme had become a closed community because of lack of acceptance by the larger community, but Gövsa argues that internal religious reasons, particularly commitment to the eighteen commandments of Shabbatai Tzevi, such as "Only marry among yourselves. Only engage in their customs and rituals so they (Muslims) see you performing them" (83), compelled them to guard their distinctness, not merely conservatism. The old walls had been torn down for some, but the other walls had become stronger (84). And at the time was writing, religious motivation continued to be primary. The Dönme did not only engage in endogamy and mutual assistance out of conservatism, Gövsa asserts, and nor were the only believers who remained elderly. On the contrary, children recited Dönme prayers, and endogamous marriage customs were central to their entire belief system (84).

As to Yalman's suggestion that the Dönme model of mutual assistance be applied to all of society, Gövsa writes acerbically: "If people who believe the same thing help each other, why would they help others who do not believe? Don't they keep a separate graveyard due to their beliefs as well? Calling it 'ridiculous' cannot cover it up. What is ridiculous is believing he [Yalman] can fool everyone." (85).

Gövsa also asserts there is no Sufi order called Dönme, and that the Dönme religion is something distinct from Islam, saying: "The *Vatan* series speaks of a Sufi order and secret society, but there is no Muslim Sufi order called Shabbatean, nor has there [ever] been such a secret society in Turkish political history." In sum, "Shabbateanism is something distinct from Islam and Judaism. Wouldn't it be more sincere to say this?" (85). He concludes by defining the Dönme as a group similar in form to a community that is formed according to beliefs, such as the non-Muslims in Turkey. Finally, Gövsa accuses Yalman of trying to protect the Dönme religion that is still living, while promoting the integration of the Dönme with the rest of society, although using language that hints at sympathy for his friend Yalman's predicament: "One can sense in every sentence of the series the stress of one who aims to cover up and protect today's living Shabbateanism, and the same time desires to mix with the rest of society" (86).

Although Dönme belief did persist in the first two decades of the Turkish Republic, not every example that Gövsa cites meant that the Dönme who engaged in these rites and rituals continued to believe in the messianism of Shabbatai Tzevi. Continued endogamous marriage also may have stemmed from a reluctance of Dönme to intermarry with Muslims, and vice versa, for reasons of class and culture as well as anxiety over racial degeneration, as well as the fact that being Dönme had a religious as well as ethnic or identity component. Continued adherence to Dönme customs may have helped to consolidate their corporate unity in their new locale and enhanced their ability to continue working together in the national and transnational economy. Finally, reciting prayers in Ladino may have given Dönme an emotional sense of grounding amid the upheaval that marked their lives in the period. It did not mean that they understood what they were saying. As Yitzhak Ben-Tzevi noted a few years after Gövsa's book appeared, the Dönme's ancient prayers had been "converted into a 'learned tradition.' Their contents were forgotten while all that remained was the holy shell, that is, the words themselves."[69]

Assessing Dönme Strategies

Less than two years after the debate that he had begun, Rüştü completely reversed himself. He claimed astonishingly that as "a person who had in actual fact left the Dönme religion and assimilated into pure Turkishness," he could now attest that "our great spiritual guide Gazi Pasha

[Atatürk]'s bombs of enlightenment had blown up the Dönme houses of worship, prayers, books, and superstitions," that the Dönme had assented to the ideal of Turkishness, had been saved from the affliction of being Dönme, and thus the Dönme problem had been solved.[70] No longer should anyone view the Dönme as a separate group. They were nothing other than Turks, the title "Dönme" should be finally buried, they deserved to appear in public like their Muslim coreligionists with nothing to be ashamed of, and "every one must know that there are no longer any Dönme."[71] He then disappeared from the historical record. Yalman, reflecting the main option available to Dönme at the time, became a prominent, fervent, and vocal Turkish nationalist.

It is understandable why Rüştü and Yalman publicly called for all Dönme to become Turks. Yet why were they not concerned only about their own personal integration? Was denigrating their origins, Dönme "superstitions," and the "charlatanism" of Shabbatai Tzevi a way to establish authenticity? Answers to these questions may come from judging Dönme actions against those of Jewish converts seeking integration in Europe. Comparing the attitudes of Jewish converts to Christianity toward Jews in contemporary Britain and Germany, Todd Endelman found that when societies are more resistant to integration, and demand that minorities prove their citizenship by freeing themselves of minority identities, individuals with minority backgrounds are compelled to distance themselves in public from unconverted members of their communities and even urge others to follow their example.[72] The experience of Jewish converts in Europe and Dönme in Turkey reflects the difficulty of converting to secular identities, both in the eyes of the converts and the majority. The main difference was that the Dönme had changed religion over two centuries prior to the period when the sincerity of their conversion was called into question. Some people from both groups publicly denounced the group that they sought to abandon in order to be accepted by the group they were attempting to join. Individuals with fractured identities, such as Rüştü and Yalman, who seek personal salvation through cultural conversion, but find that the society denies the affiliation they desire, discover a role as intermediaries between society and the community.

Moreover, Yalman's arguments call to mind those of the German Jewish intellectual Moritz Lazarus in response to the antisemitic attacks of Heinrich von Treitschke, who cast doubt on the ability of Jews to assimilate in the late nineteenth century. Lazarus, like Yalman a prolific writer for public and academic audiences alike, also promoted voluntaristic nationhood and used the widely prevalent term "tribe" to denote ethnicity, common descent and history, and communal and group consciousness, although in a positive sense. Such pockets of tribal communities, however, became a thorn in the side of nationalists who could not tolerate plurality, and for whom such differences stood in the way of national unity, which demanded the forfeiting of tribal identities and loyalties. To overcome their objections, people like Lazarus and Yalman argued that nations are not given or objective, but made and subjective, created by those, even diverse tribes, who consciously and voluntarily help build them.[73] For Lazarus, German Jews had proven themselves on the battlefield, served in parliament, in the judiciary, hospitals, and universities. For Yalman, the Dönme had also served the nation at a crucial juncture in its formation.

One is tempted to argue that rather than promoting strategies of assimilation or dissolution, Rüştü and Yalman wanted to be seen opposing Dönme separatism, when in fact they were adopting false personas, masks of secularism, the appearance of disappearance, in order to hide their true identities, maintaining their duplicity to protect the community. Rüştü's early declaration that "When people told me I was a Jew, I took it as a painful insult, sharp as a knife. Thankfully, the Turkish Republic has been established. The time is ripe. That is why I openly declared myself a Muslim" can be interpreted in this fashion.[74] So can his final public assertions that all Dönme had completely assimilated. Secret adherence to Dönme customs could be immediately disavowed when necessary. Promoting the separation of religion and state could theoretically free minority groups from being hindered in their religious practices, as a tactic to create more freedom of religion in the private sphere.

Turkey maintained distinctions between groups in order to perpetuate the rule of one group. Where groups found themselves in the position of minorities, they had to explain who they were. If they kept their ethno-religious identities, they might have negated their welcome in the new state, but they may not have wanted to or could not abandon their identity, accept an ambivalent position in a new national civil society, or completely disappear.[75] For a group that was "not fully accepted by the Turks [Muslims] and rejected by the Jews,"[76] it may have been most tempting to maintain Dönme identity. Yet how could Dönme maintain a separate culture while incorporated into a nation whose defining characteristics were based on the majority culture and religion?[77] If they did not renounce their identity, minorities were branded separatists and perceived as a "fifth column," an internal danger to the majority. Even when they attempted to play their part, minorities were not always accepted as equal citizens in practice. Accordingly, minority groups sought other strategies for maintaining their corporate identities, such as dissimulation, which allowed them to act as the majority while maintaining beliefs and rites in private.

Some Dönme saw the possibility inherent in secularism to ostensibly become secular Turks in public, just as once they had manifested themselves as normal Muslims in order to continue their religious rituals and practices in private. By donning the mask of acceptable Sunni Islam, their ancestors had managed to flourish for over two centuries. It might seem difficult for readers to accept that the Dönme would want to integrate. Perhaps, it might be suggested, they were maintaining their duplicity. If that had been the case, however, why would Rüştü go to such great lengths to attract attention to the Dönme and ultimately himself, and how could Yalman, a well-known journalist, afford to risk exposing his secret rituals if he practiced any? Yalman's strategy may have been more successful. Rather than pointing out the group's racial difference, distinct belief system, and economic strength, the series in Yalman's newspaper presented the group as a relic of the past, which would soon completely disappear, just as republicans believed all traces of the Ottoman Empire had vanished.

How much did the debate among Rüştü, Yalman, and Gövsa reflect the Dönme lived experience? Attacked for their racial origins, religious beliefs and practices, and international commercial ties, and stripped of their wealth and capital, how could Dönme set up a new life in Turkey? Were they able to maintain practices and institutions of boundary maintaining such as self-segregation and their own schools as in Salonika? Did they continue to practice endogamy? Did they find it necessary? How did the Dönme and their leaders, particularly those visible in politics, fare during the first two decades of the Turkish Republic?

§8 Reinscribing the Dönme in the Secular Nation-State

Addressing the question of Istanbul schools in his autobiography, the Karakaş Dönme Reşat Tesal, a recent migrant from Salonika, wrote:

§ Most of my classmates were children who had come from Anatolia. They looked down on southeastern Europe and people from southeastern Europe, especially Salonikans. To them, Salonikans were Greek or Jewish converts to Islam. They taunted me by calling me "Salonikan," or "Mishon" [the stereotypical Jewish name in Turkey]. While I could have responded to these attacks by either turning the other cheek, or counterattacking, I got so angry I would run away and hide.

My life became better when I transferred to Feyziye in 1927. . . . The [Karakaş] Feyziye, with which my father had good contacts, had been my primary school in Salonika, and had recently moved from the Sultanahmet area to Nişantaşı, where I lived. It was also a school where they taught English and French very well, which was quite important to my family. Unlike my previous experience at school in Istanbul, I enjoyed the experience at Feyziye. My fellow classmates in the small classes included Salonikans and I instantly became close friends with everyone, including Ali Muhsin [from the Karakaş Kibar], the son of one of the school's owners, Kibar Muhsin Bey.[1]

Despite the challenge of losing their homeland and facing vicious attacks in their new domicile, some Dönme tried to maintain their bonds of distinction after 1923 by recreating their Salonikan lives in Istanbul and establishing a new center for their ethno-religious group strengthened by all the institutions and businesses they left behind on the other side of the sea. What distinguished them from others was that relatives settled together in several neighborhoods in Istanbul such as Nişantaşı, where some continued to faithfully observe the feasts, fasts, and festivals that Shabbatai Tzevi had established, and buried their dead in distinct cemeteries.[2] Şemsi Efendi, members of the Kapancı family, and teachers and graduates of the Terakki and Feyziye were buried in the main Dönme cemetery of Bülbüldere in Üsküdar, Istanbul. Dönme served on the board of and sent their children to the originally Salonikan Dönme schools relocated in Istanbul, resided in the neighborhood, which has at its center a mosque that in some uncanny ways calls to mind the mosque they built in Salonika, and most important, attempted to maintain their textile, timber, and tobacco businesses. Yet the international financial ties of the Dönme became a liability in the nation-state, which aimed to limit the boundaries of the nation. The Turkish Republic attempted through expropriations and exorbitant taxation to facilitate the rise of a Muslim Turkish bourgeoisie at the expense of such "foreign" groups as the Dönme. Influential Dönme faced state violence.

The Ottoman Finance Minister Mehmet Cavid, former head of a Karakaş school, was an advisor to the Turkish delegation at Lausanne in 1923, and in 1924 headed a committee preparing a report for the Istanbul Chamber of Commerce. Mehmet Cavid was an economic liberal, interested in linking the Ottoman and later Turkish economies to the world economy, to encourage and protect foreign investment. Such global thinking went against early Kemalism which sought to create a self-sustaining domestic economy.

Atatürk had little tolerance of economic liberalism, or his critics. He acted swiftly to rid himself of rivals. In 1926, Mehmet Cavid and the other key Dönme figure in the CUP, Dr. Nâzım, were executed in Ankara on charges of trying to resurrect the CUP and involvement in a plot to assassinate Atatürk in Izmir.[3] Ironically, Dr. Nâzım had been allowed back to Turkey by Atatürk from exile in Berlin, where he had escaped an assassination attempt by an Armenian on account of his role in the 1915–17 deportations and massacres of that people. Dr. Nâzım and Mehmet Cavid were accused of having met with another Dönme doctor, Tevfik Rüştü Aras, to plot a return of the CUP to power. Again ironically, their enemy Rıza Nur fled to France, and then Egypt, for fear that Atatürk would have him killed, and only returned to Turkey after Atatürk died in 1938.[4]

After this purge of surviving CUP leaders, Atatürk moved to downplay his past, membership in the CUP, and the connection between the CUP and the ultimately successful nationalist movement. From 1908 to 1926, the CUP had played a leading role in Ottoman and then Turkish politics; many leading participants in the national movement were former CUP members, and the movement was the heir of the CUP legacy, but the execution of the two leading Dönme in their ranks put an end to it. Atatürk also acted harshly against two other institutions that had contributed so much to the revolution of 1908: he banned Freemasonry and outlawed Sufi orders in 1925.

Istanbul and the Early Republic

The republic turned its back, not only on Dönme revolutionaries, but on the international economic ties, religious morality, and eclectic cultural outlook exemplified by Dönme-influenced Salonika. This is reflected in the choice of capital city. The republic did not favor international Constantinople, renamed Istanbul after the founding of the Republic, but invested in dusty Ankara, a small provincial town on the steppe famous only for its mohair (the fleece of the Angora goat), a city with only one, bad restaurant.[5] Istanbul had been either a Roman, Byzantine, or Ottoman capital for over 1,500 years and residence of ruling dynasties, the seat of the religious authorities, a city that housed armies of military men and bureaucrats and attracted artisans, scholars, and above all else, merchants.[6] The city boasted the largest market in the Mediterranean, was an importing and consuming colossus, and long the largest city in Europe. In the late nineteenth century, Istanbul, whose population was majority Christian, was a crucial node in the circulation of persons, money, commodities, and ideas. Bank buildings were erected there in the international style, along with monumental foreign embassies, and the "Parisian and Italianate *art nouveau* architecture preferred by the global bourgeoisie of the period."[7] The city's bankers, merchants, and new residents "built for themselves mansions, apartment buildings, hotels, clubs, restaurants, and cafés, as well as less reputable locales for entertainment" in the district known as Pera, where foreigners and upwardly mobile Christians and Jews lived, a district separated from the "Old City" by the Golden Horn.[8] This part of the city benefited from urban planning and renewal, like the waterfront districts of Salonika, and was endowed with paved roads and sidewalks, gas lamps, and electric trolleys.

By World War I, one-tenth of the city's million inhabitants were foreign subjects and fewer than half were non-Muslim. But foreign occupation and state policy stopped the city's cosmopolitanism dead in its tracks. First came the occupation of the British, French, and Italians from the end of World War I to 1922, and then the willful isolation of the city by the new Turkish Republic, which saw it as corrupt, amoral, and foreign. Istanbul was suspect for its being "Byzantine," inhabited by "'others,' those who were not really of us."[9] Transferring the capital to an inland place "without significations," and "a neutral space devoid of history and symbolic weight" illustrates the desire to "forget and erase from memory" coastal places associated with Greeks,[10] and one might add, people such as the Dönme who came from Greece.

In this period, some considered Istanbul to be the corrupt capital of a corrupt regime, "a Sodom," in contrast with the peasant town of Ankara, which according to Ahmet Emin Yalman, had "no hotels, no electric lights, and no conveniences. You had to carry your own bed and find a space for it in the house of a friend. When it was your turn to get a bite to eat in the only restaurant, called 'Anadolu' (the Turkish name for Anatolia), you certainly were not carried away by gastronomic delight." Nevertheless, in the author's view, it was comparable to Paradise, because it meant Turks were on the path to satisfy their dreams and desires, namely, the creation of a national home purified of extraneous elements.[11]

Istanbul lost its financial capital with the closing of seaborne connections to the Mediterranean and Black Seas during World War I, and had to abandon its cultural and political capital as well. It was no longer the center of an empire that stretched from Europe to the Persian Gulf, North Africa to Iran. Neither Christians nor Muslims could look to it as the center of the world, a borderland bridge between continents and cultural zones, the conductor of international flows of goods and capital. The symbol of a great plural empire was to the Turkish revolutionaries the emblem of anti-national and obscurantist religious forces that had to be destroyed. The elements leading Istanbul's cosmopolitanism and globalization, whether foreign, Levantine, non-Muslim, or Muslim "compradors" who were middlemen for colonial capital like the Dönme, were considered inauthentic, unwelcome in the nation-state. This may have contributed to urban violence, and the discriminatory, harsh, and even violent backlash against them. The Dönme were especially despised for they were labeled pejoratively "cosmopolitan," in Antonio Gramsci's sense of being detached, disengaged, hindering the development of the national culture and economy, not an organic element that would develop the nation.[12] In the new republic, the state was opposed to precisely the kind of intercultural borrowing, exchange, and trade that the Dönme represented, and to the Dönme as well, since cosmopolitans, like capital, seem to have no boundaries.[13]

According to this way of thinking, sovereignty of the nation must be ensured by sovereignty of the economy. Atatürk declared in 1923 to an assembly of Muslim Turkish craftsmen that "Armenians have no rights at all in this prosperous country. This land is yours, the land belongs to the Turks. In history this land was Turkish, therefore it is Turkish and will remain Turkish for ever. The land has finally been returned to its rightful owners. The Armenians and the others have no rights here at all. These blessed regions are the native lands of the true Turks."[14] Accordingly, foreigners and non-Muslims were fired from foreign businesses taken over by Muslims or the state and companies working for the public good, including banks. Private companies on contract with the state and municipalities were forced to expel non-Muslims and foreigners, which affected the communications, transportation, service, and utility sectors. Then the ax fell on bars, hotels, restaurants, and cafés. The municipal government closed establishments that did not ensure that employees were Muslim Turks. Non-Muslims and foreigners were thrown out of the Istanbul Chamber of Commerce. In order to turn its back on the global flow of goods, there was an ongoing state effort to encourage the consumption of "local goods" such as by requiring the wearing of clothes made with local textiles. Laws passed by parliament between 1924 and 1928 Turkified the Ottoman Bank, a symbol of non-Muslim economic dominance, mandated that account books and business records be kept in Turkish (rather than in French, as had hitherto often been the case), and employees in state service, and directors and accountants in industry had to be Turks, shorthand for local Muslims.

Non-Muslims and foreigners in Istanbul faced the full brunt of anti-global and anti-colonial economic nationalism and pent-up anger in response to the "capitulations" that exempted resident foreigners from Ottoman law and taxation, which over time gave foreigners and their local, mainly Christian and Jewish, partners and agents unfair privileges and commercial advantages.[15] Although the Christians of Istanbul were spared from the population exchange of 1923, they still faced great pressure to leave the city. The Christian population declined from 450,000 to 240,000 between 1914 and 1927. In 1927, the main street of Pera, the Grande Rue de Péra, officially became İstiklâl Caddesi, Independence Avenue. The city lost its cosmopolitan character, not only because the minority population shrunk as the total population of the city decreased by almost one-third in the same period,[16] but because it lost its orientation, its connection between the local and the international, its openness, its choice to be that way, as well as its being the home city of mobile diasporas.

Self-Segregation

Reflecting the loss of the cosmopolitan milieu from when they were based in Salonika during the days of empire, like other transregional ethno-religious groups, the Dönme had a much more restricted diaspora after they were forced to reside in the Turkish Republic. The Dönme migrants, no matter to which group they adhered, adopted similar strategies. At the same time, boundaries between the groups, and borders between Dönme and others, began to break down.

The great Kapancı merchant families mainly settled in Teşvikiye and Nişantaşı. According to interviews I conducted with a member of the family, the descendants of the great Kapancı tobacco merchant and early board member of the Terakki school Hasan Akif—namely, the family of his granddaughter Nuriye and grandson Ali Riza, who had married each other—moved from Brussels to Istanbul in 1939. World War II broke out while they were visiting their grandmother Fatma Akif, and they ended up staying. They settled in Nişantaşı, where exchangees were given homes of Orthodox Christians who had been expelled to Greece. This family did not need government assistance, because all of their family in Istanbul lived in the neighborhood. In Nişantaşı, they imagined that the Teşvikiye Mosque, which has the same inscription over the mihrab as the Dönme New Mosque in Salonika, resembled it and made them feel at home, as did the presence of so many relatives, fellow Dönme, and other Salonikans in the neighborhood. The same interviewee claimed that in the 1920s and 1930s, Dönme religious leaders prayed and performed rituals in the basement of the Teşvikiye mosque, usually for funerals of Dönme. They were joined two or three years later by the few relatives who had remained in Salonika, Nuriye's brother Akif Fuat and his family. Hasan

Akif's descendant, who moved to Istanbul at the age of four, told me that "we were like a community, we had our own way of life, which was a little different than that of those around us, even different than the Turkish upper crust. We had parties together, socialized together, worked together in the same trades."[17]

Boundaries between Dönme were hardly as strict in Istanbul as they had been in Salonika. Kapancı and Karakaş settled and opened their schools in the same neighborhoods and buried their dead in separate sections of the same cemetery.[18] Some distinctions were maintained. The Karakaş largely settled in Bakırköy, Bayezid, and Sultanahmet. Bakırköy became a virtual Salonikan colony. In fact, the Karakaş had been there since the 1860s. Salonikans settled there for business reasons or because of government appointments in Istanbul.[19] Bakırköy may also have been the neighborhood most closely resembling Hamidiye. In 1910, to meet the needs of the growing numbers of Dönme children the wealthy Karakaş family established the Makriköy (Bakırköy) Boarding and Day Union Girls School. The Feyz-i Ata in Bayezid was united with it in 1922. İbrahim Alâettin Gövsa, who was also one of the first directors of the Feyz-i Ata, ran the Makriköy school as well.

There is a street in Sultanahmet today named for the nineteenth- century French author Pierre Loti, partly devoted to tourists, partly to residents, and partly to bureaucrats. According to the narratives of many Karakaş, from the early 1920s to the late 1940s, the area south of Divan Yolu and today's Pierre Loti Hotel, then entirely filled with apartment buildings, was crowded with members of this Dönme group. A Karakaş descendant proudly pointed to the buildings in which his family had settled after arriving from Salonika. His grandfather had owned a building on the corner of Piyer Loti and Medrese streets, and his father had been born there in 1948, thereafter joining most other Dönme when he moved to Nişantaşı. Many of the Karakaş who arrived in the city with the population exchange settled first in Sultanahmet and Bayezid.[20] Another interviewee told me that Piyer Loti Street behind the Köprülü Library in Çemberlitaş was full of Dönme families. They remained there until they moved en masse to be near what she says was their mosque, the Teşvikiye Mosque in Nişantaşı.[21] Exchangees were originally sent to places all over Turkey: Istanbul, Izmir, Ankara, Bursa, Çanakkale, Hatay (Antioch), Samsun (a center of tobacco cultivation), Adana, Trabzon (an important port), and Gümüşhane (important in commerce with

Iran), but most soon made it to Istanbul. One extended family from a town on the Greek–Albanian frontier settled in the Istanbul neighborhoods of Çağoğlu, Gedik Pasha, and Mahmud Pasha, where they lived on the main boulevard, Divan Yolu, where the Pierre Loti Hotel stands today. Other families settled in Eminönü, Beşiktaş, and Bakırköy, continuing their business relations with Dönme who had come before the exchange.[22]

According to the Records of the Mixed Commission, some of the leading Karakaş merchant families, such as Kibar Ali and his sons, Osman Fettan, Mehmet Sarım, and Halil Hikmet, who formed a hardware and metal goods company by that name, reestablished their businesses in Tahtakale in the business district of Eminönü, Istanbul.[23] Stationery upon which the powers of attorney were written allowing the liquidation of their abandoned property in Salonika is headed "Sons of the Kibar Ali Brothers, Istanbul, Kanza Han, Tahtakale, Numbers 51–2, Telegraph address: Kibars, Telephone number, Istanbul 3291–3292." The letter is stamped with the Sons of the Kibar Ali Brothers seal in Ottoman and French (Fils de Kibar Ali Frérés / Kibar Ali Kardeşler Mahdumları, Istanbul), and the Balcı Brothers stamp as well, "Mehmet Balcı Brothers, Turkish Commerce Inc. (Türk Ticaret Anonim Şirketleri),"[24] which was based in Sultan Hamam.[25] The name of the Balcı company is a sign of a quick and successful transfer to a new cultural milieu where the Dönme had to seize upon the key element of identity: Turkishness. Other powers of attorney, such as that of Kibar Ali's wife Afife, also include the stamp of the Dilberzade Brothers Istanbul in Ottoman and French (Dilberzade Kardeşleri Der Saadet / Dilber Zade Frérés Constantinople).[26] Thus we see how when they set up businesses in Eminönü (Tahtakale, Sultan Hamam) and later Şişli in their new home city, Karakaş clans continued to keep business within extended families (Karakaş, Kibar, Dilber, Balcı) and the sect (Karakaş). Moreover, the names of the companies, such as "Sons of the Kibar Ali Brothers" also illustrate the continuation of family business for a second generation, in a new homeland, an attempt to bridge family connections and customer recognition between the imperial and nation-state era.

Business relations may have been maintained, but tight communal bonds began to unravel. While some Dönme had ceased practicing endogamy in turn-of-the-century Salonika, like other groups, the larger transition toward exogamous marriage took place in the early years of the

Turkish Republic. Haldun, son of Faik Nüzhet, the last Ottoman finance minister, is a good example. I was told Haldun was born in Salonika in 1905.[27] A photograph from prior to 1913 shows Faik in a dark suit sporting a handlebar mustache, close-cropped hair, and slight smile. He sits comfortably, with his left leg crossed over his right. Behind his right shoulder stands his younger wife, Şükriye. She looks, not at the camera, like her husband, but past the camera, giving her a distracted or cool and resigned appearance. Her hair is bobbed into a short style, and she appears to wear earrings and a fashionable dark dress that would have been in style in any major European city at the time. Directly in front of her is their daughter, Feridun. She is wearing her hair in pigtails, with white ribbons that match her short, white pleated dress with oversized collar and large buttons. She has one hand on her father's left knee. In the picture, there appears to be another daughter, also with white ribbons in her long hair and an identical dress with her sister also with her hands on her father's left knee. But the second child with pigtails and a white dress is not the couple's second daughter, but Haldun, their son. He came to Istanbul with his family after Salonika fell to Greece. His father sent him abroad for his education, including Switzerland, France, and the Sorbonne in Paris. He became a Freemason like his father. He did not return to Istanbul until the 1930s, where he married a Muslim woman who was not a Dönme.[28]

According to the genealogy provided by a descendant, three of the four children of the Kapancı Sarrafzade Ahmet Tevfik Ehat, son of Sarrafzade Osman Ehat, co-founder of the Terakki school, married foreign women, and two settled abroad.[29] Reşat Tesal's brother married Atatürk's army buddy Nuri Conker's daughter. Conker was distantly related by marriage (mother's brother's wife's relative). In 1944, Tesal married a woman whose father was from Trabzon and her mother's family from Bosnia.[30] Some Dönme were marrying outsiders. If they were satisfied breaking the bonds of the community maintained for so long through endogamy, did they find the need to continue to educate their children in their own schools or bury their dead in separate cemeteries?

Separate Schools

In 1927, an elderly Dönme exchangee from Salonika explained that in her former domicile, the group had had its own schools, where the children were separated from others and thus strengthened in their belief. But in the new republic, their children had to be sent to the state-run schools, where they were excluded, ridiculed, and even beaten up by their Turkish classmates.[31] Based on the need of their terrorized youth, called Greek bastards and worse by their schoolmates, the only two Salonikan schools to survive the population exchange and bridge the transition from empire to nation-state, at least in Turkey, if not in Greece, and be reestablished in Istanbul, were the two schools founded by Dönme, the Feyziye and Terakki.[32] Yet their mission had changed: once marked by the teaching of religion and international values, in Turkey, the schools were secularized and nationalized. While they could still function to ensure communal identity, it was an identity gutted of its primary ideological substance.

FROM EXCELLENCE (FEYZIYE) TO LIGHT (IŞIK)

As Mert Sandalcı's grandfather explained to him, in the wake of the Balkan Wars, the Dönme decided to migrate to Istanbul, where they had relatives and could most comfortably continue to do business; by 1915, much of the Feyziye school's administration had resettled in the Ottoman capital.[33] First he suggests that those who left Salonika after 1912 (assuming they were Turks, and that life for Turks under Greek rule was impossible) desired to educate their children in the manner and way in which they were accustomed. Despite there being other "modern" schools in Istanbul, they thus set up their own: Yeni (1915), Feyziye (1917), Şişli Lisan (1919), and Feyz-i Ata (1921). But as seen in Reşat Tesal's autobiography, quoted at the beginning of this chapter, another reason was the way Dönme children were being mistreated in Istanbul schools.

At first, most Karakaş settled in Bakırköy. But as the number of migrants increased, they began to settle in other districts, including Sultanahmet, Gedikpaşa, Teşvikiye, and Şişli, where their children faced the problem of getting along with other children at school (140). For the Salonikans, the years between 1917 and 1923 were the most difficult, because "these migrant children were continually marked as Greeks or Jews, and not understanding why they were subject to this treatment from other children, had a hard time" (141). In addition, the fact that these migrants had financial difficulties and lived humbly, unlike their schoolmates, only exacerbated the problem.

In this context, leading Karakaş families built a school first in Bayezid. On Jacques Pervitich's 1930s map, it appears as an *école Turque* (144–45), just as Dönme cemeteries in Salonika had appeared on maps as "Turkish cemeteries." The school was just southwest of the Bayezid mosque, Bayezid Square, and the main university gate, not far up Divan Yolu from Piyer Loti Street. In 1923, the school was moved to Nişantaşı (166–67). Leading the way in donating funds to establish the school were the İpekçi and Kibar families. The Kibar Ali and Sons Business donated much money (149). A list of the one hundred or so people who donated money in 1921 includes fifteen İpekçi, nine Kibar, four Balcı, and a Karakaş (149–51), the Kibar by far being the biggest givers, donating over half the funds, followed by the İpekçi. The director of the school in Bayezid until 1928 was Nakıyye Hanım, a former CUP member and post–World War II parliamentarian, and a close friend of the well-known feminist and Turkish nationalist Halide Edip Adıvar (153, 155).

The founders of the school in Bayezid attempted to set up a commerce school, but failed (157). They did manage to replace "non-modern" Arabic and Persian with philosophy, sociology, logic, and business courses (160). According to Sandalcı, this serves as evidence that they were preparing students for the republic and the post-Ottoman future, as an important element of the national struggle was waged on the education and linguistic front.

In 1923, the school moved to the mansion of Naciye Sultan, wife of Enver Pasha, one of the leaders of the CUP, World War I minister of war (167), in Teşvikiye, next to the neighborhood's main mosque and close to the mansion that housed the Terakki school. A photograph from that time illustrates how both Dönme schools anchored what became a Dönme neighborhood. One-third of the money for the land and building came from donations of the newly established Alumni Association; half came from a mortgage from a bank, with the Dilber and Kibar acting as guarantors (170).

In 1932, the school faced a major crisis in the shape of a clash between the two leading families represented on its board, the Dilbers and Kibars, who could no longer work together amicably, notwithstanding their apparently smooth transition to Istanbul in the 1920s. The Kibars, who were in the tobacco trade, suffered great financial losses in the Depression, and as their fortunes declined, the star of the Dilbers, who were in the textile business, rose. This was a reversal of what had been the case in Salonika, where the Dilbers had lost many properties and businesses in the great fire of 1917.[34] The İpekçis, who, although not as wealthy as the others, had also made their money mainly in the textile trade,[35] likewise played a major role in school administration, both before and after the split, and İsmail İpekçi was able to bring the Dilbers and Kibars together.[36] İsmail ran the school until his death in 1936, after which Suleiman Kâni İrtem, one of the first graduates of the Feyz-i Sıbyân, headed the board until his death in 1946 (223).

The Dönme school did its best to fit into the new republic, changing its aims from ethno-religious community building and international commerce to Turkish nationalism. According to the new school regulations, the Feyziye had only educational aims, was not established for political ends, and any Turk could be a member of the board (201). In 1934, it changed its name to Işık (Light) (211). Atatürk himself sent a telegram celebrating its fiftieth anniversary, and the change of name (213), in response to a telegram the school had sent him, which alluded to its origins in Salonika with Şemsi Efendi, Atatürk's own first teacher, and noted that the school board had pledged loyalty to the republic and its leader and placed a wreath at the Republic Monument in Taksim Square. The school thus became like most others in Turkey, although its student body, if not its pedagogical aims, remained distinct.

FROM TERAKKI TO ŞIŞLI TERAKKI

The Kapancı school also survived "keeping it within the family," but underwent a major overhaul by changing to reflect the realities of the republic. In 1919 the Salonikan Terakki was reopened in Nişantaşı, Şişli, Istanbul. Reflecting this move, in 1922, its name became Şişli Terakki. The minutes of the first meeting of the board reveal that no members of the Kapancı family attended; they were still in Salonika.[37] One of the early decisions was not to allow girls wearing head scarves to attend,[38] making it one of the first Istanbul schools to demand something on which the new republic would pride itself in encouraging later. Thus one of the reasons for the Dönme schools' reputation for secularism stems from such measures enacted not in Salonika, but in Istanbul. After 1923, Salonikan Dönme arrived and enrolled in the school. In 1925, the Sertel family began to participate in the life of the school, with Sabiha Sertel serving as general inspector.[39] The board membership in 1925 reflected continuity with Salonika: its members were professionals and international merchants (tobacco, textiles), and ambassadors. Among them was Hasan Sabri of the Duhani Tobacco Company.[40] The 1933 board members continued the trend and added the banker Namık Kapancı (formerly mainly a money changer in Salonika); Faiz Kapancı, a merchant and Salonikan banker (and sales representative while in Salonika), who had served on the board of Dönme schools in his former domicile; the banker İsmail Kapancı; and Dr. Ziya Osman.[41] İbrahim Telci and Mecdi Dervish would also serve an important function at the school. The Kapancı had arrived, and they continued to play a leading role in the school, as they had in Salonika.

An article by Mecdi Dervish in 1934 on Şisli Terakki High School publicized its efforts to modernize and discussed the close connection between the Dönme community and the school at length, emphasizing the need for families and schools to work together. If they were not united, associations must be established to link families and schools, parents and teachers. "If families ruin the good habits taught at school, then what do the efforts and hard work of the teachers accomplish? That is why these associations are needed," the writer explained. Although family-school, parent-teacher, and school oversight boards were almost completely unknown in Turkey, "we have had these associations for a very long time." The best proof of this was the fact that the school was celebrating its fifty-fifth anniversary. Fifty-five years ago, "this institution saved our little children from the stick and bastinado of the fanatics who ran neighborhood schools. In order to provide them with a school suitable for the age they established the Terakki." The article is illustrated with a photo of a thirtyish Mustafa Fazıl, identified as a lawyer and one of the founders of the Salonika Terakki school. He wears a fez, symbolizing the Ottoman past, a past the school was not ashamed to claim.[42]

The Terakki school did indeed continue to be a family affair. It was "our school, our family school. Students were from our family, Salonikans, Jews," a descendant of the Salonikan tobacco merchant Hasan Akif told me in an interview. Since Hasan Akif had been one of the founding board members, members of his family continued to govern, teach in, or be educated in the school, first in Ottoman Salonika and then in Istanbul under the Turkish Republic. His son and daughter taught at the school, and his granddaughter and great-granddaughter were also students, the latter attending what had by then been renamed Şişli Terakki.[43] In Istanbul, Akif Fuat, the grandson of Hasan Akif, became a board member of the school in the 1940s.[44]

Distinct Cemeteries and Dönme Religion

THE CEMETERIES

Along with self-segregation and separate schools, cemeteries were the third way Dönme maintained their boundaries in the new republic. Hasan Akif's descendants, Mustafa Fazıl, and the leading Dönme who migrated from Salonika to Istanbul were buried in distinct Dönme cemeteries. On the Asian side of the Bosphorus, uphill from the quay of Üsküdar, past the gray-stone sixteenth-century mosque of Suleiman I's wife Roxelana, along Selânikliler Street, past a mosque in which the inscription over the prayer niche is the same as that in the last mosque dedicated in Salonika, one enters the main gate of Bülbüldere, the Valley of the Nightingales, also known as the Cemetery of the Salonikans, the main Dönme cemetery in Istanbul.

I was told the originally seventeenth-century mosque and tomb complex was remade in its present form in 1883, replacing a wooden mosque under which a spring (*dere*) flowed, and renamed in 1939–40 by a man who dedicated it to his wife. Both are buried here. Its name became Feyziye mosque, the same name as the Karakaş school. According to the web site of the Üsküdar Municipality, the "Salonikan" section of the cemetery and the mosque were established in 1882–83 by the Salonikan immigrants to Istanbul, "all of whom were wealthy."[45]

Many may have been wealthy, but the cemetery has lost its grandeur. The main part of the lower section of Bülbüldere Cemetery is neatly divided by a staircase into Kapancı and Karakaş sections. The Kapancı section, which is nearest the front gate of the cemetery, is noticeably untidy. There is no one to look after these graves anymore. Graves have crumbled, trees and weeds grow between the cracks in the cement, many graves have been opened by people searching for buried gold, and one occasionally sees bones of the deceased. One also sees bones of birds and small animals devoured by stray cats, and comes across the refuse of homeless people.

Despite its condition, the uniqueness of the Kapancı section of the Bülbüldere Cemetery immediately strikes the visitor. Two aspects make it unique. First, unlike most other Sunni Muslim tombstones, and unlike the Karakaş section, these Dönme tombstones are marked by photographs of the deceased. Soon after entering the gate of the cemetery one is met by a sea of photographs of elegantly dressed people, facing southeast, who died mainly in the 1930s, especially in 1932, at roughly the age of 50,[46] whose handsome demeanor, social status, and elegant dress contradict the shabby status into which the cemetery has fallen. It is difficult to determine why so many Dönme born in 1880–82 in Salonika passed away in 1930–32. Obituaries from the time do not give the cause of death. However, life expectancy in Turkey did not reach the fifties for another generation, until 1965–69. In fact, between 1945 and 1949, the earliest data we have, life expectancy for men was 36 and women 39. Accordingly, the Dönme were very long lived for their age, which counters stereotypes concerning their degenerate health due to endogamy, and supports Major Sadık's claims in 1919 that they boasted of people who lived to be over one hundred years old. When examining the graves at Bülbüldere Cemetery, one finds a Karakaş woman who lived 106 years, from 1836 to 1942; it is not unusual to find tombstones of Karakaş recording that they passed away in their eighties and gravestones of Kapancı who died in their seventies. In fact, despite the low life expectancy in their final resting place, Turkey, it is more difficult to find tombs of Dönme who passed away under the age of forty-five, already above the average local life expectancy.

The most impressive tombstones are those from the first generation of Salonikan Kapancı Dönme to arrive en masse in Istanbul, who died in the city within a decade. I was told after being taken in the 1920s and 1930s by Osman Murat, the photographs were sent to a porcelain factory in Italy for finishing. The tombstones from the 1920s and 1930s were made by Armenian and Greek craftsmen, particularly those employed by the firm whose signature reads "Pungis Bros. Galata Şişane Karakol." A. Turan (1893–1958), the Greek-speaking son of a Qur'an memorizer of Kayseri, possibly a convert to Islam, was trained in the art of tomb design by the Pungis Brothers. He took over their business, just as many Kayseri Muslims inherited the wealth, skills, and property of Armenians and Greeks following World War I and the establishment of Turkey, and become very wealthy from his marble business, which used marble from Marmara Island. Appropriately, he made a very large tomb for himself and his family with beautiful marble work at the center, overlooking the graveyard and his earlier works.

The second aspect that makes the Kapancı section of the cemetery unique is that most of the deceased are referred to as "Salonikan." That this marker does not distinguish Karakaş graves may lead one to speculate that the Kapancı were quicker to adopt a seemingly neutral term to publicly refer to the group, although such a term had negative social capital at the time.

The leading Kapancı families are represented here, especially the Kapancı. The list includes Namık Kapancı, the banker listed in the 1913 Thessaloníki Electoral Register, who was buried in Bülbüldere in 1932, his tombstone also describing him as a banker, and Osman Kapancı buried nearby in the same year, and the wives and daughters of Mehmet and Yusuf Kapancı.

Many of the deceased buried in the Kapancı section were professionals. One finds portly, bespectacled doctors, for example, such as the "Saloni-kan Doctor Ziya Osman" (1866–1933), who served as the school doctor at the Terakki school, selling prescriptions for a discount at board member Ethem Efendi's pharmacy,[47] "Salonikan Doctor Rıfat İnsel" (1859–1935), who had served on the board of the Terakki in 1904–5, and the joint Terakki Feyziye Commerce School in 1905–6,[48] Dr. Osman Öğütmen (1895–1940), Dr. Mehmet Vamık, and Dr. Tevfik (d. 1931), who the Greek-language *Faros tēs Makedonias* newspaper reported in 1891 had developed a cure for tuberculosis.[49] So too one finds timber and textile merchants and their descendants, also lawyers and bankers, foreign consuls, and bu-reaucrats, such as comptrollers in government offices. As we have seen, Dönme played a crucial role in the 1908 revolution. We also see here the graves of Salonikan telegraphists who may have been instrumental in that effort, such as İbrahimzade İsmail and Emin Efendi.

Another visible profession is that of schoolteacher. One finds the graves of many who taught at the Kapancı schools, women, as well as men. This includes Ahmet Mithat Efendi (1861–1932). His tombstone reads: "O visitor! Teacher Ahmet Mithat Efendi is buried here. The de-ceased taught at many schools and with great self-sacrifice served Turkish education for over half a century. May God grant his wife Raziye Hanım and his children patience, and may his soul be flooded with light." The reference to Turkish education makes sense in the light of the Dönme conversion to secular nationalism in that period. Another example is the grave of Ethem Müfit (1872–1932), a relative of Hasan Akif's, whose tombstone reads:

> Etem Müfit, one of the teachers of the Salonikan Terraki and Feyziye School, is buried here. This man with a good disposition and pure heart was a person loved by all. While young, death found him in a hotel room in exile. That must have been what God wanted. Destiny spared him the pleasure of having his own children. This great sorrow was overcome by the love of the students whom he taught, the nephews who loved him as a father, and especially the

love of his life, [his] partner Emine. O visitor! Stop for a moment before these silent stones and with a *fatiha* [prayer] send your final wishes to this traveler who will not return from the endless journey.

The gravestone of Osman Şevki (1868–1926) includes a very large open book, whose Ottoman script has unfortunately been made illegible by the elements. The inscription refers to him as a teacher who passed away after he had spent "his entire fifty-eight-year life as a teacher educating people for his native land" which is assumed to be Salonika, another reference to the lost past of the Dönme.

Famous musicians with Sufi connections were also buried in the Kapancı section. Most notable is "the great musician and composer Salon-ikan Oudi Ahmet Bey" (1870–1928), as he is referred to on his tombstone, topped by an oud. An oud also appears on the side of the tomb. The inscription reads "The deceased devoted his fifty-eight years to Turkish music. He composed over 500 works and trained hundreds of students. That delicate mind, which created the greatest songs of Turkish music of the past century, is now mingled with the earth. May God forgive the sins of the deceased within the melodies of paradise and console his wife and daughter with the reflection that his name will not be forgotten in the music world." Again it is important to note the reference to the contri-butions the deceased made to Turkish culture and how he is depicted as a teacher. As we know from other sources, this bespectacled, fun-loving man with a large, bushy mustache had a life marked by religious and political tendencies typical of Dönme in his era. Oudi Ahmet Bey was known for playing in Salonika's Mevlevi lodge,[50] more evidence of the connection between Sufis and Dönme in the city. He came to Istanbul in 1909 with the "Action Army" that put down Abdülhamid II's supporters inspired by Dervish Vahdetî's *Volkan*.

One finds a mix of women in this section of the cemetery. They range from the chador-wearing wife Hatice (d. 1935) of the Ottoman consul to Iran Abdi Efendi (fig. 8.1) to young women wearing low-cut formal dresses and bobbed hairstyles, such as Vahide Kara Ali (d. 1928), who offers the camera a profile and exposed right shoulder (fig. 8.2); formal dresses, such as worn by a stunning woman named Sabite (1886–1934) (fig. 8.3); fur and earrings such as worn by Atiyye Zeki (1886–1932) (fig. 8.4); just as one sees a range of men, some in fezzes and bow ties, others with exposed heads and ties.

FIGURE 8.1   Tombstone portrait of the Kapancı Dönme Hatice, Istanbul.
Photo by author.

FIGURE 8.2   Tombstone portrait of the Kapancı Dönme Vahide, Istanbul.
Photo by author.

FIGURE 8.3   Tombstone portrait of the Kapancı Dönme Sabite, Istanbul.
Photo by author.

FIGURE 8.4   Tombstone portrait of the Kapancı Dönme Atiyye, Istanbul.
Photo by author.

The Karakaş section of the lower level of the cemetery, in great contrast to the Kapancı section, is far tidier, the flowers in the middle of the graves are watered, and there is hardly a weed or broken grave. It is obvious that the graves are cleaned regularly. What is also noticeable about the Karakaş section is how few photographs there are and the near complete absence of the identifier "Salonikan." The leading Karakaş families are represented here: İpekçi, Dilber, Mısırlı, Kibar, and Balcı. For example, one finds the simple grave of Ali Macit Karakaş (1876–1936), the son of Mehmet Karakaş, which is plain, without any adornment, only the name and dates. One finds in this section the graves of leading Karakaş school administrators and educators, such as İpekçi İsmail (d. 1936). İpekçi's tomb is a mainly plain gravestone, decorated only with a floral motif, and there is no photograph, just black, thick, art deco letters stating his name and birth and death dates. As will be explained below, however, many Karakaş tombs, befitting the most antinomian of Dönme groups, contain striking religious language.

The Karakaş and Kapancı dead lie in the Valley of the Nightingales. The first generation of the population exchange who were members of the Yakubi group buried their dead in a small cemetery in the neighborhood of Maçka. I visited the cemetery with a descendant of the Kapancı who has extensive knowledge of all three Dönme groups. The cemetery consists of several hundred graves, many of which have been robbed, or their tombstones toppled over. It is overrun with weeds and trees. There is no caretaker, only a homeless man who resides in the cemetery with five dogs and four cats. Most photographs have been chipped away, and few remain. Some tombstones are inscribed in the Latin alphabet, but most are in Ottoman. Many of the people buried in this cemetery are identified as "Salonikan," and most were government officials, military men among them. Like most of those buried in the Kapancı section of Bülbüldere, most in the Maçka cemetery were born in Salonika (or, less frequently, in Monastir, Skopje, and other places in Macedonia) in the 1870s and 1880s and died in Istanbul between 1927 and 1931. Most were buried in 1931. The newest tombstone seems to be from 1950. Since that time, most Yakubis, the smallest group of the remaining Dönme, have been buried in the main Muslim cemetery in Feriköy.

REMEMBERING SALONIKAN ORIGINS

Establishing a cemetery is an act of staking a claim to a locality, especially when those who bury their dead bring the bones or gravestones of members of their group from elsewhere. A handful of turban-topped late seventeenth-century Balcı and Dilber family headstones (Ali Agha, son of Abdullah, 1690; Ali Agha, 1697) stand smack in the middle of the Karakaş section of the Bülbüldere Cemetery. It is most likely that the tombstones were brought here by Karakaş between 1917 and 1923, because I have only been able to trace the main Karakaş presence in the city back to the mid-nineteenth century. Karakaş left their most important tomb, however, that of Osman Baba, in Salonika, and returned to that city on pilgrimage.

Graves or tombs are "places of return" for a dispersed group when they are made into pilgrimage sites.[51] The most important tomb for many Dönme, especially the Yakubi and Kapancı, was that of Shabbatai Tzevi in Ulcinj in what is now Montenegro. Kapancı insistence on labeling themselves "Salonikan" on their Istanbul gravestones so soon (less than a decade) after their arrival en masse in the city points to a motive of return. It also points to a sense of desire, longing, and absence and loss (they were expelled from the city where they had emerged and then been established for nearly two and a half centuries), a code word for a secret identity (Dönme), a way of perpetuating that identity, a continued sign of their sense of togetherness, and a displaying of their rootedness in and identification with one space, even while in exile. It also marks a Dönme myth of origin that was distinct from that of the Jews, whose myth of origin and return was not centered on the Aegean Sea. Although Jews were in diaspora, their imagined origin and place of return (at least in a theological, religious if not material sense) referred also to a distinct yet different place. When the Dönme had to leave Salonika, their center, their world, their community, collapsed in an Istanbul that was itself stripped of its cosmopolitan features in the nation-state, could not be a new center. Living in Istanbul affected the choices available to them, especially issues of mobility.

"In a society of migrants, what is important is not where you were born, but where you die . . . place of death is important because it often becomes the site of burial. Tombstones abroad acknowledge the shift in allegiance—from origins to destinations—that migrants take whole lifetimes or more to come to terms with," Engseng Ho contends.[52] This is contradicted in the Dönme case, especially the Kapancı, by their insistence on articulating their Salonikan origins. The Dönme used the tombstones to mark not only their place of birth, their Salonikan origins, and their place of death, Istanbul, their end, but also identified themselves as being from their place of origin, although it was outside the boundaries of the nation-state to which they now belonged. Tombstone inscriptions mark a life's journeys and final return, even if symbolic, to one's true home. Graves marked "Salonikan" urge the visitor to imagine that the deceased, and thousands lying next to him or her, may have died in this land, but belonged somewhere else. Burial marked the loss of the ability to return. Kapancı Dönme remembered, did not wish to forget their origin. The grave of Kapancı Nuri Rasim has a section that speaks in the voice of his brother Etem:

> I spent my life suffering from many illnesses. I learned English, French, and German language and literature. Shortly after we inherited our father's father's business in Manchester, I left it to my brother Nuri, the true inheritor of my success, who elevated the family. I was buried at the age of twenty-two in Salonika. Now, not even my bones remain. In order to remember my name, they put my photograph on Nuri's grave.

Etem's disembodied voice speaks to Salonikan mobility, mentioning England and Turkey, but ultimate belonging in Salonika where his body lies. The Dönme lost their city and even the desiccated bones of their dead, but not the memory of their origins.

It is not unusual to find headstones of Dönme graves from the 1920s that speak to a life of mobility. Mobility also means that people may die far away from their homelands. Written in her voice, the tombstone of the seven-year-old Kapancı Aisha, daughter of Asıf Efendi, mentions how "my father died in a foreign land." "Graves, while they are endpoints for migrants, are beginnings for their descendants, marking the truth of their presence in a land," Ho observes.[53] The era of cosmopolitanism was at an end. The Dönme had to acknowledge that they would not be able to return to Salonika. By the 1930s, the distinct Dönme cemeteries in Istanbul had become the new locus of Salonikan life, among the few places where Dönme rituals were perpetuated, whether openly or secretly, under Islamic cover.

Tombstones not only mark beginnings and endpoints, but can be used to mark distinction, difference, transregional identity, and continuing dispersal and diaspora. The oval photograph on the grave of Kapancı Osman Nusret (d. 1936) is ringed by many Ottoman postage stamps and a single Turkish one, presenting an intriguing mix of Ottoman and Turkish symbols (fig. 8.5). Represented on the Ottoman stamps are famous sights in Istanbul: Hagia Sophia, the greatest church in Christendom

FIGURE 8.5 Tombstone portrait of the Kapancı Dönme Osman Nusret, Istanbul. Photo by author.

converted into the greatest mosque, and finally into a museum; Rumeli Hisarı, the fortress that Mehmet the Conqueror built prior to conquering Constantinople from the Byzantines; an ancient column located at the Hippodrome; stamps with the sultan's monogram; Leander's Tower; and two fez-wearing military men. There is also a stamp depicting a nearly naked man with the female wolf Asena that led the Turks out of Central Asia to Anatolia, looking to the future, in Turkic mythology. The latter stamp is from the Turkish Republic, yet it is also inscribed in Ottoman writing. Nevertheless, its image is a striking nationalist intrusion on the other stamps. Along with the thin, brushlike mustache in the center of Osman Nusret's upper lip, it is the only clue that this is a tombstone from the 1930s. And despite the fact that eight years had passed since the language reform replacing Ottoman written in Perso-Arabic script with Turkish written in the Latin alphabet, and thirteen years since the empire had been replaced by the nation-state, Osman Nusret chose (or those who buried him chose) to include Ottoman stamps in the Ottoman and French languages to decorate his tomb.

The Salonikan might have become an Istambuli, but the "Salonikan" badge still identifies and marks the journey and genealogical precedence of Salonika. Resisting strong pressure to disappear, those who were buried in the 1930s had wanted their descendants to know of their origins—to maintain the asymmetry between themselves and other Turks at a time when the state and social pressure worked to abolish it. As Ahmet Emin Yalman argued regarding endogamous marriage in Salonika, discrimination reinforced it. In burying relatives, Dönme descendants accepted the label "Salonikan" when they paid for tombs that bore it, expressing a wish to mark their trajectory despite the nation-state. One suspects some hoped they would one day be able to return to Salonika.

TRAVELING ON THE SUFI PATH

It is notable that there are few references to religious themes on Kapancı gravestones. Occasionally, one finds instead a combination of science and knowledge (*ilm ve irfan*), the latter perhaps meaning spiritual knowledge. Occasionally, too, the visitor is asked to recite a *fatiha* for the deceased, and one sometimes comes across the phrase "Ruhu için, dua edin" (Pray for their soul) in place of the more typical Sunni Muslim *fatiha*. But *fatiha* are few and far between. Often no prayer is included. Some, however, ask God (*Tanrı*) for forgiveness, or the head of the tombstone reads "Hüve'lbaki" (God is everlasting), but in many tombs, even this is absent.

It would be incorrect to label them atheist, for at the same time, the few references to religion are striking. The beautifully ornate tombstone that contains the photo of a bareheaded, mustachioed man in suit and tie from the 1910s, engraved with Persianate Sufi couplets, reads in part: "In this perfect devotee [or a novice on the spiritual path] every part of his heart was a wide open vacant space for God [or the spiritual teacher] to fill with love. He was exceptional such that his haste in fulfilling the spiritual path cannot be perceived with words or even with silence. In spirituality, if speech is silver, than silence is golden." These are clear references in Sufi language to one who has traveled quite a way on the path of reaching unity with God, so far that he has had his heart emptied of all that is black or negative, cleansing it so that it can be a pure receptacle for receiving God. The silence of the one who has knowledge is fitting for a Dönme tombstone inscription for one who had complete mastery and knowledge of the Dönme tradition. One wants to know what he learned, from whom he learned it. One can only determine that this meant that Dönme religion was actively transported from Salonika to Istanbul between the waning years of empire and early years of the nation-state and that the secret of Dönme identity was taken to many a grave.

The tombstones in the Karakaş section, in great contrast, are full of religious, especially Sufi references. Many tombstone inscriptions are similar to that of Mustafa Tevfik. Mustafa Tevfik (1851–1934) was the son of Mısırlı Zeki Efendi. His tombstone reads

> O visitor! This is an exalted grave that preserves the esteem of a great soul which has now reached God's lights. He was a perfect human being [*bir kâmil insandı*] and elevated soul who dedicated his entire being to his own kind's [*kendi cinsinin*] good and well-being, and worshipped God [*hakk*] and truth [*hakika*]. Among his many good works that he established to benefit future generations, he is also the one who founded the Feyziye school. This blessed being whose hand and heart [*eli dili*] advanced good has now reached his God [and master]. He has attained God's light. How happy is he.

The language of this tomb is striking for its Sufi metaphors. The concept *kâmil-i insan*, is a well-known Sufi phrase for the perfect spiritual guide used for such diverse people as Rumi and Ibn al-Arabi and calls to mind Major Sadık's defense of Shabbatai Tzevi's spirituality. The play upon the words for God and truth are also common in Sufi hagiography. Finally, suitable for a Karakaş Dönme, the sect closest to Bektaşi Sufis, central to Sufi morals, especially Bektaşi, is control over one's hands, tongue (or heart), and loins, in other words, not stealing, slandering, lying, or engaging in inappropriate sexual behavior. References are made to the first two here. A link is made in this inscription between Dönme spirituality and Dönme schools, and offers evidence for this man being a Dönme religious leader as well as educator, again emphasizing how important religion was for the group and pointing to one of the main reasons for their establishing their schools. The schools were not established for all children, but for Mısırlı Zeki Efendi's "own kind." A Karakaş interviewee, descendant of Mustafa Çelebi, the man who established the Karakaş sect, pointed out a grave of a close relative, who was born in Salonika in the 1880s and died just after World War II in Istanbul, which reads in part "This human who put into practice the morals of his elite ancestors now stands before you in the form of a perfect monument. Pray so that he may complete his final journey to perfection." The second sentence is another Sufi reference, as it is inferred that the deceased is still traveling after his death en route to reach God.

Secularizing Şemsi Efendi

A crack runs from left to right directly beneath the lower lip of the aging, fez-wearing educator Şemsi Efendi—his white beard closely cropped, his eyebrows still dark—in the oval portrait on his grave in the Karakaş section of the Bülbüldere Cemetery, facing the Kapancı section across a flight of stairs (fig. 8.6). This placement is evidence both of his efforts to reconcile the two groups, and his many years working for the educational advancement of youth of both. Unfortunately, the black Arabic letters lightly etched into the plain outer fez-topped gravestone have been so worn out, whether by people's fingers touching the stone while on pilgrimage after he was buried in 1917, or by the weather, that the original inscription is now completely illegible. Not a single word is readable on the outer tombstone of the man who spent decades educating youth in Salonika and then Istanbul. Sometime after the 1930s, a new inscription was added in Turkish in Latin characters above the floral design on a second tombstone, which bears his ceramic photograph. The later inscription reads "Atatürk's teacher, Teacher Şemsi Ef." It is as if the republic had

FIGURE 8.6   Grave of Şemsi Efendi, Istanbul. Photo by author.

erased the Ottoman elements of his past, reducing everything to a teleo-logical reading of what he had done to contribute to the establishment of the Turkish nation-state, implying teaching secular ideas to its founder. A direct connection is thus made between Şemsi Efendi and the secular Republic. His daughter Marufe (1876–1936) is buried nearby, her photo-graph depicting a plain woman with short hair and her father's oval face and dark eyebrows. On her grave, her father is referred to as "the sheikh of teachers," a curious mix of Sufi title and modern profession.

The Dönme who desired to do so were initially able to establish some of their traditional boundary-maintaining mechanisms in Turkey: living together, running their own schools, and burying their dead in distinct cemeteries. Yet they had to abandon two of their primary markers, reli-gion and transnationalism, which were to be replaced by secularism and nationalism. Few Dönme tombstones have mainstream Sunni Muslim religious references. The transregionalism of the Dönme can be seen in the forms they filled out when forced to leave Salonika. For example, the documentation of the Mixed Commission set up to assess the value of Salonikan Muslims' wealth and property invariably lists their *memleket*, homeland, as Salonika, the same concept expressed on many Kapancı tombstones inscribed a decade later.

§9 Forgetting to Forget,
1923–1944

Loyal Greeks or Crafty Imposters?
Denying Dönme in Thessaloníki, 1923–1941

As many as a hundred Muslims, among them an indeterminate number of Dönme, remained in Thessaloníki after the population exchange. How did they fare? How did debates about their place in society and their lived experience compare with those in Turkey?

Greece's Prime Minister Eleuthérios Venizélos noted: "Turkey herself—new Turkey—is the greatest enemy of the idea of the Ottoman Empire. New Turkey does not wish to hear anything about an Ottoman Empire. She proceeds with the development of a homogeneous Turkish national state. But we also, since the catastrophe of Asia Minor, and since almost all of our nationals from Turkey have come over to Greek territory, are occupied with a similar task."[1] In Greece, the Muslim population declined from 20 percent in 1920 to 6 percent less than a decade later.[2] Following the population exchange, the Athens government provincialized Thessaloníki by marginalizing and ignoring its businesses and merchants, and through such measures as briefly prohibiting the export of tobacco, and redirected its economy away from traditional markets such as Istanbul and toward the Greek national economy.[3] Similarly, the Turkish government taxed imported timber from northern Greece, another market niche dominated by Dönme, heavily in order to decrease its use and promote demand for and drive up the prices of Anatolian timber, which would monopolize the market.[4] Beyond Greece, political changes meant disruptions to the southeastern European, Black Sea, Anatolian, and Middle Eastern markets of the Dönme. Ideological conviction within Greece ensured that their economic loss was complete.

Uncomfortable with the fact that Greeks were a minority in Thessalon´ıki, the Greek government also refused to allow the Dönme to remain in Greece. It wanted to be rid of this significant non-Greek economic element. Yıldız Sertel's memoir claims that the Greek authorities aimed to prevent wealthy Dönme (and by extension, Turkey) from profiting by selling their goods and properties before they left for Istanbul, so it confiscated their immovable goods and disallowed the sale of property on the market, promising to safeguard it.[5] Article 14 of the Treaty of Lausanne required that "the emigrant shall in principle be entitled to receive in the country to which he emigrates, as representing the sums due to him, property of a value equal to and of the same nature as that which he has left behind." The Dönme were supposed to have their moveable and immovable property valued in gold currency and to receive a declaration in Thessalon´ıki from the Mixed Commission for the Exchange of the Greek and Turkish Populations created under the Lausanne Treaty stating the value of the property that had been expropriated by the Greek government. They were to present this valuation once they arrived in Turkey. The question was not whether the Greek government would protect their liquidated property, because it was irrevocably lost, but rather whether the Turkish government would live up to the Lausanne Treaty and recompense them accordingly.

The Dönme, estimated to number from ten to twenty thousand people,[6] were compelled to abandon their native city as part of the population exchange between Greece and Turkey. In Greece, the population exchange was referred to as the "catastrophe," which literally means "a sudden ending," a fitting description of the fate of the Dönme in Thessalon´ıki. With few exceptions, Thessalon´ıki's Muslim inhabitants, who had formed one-third of the population when Greece took control of the city in 1912, were all deported and replaced by Orthodox Christians, whose proportion of the population had risen from a mere quarter to three-quarters of city residents by 1928.[7] For the first time since the Byzantine era five hundred years before, the city had a Greek majority.

By the beginning of 1925, according to Thessalon´ıkan police records, only ninety-seven Muslims remained in the city, exempted from deportation by Serbian or Albanian papers.[8] To be considered Albanian, one had to have residence in Greece, be a Muslim, have a father born in Albania, and not regard oneself as Turkish. Accordingly, satisfying these criteria, a handful of notable Dönme, such as Ahmet Kapancı's son Mehmet Kapancı (and not Ahmet Kapancı himself, as is commonly thought in Greece), managed to remain. According to a Kapancı interviewee, some members of her family, who were important timber merchants, were able to remain in Thessaloníki after the population exchange because they had obtained either Albanian or Serbian citizenship.[9]

The situation faced by the Dönme who remained in Thessaloníki was similar to that facing the Dönme who were beginning a new life in Istanbul. The period after the founding of the Turkish Republic was much worse for the Dönme in Thessaloníki than the era between the Greek conquest of the city and the population exchange, when some Dönme at least were able to retain their posts and properties. Articles in the Greek newspaper *Efēmeris tōn Balkaniōn* (Newspaper of the Balkans) from the years immediately following the population exchange provide testimony to the negative sentiment the Dönme faced in the city that had once been their main home. One notable article from 1923, entitled "The Trial of Osman Said," informs us that the last Ottoman mayor of the city was put on trial, and charged with high treason.[10] Osman Said had been arrested and imprisoned along with the mufti of Thessaloníki following the rout of the Greek forces in Anatolia and the burning of Izmir in 1922. Both men were released, however, and Osman Said left Thessaloníki that summer after being acquitted of all charges.[11] The mayor's sisters were apparently inconsolable over having to leave their beloved city for Turkey.[12] One reason may be how comfortably they lived. The Mixed Commission records provide evidence of the extent of the family's property and wealth. Safiye, Osman Said's wife, owned so much property that she had to insert additional pages into the standard form.[13] The family of Osman Said's brother Osman Adil also owned much property.[14] In 1925, Anatolian exchangees were allocated land on the estate of Hamdi Bey, Osman Said's father, as part of the process of the state expropriating land and handing it over to refugee groups, who built homes on it. Ironically, this included sixty refugee tram drivers, who thus settled on the estate of the architect of Salonika's tramway system.[15]

That same year the *Efēmeris tōn Balkaniōn* published several inflammatory articles concerning another significant Dönme family when it ran stories about Mehmet Kapancı, the son of Ahmet. It questioned Mehmet Kapancı's citizenship and right to own property. If Mehmet Kapancı was a Greek citizen who was Muslim, then he should have been expelled to Turkey and his property confiscated by the government for the purpose of redistribution to Orthodox Christian expellees from Turkey. But if he had neither Greek nor Turkish citizenship, he could remain in Greece and keep his property, at least for the time being. The newspaper sides with the refugees from Anatolia and attacks the ministers handling the population exchange.

In an article entitled "The Kapancıs Have Become Serbian subjects As Well, a Manifest Scandal," the newspaper expresses outrage that "the Ministry of Agriculture has sent an order to the local Mixed Commission for the Exchange of the Population by which it makes it known that one of the Kapancıs [Mehmet Kapancı, son of Ahmet Kapancı] is a Serbian subject and that his property should therefore continue to belong to him. Once known, this scandal has upset the refugees and those that know the Kapancı family. It would not be strange if the rest of the Turks of this family were to become Serbian subjects."[16]

Four days later, the newspaper continues to fan the flames of outrage in an article with the long heading "Unexplored Matters: The Refugee and Public Properties. Some Are Plundered and Others Are Ignored. Mehmet Kapancı [son of Ahmet Kapancı] Has Began to Take Action—Uproar and Protests—The Scandal Has to Be Dealt With. . . . Someone Has to Talk." The article begins by claiming that immediately after the order given by the Ministry of Agriculture for the restitution of the property of Mehmet Kapancı, he, or rather his wife, had visited the tenants of her lands and demanded that they either pay their overdue rents or evacuate the properties. Most of the tenants began to protest and express their outrage in various ways to both the police and the Mixed Commission. The newspaper declares "that the scandal has to be dealt with with force equal to the impudence with which the ministry has provoked it. We regret that we have recently learned that along with Mehmet Kapancı's successful claim, other wicked acts are occurring with the connivance and culpability of the ministry."[17] It argues that such important scandals harm the rights of the refugees to receive their just compensation.

The following day, the newspaper continued to focus on Mehmet Kapancı. In an article entitled simply "The Pillaging," it writes that Mehmet Kapancı has usurped a property that is not his and lists what the writer of the article considered his unjust claims: a mansion on Leōforos Dēmokratias (Republic Avenue; the new Greek municipality had Hellenized the names of Thessaloníki's streets and squares, some of which it had rebuilt after the great fire of 1917); the Hotel Olympos Palace on Plateia Eleutherias, the city's main square; the building on Plateia Eleutherias where the Pâtisserie Flokas was located; a textile factory next to the building of the Second Police Station; and a building plot next to a brick factory, only 35 percent of which he was entitled to. Yet from these properties "he gains 2.5 million Turkish pounds, which according to the Lausanne Treaty and the dictates of reason and justice rightfully belong to the refugees. But who among those responsible for the fate of the refugees has ever contemplated the extent of this colossal theft?"[18] This article both questions the loyalty of the Dönme and provides evidence of the wealth of Mehmet Kapancı. He owned a mansion, a hotel (from whose balcony the Constitutional Revolution had been cheered less than two decades before), a commercial building, a textile factory, and another presumed factory or commercial building.

Soon after that piece appeared, A. Theodoridis, most likely a representative of the refugees and member of the Bureau of Exchange of Refugee Property who was frustrated by the bureaucrats in the Ministry of Agriculture, wrote an article entitled "Check the Properties." In it, he attacks Mehmet Kapancı for becoming a Serbian subject for cynical reasons, his real and sinister purpose being to usurp refugee property. But the writer is concerned that the Mehmet Kapancı case is only the tip of the iceberg, for "beyond this theft, other scandals are being revealed daily, other attempts to usurp properties at the expense of the state, on the one hand, and the miserable refugees on the other."[19]

Two years later, the *Efêmeris tôn Balkaniôn* again took up the scandal of Kapancı citizenship and property ownership in an article entitled "The Scandal of the Exchangeable Property of Kapancı. How the Property of the Refugees Slips Away." The writer aims to bring to public attention the scandalous affair "of the well-known Dönme Kapancı," Mehmet, the son of Ahmet. The author argues "The Kapancı family, and more precisely the father of the Kapancı [Ahmet Kapancı] now residing here [in Thessaloníki, Mehmet Kapancı], in whose father's name all of his real estate property in Thessaloníki was registered, including the well-known mansion where the Spanish Consulate is currently housed on Leôforos Eleutherias [Liberty Avenue], and large parts of important buildings in Plateia Eleutherias [Liberty Square], was a Greek citizen." The newspaper says it has had this certified by the former head of the Directorate of Real

Estate of the Provisional Government of Thessaloníki during 1917, who is now residing in Athens. This [former] director informs the paper "that when in 1917 the aforementioned real estate property of Kapancı was to be confiscated by the Greek state, because it allegedly belonged to an Austrian citizen (as Kapancı led others to believe) and therefore a citizen of an enemy country, the aforementioned father of Kapancı [Ahmet Kapancı] came to the Department of Public Land and declared that he was not an Austrian citizen, and he produced a relevant certificate of his Greek identity." The author of the article asserts that it "is therefore worth questioning how the department did not consider this fact and thoughtlessly proceeded in restoring the property of Kapancı, which is estimated to be [worth] several million [drachmas] and which should have devolved to the refugees, because it belongs to an Ottoman Greek citizen and therefore an exchangeable person."[20] Kostas Tomanas's *Chroniko tēs Thessalonikēs* [Chronicle of Thessaloníki], written during World War II, asserts that "Turks departing from the villages and towns of Macedonia sold whatever they could and came to Thessaloníki [en route to Istanbul]. . . . However, many rich notables suddenly 'discovered' their Albanian origins, and with the help of cunning lawyers and the bribing of senior civil servants, they managed to remain in Greece and retain their huge properties," such as in the case of the Kapancı family.[21]

The impression given the reader of Tomanas's history and of the final *Efēmeris tōn Balkaniōn* article from the 1920s is that the Dönme, in particular members of the Kapancı family, switched their citizenship at will according to whichever way the political winds were blowing. The Kapancı had become Austro-Hungarian subjects in the late Ottoman Empire in order to benefit from treaty clauses that gave residents who were not Ottoman subjects great commercial and juridical advantages. In the autumn of 1888, on the orders of the Austrian government, the Austrian consul had organized a train trip from Salonika to Vienna and Budapest, which had included many "fabulously rich merchants," honorary consuls, and "the Ottoman Kapancı, of Jewish origin (Dönme), who was president of the Austrian Chamber of Commerce."[22] In Budapest, Mehmet Kapancı had delivered one of the most important speeches launching the chamber.

The Greek Foreign Ministry took up the matter of Kapancı citizenship and property rights. The Archive of the Ministry of Foreign Affairs in Athens contains two files on the subject. The first, from 1934, is labeled

"File B/2/IV: File of the property of Mehmet [son of] Ahmet Kapandji, Yugoslav citizen, resident in Thessaloníki." The second, from 1935, is labeled "File B/13δ/I: File of Mehmet Kapandji (1925–1935)." The label of the first file serves as evidence that the Greek government accepted Mehmet Kapancı's claims to Serbian citizenship and thus conceded his right to stay in Greece and to hold on to his property.

By acquiring foreign citizenship, some members of the Dönme elite were able to resist deportation and confiscation of their wealth and property. But nothing could be done to save the resting places of thousands of deceased Dönme. Soon after the devastating 1917 fire, the Dönme began to lose their cemeteries. Ernst Hébrard's plan for the reconstruction of the city included the expansion of Aristotle University across the Jewish cemetery. The Kapancı cemetery, which lay adjacent to the Jewish cemetery, was also located within the area of planned growth.[23] Seven years later, after all of the Kapancı had been officially expelled, a law was passed legalizing its confiscation, and the remains were moved to a new site. The Karakaş cemeteries in the northwestern part of the city, near the Mevlevi Sufi lodge, which along with its cemetery was soon demolished, were also expropriated by municipal authorities, probably between 1927 and 1932, and as with the former Kapancı cemetery and Mevlevi lodge, not a trace remains of them.[24]

The depiction of Jews in Greek Thessaloníki during these years resembles that of the Dönme in Turkish Istanbul, especially Rüştü's version. Writing in 1927, Wladimer Gordlevsky noted how "Salonika's situation had changed. One witnessed the rise of fanatical nationalism. The Greeks, to whom the city now belonged, persecuted the Jews and supported the establishment of antisemitic associations."[25] In 1929, the newspaper *Makedonia* (Macedonia), which promoted the conspiracy theory that Jews planned to take over all Greek institutions, had infiltrated the economy, and were secretly running the state, warned: "Either they will acquire a Greek consciousness, identifying their interests and expectations with ours, or they will have to seek a home elsewhere, because Thessaloníki is not in a position to nurse in its bosom people who are Greeks only in name, whereas they are the country's worst enemies."[26] This is similar to Rüştü's asking at about the same time: "Do you think that the leaders of the nation, who pay attention to such minute details, will be able to retain in its breast a mass of foreigners? No individual who is able to tolerate this any longer has been found or will be found." *Makedonia*

was critical of Jews' apparent lack of assimilation, saying that their Ottoman mentality was manifested in the desire to retain a separate corporate
identity. Asserting that Jews could never be Greeks, it whipped up anti-
Jewish animosity and played a prominent role in the 1931 Campbell riot,
in which members of the extreme nationalist National Union of Greece,
founded by refugee merchants, attacked an area of the city populated by
Jews who had settled there following the 1917 fire. The editor in chief
of *Makedonia* was put on trial following the riot.[27] Claiming that Jews
despised Hellenism, his paper imagined that they were conspiring to take
over the city and undermine Greece, just as Dönme were beginning to be
depicted as playing a sinister role behind the scenes in Turkey.

Aristotle University, originally housed in the Allatini villa, where Abdülhamid II had lived under house arrest, was granted the land of the Jewish
cemetery in 1937. Disinterments were carried out. As Nicholas Stavroulakis graphically relates, "The great necropolis resembled a pockmarked
valley on the moon. Across its ravaged surface could be seen shattered
fragments of marble, piles of earth and bricks intermingled with remains
of the dead."[28] In 1941, the Nazis seized the city, and the fate of the cemetery reflected that of Thessaloníki's Jews. The following year, Nazis and
Greek municipal officials expropriated two large sections of the Jewish
cemetery, demolished graves, disinterred bodies, and then destroyed the
rest of the cemetery. Many gravestones were incorporated into the reconstruction of St. Demetrius, the church of the city's saint, his tomb recently
tended by Mevlevi Sufis. Gravestones were even used in the dance floor
in a taverna located in the former cemetery.[29] In 1943, the deportations
of Jews began. Among all of the Jews of Europe deported to Auschwitz,
those of Thessaloníki faced one of the highest death rates. By the end of
summer, Thessaloníki "was a city rid of its Jews and all that was left of its
rich Sephardi history was to be found in empty graves, shops, and homes.
The last vestige of pluralism had vanished almost without a trace."[30]

A Karakaş interviewee related the story told in his family about their
factory or workshop in Sultanahmet, Istanbul which received most of its
raw material from Germany. In the early 1940s, the material stopped arriving. The factory manager wrote to the supplier in Germany. Months
passed. Finally, he received a curt response stating; "We can no longer do
business with you because you have Jewish origins."[31] In 1942–43, the businessman Mümtaz Taylan Fazlı, whose firm Orak was on the fashionable
Kurfürstendamm in Berlin and was a member of the executive committee

of the Turkish Chamber of Commerce for Germany, protested to Nazi authorities that his business was classified as a "Jewish business" although he was not a Jew, but a Dönme.[32] These two examples serve as evidence that the Nazis considered the Dönme Jews, which would have had disastrous consequences for them had they not been deported en masse as part of the population exchange two decades before the Nazis occupied Thessaloníki.

Attacks on Prominent Dönme Intensify

In the early Turkish Republic, many Dönme former CUP members were dismissed from their jobs, imprisoned, and banned from journalism. The Yakubi CUP member and Freemason Fazlı Necip, a contributor to the literary magazine *Gonca-i Edeb*, moved to Istanbul in 1909 in order to run his newspaper, *Asır*. Yet after World War I, he was not allowed to return to journalism. In 1919, Ahmet Emin Yalman was taken into custody by the Allied occupiers and exiled to British Malta for three years, along with nationalists, state officials, members of the CUP, and war criminals. Upon his return, he had a falling out with his partners at the newspaper *Vakit*, so he established *Vatan* in 1923. It only lasted two years before it was closed under the "Statute for the Establishment of Public Order" passed in the wake of the Kurdish Sheikh Said rebellion in southeastern Anatolia and political opposition to Atatürk, since the newspaper was thought too critical of the new Turkish government.[33] Yalman was tried at an Independence Tribunal and acquitted, but banned from journalism. He was not able to return until the mid 1930s and then only with the permission of Atatürk.[34] Mehmet Zekeriya was also allowed to again practice journalism the same year.

Mehmet Zekeriya and his wife Sabiha, adopting the surname Sertel, were frequent targets of the government. They published *Resimli Gazete* (Illustrated Monthly) between 1924 and 1930. Like *People* magazine in the United States, this journal appealed to a wide audience, was written in popular language, addressed issues of general concern, and was easy to read, because it featured many photographs and illustrations.[35] Unlike *People*, the journal was also critical of the government, and faced constant lawsuits and censorship, and some of its writers served time in jail, apparently on charges of inciting class conflict. Mehmet Zekeriya Sertel had been tried for inciting soldiers to rebel, and sentenced to three years' exile; in 1930, he was again banned for three years from journalism.[36]

In 1934, the socialist Mehmet Zekeriya Sertel and the liberal Ahmet Emin Yalman purchased *Tan* (Dawn), and ran it together for two years; Yalman becoming the head writer and Mehmet Zekeriya and his wife Sabiha Sertel writers for the paper. The writers of *Cumhuriyet*, stalwart Kemalist nationalists, especially the double-chinned owner and head writer Yunus Nadi (d. 1945), like Yalman close to Atatürk, and a former member of the CUP, began attacking these Dönme journalists. The late 1930s and first half of the 1940s witnessed numerous lawsuits filed by one newspaper or writer against another, and frequent closings of papers.[37]

Race was never far from the minds of those who attacked the Dönme. In 1937, a great dispute broke out between Yalman's *Tan* and Nadi's *Cumhuriyet*.[38] After *Tan* accused *Cumhuriyet* of defending fascist propaganda in Turkey, *Cumhuriyet* quickly shot back, accusing *Tan* of spreading Communist propaganda.[39] Moreover, despite Yalman's repeated efforts to distance himself from any associations with Jews, *Cumhuriyet* also compared *Tan* to a noisy synagogue.[40] The same year, Yalman again criticized the remnants of the Ottoman cultural mosaic when he wrote a front-page article in *Tan* entitled "Turkish in Public Places," in which he excoriated Jews for declaring their foreignness by preferring to speak Spanish (Ladino) and French in public, rather than Turkish.[41] Jews were also publicly urging their co-religionists to speak Turkish in public during these years, the best-known example being Avram Galanté / Galanti's book *Vatandaş Türkçe Konuş!* (Speak Turkish, Citizen!).[42] While it was no secret that Galanté was Jewish, the fear about Yalman was that he was a secret Jew. Nadi attacked Yalman personally, arguing he was the grandson of the Jewish rebel Shabbatai Tzevi who had superficially converted to Islam in order to save his life. Like Sabiha Sertel, Nadi added, Yalman was not a Turk, but belonged to a people who, although they were of a different race, mentality, and identity, hid under the Turkish name.[43] No matter how much Yalman attempted to avoid the topic of the Dönme, his enemies endlessly reminded him of his background. In 1924, as reported in the Islamist *Sebîlürreşat* (Straight Course), Nadi asserted that Yalman was a "blood brother" of Rüştü, repeating the latter's rhetoric from two decades before.[44]

Finally, Yalman used the term Dönme in print for the first time. A member of the most Muslim of the Dönme sects, the Yakubi, which he had claimed a dozen years earlier had completely assimilated into the Muslim community, Yalman defended himself (and by extension Karakaş Sabiha Sertel): "You say, 'You are not a Turk, you are a Dönme, you have no right to open your mouth.' Yet for three centuries my ancestors have taken their place in the Turkish and Muslim community, people who always spent their lives serving the state. How many other peoples could claim this?"[45] He continues: "I heard the term Dönme very few times in my life. Those using the term were always men whose interests were harmed in the campaigns I started in the name of the national interests of the Turkish nation."[46] Thus he acknowledges being of the community, turns it to a point of honor, and reveals that the term is derogatory and used as a last resort, usually by those who were the targets of his journalistic exposés of corruption.[47] Asserting that the Dönme had always served the state might prove their loyalty, but it did not refute the claim that they were not sincere Muslims; nor did the assertion solve the problem of Dönme religious or racial identity. To solve these dilemmas, he would have had to argue that the Dönme had been Muslim for three centuries and thus longer than those whose ancestors had more recently converted to Islam.

But Nadi and other writers in *Cumhuriyet* continued the personal attacks against Yalman. One writer claimed Yalman "never had the courage to say, 'I am a Turk,' like a true citizen; he is a Dönme, he does not serve the Turkish nation, rather, he sabotages it. This is why he was tried [by the Independence Tribunal]." Afterward other writers put these words into his mouth: "'In accordance with the essence of my race, I did all of this because I am Jewish.'"[48]

For Sabiha Sertel, being accused of being a Dönme was a terrible, serious accusation, and she sued *Cumhuriyet*. Atatürk wanted the dispute between the two newspapers to end, and Yalman and Nadi agreed to comply with the wishes of the leader of the nation.[49]

During World War II, *Vatan*, reestablished by Yalman in 1940, was closed twice. The newspaper was shut down in 1942 for discussing Charlie Chaplin's film *The Great Dictator*, which made fun of Hitler, criticized fascism in stark language, and sympathized with the persecuted Jews of Europe. Again in 1944, the paper was indefinitely closed for criticizing the wealth tax.[50]

The Wealth Tax, 1942–1944

After Fazlı Necip was banned from a career in journalism, he served as a branch director of the state tobacco company. Other Dönme also continued to work in the same industry. According to interviews I conducted, the reassembled members of the family descended from Hasan Akif were

able to work in the tobacco business, as they had begun doing in Salonika in the late nineteenth century and then in western and central Europe prior to World War I, in Istanbul until the 1960s.[51] Akif Fuat, Hasan
Akif's grandson, continued the business in Thessaloníki until 1941 or 1942,
buying and selling the tobacco in Drama and Kavala. When he finally
left Thessaloníki for Istanbul, he established the Akev Tobacco company
in Tophane, Istanbul. It lasted for two decades. Thus for close to eighty
years, Hasan Akif's family owned its own business, without partners, in
the words of the descendant, "running the company entirely with close
and not-so-close relatives."

Along with tobacco, textiles were also a signature Dönme concern in
the new Turkish Republic. A Karakaş descendant told me that her family had boasted of quite wealthy textile merchants in Salonika.[52] The
family also had a tobacco business in Bulgaria. Their wealth stemmed
from the fact that her grandfather had been sent by the government to
Germany to study textile engineering. When he returned, he was able to
open factories in Salonika. As part of the population exchange, the family, including the interviewee's father born in 1917, were sent to Kayseri
in central Anatolia. The family quickly relocated to Istanbul, where her
grandfather was able to open several textile factories.[53]

Such success does not mean that all Dönme were able to prosper economically, fully assimilate, and pass as Muslims or Turks. The lack of
Dönme integration was proved by the 1942 implementation of the wealth
tax. Recreating a meeting at the Office of the Prime Minister in September 1944 will help us to understand the atmosphere at that time:

§ The middle-aged Turkish man glances through eyes framed by thick
eyebrows and heavy bags at the headline of the American newspaper on
the desk: TURKISH TAX KILLS FOREIGN BUSINESS. Capital Levy
Up to 232 Per Cent Is Required to Be Paid in Cash Within a Month.
RATES SECRETLY LAID. Inequities Are Attributed to Local Boards
From Which There Is No Appeal.[54] He takes a drag on his cigarette,
and then a sip of tea. He thumbs through three articles of his own that
have just appeared in the Turkish press, which although critical of the
extraordinary tax, appear to him to be far more objective.[55] The articles
make the point that "the sole distinction that can exist between one
citizen and another resides in whether or not a citizen fulfills his patriotic
duties." One needs to "save the honorable man from being considered
dishonorable or worse." He thinks it is tragic that "those who love and

embrace the homeland, perform military service, and speak Turkish at home have been treated the same as those who betrayed the fatherland."[56]

Repeating to himself that he has only been doing his patriotic duty, he finishes dressing in his brown three-piece suit, which hangs loosely from his stocky frame. He ties his best yellow polka-dotted silk tie and pats down his short, dark hair while looking in the hotel mirror, bends over to polish his shoes, purchased while in two-year exile in America during the recently ended banning of his newspaper, and steps out into the hot and dusty afternoon. It is early autumn in Ankara, the remote, quiet, yet ever dusty new capital of the Turkish Republic, established on the ruins of the Ottoman Empire in 1923. How many times will he have to shine his shoes to look respectable before arriving at his important meeting?

For over two decades he has been a vocal Turkish nationalist, yet there have always been people who doubted him. Today is no different. Walking out of the hotel, he runs into a parliamentarian who shouts from close range, "They should lynch you for what you wrote."[57] Unshaken, he realizes how much the World War has changed the city. It has become meaner, more isolated and insular, more closed into itself than before, if that were possible. He does not have time to stop to greet the owners of some of his favorite shops, but that is pointless anyway, as they have been deported to labor camps in the east, and their businesses taken over by others whom he does not know.

The doorman hails a taxi, which drives across the city to the Parliament building. When he arrives at the monumental, symmetrical, cut-stone building, the white-helmeted, goose-stepping guards recognize him. Ahmet Emin Yalman is the editor of *Vatan*, the second leading daily in the nation—when it is not banned. They wave him in to the grounds, and others escort him to the Office of the Prime Minister. Şükrü Saracoğlu is not his favorite politician. He is very unlike the recently deceased Atatürk, whose corpse lies at the Ethnography Museum. The nation's founder had been on very good terms with Yalman, a fellow Salonikan, whose father had been Atatürk's penmanship and calligraphy teacher.

Saracoğlu looks up from what he is writing at his oversized desk. He is prime minister during the worst of times, the war years, and it has taken its toll. Although his appointment as prime minister had been met with great hope, two years of wartime policies have changed people's opinions of their leader; the stress has changed him as well. Gone are the pleasant demeanor, the little jokes and stories he used to deploy to lighten tense moments, the gift of gab.[58] The office is beyond his abilities, he can't handle it. He is exhausted. His dark hair is already receding, his tightly stretched skin seems taut to the breaking point.

Turkey is in awful shape. It has faced only economic hardship as a result of being neither allied with Great Britain, the United States, and the USSR nor openly siding with the Nazis, although the prime minister hopes for their victory.[59] Turkey's decision to declare war on Germany will not come for another five months. Saracoğlu has implemented the tax to take wealth away from the Christians, Jews, and foreigners and put it in the hands of the Turks (Muslims) and state economy, but this has not produced the expected results, only causing foreigners to lose their respect for Turkey and vocal minorities to criticize his beloved nation. He has turned on the local press. He had no tolerance of criticism either of his plan to crush the minorities or of those who criticize the Nazis. They had to know their place. When they went beyond it, they had to be punished.[60]

He beckons the man in the dusty shoes who waits at the threshold of the door to enter his office. Unfortunately, it is that journalist, the grandson of Shabbatai Tzevi. Hasn't he given up yet? The prime minister greets him with the scowl he deserves.

The journalist thinks the man is drunk with power like a dictator.[61] He has just suspended his newspaper indefinitely. Yalman quickly launches into a defense of his writing.

"I wrote those last three articles to protect our national honor in the face of world opinion. I was only doing my duty for our great nation."

The prime minister has a country to run and no time to hear pleading from people who have no right to criticize his administration.
"The wealth tax was implemented in order to put the minorities in their place and bring those to justice who, under cover of the war, used their privileged place in the economy to profit as black marketeers," he says.

Yalman tries to soften the atmosphere. "It is the right of the government to prevent black marketeering and to tax profiteering during war, but a state cannot do so arbitrarily . . ."

The prime minister cuts him off, recognizing a plan that can cut his enemy to the quick and preclude having to read his naysaying any more. Pleased with himself, he says, "Write 'We are a minority newspaper' and I will immediately rescind the suspension decision."[62]

The journalist looks at him blankly. The prime minister wants Yalman to tell the Turkish nation that he does not belong to it, to confirm what is widely believed, that he is neither a true Muslim nor a true Turk, that he is in fact a secret Jew. Unable to speak, the normally vociferous journalist stands up to leave.

The prime minister had earlier declared Christians and Jews, like parasites, had "grown rich by taking advantage of the hospitality shown by this country."[63] This was not too dissimilar from Yalman's views. He would later defend the motivation behind the levying of the tax, writing: "It was true that huge amounts of illicit money had accumulated during the war in the hands of a few at the expense of the general public. . . . It was also true that much of this money was in the hands of minorities and foreigners, who predominated in certain commercial fields. Many of these people, not entrusted to share in the defense of the country in armed military service, were not proving themselves loyal citizens."[64]

What was so shocking about what the prime minister had said was that he lumped him together with Christians, Jews, foreigners, and traitors to the nation. But Yalman saw himself as none of these! This was precisely what he had written against. It was unjust that innocent, patriotic people, such as himself, were considered non-Turks. And in that era, to be a non-Turk was to be an enemy of the race, an enemy of the nation. According to the xenophobic *Cumhuriyet*, the government's Nazi-sympathizing mouthpiece, the tax was meant to punish those of "alien blood" and those who were "Turks only in name." And that included the Dönme.

For purposes of administering the tax, Faik Ökte, director of finance for the Province of Istanbul, divided society into four categories, Muslim, non-Muslim, foreigner, and Dönme.[65] The Dönme category was reserved for descendants of Jews who had converted to Islam in the wake of the movement of Shabbatai Tzevi. Contrary to popular view, it did not include all descendants of converts to Islam or recent converts.[66] Prominent Turks denounced Dönme in general and Yalman in particular. The British ambassador in Ankara was told that Dönme "were worse than Jews because they pretended to be Turks and wanted to have the best of both worlds. Denunciation fits in very well with imposition of tax on wealth since wealthiest men in Istanbul (Constantinople) and particularly Izmir (Smyrna) are Dönmes [*sic*]." He informed the Foreign Office in London: "These Islamised Jews played a very prominent part in young Turks revolution and in subsequent activities of the Committee of Union and Progress. Although in 1926 two of their leading personalities Dr. Nazim and Javid Bey, were executed on specific instructions of Mustafa Kemal, other Dönmes continued to play important part in Kemalist movement and M. Yalman in particular was always a leading Kemalist publicist."[67]

The imposition of the tax and Turkish and foreign musings about the Jewish nature of the Dönme twenty years after their arrival in the republic demonstrate how unsuccessful Dönme efforts to integrate, or appear to integrate were. It has been argued that the Dönme "remembered to forget" their identity, and believing that others had forgotten their origins, too, imagined they had become indistinguishable from other citizens of Turkey.[68] That may have been the case for many Dönme, who were utilizing what Michael Taussig calls public secrecy. But the government and Muslims *forgot* to forget that the Dönme formed a separate ethno-religious group. Instead, they remembered that their ancestors were converts from Judaism. Unlike the Dönme themselves or people who actually were Jews, Muslims considered the Dönme simply as Jews.

When Dönme, people who were descendants of Jews but did not consider themselves Jews, arrived in the early Turkish Republic, they made a public commitment to become Turks and Kemalists. Two decades of efforts to assimilate turned to smoke overnight when the wealth tax was announced. Neither their neighbors nor the state recognized them as Turks (i.e., ethnicized Muslims). Political loyalty, service to the nation, public Turkishness, nothing seemed to matter when compared with the unforgiving truth of racial origins. Seen as internal enemies, the Dönme were placed nearly in the same position as Jews in Turkey, who, after the massacres and deportations of Armenians and Orthodox Christians remained the largest non-Muslim community in the country.

In the early republic of the 1930s and 1940s, Jews felt the full brunt of Turkish racialized nationalism. Measures promoting the speaking of Turkish in public sometimes led to violent encounters between Muslims and Jews, and there was a pogrom in Thrace in 1934, part of a long-term government plan to discourage Jews, viewed as a potential fifth column, from living in the sensitive border region. According to the Statute of Relocation, passed in parliament two weeks before the pogrom, the government planned to deport Jews from Thrace and replace them with Turks.[69] There was little sympathy for Jews, foreign or local, in Turkey. In the spring of 1941, non-Muslim men between the ages of twenty and forty-five, especially those who owned businesses in Istanbul, were conscripted into special army reserve units, but not given any weapon training, instead assigned to road repair work in the interior.[70] Conscription lasted one year. Then soon after the conscription ended, the wealth tax was implemented. In 1942, German Embassy reports from Ankara to the Foreign Office in Berlin noted the increase in antisemitism in Turkey evidenced by the tax and the prime minister's response to the pleas of Jewish refugees in Nazi-occupied Europe.[71] In response to their plight, the prime minister declared: "Turkey cannot be a homeland for those who are unwanted elsewhere." He made this statement after the *Struma*, a ship carrying nearly 1,000 Jewish refugees from Romania was not permitted to disembark its passengers in Istanbul, but instead, after over two months, was towed through the Bosphorus to the Black Sea, set adrift, and later torpedoed and sunk by a Soviet submarine, killing all but one passenger.[72] Such sentiment was reflected in Turkish foreign policy and its treatment of Turkish Jews abroad. In the 1930s and 1940s, the Turkish Republic denaturalized most Jews with Turkish citizenship living in Europe, half of whom lived in France, and forbade them to reenter Turkey, which allowed the Nazis to send them to their deaths between 1942 and 1944. This occurred after the Nazis had asked Turkish embassies to repatriate their nationals, lest they be subjected to anti-Jewish measures. Most denaturalizations occurred after German authorities sent the Turkish embassy lists of Jews, inquiring about their status. Turkish embassies were even asked about the status of Jews held in detainment camps in western Europe prior to their deportation to certain death in the east.[73] Some Jews were saved here and there by Turkish consular officials, and Turkey welcomed up to one hundred German Jewish scholars during these years. However, due to the lack of intervention of Turkish authorities on their behalf, because its diplomats were ordered "not to send trains full of Jews to Turkey," several thousand Turkish Jews were instead sent to Auschwitz, never to return.[74]

Such contemporary views of and policies toward citizens who were not Muslims, especially Jews, hindered the full realization of the project to create equal citizens in the republic.[75] The ruling Republican People's Party's view of Jews crippled the success of the government's social blueprint and secular rhetoric. Already in the early 1930s, the party's organ, *Ülkü* (Ideal) cited and emulated ideas from fascist Italy and Nazi Germany.[76] A party report written in 1944 argued that non-Muslims did not integrate, spoke their own languages, had played no role in the foundation of the republic, served the interests of foreign powers, and never demonstrated their loyalty to Turkey.[77] The report states that Jews never mixed with others, since they remained separate, their only goal being to earn money. The report proposes that Turkey should not permit the Jewish population to grow, but ease Jewish emigration, decrease their population, and remove them from important spheres of the Turkish economy. As an MP and former justice minister remarked, the environment created by Nazi successes in Europe offered "the last opportunity Turkey would have for several years to eliminate Jewish domination of Turkish commerce."[78]

The wealth tax can be viewed as the culmination of an effort to win a "second" War of Independence" by "liberating" the economy of the last remaining non-Muslims and creating a Turkish bourgeoisie. The Turkish government created the wealth tax in 1942 ostensibly to tax the excessive profits of war profiteers whatever their religious or ethnic backgrounds. In practice, its discriminatory implementation demonstrates how it was aimed at creating a Muslim Turkish bourgeoisie at the expense of the remaining foreign, Christian, Jewish, and Dönme businessmen and industrialists in Istanbul.[79] Of the two people charged the highest tax, one was Jewish, the other Dönme.[80] As two-thirds of the tax was assessed in Istanbul, and especially targeted the import and export trade, the tax served as yet another method for the nationalist state to provincialize the cosmopolitan city and pass from an economy based on private enterprise to a state-controlled economy.[81] After 1923, Istanbul remained the last link of the Turkish state to the rest of Europe. Concentrated there were what remained of Ottoman era wealth, capital, Christians, and Jews. By taxing or confiscating this wealth, the state could strike the death blow to cosmopolitanism. In 1925, the architects of the republic had hoped Muslim Turks would occupy the commercial and financial vacuum left by the deported or murdered Greeks and Armenians. Instead, their place had been filled by Jews and then Dönme.[82] The financial crisis of the war years allowed the government to complete the goal of ruining their economic position. "This law is also a revolutionary law," the prime minister declared. "We now face an opportunity which can win us our economic independence. We will in this way eliminate the foreigners [foreign citizens resident in Turkey and non-Muslim citizens] who control our market and give the Turkish market to the Turks."[83] Only then would the main street of Istanbul be Turkified, meaning that the Christian and Jewish names of stores would be replaced by those of their Muslim business rivals.[84]

The government and its citizens who implemented the wealth tax failed to live up to the founding principle of secular citizenship and equality. Converting to secularism, the Dönme gambled that losing their religion would be offset by being treated as equals. Many Dönme abandoned Dönme religion and gave up all that they valued, yet did not receive full equality in return. The tax seems in some respects to be a transformation of the poll tax (*jizya*) Christians and Jews had to pay in the Ottoman Empire, one of the differences being the addition of an added racial qualifier making the Dönme liable. The Dönme were reminded not only of their difference but of the fact that they were Jews by blood. Faik Ökte checked Muslims' backgrounds to see if they were Dönme, and when he believed they were, he taxed them at a higher rate, making them pay twice as much as Muslims, yet half as much as Christians and Jews. Three of the four categories of the tax he imposed in Istanbul included Jews, or those perceived as Jews: non-Muslim (Armenians, Jews, and Orthodox Christians), foreign (including Jewish refugees from Germany), and Dönme (Jewish converts to Islam). Ökte's actions clearly indicate a racial understanding and inquisitorial mentality; after all, Dönme were descendants of people who had converted three centuries before.

Many argue that the tax was implemented because of the close relations between Turkey and Nazi Germany and Nazi sympathy prevalent among many Turks, including the prime minister. But anti-Dönme sentiment and fears of Dönme economic power existed two decades before the tax was applied. In the 1940s, the state did not forget that the Dönme had been distinct and a potential economic threat. Popular perceptions of secret Jewish economic power and treachery for not using their wealth to help in the struggle for independence dovetailed with conspiracy theories of Dönme power, which still had resonance twenty years after the group arrived en masse in Turkey. The fact that some Dönme also did not keep their end of the deal by not becoming sincerely secular and continued to pursue a separate identity also played a role in their being categorized as a distinct group. The Turkish nation-state reactivated an Ottoman practice of social division by demarcating Muslims from non-Muslims, but then added a modern touch by separating Dönme from Muslim.

How did the state know who was a Dönme? Many have speculated that the Dönme carried a special number on their identity cards that identified them as Dönme, that the state marked them when they arrived in 1923 and 1924. In fact, more important than the state were the neighbors of the Dönme who implemented the tax. Secret commissions met behind closed doors to draw up lists of those liable to the tax and to fix an arbitrary amount that taxees had to pay in cash within two weeks. The tax was implemented by neighborhood committees. The people among whom the Dönme resided turned them in to the authorities. This meant that their neighbors always knew of their identity. The Dönme had arrived in Turkey at the end of the population exchange in clusters of Kapancı, Karakaş, and Yakubi family groups. Their arrival was accompanied by the spirited debate in the press—kicked off by one of their own, Rüştü—about their racial and religious identity. When the time came, their neighbors and business rivals were able to settle scores. It is lucky for the Dönme that despite the spate of newspaper articles about the group in the 1920s and 1930s none of the journalists got their hands on a genealogy that would have done the most to boost their claims about the racial origins and lack of mixture of the group. One wonders, however, whether any were used in the 1940s during the implementation of the wealth tax, whether any self-hating Dönme types like Rüştü passed them on to those searching the origins of the black marketeers.

The behavior of some Dönme during the implementation of the tax again highlights the poor relations they had with Jews. Although it is said that Dönme families, such as the Kapancı Bezmen, who were important in the textile industry, paid a heavy price overall, some Dönme, including Refik Bezmen, benefited from the Jews' plight by buying their business partners' shares at rock bottom prices and not returning them after the war.[85] An interviewee's father suffered during the collection of the tax as well. Having been assessed a large amount, he faced great financial losses, but Dönme helped one another pay their debts. The interviewee also says that because the Dönme had been in the country less time than the Jews and Greeks, they faced less opposition than the others confronted, whose enemies sought to rid themselves of their economic rivals and take over their businesses, reveling in their being bankrupted.[86]

According to Turkish government figures, Muslims were assessed 4.94 percent of their assets, Orthodox Christians 156 percent, Jews 179 percent, and Armenians 232 percent.[87] Since most possessed wealth in the form of goods or real estate, it is difficult to imagine how they could be expected to come up with so much money in such a short time. It seems clear that the goal was to ruin them. The assessments and decisions of the commissions were irrevocable. Those unable to pay the excessive tax, anywhere from 100 to 500 percent of their estimated assets, even after having to sell everything they owned, lost all their assets and were sent to hard labor camps in remote eastern Anatolia, such as at Aşkale. Not a single Muslim Turk was sentenced like a convict to an unlimited period of hard labor. Clearing roads of snow in winter and building roads in summer, these men, some as old as eighty, earned 1 lira per day. If a man had been taxed 10,000, 100,000, or even 1 million lira, one could calculate how long it would take to pay off the debt. This drove Christians and Jews out of business and commercial life, and the financial and psychological damage it caused broke Armenian, Greek, and Jewish men. Indeed, as Rıfat Bali relates, this tax served as one of the main impulses for the rapid emigration of half of Turkish Jewry in the ensuing years.[88] Coming at the end of a series of anti-Jewish measures, and not followed by apology or compensation, it made Jews, considered parasites, realize that they would never be treated as equals, and thus that they had no future in Turkey.

A meeting at the Office of the Head of the Industrial Study Board in Istanbul in autumn 1944 toward the end of the wealth tax's imposition is illustrative of the mood of the time. Şevket Süreyya Aydemir serves as the head of the Industrial Study Board. He is meeting with Avram Galanté and another leading Turkish Jew about the implementation of the wealth tax. Galanté, despite being a vocal Turkish nationalist and vociferous proponent of the Turkification of the Jews, lost his property to the wealth tax. He went to Aydemir to appeal the confiscation of his property. Aydemir is very blunt, asserting: "We Turks, because for centuries we have been busy fighting thousands of wars, have never found time for industry, or for accumulating money and wealth. All of you minorities have done this. We protected you from wars. You did not send any soldiers to the front. Sometimes you even found a way not even to pay taxes." Accordingly, ethno-religious minorities "gathered all commerce, industry, imports and exports, money and wealth in your hands. This was done at the cost of the blood we spilled for centuries—even after the Tanzimat [Reform Decree of 1839 establishing equality of Christians, Jews, and Muslims under Ottoman law] you were able to preserve the opportunities that you minorities have gathered unto yourselves. The Tanzimat Decree itself was not proclaimed in order to save us from these wars, but in order to preserve 'the security of your property and person.'"Then Aydemir draws up an imaginary account book. He says: "If you were to compare the blood that we have spilled for centuries against the one or two million lira that you will hand over for this wealth tax, and if we were even to call it the 'Blood Tax,' do you think our reckoning would be very oppressive? What do you say? If you wish, let's weigh the blood we've spilled and our endless military efforts against a little extra taxing, or our accumulated blood and rights as soldiers against the wealth you've accumulated and see if ours adds up. If we are being unjust, your taxes will be abolished. What do you say?"[89]

As illustrated by Aydemir's argument, World War II and the wealth tax coincided with the return of the parasite motif to the forefront of public discourse. At the end of 1940, when the RPP debated what to do in the event Nazi Germany should invade and occupy Istanbul, an outspoken Istanbul MP named Kâzım Karabekir argued that non-Muslims "who suck the blood of Turks," would be fifth columns, so they should be deported to the interior and replaced with Muslim Turks.[90] The prime minister's statements during the implementation of the tax confirm the prevalence of the parasite theme. In an interview with *The Times* (London) at the beginning of 1943, Saracoğlu declared that the non-Muslims had "grown rich by taking advantage of the hospitality shown by this country."[91] Moreover, he admitted, "If these fortunes have been made in Istanbul and if their owners are in the proportion of 75 per cent Jews and non-Moslems, that is a coincidence which the Turkish Government will be the first to deplore." That is to say, deploring the fact that so many Jews and Christians have become rich in Istanbul.[92]

Ahmet Emin Yalman wrote the only critical words about the tax in the Turkish press, focusing especially on its inequitable administration.[93] His statements remind the reader of what he had written as the anonymous author of the series on the Dönme twenty years previously, that loyalty and patriotism should be the only litmus test of belonging to the nation. He still had a hard time convincing others of his definition of who was a Turk. Yet he waited until after the tax was abolished and had much positive to say about the tax as well.

In his English-language autobiography, written a little over a dozen years after the war, Yalman criticizes the wealth tax without mentioning the Dönme or his relatives who suffered from it. He called it one of the greatest shocks of his life. Yet he defends its motivation.[94] This echoes another remark he makes in the book, that it was all too vividly remembered how during the foreign occupation of Turkey following World War I, "minorities had not behaved generally as loyal citizens." These were some of the same false charges that Yalman had been countering for three decades, but here he seems to be accepting their validity. He did complain of the unjust way the wealth tax was implemented, including "discriminations of a political or religious character" and its enforcement "in an atmosphere of terror."[95]

In his Turkish-language autobiography, written thirty years after the war, Yalman devotes a number of pages to the wealth tax, but again avoids mentioning that Dönme were made to pay twice as much as Muslims.[96] He explains how it was intended to crush the economic power of minorities and was inequitably applied: even Christians and Jews who were not rich and who spoke Turkish and had served in the military had to pay. Because of this, he was ashamed to be a Turk and met with the prime minister to convince him that something had to be done, since Turkey looked bad in the eyes of the foreign press. Yalman says in his autobiography that he twice happened to visit Aşkale, and that those deportees were treated well by local people and lived comfortably and in healthy conditions.[97] From his description, one would think he was describing a Swiss spa.[98] From the passage, it is not clear whether he was sent there as a deportee or went there as a news reporter. One writer even says that he was sent there as a punishment for not being able to pay his tax.[99] Nevertheless, in the preceding pages, he describes his immense disappointment with the "racist" tax. It was most crushing to him personally, since it targeted those "model minorities," that is, the Jews, who identified with and loved the homeland, served in the military, and spoke Turkish at home. Nevertheless, he was heavily criticized in other papers, but does not say how. He implies, however, that others labeled *Vatan* a "minority" newspaper, which was what the prime minister wanted him to admit.[100]

Dönme Claiming Turkishness and Islam: Ahmet Emin Yalman and Sabiha Sertel

In the 1920s, Yalman's strategy was to claim that the Dönme had been almost entirely assimilated into the Turkish Muslim nation. Yet for the next decade, despite his efforts, Yalman was continuously attacked in the pages of *Cumhuriyet* for being a Dönme, a "fake" Turk, and in essence, a Jew.[101] This caused him to try another approach, beginning in the 1940s, to assert his own Muslim and Turkish identity and deny his Dönme background. This approach is especially evident in his two autobiographies. In his English-language autobiography, Yalman introduces himself by writing, "I am a Turkish journalist."[102] He also notes how he was born on the last Friday of Ramadan, which coincided with the Day of Fate, when Muhammad received the first revelation, at the time when the muezzins were calling from the minarets for the midday prayer.[103] Yalman also discusses his circumcision according to Muslim rituals.[104]

Yalman's two volumes and nearly two thousand pages of Turkish autobiography contain not a single reference to the Dönme, nor to the eleven part series he wrote about the group, nor to debates in the press in which he was called a Dönme. Yalman refers to Salonika, which when he was born had a majority Jewish population and the largest concentration of Dönme, as "a Turkish city, very much part of the homeland" and mentions that it was also the birthplace of Atatürk.[105]

Yalman, looking back much later on his Feyziye education, argues Şemsi Efendi instilled Turkish national feeling into him, an implausible claim.[106] The aim of Yalman's autobiography was to establish himself in the minds of the public as a patriotic Turkish Muslim who had devoted his life to fighting for the Turkish nationalist interest. The Dönme are not mentioned in the place one would expect, the section on Salonika. The only hint is his discussion of there being two worlds at home, one conservative and old-fashioned, the other progressive and new.[107] But this mirrors Atatürk's own analysis of his childhood in the city and merely serves as a generalization about the era.[108] Yalman even avoids mentioning the anti-Dönme slurs hurled at the CUP by parties opposing it. Yalman only mentions they were called Freemasons.[109] Yalman displays his patriotism by writing about Armenians and Orthodox Christians as subversives.[110] Only Turks, he declares, were willing to sacrifice for the nation; the rest were separatists. Worse, the minorities were gaining economic power.[111]

Yalman's autobiography is remarkable more for what is left out than what is included. He repeatedly asserts that his aim, manifested in the newspapers he founded and for which he wrote, was to support the national struggle and national unity, and hinder the enemies of the Turkish nation.[112] He asserts that he had always supported Atatürk and his principles. When the Allies left Istanbul, the headline in *Vatan* declared that Beyoğlu, the district of the city with perhaps the most prevalent non-Muslim population "has become Muslim."[113] He praises the spiritual leaders of the minorities that had gone astray under occupation, but who participated in military ceremonies and made speeches peppered with patriotic phrases in 1922.[114] He celebrates the heroism of Turkish soldiers, the success of the independence struggle, and the power of Turkish unity in the face of foreign intrigue.[115] Denying the Dönme background, avoiding any mention of Jews, even in Salonika where they predominated, and asserting his Muslim and Turkish bona fides, perhaps Yalman did not wish to resurrect the bitter, painful personal attacks he faced at the time, which culminated in an attempt on his life decades later.

The story of the Sertels is more dramatic, and ultimately, more tragic. On the occasion of Atatürk's death in 1938, Sabiha Sertel wrote an elegy demonstrating her transformation into a nationalist and secularist.[116] She praises Atatürk's founding of Turkey, bringing down the sultanate and caliphate, replacing Shari'a with secular law based on western European law codes, which saved Turkey, bound to Islam due to Shari'a, from the tyranny of Islamic law, separating religion and the state, and removing religion's reactionary hold over education. Moreover, Kemalist nationalism, she says, was, like the nationalism of 1908, not based on race.[117] Yet her enemies proved the popularity of racialized nationalism.

Like Yalman, the Sertel couple also faced many lawsuits, especially in the early 1940s. The cases usually concerned slander, and pitted the socialist Sertels against fascists, such as the writers of *Sebîlürreşat*.[118] In 1941 and 1942, Sabiha Sertel was forbidden to write. In fact, Yalman was permitted to continue bringing out *Tan* only on condition that he publish nothing she had written. At the time, Turkey was seeking to be on good terms with Nazi Germany, and the government could not stomach her antifascist pieces. For example, she had written, "Hiding behind the mask of nationalism, racists defend Nazi ideology, praise the wealth tax, and propagate anti-minority views."[119] Saracoğlu was gleeful when the Nazis attacked the USSR. Seeing the Nazis as the liberators of Soviet Turks, in one speech he stated: "Turkish nationalism is not a peaceful nationalism. Just as we have close relations with Turkish races living abroad, so, too is it every Turk's duty to wish for their good fortune. We are Turkists and we will remain Turkists."[120] He advocated a Greater Turkey and did not arrest Pan-Turkists until February 1945, when it was clear the Nazis were en route to being destroyed. *Cumhuriyet*, the mouthpiece of the regime and thus close to Saracoğlu, labeled Sabiha Sertel a Bolshevik and Gypsy. Sabiha Sertel was only allowed to write again when Turkey became officially neutral in 1944.[121]

This incessant critic of the one-party state and advocate of multi-party democracy became the enemy of the ruling RPP party, which had frightening consequences. On a sunny, but cold day in the autumn of 1945, a furious mob of 10,000 fascist university students organized by the RPP gathers first before the main gate of Istanbul University. It coalesces in Bayezid Square, and then marches down Divan Yolu past where many Karakaş Dönme had settled after being deported from Salonika, toward the building of the newspaper *Tan* in Çağoğlu. Shouting "God damn Communism" and "God damn the Sertels," they first destroy a bookstore selling communist books and then *Tan*'s offices and press.[122] The students roam the building, destroying everything in it, asking where the Sertels are. They intended to strip the couple naked and paint them red with the bottles of ink they had brought and then parade them through the streets saying, "Here are your Reds."[123] Hüseyin Cahit Yalçın, the enemy of the Sertels, had published a call to arms in *Tanin* using the phrase "Rise up, O citizen," which Namık Kemal had used to incite Ottomans against Abdülhamid II's tyranny before 1908; ironically, here it was used to incite a mob against those fighting for democracy.[124]

No assailants were arrested for the looting and burning to the ground of *Tan*'s office and press building. The Sertels, at home in the Asian suburb of Moda, were told the mob had boarded ferries and was on their way to their home. The police redirected the boats to the Princess Islands, home to large Armenian, Greek, and Jewish populations. The Sertels were placed under house arrest and then imprisoned. They were put on trial the following year for slander, actually their harsh criticism of the government, especially its silencing of opposition and the press.[125]

The Sertels continued to advocate for free elections and a multi-party democracy, main themes of Ahmet Emin Yalman's writing as well. Sabiha Sertel compared Turkey to a fascist state and claimed it was not democratic, since citizens' mouths, wrists, and ankles were bound, and were not permitted to think, speak, or act. The government wanted to silence this forceful critic of "freedom in chains."[126] Fortunately, the Sertels were exonerated and released. Nevertheless, life in Moda was like a prison, as police controlled their movements and screened all visitors. In 1950, the couple decided to travel to Paris; Sabiha Sertel never returned to Turkey.[127]

The Double Bind of the Dönme: Race and Religion

The problems Ahmet Emin Yalman and Sabiha Sertel faced were representative of the nearly impossible double bind of being Dönme in the early Turkish Republic. Their acceptance required a two-phase conversion: they had to first of all prove their sincerity as Muslims, and then, after being recognized as Muslims, the Dönme were compelled to abandon this accepted religious identity for a secular Turkish one. But they faced handicaps in the process of being recognized as Muslims and becoming Turks. The persistence of their imagined and real religious beliefs and practices marked them as distinct from other Muslims at a time when being Muslim did not include formerly acceptable practices and affiliations, including Sufi ones. The Dönme were foreign, having arrived from Greece. For this group at least, the limits of Turkishness stopped at the newly drawn Turkish border. They were not of the Turkish race, since they had until recently only intermarried among themselves, descendants of Jewish converts. Thus by blood and lineage, they could not be considered Turks, who did not include non-Muslims.

In other words, the two main road blocks to acceptance of the Dönme were racialized nationalism and ethnicized religion. A belief in biological race, not merely ethnicity,[128] made the boundaries separating groups far more rigid in the republic than they had been in the empire. With the introduction of the idea of racial difference in the latter years of the empire, the possibility of cultural conversion became far more difficult for groups considered racially different than the core group that was to constitute the nation in the republic. Whereas in the empire, the religious convert was able to reap the benefits of conversion—individual transformation, a new identity, joining another community—in the republic, the cultural convert faced social and political constraints that hindered his or her ability to be fully of the community he or she desired to leave and the one he or she desired to join.[129] Turkey applied an ethno-national model to those considered non-Muslims and non-Turks. Yet even if the nation-state had employed a civic model of nationness for these groups, because of the deployment of racial thinking, in the Turkish case there are great similarities between the secular and communal ideas of nationhood. Neither tolerates the multiple identities that had existed in the plural society of the empire they replaced nor allows for any exit strategies such as cultural separateness.

The problem the Dönme faced was that pluralism based upon accepting and maintaining cultural difference, religious identity, corporate autonomy, and non-ethnically homogeneous communities was replaced by an attempt to create a nation based upon ideas of race that excluded formerly integral components of the whole. The nation that was the direct successor of the empire was unwilling in its first decades to sustain the pluralism that had accommodated separateness and multiple identities. The end of empire spelled the end of the tolerance of difference. The modern nation-state requires transparency to rule. As we see in the implementation of the wealth tax, no matter what approach the Dönme pursued, their identity could no longer be an open secret. The logic of Turkish racialized nationalism ensured that the Dönme had to become a "mysterious page of history" as Yalman wrote in a newspaper series, a disappearing relic of the Ottoman past.

As the category of religion (Islam) was reconceived, the term "Muslim" was reconceptualized. "Muslim" signified the ethnic core of the Turkish nation, whose public practices were avowedly secular. A term that had denoted religious identity in the Ottoman Empire became an ethnic marker in the nation-state of Turkey, whose civic religion is secularism. Thus religious Muslims bore the brunt of the state's concern with controlling religion in all its manifestations, from education to prayer, since secular elites were under the spell of the secularization thesis and laicization, the transfer of institutions from religious to centralized state authority. Yet asking religious minorities to assimilate means they have to abandon their own beliefs and identities, while the majority does not have to. Even in the Turkish case, where religious Muslims had to convert to secularism, to be Turkish meant to be ethnically Muslim.

Ethnicized religion was expressed in an Ottoman parliamentary debate from 1920, when one MP asked, "Is not Turkish the same thing as Muslim?" and another responded, "Sir, when one says Turkish one *is* saying Muslim."[130] The late Ottoman and early republican statesman Celal Nuri argued that "the true citizen was a Hanefi Muslim and spoke Turkish."[131] Although the Dönme appeared as Muslims, persistent rumors and their own testimony, especially that of Rüştü, suggested that they maintained a set of beliefs and communal consciousness—also manifested in their self-segregation, separate schools, and distinct cemeteries—inappropriate for people whose ancestors had converted to Islam centuries earlier.

The politics of secularization require that ethical moralities supersede theocentric ways of being based on corporate communities.[132] In Turkey, this meant converting religious Muslims to secular Kemalists and compelling people to abandon Islamic morality and ethics and replacing these with lay morality and ethics.[133] State-imposed morality replaces individual moral conscience. The nation-state requires a self-determining citizen, but it is an illusion of freedom, since citizens are presented with a set of propositions to which they must assent.[134] The clash between self-ascribed religious identities and state-granted rights that deny subjectivity and the ability to define the self exacts a heavy price, because it allows people fewer alternatives and less flexibility in determining their identities.[135] The apparently liberating aspects of state-enforced secularism, which was used as a pillar of the nation-building process in the transition from multi-religious empire to homogenizing, secular nation-state led to the transformation of religious identity into an ethnic category and made cultural conversion a limited possibility for those groups wishing to undertake it for the sake of integration.

Although secular nation-states attempted to remove manifestations of religion that did not support the modern state project from the public sphere and to restrict them to the private, this process ironically increased the significance of religion and religious identity and made them issues of public debate. In theory, the problem of how minority citizens related to the state and civil society would be resolved by their subjective choice to integrate. In practice, racialized nationalism and ethnicized religion hindered their earnest efforts.

The waning years of the Ottoman Empire witnessed changing perceptions of religious difference and the rise of race-based nationalism, which serve as the background for how the Dönme were treated in the new nation-state of Turkey. The Dönme flourished when they were allowed to be religious international merchants in plural Ottoman society, but were pressured to dissolve as a group when bearing stigmatized racial and religious status in the secular nation-state of Turkey.[136]

Conclusion

From Cosmopolitanism to Nationalism

Turkish historiography is dominated by a history of becoming, from the point of view imagining how the Turkish Republic was established and how secular nationalist Turks became who they are. The past is reread in terms of the present, and events and personalities are highlighted only when they are considered stepping-stones to what happened later. Aspects of those people and events that do not fit the teleology are ignored, or only given value when it is assumed that they contributed to the future. Adopting this way of thinking, one might suppose that Mustafa Kemal Atatürk's reform efforts built upon the foundation previously forged by the Dönme in Salonika, and in which he was instructed as a young boy while a student of the Dönme religious leader Şemsi Efendi. Yet Atatürk and other founders of the Turkish Republic emphasized radical secularism (laicism) and nationalism in the new nation-state, whereas the Dönme incorporated religion into their way of being and expressed no manifestations of nationalism.

It is hard to imagine the earlier, very different world the Dönme inhabited from our nation-state or post-nation-state vantage point. Much is lost in narratives that cannot without suspicion or omission conceive of the mode of being, role, or aims of a group such as the Dönme. They are seen as either simply Jews or secular nationalists, not who they were, religious cosmopolitans who forged an ethno-religious identity syncretizing Jewish (Kabbalah) and Islamic (Sufism) mysticism.

Religion and religious people played a crucial role in the modernizing of the Ottoman Empire, culture, and society and in making it cosmopolitan.

Accepting that religion was a vital element, we can avoid false dichotomies between progress and reaction, modern and traditional, secular and religious, or linking tradition to religion and irrationality, modernity to secularism and rationality, and secularism to cosmopolitanism. Secularity assumes links to progress, liberty, tolerance, democracy, and the public sphere.[1] Ignoring the practice of plural, religious empires, modern secularists see religion as a threat to freedom of thought and expression, and secularism as "a necessity for the democratic life of religiously diverse societies."[2] Accordingly, they assume a religious majority poses a greater threat than a secular majority, that a religious society cannot be tolerant, that only a secular society can be free of violence, coercion, and persecution.[3] The history of the twentieth century and the experience of the Dönme argue to the contrary, that secularism guarantees neither democracy nor tolerance of minorities.[4]

Unfortunately for the Dönme, they contributed to a revolution that set in motion processes of secularism and nationalism. Accordingly, the transregional impact of the transcultural Dönme, which extended as far as Paris and Berlin, ran into a wall after Salonika fell to Greece in 1912 and was Hellenized, and the Turkish Republic replaced the Ottoman Empire just over a decade later. Ottoman Salonika became Greek Thessaloníki, and Istanbul became a predominantly Turkish city. Because they were proponents of and represented cosmopolitanism, the Dönme had no place in the nation-states of Greece and Turkey.

The world the Dönme had helped create was a heterogeneous one, based on continuities, connections, and mobility. The Dönme forged a wide commercial space, whose home base, Salonika, was also their main site of religious pilgrimage, along with the small town of Ulcinj (in present-day Montenegro), where their messiah is buried. Pilgrimage did not take them to Jerusalem, and few to Mecca. Their lives were marked by movement and travel and transregional itineraries.

Then, abruptly, there was spatial break. People who had once belonged to many places no longer truly belonged anywhere. A map of the Dönme world before 1923 was centered on Salonika. It had axes running north and south, from Manchester to Munich, and west and east, from Paris to Istanbul. After 1923, their world was centered in Istanbul, and connected only to minor Turkish cities such as Samsun, Trabzon, Ankara, and Izmir. The Greco-Turkish population exchange of 1923–24 was a catastrophe, a major rupture that ended the possibility of a cosmopolitan mode of being. Dönme routes were stopped by rigid nation-state borders. Their circulation was frozen and blocked. They were redirected to a new pilgrimage destination: Ankara, later the site of Atatürk's mausoleum. The Dönme had to eke out a living in a narrow, landlocked commercial space. The world the Dönme were forced to live in was based on homogeneity, discontinuity, disconnection, and rupture.

By World War II, at the latest, the Dönme had ceased to be a real presence in Greece and Turkey, two of the successor states of the Ottoman Empire, and Salonika and Istanbul had lost their cosmopolitan nature. Whereas turn-of-the-twentieth-century Salonika had had the smallest Muslim population among major Ottoman cities, and one of the largest Jewish ones, Istanbul had had one of the largest Greek populations. At the beginning of the twenty-first century, however, there were only 1,000 Jews (and no Dönme) in Thessaloníki, a city of over 800,000 inhabitants, and 2,000 Orthodox Christians (and an unknown number of Dönme descendants) in Istanbul, a city of over twelve million people. Istanbul would not again become a globally connected city until the 1980s, after the Turkish Republic abandoned the extreme nationalism of the early republican era. These processes occurred long after the disappearance of the Dönme.

Contrary to what it had been half a century before, the cosmopolitan nature of Istanbul became a source of pride for Turkish nationalists, something that put Turkey on a par with Europe, a status to be embraced, not disparaged or expunged. Moreover, in the 1990s, descendants of Dönme and others began publishing works explaining the history, culture, and religious beliefs of the group.[5] Esin Eden and Nicholas Stavroulakis's *Salonica: A Family Cookbook*, based on Ottoman-language recipes prepared in the nineteenth century by two of Eden's great aunts, was published first in Greece in English, and then in Turkish in Turkey. However, the historical section explaining the history of the Dönme is omitted from the Turkish version. This disparity, according to the preface, "was felt necessary given the quite different milieux in which the two versions were going to appear."[6] This change is evidence not only of a concern to avoid adding fuel to the widespread fear and hatred of the Dönme in Turkey, but also displays the secularization of ritual, because food formerly had secret, sacred, mystical meanings for the Dönme.[7] Similarly, Dönme genealogies compiled since the 1990s are also without religious significance, being instead the work of family nostalgia. Turkish public interest in the Dönme only became possible when the group had practically disappeared from society, when cultural and religious pluralism could be viewed as a positive feature, and when Turks began to once again imagine connections with the world well beyond the boundaries of the nation-state.

Hellenized Thessaloníki was designated European Capital of Culture for 1997, after city planners and leaders in the former domicile of the Dönme spent decades at best neglecting and at worst erasing almost every trace of its Ottoman past, including its Dönme, Muslim, and Jewish elements. The city's most obvious Ottoman symbol, the White Tower, constructed on orders of Sultan Suleiman I in the sixteenth century, was converted into a Byzantine museum. The exhibit explains the city's history only until 1430, when it became a part of the Ottoman Empire, labeled the period of Turkish occupation. A panel at the entrance of the museum declares the tower was built in the sixteenth century, but it does not state who built it. In the 1920s, the city's Sufi lodges, including the Mevlevi, were torn down. The Véritas and L'Avenir de Orient Masonic lodges did not survive the rise of antisemitism and the Metaxas dictatorship.[8] Between 1922 and 1925, the Dönme mosque was shorn of its minaret, made to house refugees from Anatolia and then turned into a museum and gallery.[9] The Dönme cemeteries disappeared beneath the new concrete skin of the city. During the Nazi occupation Ahmet Kapancı's villa, draped on the street side in a black banner marked *SS* and by another in the courtyard with the Death's Head, was where Alois Brunner and Adolf Eichmann's close aid Dieter Wisliceny organized the deportation of the city's Jews to Auschwitz.[10] The international trader Mehmet Kapancı's villa, after housing a parade of Greek royalty and politicians, ultimately became the National Bank of Greece's Cultural Center for Northern Greece. Dönme schools were forced to close in accordance with the Treaty of Lausanne, and the Dönme presence in the city was erased from the local Greek historical record.[11]

Greek letters above the door of the New Mosque, the most modern and last mosque built in the city, announce "Archaeology Museum" (fig. C.1), marring its esthetic appearance and bearing witness to how the modern Dönme presence, if recognized, has been relegated to the ancient past. At the same time, this latest cultural layer marks the building as local, confining it to a fixed, absolute time and space, not the space-time that connected Dönme from Salonika to many elsewheres, and thus obscuring the mobility of the people who built it.[12] In 1997, the mosque became one of the sites chosen to host exhibits celebrating the selection of the city as Cultural Capital of Europe.

Today Thessaloníkan city maps mark the Dönme mosque as the former municipal art gallery, or as an archaeological museum. Tourist maps produced by the municipality do not mark the building at all; in fact, the keys of these maps do not mark any Ottoman buildings. Acknowledgement of the Dönme-built structure reappears only in contemporary tourist maps produced by members of the two religious groups from which the Dönme emerged: Jews and Muslims. A recent version of the Jewish-owned Molho

FIGURE C.1 Entrance to the New Mosque in Thessaloníki. Photo by author.

bookstore's map "Sites of Jewish Interest" marks the city's Jewish museum, community center, Holocaust memorial, and Dönme mosque and villas alike with Stars of David, erasing the difference between the Jewish and Dönme past. The latest map still places a Star of David over Mehmet Kapancı's villa. The map produced by the Turkish Consulate (housed in Atatürk's first home), denotes the same Dönme buildings as "Turkish" works, nationalizing the memory of the Dönme and blotting out the Muslim nature of the group.

After spending so much effort maintaining their genealogical, moral and ethical, social, economic, and spatial distinction in Salonika, the Dönme had to expend even more effort to dissolve their religion and social distinctions in the early Turkish Republic. The state and social pressure assisted these efforts by ridding them of the wealth and power they had had in Salonika.

It would seem that the Dönme could be very useful to the new Turkish Republic. They had received educations at the best schools in Salonika, spoke many foreign languages, and had many contacts in western and central Europe. If one assumes that they were already proponents of secularism in Salonika, then one can imagine that the transition to the Turkish Republic would be a smooth one. It is often argued that the new republic, in desperate need of personnel to fill government positions with qualified people, turned to the Dönme.[13]

The Dönme were suitable to the task, so the argument goes, and especially to positions in the Foreign Ministry, because they were secular, had turned away from religion, thus becoming modern and "Western-leaning." In fact, one of the republic's first (1925–38) foreign ministers was Dr. Tevfik Rüştü (Aras), a descendant of the Karakaş. Some Dönme were able to make the transition between Salonika and Istanbul better than others. Despite having served the sultan in occupied Istanbul as the last Ottoman finance minister, the taciturn Faik Nüzhet was considered to have valuable financial knowledge and became an advisor to Atatürk.[14] Based on such examples, the above scenario supports a triumphalist, teleological, presentist thesis that it was only in the Turkish Republic that the Dönme, for the first time in their history of over two centuries, were able to live without any major problems, free and unoppressed. It is claimed only the new modern model of citizenship permitted this freedom, as a result of which the Dönme became idealized, model, secular, nationalist citizens and represented in their lives the basic principles of the secular nationalist state.[15] Because the way religion, education, and culture were viewed in the Turkish Republic were the same as the modern life the Dönme promoted, especially in Salonika, it is claimed, they had no problems in the new state and were never oppressed. Although they had to suppress their identity in the process, Dönme were not harmed by policies of Turkification and succeeded in being considered part of Turkishness. According to this understanding, the term "Dönme" can be so watered down to mean any "Western-leaning" secular Turk in contemporary Turkey.

The problem with this thesis is that it is based on looking at the present situation of the descendants of the Dönme and ironing over the painful process of Turkification their families experienced in the first two decades of the Republic. And if they had to suppress their Dönme identity and lose their Dönme religion, was it a success from the perspective of the Dönme or of the Turkish state? Oddly, it is claimed that the enemies of the Dönme were not secular nationalists, but Islamists and Kurds.[16] Perhaps those who argue this thesis are themselves an example of the Dönme assimilation of Turkish nationalism, and identification of state interests with their own. It is hard to imagine how the two most ruthlessly suppressed groups in the early republic, Islamists and Kurds, could have affected the Dönme more than the state. Taking the present for the 1930s, one cannot see the past in its own terms. Assuming that the Dönme had already long been secular in Salonika allows one to make this assertion. But because the Dönme were religious and cosmopolitan, and not secular Turkish nationalists, the thesis that the Dönme paved the way for the republic falls apart. It was the Islamic, plural empire, not the secular nationalist state that tolerated them, did not examine their background or beliefs and allowed them to rise to the top.

Turkish racialized nationalism that replaced Ottoman pluralism was reflected at the symbolic level in the new slogan: 'Unity in language, culture, and blood.'[17] Such sentiment was a bad omen for the Dönme. In a homogeneous nation, diverse ethnic identities were to be superseded by one racial identity; those who were born without the genealogy of the majority had no right to be citizens. In 1921, the future justice minister Mahmut Esat (Bozkurt) wrote, "We are Turks not only by religion, but mainly by race."[18] Following the 1925 Sheikh Said Kurdish rebellion, Prime Minister İsmet İnönü declared: "Our duty is to make all those living in the Turkish fatherland into Turks. We will cut out and discard all those minorities who oppose Turks and Turkism."[19] During another Kurdish uprising, in 1930, Mahmut Esat argued: "All, friends, enemies, and the mountains shall know that the Turk is the master of this country. All those who are not pure Turks have only one right in the Turkish homeland: the right to be servants, the right to be slaves."[20] In this view of nationalism, minorities were to be purified from the body politic, and extraneous elements were to become parasites. Kurds were not the only problem. To Esat, "For me a Turk has more value than all the Jews of this world, not to say the whole world."[21] And for many Muslims in the early republic, as well as today, there is no difference between Jews and Dönme.[22]

The secular Turkish state sought to undermine transnational loyalties constructed on the basis of shared religious identity—Jewish, or Dönme, for example—so that citizens would cultivate loyalty exclusively to the nation. The rise of the secular Turkish Republic and the emergence of a public sphere where "unifying sets of rituals and ideas" served to "define new political communities" made "new, modern forms of freedom and unfreedom, tolerance and intolerance, possible."[23] Religious minorities were tolerated only to the extent that they dropped their former commitments and loyalties. If they did not in fact do so, they had at least publicly to appear to be non-religious, which reflects the adoption of the privatization component of the secularization thesis by the architects of the Turkish Republic. They believed that where religion survives in the modern world, it should do so only in the protected space of the home and not in the public sphere.

No matter what approach the Dönme pursued, their identity could no longer be an open secret. In order to avoid public attacks, the Dönme could claim that although others might label them Dönme, they did not adopt that identity themselves. They could deny having any knowledge of the group, or refuse to talk about it. They could claim that their own sect was defunct, although another one was still active. They could use the term "Salonikan" either to claim social capital as cultivated, progressive Europeans, or as a geographical label, making them indistinguishable from other Muslims who originated in Greece.[24] They could tell others they were sincere Muslims. All of these options were available to them. Ahmet Emin Yalman's sophisticated defense of the group used many of these strategies. He called members of the group "Salonikans." He claimed that only members of another sect still engaged in Dönme practices, whereas the rest (including his own) were on the path to becoming sincere Muslims, because old beliefs were dying out. Yet by acknowledging their differences, even if depicted as being mainly historical, Yalman fed the flames of doubt about the group's sincerity.

The logic of Turkish nationalism ensured that the Dönme had to become a disappearing relic of the Ottoman past. To overcome this handicap in the new republic, prominent Dönme publicly proclaimed their Turkishness through words and deeds, even as some Dönme quietly perpetuated their beliefs. Yalman disavowed their unique religion by redefining it as harmless culture, a matter of antiquarian interest, comparable to the recently dissolved Sufi brotherhoods. Yet even minimal adherence to prior communal identities was considered a threat to national integrity that complicated the integration of the Dönme into the Turkish national fabric. While the Dönme could publicly adopt the civic religion of secularism, they could not be accepted as ethnic Muslims because of their Jewish roots. What was acceptable in the Ottoman Empire appeared in the Turkish Republic as a sinister form of dissimulation. The conversion of the Dönme to secular Turkish nationalism involved engaging with diverse new visions of what religion and race are or ought to be, where conversion serves to remake the categories that define identity.[25]

Religious syncretism is a temporary phenomenon; eventually, one of the competing paramount values comes to the fore. As Richard Eaton argues, at first the new beliefs or practices can be included and accepted, then over time they become identified with or merge with previous ones, and finally, they displace or replace them.[26] The Ottoman authorities recognized this fact, and did not much concern themselves with apparent groups of crypto-Jews or crypto-Christians, or at least the lax practices of new converts over the last three centuries of the empire's existence. Would not the neophytes become Muslims in the long run anyway?[27] The Dönme bucked this trend. Although some Dönme had already made mainstream Islamic values their own by the turn of the twentieth century, this defection was not enough to dissolve the group. Because they were an ethnic as well as religious group, the Dönme lasted longer than expected. Reversion to Islam and the pressure of secularization affected them greatly. But it was the end of endogamy that made the Dönme way of being no longer tenable. Dönme began to choose to dissolve through intermarrying; Dönme interviewees estimate as many as 50 percent of marriages were with non-Dönme following World War II. For such secret groups, the abandoning of endogamy and the "dilution of identity" go together.[28] In other words, "when men and women from the same ethnic group choose to marry outsiders, we have a good hint that the morale of that group is low."[29]

The internal factor of marrying secular Turks, along with several external factors, served to allow Dönme disappearance into Turkish society. The Dönme lost some of their wealth to the exorbitant wealth tax, whose implementation created an emotional as well as financial loss. They lost control over the content of the education in their schools, because all schools were controlled by the secular nationalist central state. Their disappearance is evidence of the success of the Turkish secularization project, at least with this community. They could no longer give their youth the same education, and their students were open to outsiders in larger numbers than ever before.

The Dönme could not recover from the forced migration and the straitjacket of the nation-state mode of being. Due to the conflation of ethnicity (Greek or Turkish), religion (Orthodox Christian or secular Islam), territory (Greece or Turkey), and imagined origins in a pure, ancient past (whether ancient Greece or Hittite and Sumerian), in Greece, to be Greek is to be Orthodox Christian; in Turkey, to be Turkish is to be (secular) Muslim. According to this understanding, it is simply inconceivable for one to be Jewish or especially Muslim *and* Greek; likewise, one cannot be Jewish or especially Christian *and* Turkish.[30] Any other identity means not being local, not belonging, making oneself unwelcome, and presenting oneself as a Trojan Horse, a dangerous internal threat left behind by a rival nation.[31]

The experience of the Dönme in the Ottoman Empire and early Turkish Republic invites comparison with other groups. Of all the comparisons that can be made, that between the Dönme and the Alevi, a sect of Twelver Shi'i Muslims who number many millions in Turkey, is most apt.[32] One cannot convert to either group; membership is determined by birth. Neither faith is a universalizing religious movement or seeks to engage in a universal civilizing process by bringing its religion to others. Historically, members of neither married women of other religions. The Alevi and Dönme were both also frequently accused of having secret immoral rituals.[33]

What is most significant is how the Alevi and Dönme historical experiences are mirror images. In the Ottoman Empire, the rural Alevi were considered disloyal for supporting the Shi'i Safavi dynasty of Iran and consequently persecuted and massacred (especially in the sixteenth century) and were the targets of Sunni Hanefi conversion efforts (especially in the nineteenth century) on grounds of their heretical beliefs, including allegedly engaging in ritualistic orgies. Like the conversos, who promoted secularism since it seemed to fulfill their highest hopes, a society free of the religious persecution of ecclesiastical society,[34] because of four centuries of documented persecution, the Alevi supported the creation of the new, secular Turkish Republic. They believed it would relieve them of Sunni Hanefi oppression and allow them the freedom to practice their own religion in private. Alevi deemed only a secular state that established no religion, but protected the freedom of all, could relieve them of oppression and allow them to maintain their unique religious identity. For this reason, they wholeheartedly joined the Kemalist revolution, many seeing it as a chance to no longer be a central concern of an oppressive state. And in the new republic, they were considered Turks by race, if formerly schismatic Muslims, and an important ethnic building block of the new nation.[35] Many of those who publicly abandoned an Alevi identity and embraced secular nationalism were able to integrate into Turkish society, although the state has not recognized, or allowed them to maintain their religious institutions and practices and continues to Islamize them through compulsory religious education and mosque building in Alevi villages.[36]

Unlike the Alevi, the urban Dönme were tolerated, their beliefs not being an issue, and they supported Ottomanism in which all the elements of society belonged to an overarching identity. The Dönme, who had thus thrived in the empire, were opposed to its dissolution and the construction of nation-states in its place. In the Turkish Republic, they were targeted due to their beliefs, including allegedly engaging in ritualized orgies, and were not accepted as true Muslims. They were discriminated against as Jews and foreigners. Dönme were not in practice accepted as Turks and were distrusted on account of their international commercial connections, which were severed or confiscated.

Because of their very different experiences at the hands of the Turkish Republic, the Alevi underwent a renaissance and today they thrive, while the Dönme have dissolved as an organized community. The Dönme and Alevi, therefore, faced historically opposite pressures, since the latter were persecuted by the imperial state for their religious beliefs, but were not a primary concern of the secular state, which approved of their racial identity.

The dissimilar experiences of the Alevi and Dönme point to their essential difference in the modern period. "Service nomads" are seen as internal enemies during the nation-state era. The rise of the nation-state highlights their anomalous position. Such "internal strangers were potential traitors. They might, or might not, be allowed to assimilate, but they had ever fewer legitimate arguments for continued difference and specialization. In a nation-state, citizenship and nationality ('culture') became inseparable; nonnationals were aliens and thus not true citizens."[37] "Parasitic" groups such as Dönme became victims. The restless pursuit of wealth and learning for the tribe, and filling occupational niches as merchants, bankers, doctors, pharmacists, lawyers, and journalists made them vulnerable to nationalisms that sought to obtain their capital—economic and social—and put suitable nationals in these leading positions shaping society.[38]

From Racism to Antisemitism

Janet Jacobs has found that the genocide of European Jews during World War II renewed a desire for secrecy and denial among "crypto-Jews" in New Mexico. "Whatever might have been more out in the open went underground after the war," one of her interviewees said. His father realized that "it was bad to be a Jew in 1945, so he probably decided better to erase any connections with Judaism until this whole thing clears up."[39] Jacobs argues that the Holocaust led to a fear of antisemitism and bodily violence, which in turn caused the re-creation of a culture of secrecy. In this construction, antisemitism (both medieval and in modern Mexico) is the lens for understanding crypto-Jewish behavior, both violence and the internalization of antisemitic ideologies, for it is the trauma of Jewishness that shapes them: "As a consequence of the persistent threat of violence against the Jews, a deep-seated ethnic anxiety appears to have survived among modern descendants of the crypto-Jews."[40] This found its expression in "the creation and maintenance of family cultures that, through silence and secrecy, conveyed a sense of difference, isolation, and danger to succeeding generations." Thus "crypto-Jews" in the American Southwest were secret about Jewishness for reasons of self and group-preservation. They feared exposure, which could cause ostracism at best, death at worst. Instead, they choose to use protective assimilation, ethnic deidentification.[41] Similarly, Hilda Nissimi finds that the trauma of an initial forced conversion, the fear of being caught and punished by death, and the anxiety of remembrance combined to impel the Mashhadis to maintain endogamy and an identity as crypto-Jews in modern Iran.

Jews who had accommodated or assimilated and passed as non-Jews in western Europe and the United States had a great deal of internalized ethnic anxiety, which they projected onto eastern European Jews, who embodied all the characteristics they feared the discovery of in themselves, Sander Gilman contends.[42] This argument may also be applicable to Iran, which has a sorrier record concerning tolerance of Christians and Jews than the Ottoman Empire. But this was not the case in the Ottoman Empire, where unlike in Spain, there had been no mass forced conversion, no Inquisition, no burning at the stake for secretly practicing Judaism after converting, no expulsion, no taking refuge disguised as Christians halfway around the world in a new land. The voluntary converts known as Dönme did not have a history of religious victimization because they were Jews. They faced the trauma of exile from their homeland of Salonika, but this was not based on their racial identity. The antisemitism they faced in Turkey was not part of Christian cultures that blamed Jews for the crucifixion of Jesus and the murder of God. But it was antisemitism nonetheless. In the 1930s in Turkey, the extreme rightists Cevat Rıfat Atilhan and Nihal Atsız, publishers of the rabidly antisemitic newspapers *Orhun* and *Millî İnkilâp*, respectively, publicly called for those who were not Muslims to be expelled, since they could not be assimilated. Atsız argued "just as we never expect Jews to be Turkified, nor do we want it. For just as no matter how long you bake mud, it will never turn into iron, a Jew can never become a Turk, no matter how much he struggles."[43] Atsız also attacked Yalman, the most visible Dönme in the early Republic, claiming although he carried a Turkish passport as a Turkish citizen, he was "not a Turk and not a Muslim," but a Jew.[44]

Unlike the conversos, the Dönme were never accepted as Jews by Jews, nor accused of having close relations with Jews. They were not charged with judaizing, of believing in Judaism and secretly fulfilling its commands, rituals, and customs. Their crime lay less in their actions, and more in their inherited genes. In the end, they were attacked, not for acting like Jews, but for being Jews, for their racial identity, which allegedly caused them to spread bad morals. This was similar to the situation in fifteenth-century Spain, where "the mere presence of Jewish blood in that individual [the New Christian] was seen as creating a proclivity to undermine the Church."[45]

The Dönme are similar to conversos in that viewed from the group they left and, eventually, the group they joined, they were outsiders "whose origins deprived [them] of full membership in the community."[46] Tomas Atencio uses the theory of estrangement to describe how conversos had an ambiguous place on the border between Catholics and Jews; to Jews, they were Jewish apostates practicing Catholicism, to Catholics they were heretical Christians practicing Judaism.[47] Like the early modern crypto-Jews, Dönme were considered "a ship with two rudders," a group willing to trim its sails to the prevailing religious and political winds.[48] Others could not fathom their background or what they truly believed. They imagined the worst. The similarity to the perception of the Dönme by Jews and Turks beginning after 1908 and Greeks after 1912 is clear.

The Dönme emerged with the promise of a new messiah and the end of days, saw its members, their religious identity unquestioned, become the leaders of a cosmopolitan city in a crucial era, and offered the possibility of non-nationalist, international belonging. The group eventually dissolved with the fall of the plural religious empire and rise of the homogeneous secular nation-state that preferred to see them as Jews. The wealth tax imposed in 1942–44 was a reminder that others saw through their Turkish veneer to the Jewish blood that ran in their veins. When considering the situation of the Dönme in Turkey during World War II, it is helpful to bear in mind Jean-Paul Sartre's observation: "It is not the Jewish character that provokes anti-Semitism, on the contrary, it is the Anti-Semite who creates the Jew."[49]

The Holocaust and treatment of Jews in Turkey may have also led to Dönme fearing the discovery of their Jewish origins and blood. Jews in Balat, the predominantly Jewish neighborhood of Istanbul, panicked in 1942 when rumors about the grim ends to which a giant oven being built in the neighborhood was to be put to use, causing many to panic and think they were going to be murdered, as in Nazi-occupied Europe. The newspapers were filled with veiled threats about what would befall Jews if they failed to Turkify and grotesque antisemitic cartoons during the building of the giant oven (which in fact turned out to be for a new bread factory).[50] That same year, the wealth tax, three of whose four categories targeted those considered Jews, began to be imposed, and those (especially Jews) who could not pay sent to faraway Aşkale. Jewish men had been sent on road-digging crews as well, reviving memories of how Armenian men had been sent away on false military call-ups in 1915, only to be murdered. Fear of the "oven" shows the widespread insecurity of Jews in Turkey at the time.

Had the Dönme remained in Salonika, they probably would have been sent to Auschwitz, the horrible fate of most of Salonika's Jews during Nazi occupation. The racial logic of the Nazis was clear: as of 1942 in Salonika, in the words of the local Nazi commander, "Whoever belongs to the Jewish race is considered a Jew, regardless of what religion he professes."[51] Northern Greece was among the regions in Europe that lost the highest proportion of its Jews, despite the fact that the archbishop and heads of professional and public institutions in Athens publicly and the metropolitan of Salonika privately protested the deportation of Jews.[52] It is possible that as in Poland, where Rabbinate Jews, when asked to verify the Jewishness of the Karaite sect, claimed they were not Jews by blood, saving their lives, the Jewish council appointed by the Nazis in the city could have done the same. Yet considering poor relations between Jews and Dönme in the city, this was not guaranteed. The population exchange saved the Dönme from near certain murder at the hands of the Nazis— over 95 percent of Salonikan Jews were deported to Auschwitz and most gassed within hours of arrival.

Despite escaping that danger, they lost their religion after being forced to migrate to Turkey. How could the group have dissolved so quickly? After having had survived for almost three centuries, how could they give up their religion and identity? There were earlier disturbances, as noted by Paul Bessemer: the fall of Salonika to Greece severed the city from the Ottoman capital, culturally and economically, the fire of 1917 destroyed precious Dönme archives, religious books, relics, tombs, and religious objects, and, finally, there was the population exchange.[53] In the Turkish Republic, several reasons present themselves. Being Dönme was no longer an advantage. Where once it had served them well in Ottoman Salonika, allowing them to rise to the top of society while preserving their difference, in the Republic of Turkey they could no longer rise to the top, and maintaining their difference was difficult. One might suppose that they passed as secular Turks where once they had passed as Ottoman Muslims. But after World War II, there is hardly any evidence of this strategy of dissimulation. Part of the reason was internal, part external. As one Karakaş descendant informed me, the Karakaş went underground beginning in 1924 in the wake of the Rüştü affair.[54]

The desire to ensure secrecy about the group's origins stemmed from many causes. These include the threat of violence, the first the Dönme had faced in their nearly three centuries of existence. The economic discrimination of the wealth tax alerted them that their efforts over two decades at assimilation had failed; their ancestors were known to be Jews, causing them to be considered masked or hidden, secret Jews. Fear of the Holocaust made them realize the danger of being regarded as Jews, leading to ethnic anxiety and the internalization of racism.[55] Unlike in the case of the Southwestern crypto-Jews, such a context did not reinforce their identity, but instead combined with the other factors, including the difficulty of maintaining their religion in a new homeland, and constant pressure to become secular Turkish nationalists, served as cause for the ultimate weakening of the religious bonds that had once been their reason for being. Facing strong prejudice, many Dönme decided to abandon their separate ethno-religious identity to defend themselves (and their descendants) from hatred and violence. Difference and stigma had the effect of marginalizing a people living in an environment that stressed homogeneity. One might think that this would help the Dönme remain isolated and cohesive as a corporate body, as in Salonika. In fact, realizing after two decades in Turkey that the pressure on them would not relent, and that the only choice was to become secular nationalists, Dönme identity and religion to all intents and purposes largely dissolved after World War II, and they intermarried.

Postscript

The Shooting of Ahmet Emin Yalman

The main place where the Dönme refused to disappear in Turkey was in the minds of their enemies, where obsession with them was given a new lease on life with the country's democratization and liberalization, especially the freeing of the press and the return of fascist and antisemitic journals in the 1950s. Ahmet Emin Yalman bore the brunt of the attacks.

§ When Yalman visited Malatya in Turkey's heartland in the summer of 1952, he was unaware that he was being followed by a group of plotters against his life. One evening after dinner, as he started in the direction of his hotel on the opposite side of a spacious square a little before midnight, he "suddenly had the sensation of being showered with pebbles. I had heard no noise; nobody was in sight. Having had no previous experience of being shot at, everything seemed to me rather uncanny. My first thought was that some boys were throwing pebbles at each other from hiding places, so I stretched out my hand and cried: 'Stop that nonsense.' Then I somehow felt that I was in danger and ran toward my hotel. I suddenly became aware that my right hand was full of blood, and something warm was dripping from my abdomen and legs. Noticing a group of men at the hotel entrance, I cried, 'Doctor! Taxi!' They made no response. Judging, therefore, that they must be associates of my unknown assailants, I started to run in the opposite direction, only to fall to the ground, unconscious."[1]

Yalman took his brush with death in his stride. Although shot in his right hand, abdomen, and both legs from close range, the wounds were not serious. On the second day after the attack, before a wall of newspaper reporters and cameramen, and his intrepid wife, he addressed his young attacker: "Hüseyin, you pretend to be a good believer. As such, you must know that God is the only acceptable judge in moral matters. You usurped his prerogatives and felt entitled to judge my acts, to condemn them, and to execute a sentence of death against me. Would it not have been the right thing to give me a hearing before you carried out the sentence?"[2]

"From a bed in a hospital, where five bullets were removed from me, I saw in retrospect the strange, kaleidoscopic patterns of Turkey's career and mine," Yalman writes. "Once more, Turkey's fate and mine were inextricably interwoven."[3]

Vicious anti-Dönme and antisemitic articles in the Turkish press in the early 1950s created a dangerous atmosphere for Dönme in general and Yalman in particular. Representative articles include stories of Jews attempting to use bacteria produced in Soviet labs to poison the Well of Zamzam in Mecca to kill Muslims during the hajj—ironically, at a time when Jewish physicians were being purged in the USSR for allegedly spreading contagion.[4] Hateful cartoons of Mason Kapancı stockbrokers were published.[5] Articles labeled Yalman an "Avdeti," and claimed he prostituted Turkish Muslim women to American Jews by sponsoring beauty contests, graphically illustrated in a cartoon in which Yalman appears as a spider trapping naked women in his web.[6] Like the Dönme caricaturized in the anonymous 1919 treatise, Yalman was depicted as the main disseminator of immorality. It is not surprising that within months of *Büyük Doğu* (Great East) publishing a cartoon of an arrow with the newspaper's name on it piercing the heart of a supine man wearing a Star of David and labeled a Freemason, a far-right militant wounded Yalman in an assassination attempt.[7] The seventeen-year-old Hüseyin Üzmez who shot Yalman in Malatya had been influenced by *Volkan* and claimed that he had acted in the name of all Muslims to rid the earth of a Freemason (shorthand for atheist Jewish communist), "infidel," and Dönme who had insulted Islam and the nation.[8] Yalman's newspaper *Vatan* was accused of pimping Turkish girls for American Jews because it *had* sponsored the competition in Turkey for the 1952 Miss Universe contest and run revealing pictures of Turkish women, and Yalman thought that the assassination attempt might have been triggered by this.[9] He and his brother had also been Turkish agents for American companies, including Goodyear and Caterpillar, importing American products to Turkey, and he had as a result been called an American spy. Typical of the era, Yalman contends that Moscow was behind the plot, using "the camouflage of religious reaction and national chauvinism" to attack the dynamic, progressive, modern, secular Turkey he personified.[10] In 1953, the year after Üzmez shot Yalman, *Vatan* criticized a series from Moscow published in the paper *Yeni Sabah* (New Morning), which responded by calling him a kike and a traitor, not a Turk, and asking: "Don't twenty-two million Turks know what nation this Jew is from?"[11]

Despite a lifetime of dedication to Turkey, Yalman is remembered primarily as a Dönme by many rightists and Islamists, in this respect resembling his contemporary and fellow CUP member Tekinalp, who was also from Salonika. Tekinalp was a dedicated superpatriot of Jewish origin who devoted his life to the Turkish cause, penning a "ten commandments" of Turkishness for Jews. Regardless of a passionate life devoted to this aim, he is rarely remembered for his role in helping form secular Turkish nationalism. This broken man—stripped of his wealth by the wealth tax of 1942–44—died in exile in France and is often considered to be, not the Turk Tekinalp, but the Jew Moiz Kohen.[12]

Notwithstanding the revival of fear of the secret Jews in the 1950s, and its resurgence in the past decade, Dönme religion has become a *foi de souvenir*, a faith of memory. Religion was transformed into a culture of memory.[13] Long after their religion disappeared, some Dönme and others still maintained the memory of their being Dönme, which became a term without religious meaning, instead having social meaning, knowing with whom one could socialize. As with the conversos in Brazil and Mexico analyzed by Nathan Wachtel, the "forgetting" of the Dönme first effaced the beliefs, the significance of the rites and the rules, and then affected the customs themselves. Although "the significance of certain customs is lost," they can still be transmitted as family traditions, even though no one remembers exactly where they came from. Their justification "becomes like that of all tradition: it is done this way because it has always been done this way." In the interplay between continuity and forgetting, what persists is "the obscure sentiment of a duty and the halo of a secret."[14]

Duty and secrecy: "I hid my burden, I did not tell it to anyone, I secretly put it to rest" reads an undated inscription on the back of a family grave used between 1938 and 1992 in the Karakaş section of the Dönme Bülbüldere Cemetery in Istanbul.[15] Despite all that has happened, one can still identify the Dönme today. Yet when descendants of the now global Dönme diaspora come to pay respects to their ancestors, their cemetery is the only place where the existence of the Dönme is really manifested as a distinct group.[16]

In 2005, the Üsküdar Municipality finally contracted with a private security firm to hire guards to police the cemetery and keep away vandals who come to break the oval porcelain photographs on the tombstones, believing that it is a sin to display photographs of the dead. Despite the guards, however, the pictures of Dönme on the gravestones marked with the word "Salonikan" are being chipped away one by one. Barely discernable among the clamor of conspiracy theories, the voices of the past carved in the stones are just about all that remains. Having lost their pictures and Salonika, their ghostly home city, to which there is no returning, the graves in the Valley of the Nightingales still call out: "O visitor! . . ."

Reference Matter

Notes

Preface

1. Soner Yalçın, *Efendi: Beyaz Türklerin büyük sırrı*, 72nd printing (148,000 copies sold) (Istanbul: Doğan, 2006); id., *Efendi 2: Beyaz Müslümanların büyük sırrı*, 39th printing (Istanbul: Doğan, 2007).

2. Ergün Poyraz, *Musanın çocukları Tayyip ve Emine* (Istanbul: Toğan, 2007).

3. For an analysis of the demonization of Dönme in contemporary Turkey, see Rıfat Bali, *A Scapegoat for All Seasons: The Dönme or Crypto-Jews of Turkey* (Istanbul: Isis Press, 2008). For an example of a similar phenomenon—the widespread dissemination of and belief in conspiracy theories about secret Jews—in a society with virtually no Jews, see David G. Goodman and Masanori Miyazawa, *Jews in the Japanese Mind: The History and Uses of a Cultural Stereotype* (New York: Free Press, 1995).

4. Publicly referring to Atatürk as a secret Jew or Dönme would be considered insulting or cursing his memory and thus violate the 1951 Turkish penal code statute 5816, "Concerning Crimes Committed Against Atatürk."

5. See esp. Gershom Scholem, *Sabbatai Sevi, the Mystical Messiah, 1626–1676*, trans. R. J. Zwi Werblowsky (Princeton: Princeton University Press, 1973). For the most recent account, see Cengiz Şişman, "A Jewish Messiah in the Ottoman Court: Sabbetai Sevi and the Emergence of a Judeo-Islamic Community (1666–1720)" (Ph.D. diss., Harvard University, 2004).

Introduction

1. See copy of a contemporary Ottoman miniature in *Padişahın portresi: Tesavir-i Âl-i Osman* (Istanbul: Türkiye İş Bankası, 2000), 360.

2. Sir Paul Ricaut, *The History of the Present State of the Ottoman Empire*, 4th ed. (London: John Starkey and Henry Brome, 1675), 262.

3. See the main Ottoman account of the conversion—Abdurrahman Abdi Pasha, *Vekâyi'nâme*, Köprülü Library, Istanbul, MS 216, fols. 224a–b—translated for the first time into English in Marc David Baer, *Honored by the Glory of Islam: Conversion and Conquest in Ottoman Europe* (New York: Oxford University Press, 2008), 127. Unless otherwise noted, all quotations in this vignette are from this source; the wording has in part been modified.

4. On Shabbatai Tzevi's "manic depression," see Scholem, *Sabbatai Sevi*, 125–38.

5. *The Memoirs of Glückel of Hameln*, trans. Marvin Lowenthal (New York: Schocken Books, 1977), 45. This is an allusion to Isaiah 26.

6. See Elisheva Carlebach, *The Pursuit of Heresy: Rabbi Moses Hagiz and the Sabbatian Controversies* (New York: Columbia University Press, 1990).

7. See Jacob Barnai, "Messianism and Leadership: The Sabbatean Movement and the Leadership of the Jewish Communities in the Ottoman Empire," in *Ottoman and Turkish Jewry: Community and Leadership*, ed. Aron Rodrigue (Bloomington: Indiana University Press, 1992), 167–82; and Esther Benbassa and Aron Rodrigue, *Sephardi Jewry: A History of the Judeo-Spanish Community, 14th–20th Centuries* (Berkeley: University of California Press, 2000), 59.

8. I agree with the finding of Festinger et al.: "when people are committed to a belief and a course of action, clear, disconfirming evidence may simply result in deepened conviction and increased proselytizing." Leon Festinger, Henry W. Riecken, and Stanley Schachter, *When Prophecy Fails: A Social and Psychological Study of a Modern Group That Predicted the Destruction of the World* (New York: Harper Torchbooks, 1956), 12.

9. Esriel Carlebach, "Ohne Messias: Dönmehs," in id., *Exotische Juden: Berichte und Studien* (Berlin: Welt Verlag, 1932), 169.

10. See Harris Lenowitz, *The Jewish Messiahs: From the Galilee to Crown Heights* (New York: Oxford University Press, 1998), 98–100.

11. Matt Goldish, *The Sabbatean Prophets* (Cambridge, MA: Harvard University Press, 2004), 46. News of Shabbatai Tzevi's messianic calling was often disseminated by former conversos, and some of the convincing evidence for the veracity of the movement came from former converso Shabbatean prophets. Ibid., 49.

12. Scholem, *Sabbatai Sevi*, 915.

13. Abraham Danon, "Une secte judéo-musulmane en Turquie," *Revue des études juives* 35 (1897): 275. The reference in the Talmud is Pesahim 49b.

14. Meir Benayahu, "Ha-tnu'a ha-Shabta'it be-Yavan," *Sefunot* 14 (*Sefer Yavan* IV, 1971–77): 107. On this point, see also Gershom Scholem, "Teuda hadasha me-reshit ha-tnu'a ha-Shabta'it," in id., *Mehkerim u-mekorot le-toldot ha-Shabta'ut ve-gilguleha* (Jerusalem: Mosad Bialik, 1982), 218–32.

15. Evliya Çelebi, *Seyahatname* (Istanbul: Orhaniye Matbaası, 1928): 8: 159–60.

16. Suraiya Faroqhi, "Selānīk," *Encyclopaedia of Islam*, new ed., vol. 9, fasc. 149–50 (Leiden, 1995), 122–26.

17. Cheskel wi Klotzel, *In Saloniki* (Berlin: Jüdischer Verlag, 1920), 40. The author of this book taught at the Hilfsverein der deutschen Juden in Salonika.

18. Approximately a century before Shabbatai Tzevi's movement, Salonika had witnessed the messianic fervor of Portuguese converso prophet and purported messiah Solomon Molkho, whose sermons appealed to Christians as well as Jews. Lenowitz, *Jewish Messiahs*, 93–123.

19. Leon Sciaky, *Farewell to Salonica* (1946; repr., Istanbul: Isis Press, 2000), 24–26.

20. Gershom Scholem, "Doenmeh (Dönme)," *Encyclopaedia Judaica* (Jerusalem: Keter Publishing House, 1972), 6: 151. The greatest difference between the two movements as they evolved was, however, that Dönme religion remained secret and ethnically defined, whereas Christianity eventually replaced the ethnic nature of Judaism with universal membership.

21. Moshe Perlmann, "Dönme," *Encyclopaedia of Islam*, new ed., vol. 2, pt. 2 (Leiden, 1965), 615–16.

22. Howard Clark Kee, "From the Jesus Movement Toward Institutional Church," in *Conversion to Christianity: Historical and Anthropological Perspectives on a Great Transformation*, ed. Robert Hefner (Berkeley: University of California Press, 1993), 63. Comparing the Dönme to early Christians becomes difficult after the first few generations, for unlike the Dönme, Christians married outsiders and accepted converts.

23. See Fred Donner, "From Believers to Muslims: Confessional Self-Identity in the Early Islamic Community," *Al-Abhath* 50–51 (2002–2003): 9–53.

24. Hope had been placed in Shabbatai Tzevi's son, Ishmael, but he studied in a yeshivah and became a Salonikan rabbi, not his father's successor. For widespread Jewish belief in transmigration of souls, see *Spirit Possession in Judaism: Cases and Contexts from the Middle Ages to the Present*, ed. Matt Goldish (Detroit: Wayne State University Press, 2003).

25. Irene Melikoff, "L'Islam heterodoxe en Anatolie," *Turcica* 14 (1982): 142–54.

26. Interview, summer 2007.

27. Danon, "Une secte judéo-musulmane en Turquie," and Gershom Scholem, "The Sprouting of the Horn of the Son of David: A New Source From the Beginnings of the Doenme Sect in Salonica," in *In the Time of Harvest: Essays in Honor of Abba Hillel Silver*, ed. Daniel Jeremy Silver (New York: Macmillan, 1963), 370.

28. Scholem, "Sprouting of the Horn of the Son of David," 385.

29. *Dönmeler: Hunyos, Kavayeros, Sazan* (Istanbul: Şems Matbaası, 1919), 15; Avram Galanté, *Nouveaux documents sur Sabbetaï Sevi: Organisation et us et coutumes de ses adeptes* (Istanbul: Société anonyme de papeterie et d'imprimerie [Fratelli Haim]), 1935), 67; and Nicholas P. Stavroulakis, *Salonica: Jews and Dervishes* (Athens: Talos Press, 1993).

30. On how an emerging religion elaborates a distinct identity through funerary rites, see Leor Halevi, *Muhammad's Grave: Death Rites and the Making of Islamic Society* (New York: Columbia University Press, 2007), 4.

31. Kurt H. Wolff, *The Sociology of Georg Simmel* (Glencoe, IL: Free Press, 1950), 330, quoted in Janet Liebman Jacobs, *Hidden Heritage: The Legacy of the Crypto-Jews* (Berkeley: University of California Press, 2002), 21.

32. Michael Taussig, *Defacement: Public Secrecy and the Labor of the Negative* (Stanford: Stanford University Press, 1999).

33. Elliot Wolfson, "Introduction," in *Rending the Veil: Concealment and Secrecy in the History of Religions*, ed. id. (New York: Seven Bridges Press, 1998), 3.

34. Margaret Jacob, *Strangers Nowhere in the World: The Rise of Cosmopolitanism in Early Modern Europe* (Philadelphia: University of Pennsylvania Press, 2006), 98, 100.

35. Yitzhak Ben-Tzevi, "Preface," *Sabbatean Hymnal* (in Hebrew), trans. M. Attias, annotated by Gershom Scholem (Tel Aviv: n.p., 1947), trans. into English in Harris Lenowitz, "Leaving Turkey: The Dönme Comes to Poland," *Kabbalah: Journal for the Study of Jewish Mystical Texts* 8 (2003): 69–70.

36. Lenowitz, *Jewish Messiahs*, 4. For comparison, the twelfth-century Kurdish Jewish messiah David Alroy of Diyarbekir was either executed by the Seljuk governor or killed on his behalf by Jews. Ibid., 81–91.

37. See Jacobs, *Hidden Heritage*, chap. 1.

38. Lucette Valensi, "Conversion, intégration, exclusion: Les Sabbateens dans l'empire ottoman et en Turquie," *Dimensioni e problemi della ricerca storica* 2 (1996): 175.

39. Galanté, *Nouveaux documents sur Sabbetaï Sevi*, 60; Scholem, "Doenmeh (Dönme)," 149.

40. Gershom Scholem, "Barukhya, rosh ha-Shabtaim be-Saloniki," *Zion* 6 (1941): 143–47.

41. Paul Fenton, "Shabbatay Sebi and His Muslim Contemporary Muhammad an-Niyazi," in *Approaches to Judaism in Medieval Times*, ed. David Blumenthal (Atlanta: Scholars Press, 1988), 3: 84.

42. Abdülbaki Gölpınarlı, "Niyâzî," in *İslâm Ansiklopedisi* (Istanbul: Maarif Matbaası, 1940–86), vol. 9 (1960): 305–7; Baha Doğramacı, *Niyazi-yi Mısrî:*

Hayatı ve eserleri (Ankara: Kadıoğlu Matbaası, 1988); Michel Balivet, *Byzantins et Ottomans: Relations, interaction, succession* (Istanbul: Isis, 1999), 227.

43. Gershom Scholem, "The Crypto-Jewish Sect of the Dönmeh (Sabbatians) in Turkey," in id., *The Messianic Idea in Judaism and Other Essays on Jewish Spirituality* (New York: Schocken Books, 1971), 151. Hasluck says the Bektaşi lodge in Salonika was on the western outskirts of the city. F. W. Hasluck, *Christianity and Islam Under the Sultans*, ed. Margaret Hasluck (Oxford: Oxford University Press, 1929; repr., New York: Octagon Books, 1973), 2: 525.

44. Kee, "From the Jesus Movement Toward Institutional Church."

45. Robert Hefner, "Introduction: World Building and the Rationality of Conversion," in *Conversion to Christianity: Historical and Anthropological Perspectives on a Great Transformation*, ed. id. (Berkeley: University of California Press, 1993), 17.

46. Yıldız Sertel, *Annem: Sabiha Sertel kimdi neler yazdı* (Istanbul: Yapı Kredi Yayınları, 1993), 24.

47. Nahum Slousch, "Les Deunmeh: Une secte judéo-musulmane de Salonique," *Revue du monde musulman* 6 (1908): 494.

48. [Ahmet Emin Yalman], "Tarihin esrarengiz bir sahifesi," *Vatan*, January 19, 1924, 1; Galanté, *Nouveaux documents sur Sabbetaï Sevi*, 60; Scholem, "Crypto-Jewish Community," 155.

49. Galanté, *Nouveaux documents sur Sabbetaï Sevi*, 60.

50. For the important role women played in other secret convert societies, see Hilda Nissimi, *The Crypto-Jewish Mashhadis: The Shaping of Religious and Communal Identity in Their Journey from Iran to New York* (Portland, UK: Sussex Academic Press, 2007), 44–51; and Mary Elizabeth Perry, *The Handless Maiden: Moriscos and the Politics of Religion in Early Modern Spain* (Princeton: Princeton University Press, 2005), 65–87. Mashhadi and Morisca women had an even larger role to play in leadership of the community and transmission of the religion than Dönme women.

51. Scholem, "Crypto-Jewish Community," 152.

52. She was used as a decoy and a sentry, not unlike in Mashhadi society. See Nissimi, *Crypto-Jewish Mashhadis*, 45–46.

53. Wladimer Gordlevsky, "Zur Frage über die 'Dönme' (Die Rolle der Juden in den Religionssekten Vorderasiens)," *Islamica* 2 (1926): 215.

54. Slousch, "Deunmeh," 493.

55. J. G. von Hahn, "Über die Bevölkerung von Salonic und die dörtige Secte der Deunme," in id., *Reise durch der Gebiete des Drin und Wardar, im Aufträge der Kaiserlichen Akademie der Wissenschaften unternommen im Jahre 1863* (Vienna, 1869), 154–55, cited in Şişman, "A Jewish Messiah in the Ottoman Court," 365.

56. Başbakanlık Osmanlı Arşivi [The Prime Minister's Ottoman Archives

(BOA)], Istanbul, A.MKT.UM 572/1, cited in Şişman, "A Jewish Messiah in the Ottoman Court," 366. The translation is my own. "If a Dünméh girl be led astray by an outsider, no effort is spared to recover the erring one, who, it is said, is tried, condemned, and executed for her sin by a secret tribunal of her own people," writes Lucy Garnett, *The Women of Turkey, and Their Folk-lore* (London: David Nutt, 1890), 104–5. She also mentions the windowless meeting houses of the group.

57. Slousch, "Deunmeh," 493, would also claim each group had its own separate law court.

58. On the opinions of the British Protestant missionary Benjamin Barker, who wrote about the Dönme in 1827 and again in 1847, and to whom these opinions are attributed, see Esra Danacıoğlu, "Selânik Yahudileri ve Dönmeler hakkında 3 mektup," *Toplumsal Tarih* 4 (April 1994): 26–28.

59. Kaufmann Kohler and Richard Gottheil, "Dönmeh," *Jewish Encyclopaedia* (New York: Funk & Wagnalls, 1901–6), 2: 639. Also at www.jewishencyclopedia.com/view.jsp?artid=438&letter=D (accessed March 20, 2009).

60. Joseph Jacobs, *Studies in Jewish Statistics: Social, Vital, and Anthropometric* (London: David Nutt, 1891), ii, quoted in John M. Efron, *Defenders of the Race: Jewish Doctors & Race Science in Fin-de-Siècle Europe* (New Haven: Yale University Press, 1994), 90.

61. *Vatan*, January 19, 1924, 1.

62. Mark Mazower, *Salonica, City of Ghosts: Christians, Jews, and Muslims, 1430–1950* (New York: Vintage Books, 2006), 59.

63. On the Dönme religious calendar, see Şişman, "A Jewish Messiah at the Ottoman Court," 345–57.

64. Matt Goldish, "Varieties of Deviance Among Early Modern Ottoman Jews" (paper presented at "Jewish Religion in Ottoman Lands," August 21–22, 2007, Indiana University, Bloomington).

65. Ben-Tzevi, "Preface," 71n12.

66. Julie Cohen, personal communication, spring 2008.

67. Summarized in Joseph Nehama, *Histoire des Israélites de Salonique* (Thessaloníki: Molho, 1935–78), 5: 73.

68. See Stavro Skendi, "Crypto-Christianity in the Balkan Area under the Ottomans," *Slavic Review* 26 (1967): 227–46.

69. Jacobs, *Hidden Heritage*, 4.

70. Maurus Reinkowski, "Hidden Believers, Hidden Apostates: The Phenomenon of Crypto-Jews and Crypto-Christians in the Middle East," in *Converting Cultures: Religion, Ideology and Transformations of Modernity*, ed. Dennis Washburn and A. Kevin Reinhart (Boston: Brill, 2007), 413.

71. Jean-Paul Sartre, *Anti-Semite and Jew*, trans. George Becker (New York: Schocken Books, 1976), 143, quoted in Ella Shohat, "Post-Fanon and the Colo-

nial: A Situational Diagnosis," in id., *Taboo Memories, Diasporic Voices* (Durham, NC: Duke University Press, 2006), 253.

72. See, e.g., Scholem, "Crypto-Jewish Sect of the Dönmeh (Sabbatians) in Turkey"; Yehuda Liebes, *Studies in Jewish Myth and Jewish Messianism*, trans. Batya Stein (New York: State University of New York Press, 1993); Jacob Barnai, "The Outbreak of Sabbateanism—The Eastern European Factor," *Journal of Jewish Thought and Philosophy* 4 (1994): 171–83; id., *Shabta'ut: Hebetim hevratiyim* (Jerusalem: Shazar Center, 2000), which mainly concerns the reasons for the rapid and successful diffusion of the movement among Jews; Moshe Idel, "'One from a Town, Two from a Clan'—The Diffusion of Lurianic Kabbala and Sabbateanism: A Re-Examination." *Jewish History* 7, no. 2 (Fall 1993): 79–104; and id., *Messianic Mystics* (New Haven: Yale University Press, 1998). When scholars turn to non-Jewish factors, they mainly consider European and Christian and not Ottoman and Muslim ones. See Jacob Barnai, "Christian Messianism and the Portuguese Marranos: The Emergence of Sabbateanism in Smyrna," *Jewish History* 7, no. 2 (Fall 1993): 119–26. An exception is the work of Paul Fenton, who explores the contact between Jewish and Muslim esotericists and their bilateral influence. See his "Judaism and Sufism," in *The Cambridge Companion to Medieval Jewish Philosophy*, ed. Daniel Frank and Oliver Leaman (New York: Cambridge University Press, 2003), 201–17.

73. Ben-Tzevi, "Preface," 67.

74. Perlmann, "Dönme" (cited in Introduction, n. 21, above).

75. Abdurrahman Küçük, *Dönmeler ve Dönmelik tarihi* (1979; repr., Istanbul: Hamle, 1997), 78. His later encyclopedia article is more factual. See Abdurrahman Küçük, "Dönme," in *İslâm Ansiklopedisi* (Istanbul: Türkiye Diyanet Vakfı, 1988–; 1994), 9: 518–20.

76. See the collection of hymns transcribed from Hebrew into Latin script in Moshe Lazar, "Ladino Hymns of the Sabbatean Dönmeh Sect," in *Sefarad in My Heart: A Ladino Reader*, ed. id. (Lancaster, CA: Labryinthos, 1999), 783–805.

77. For a discussion of paramount values, see Joel Robbins, *Becoming Sinners: Christianity and Moral Torment in a Papua New Guinea Society* (Berkeley: University of California Press, 2004), 11–13.

78. Meir Benayahu, "Introduction," *Sefunot* 14 (1971–77): 6.

79. This fact goes against much literature pertaining to conversos. See Thomas F. Glick, "On Converso and Marrano Ethnicity," in *Crisis and Creativity in the Sephardic World, 1391–1648*, ed. Benjamin Gampel (New York: Columbia University Press, 1997), 59–76.

80. For a comparison with conversos defined as politically, economically, and religiously liminal people who were neither fully insiders nor fully outsiders, yet inhabitants of both Jewish and Christian worlds, see David Graizbord, *Souls in*

Dispute: Converso Identities in Iberia and the Jewish Diaspora, 1580–1700 (Philadelphia: University of Pennsylvania Press, 2004), 1–7, 171–78.

81. Ricaut, *History of the Present State of the Ottoman Empire*, 147–54.

82. Ibid., 147–48.

83. Ibid., 148.

84. See Reinkowski, "Hidden Believers, Hidden Apostates," 409, 420–21; and Hovann Simonian, *The Hemshin: A Handbook* (London: Routledge, 2006).

85. See Reinkowski, "Hidden Believers, Hidden Apostates," and Bojan Aleksov, "Adamant and Treacherous: Serbian Historians on Religious Conversions," in *Converting Cultures*, ed. Washburn and Reinhart, 99.

86. Scholem, "Crypto-Jewish Sect of the Dönmeh," 151.

87. Liebman, *Hidden Heritage*, 10.

88. Nissimi, *Crypto-Jewish Mashhadis*, 26–8. Her analysis raises a paradox, however: how could Muslims be both so intolerant that they forced Jews to convert to Islam, yet so tolerant as to overlook the obvious apostasy exhibited by the Mashhadis? See Reinkowski, "Hidden Believers, Hidden Apostates," 426–27.

89. Nissimi, *Crypto-Jewish Mashhadis*, 83.

90. Ilgaz Zorlu had to convert to Judaism in order to officially change his religion. The Turkish chief rabbinate reluctantly accepted his decision. See Ilgaz Zorlu, *Evet, ben Selânikliyim: Türkiye Sabetaycılığı üstüne makaleler* (Istanbul: Belge Yayınları, 1998), and Marc David Baer, "Revealing a Hidden Community: Ilgaz Zorlu and the Debate in Turkey over the Dönme / Sabbateans," *Turkish Studies Association Bulletin* 23, no. 1 (Spring 1999): 68–75. The topics of Dönme in post 1950s Turkey and post-1948 Israel are beyond the subject of this book.

91. Peter van der Veer, *Imperial Encounters: Religion and Modernity in India and Britain* (Princeton: Princeton University Press, 2001), 14–29.

92. Talal Asad, *Genealogies of Religion: Discipline and Reasons of Power in Christianity and Islam* (Baltimore: Johns Hopkins University Press, 1993), 40–41.

93. Sir James Porter, *Observations on the Religion, Law, Government, and Manners of the Turks* (London, 1768), 2: 40–41.

94. James Gelvin, "Secularism and Religion in the Arab Middle East: Reinventing Islam in a World of Nation-States," in *The Invention of Religion: Rethinking Belief in Politics and History*, ed. Derek Peterson and Darren Walhof (New Brunswick, NJ: Rutgers University Press, 2002), 122–23; Jens Hanssen, *Fin de siècle Beirut: The Making of an Ottoman Provincial Capital* (New York: Oxford University Press, 2005), 69–70; Eugene Rogan, *Frontiers of the State in the Ottoman Empire: Transjordan, 1850–1920* (New York: Cambridge University Press, 1999), 197–201; and Selim Deringil, "The Struggle Against Shi'ism in Hamidian Iraq," *Welt des Islams* 30 (1990): 45–62.

Chapter 1

1. Yıldız Sertel, *Annem*, 66.

2. Ibid., 67.

3. Ibid., 85.

4. Mehmet Zekeriya Sertel, *Hatırladıklarım (1906–1960)* (Istanbul: Yaylacık Matbaası, 1968), 54.

5. Ibid., 88.

6. Ibid., 90.

7. Yıldız Sertel, *Annem*, 90.

8. Mehmet Ö. Alkan, *İmparatorluk'tan Cumhuriyet'e Selânik'ten İstanbul'a Terakki Vakfı ve Terakki Okulları, 1877–2000* (Istanbul: Terraki Vakfı, 2003), 48.

9. Nissimi, *Crypto-Jewish Mashhadis*, 11.

10. Ibid., 13.

11. Engseng Ho, *The Graves of Tarim: Genealogy and Mobility Across the Indian Ocean* (Berkeley: University of California Press, 2006), 140.

12. Ibid., 140–41.

13. Ibid., 141.

14. Ibid., 197–99.

15. Esra Özyürek, "Introduction: The Politics of Public Memory in Turkey," in *The Politics of Public Memory in Turkey*, ed. id. (Syracuse, NY: Syracuse University Press, 2007), 1–15.

16. A Kapancı descendant and others today are using genealogies to stake their claims to the disposal of a valuable parcel of land centrally located in Thessaloníki. Greek lawyers and judges are being asked to validate and verify the religiously based genealogical claims of thirty-seven descendants of an Ottoman imperial group. Millions of dollars are at stake, and descendants of Kapancı in Turkey and France are being traced. Interview, summer 2006.

17. The document from 1862—BOA, A.MKT.UM 572/1—is cited in the Introduction, n. 54, above. The 1891 document is BOA, Meclisi Vükela Mazbatası 68/44, discussed in Selim Deringil, *The Well-Protected Domains: Ideology and the Legitimation of Power in the Ottoman Empire, 1876–1909* (London: I. B. Tauris, 1999), 81.

18. *Istoria tēs epicheirēmatikotētas stē Thessalonikē*, ed. Efrosini Roupa and Evangelos Chekimoglou, vol. 3: *ē epicheirēmatikotēta stēn periodo 1900–1940* (Thessaloníki: Politistikē Etaireia Epicheirēmatiōn Boreiou Ellados, 2005), 280–83.

19. Interview, summer 2006.

20. Mazower, *Salonica, City of Ghosts*, 285.

21. *Arazi ve Emlaki Esasi Defteri* [1906 Register of Lands and Properties], Historical Archive of Macedonia, Thessaloníki, 1: 162, 2: 17–20.

22. Basilēs Dēmētriadēs, *Topographia tēs Thessalonikēs kata tēn epochē tēs*

Tourkokratias, 1430–1912 (Thessaloníki: Etaireia Makedonikōn Spoudōn, 1983), 150–51n160.

23. Gordlevsky, "Zur Frage über die 'Dönme,'" 212.

24. Interview, summer 2006.

25. Muhtelit Mübadele Komisyonu Tasfiye Talepnameleri (MMKTT), Cumhuriyet Arşivi, Ankara, code 130.16.132, dossiers 32441, 32442. Hereafter only the MMKTT dossier number will be listed, because all documents I used have the same code number.

26. Alkan, *Teraki Vakfı ve Terakki Okulları*, 59.

27. *Arazi ve Emlaki Esasi Defteri,* 1: 93; 1: 119.

28. MMKTT, 34632, A34655, A34668, 34656.

29. MMKTT, 33270.

30. *Arazi ve Emlaki Esasi Defteri,* 7: 108.

31. Dēmētriadēs, *Topographia tēs Thessalonikēs*, 226.

32. Meropi Anastassiadou, *Salonique, 1830–1912: Une ville ottomane à l'âge des réformes* (Leiden: Brill, 1997), 118.

33. Dēmētriadēs, *Topografia tēs Thessalonikēs*, 226.

34. Esin Eden and Nicholas Stavroulakis, *Salonica: A Family Cookbook* (Athens: Talos Press, 1997), 22.

35. *Arazi ve Emlak Esasi Defteri, Müsvedde,* 6: 5a.

36. An article based on interviews with the same person was published by a Turkish scholar. See Okşan Özferendeci, "Tütüncü Hasan Akif ailesi," *Albüm* 1 (April 1998): 101–10.

37. *Arazi ve Emlak Esasi Defteri, Müsvedde,* 6: 11a.

38. *Selânik Vilâyeti Salnamesi* [Yearbook of the Province of Salonika; hereafter *SVS*] (Salonika: Vilâyet Matbaası, 1900–1901), 361.

39. *Arazi ve Emlak Esasi Defteri, Müsvedde,* 6: 11a, 12a; *SVS*, 1902–3, 419.

40. Alkan, *Terakki Vakfı ve Terakki Okulları*, 106–7.

41. Dēmētriadēs, *Topographia tēs Thessalonikēs*, 232.

42. Hanssen, *Fin de siècle Beirut*, 221, 223.

43. Reşat D. Tesal, *Selânik'ten İstanbul'a: Bir ömrün hikâyesi* (Istanbul: İletişim, 1998), 11.

44. Anastassiadou, *Salonique*, 131.

45. Basilēs Kolonas, "ē ektos tōn toichōn epektasi tēs Thessalonikēs: Eikonografia tēs sunoikias Hamidye" (Ph.D. diss., Aristotle University of Thessaloníki, 1991), 1: 159. At around the same time, the textile merchant Osman Dervish (son of İsmail Dervish), a Kapancı Dönme, one of the founders of the Terakki school, and secretary of the province's Department of Finance, built his mansion close to those of Ahmet and Mehmet Kapancı. Mehmet's daughter Hasibe, who had also married a first cousin, built her home on a plot she purchased opposite her father's home.

46. See Dēmētriadēs, *Topographia tēs Thessalonikēs*, 332–36, for photographs of the inscriptions of the foundation stone of the mosque and the mosque's sundial.

47. Alexandra Yerolympos and Vassilis Colonas "Un urbanisme cosmopolite," in *Salonique, 1850–1918: La "ville des Juifs" et le réveil des Balkans*, ed. Gilles Veinstein (Paris: Autrement, 1993), 168–69; Elçin Macar, "Selânik Dönmelerinin yaşayan simgesi: Yeni Cami," *Tarih ve Toplum* 28.168 (1997): 28–29; Mazower, *Salonica, City of Ghosts*, 76.

48. Marc David Baer, "Selânik Dönmelerinin camisi: Ortak bir geçmişin tek yadigârı," trans. Esra Özyürek, *Tarih ve Toplum* 28, no. 168 (1997): 31.

49. Yıldız Sertel, *Annem*, 35.

50. Alkan, *Terakki Vakfı ve Terakki Okulları*, 331.

51. Gershom Scholem, "Sprouting of the Horn of the Son of David," 385.

52. José Faur, *In the Shadow of History: Jews and Conversos at the Dawn of Modernity* (Albany: State University of New York Press, 1992), ix; my emphasis.

53. Ahmet Emin Yalman, *Turkey in My Time* (Norman: University of Oklahoma Press, 1956), 10–11.

54. Stavroulakis, *Salonika: Jews and Dervishes*, 14.

55. *In memoriam: Hommage aux victimes juives des Nazis en Grèce*, publié sous la direction de Michael Molho, rabbin de la Communauté juive de Thessalonique, 2nd ed. (Thessaloníki: Communauté israélite de Thessalonique, 1988), 380, 382; Stavroulakis, *Jews and Dervishes*, 17, 24.

56. *In memoriam*, 382; Stavroulakis, *Jews and Dervishes*, 47.

Chapter 2

1. Ahmet Emin Yalman, *Yakın tarihte gördüklerim ve geçirdiklerim*, ed. Erol Şadi Erdinç, 2nd ed. (Istanbul: Pera Turizm ve Ticaret A.Ş, 1997), 1: 697–700.

2. Ibid., 1: 700–701.

3. Mert Sandalcı, Feyz-i Sıbyân'dan Işık'a Feyziye Mektepleri (Istanbul: Feyziye Mektepleri Vakfı, 2005), 82–83

4. In the late nineteenth century, American and European missionaries and nationalists, Ottoman Christians and Jews, and the Ottoman state opened schools in Salonika to reform and modernize segments of the city's population. Ben Fortna, *Imperial Classroom: Islam, the State, and Education in the Late Ottoman Empire* (New York: Oxford University Press, 2002); Anastassiadou, *Salonique*, 183; Faroqhi, "Selānīk," 125.

5. Hanssen, *Fin de siècle Beirut*, 176, 188.

6. Sultan Abdülhamid II expanded state education, employing modern methods and subjects such as the sciences while emphasizing Islam, religio-moral conduct, ethics, and sense of propriety. See Fortna, *Imperial Classroom*, 12, 16–18, 219.

7. "Muallim Şemseddin Efendi Mektebi Şâkirdânın Sûret-i Harekâtı," in Alkan, *Terakki Vakfı ve Terakki Okulları*, 328.

8. Yıldız Sertel, *Annem*, 30–31.

9. Ibid., 48.

10. Şemsi Efendi's efforts may be compared to those of Selim Sabit Efendi, who established the new method of education (*usul-i cedid*) and incorporated positivist scientific education and moral education. See Selçuk Akşin Somel, *The Modernization of Public Education in the Ottoman Empire, 1839–1908: Islamization, Autocracy, and Discipline* (Leiden: Brill, 2001).

11. Sandalcı, *Feyz-i Sıbyân'dan Işık'a Feyziye Mektekpleri*, 25.

12. Aron Rodrigue, *French Jews, Turkish Jews: The Alliance israélite universelle and the Politics of Jewish Schooling in Turkey, 1860–1925* (Bloomington: Indiana University Press, 1990); Rena Molho, "Le renouveau," in *Salonique, 1850–1918*, ed. Veinstein, 76.

13. Özcan Mert, "Atatürk'ün ilk öğretmeni Şemsi Efendi (1852– 1917)," XI. Türk Tarih Kongresi (Ankara: Türk Tarih Kurumu Yayını, 1994), 2415; Alkan, *Terakki Vakfı ve Terakki Okulları*, 329; Sandalcı, *Feyz-i Sıbyân'dan Işık'a Feyziye Mektekpleri*, 35.

14. Alkan, *Terakki Vakfı ve Terakki Okulları*, 329.

15. Ibid., 58, 63.

16. Sandalcı, *Feyz-i Sıbyân'dan Işık'a Feyziye Mektekpleri*, 32.

17. Vamik Volkan and Norman Itzkowitz, *The Immortal Atatürk: A Psychobiography* (Chicago: University of Chicago Press, 1984), 30–35.

18. Alkan, *Terakki Vakfı ve Terakki Okulları*, 23.

19. *SVS*, 1900–1901, 341–42.

20. Alkan, *Teraki Vakfı ve Terakki Okulları*, 60.

21. *Terakki Vakfı Şişli Terakki Lisesinin dünü bugünü yarını, 1879–1979* (Istanbul: Yenilik Basımevi, 1979), 17.

22. Alkan, *Teraki Vakfı ve Terakki Okulları*, 329.

23. *SVS*, 1900–1901, 343; *SVS*, 1906–7, 262.

24. Alkan, *Terakki Vakfı ve Terakki Okulları*, 64; Sandalcı, *Feyz-i Sıbyân'dan Işık'a Feyziye Mektekpleri*, 25.

25. Interview, summer 2002.

26. *Annuaire commercial & administratif du Vilayet de Salonique* (Salonika: J. S. Modiano / Chambre de commerce de Salonique, 1908), 163, 180.

27. Alkan, *Terakki Vakfı ve Terakki Okulları*, 86. Osman Telci died in Salonika, but his body was later moved to the Dönme cemetery in Istanbul.

28. Ibid., 76.

29. Dēmētriadēs, *Topografia tēs Thessalonikēs*, 233.

30. Alkan, *Terakki Vakfı ve Terakki Okulları*, 91.

31. Sandalcı, *Feyz-i Sıbyân'dan Işık'a Feyziye Mektekpleri*, 40.

32. Interviews, autumn 2005, summer 2006.

33. Sandalcı, *Feyz-i Sıbyân'dan Işık'a Feyziye Mektekpleri*, 41. The first board, presided over by Mustafa Tevfik Efendi, consisted of Kitapçi Mustafa Efendi, Mustafa Faik Efendi (lawyer), Mustafa Cezar Efendi (merchant), Karakaş Mehmet Efendi (merchant), İpekçi İsmail Efendi (merchant).

34. Sandalcı, *Feyz-i Sıbyân'dan Işık'a Feyziye Mektekpleri*, 42, 190. Sandalcı gives the year 1937, although his tombstone reads 1936.

35. Bernard Lewis, *The Emergence of Modern Turkey*, 2nd ed. (London: Oxford University Press, 1968), 206.

36. *Terakki Vakfı Şişli Terakki Lisesinin dünü bugünü yarını*, 24.

37. Ibid.; Fortna, *Imperial Classroom*, 138.

38. *SVS*, 1897–98, 273.

39. Ibid.

40. *SVS*, 1907–8, 486.

41. *SVS*, 1895–96, 142.

42. *SVS*, 1894–5, 133–39.

43. Sandalcı, *Feyz-i Sıbyân'dan Işık'a Feyziye Mektekpleri*, 51–52. "No girls' school of any description seems to have existed until some dozen years ago, when an intelligent member of the community, Shemsi Effendi, determined to remove this cause of reproach from his people, succeeded in opening one on a small scale at Salonica, which he personally supervised" (Garnett, *Women of Turkey*, 103–4).

44. Alkan, *Terakki Vakfı ve Terakki Okulları*, 102.

45. Ibid., 108.

46. *SVS*, 1900–1901, 337–41; *SVS*, 1904–5, 317.

47. Sandalcı, *Feyz-i Sıbyân'dan Işık'a Feyziye Mektekpleri*, 57.

48. July 14, 1897, quoted ibid., 330–31.

49. Ibid., 62.

50. Yalman, *Turkey in My Time*, 17.

51. Sandalcı, *Feyz-i Sıbyân'dan Işık'a Feyziye Mektekpleri*, 30, 38, 39, 54, 66. See also Ilgaz Zorlu, "Atatürk'ün ilk öğretmeni Şemsi Efendi Hakkında bilinmeyen birkaç nokta," *Toplumsal Tarih* 1 (1994): 59–60.

52. *SVS*, 1897–8, 272.

53. *SVS*, 1907–8, 485.

54. İlber Ortaylı, "Ottoman Modernisation and Sabetaism," in *Alevi Identity: Cultural, Religious and Social Perspectives* (papers read at a conference held at the Swedish Research Institute in Istanbul, November 25–27, 1996), ed. Tord Olsson, Elisabeth Özdalga, and Catharina Raudvere (Istanbul: Swedish Research Institute in Istanbul, 1998), 99.

55. September 6, 1897, quoted in Sandalcı, *Feyz-i Sıbyân'dan Işık'a Feyziye Mektekpleri*, 56.

56. *Journal de Salonique*, August 11, 1898, quoted in Sandalcı, *Feyz-i Sıbyân'dan Işık'a Feyziye Mektekpleri*, 332; Sandalcı, *Feyz-i Sıbyân'dan Işık'a Feyziye Mektekpleri*, 63.

57. *Journal de Salonique*, September 4, 1899, quoted in Sandalcı, *Feyz-i Sıbyân'dan Işık'a Feyziye Mektekpleri*, 333.

58. *Annuaire commercial & administratif du Vilayet de Salonique*, 174, 178; and Horton to State Department, June 2, 1910, "Incoming Correspondence (from State Department) (Dec. 14, 1909–Dec. 20, 1910)," National Archives of the United States, microfilm MMA4/b/11.

59. Alkan, *Terakki Vakfı ve Terakki Okulları*, 80.

60. Ibid., 70.

61. *SVS*, 1897–98, 273.

62. Ibid., 278.

63. Fortna, *Imperial Classrooms*, 229.

64. Alkan, *Terakki Vakfı ve Terakki Okulları*, 328.

65. Ibid., 330.

66. The title of the journal, *Gonca-i Edeb*, also connotes the flower of proper education, learning, and manners.

67. *Gonca-i Edeb* (Salonika: Vilayet Matbaası, 1883), no. 1 (March 1, 1883): 1; and Cengiz Şişman, "*Gonca-i Edep'*ten iki 'söz,'" *Tarih ve Toplum* 38.223 (2002): 10–11.

68. Fazlı Necip, "Edeb veya edebiyat," *Gonca-i Edeb*, no. 1 (March 1, 1883): 3.

69. *Gonca-i Edeb*, no. 10 (February 15, 1884): 154.

70. *Gonca-i Edeb*, no. 8 (June 15, 1883).

71. "İfade," *Gonca-i Edeb*, no. 1 (March 1, 1883).

72. Ibid.

73. *SVS*, 1889–90, 101; *SVS*, 1892–93, 32; *SVS*, 1904–5, 79; *SVS* 1907–8, 123; *SVS*, 1895–96, 58. For a list of honors, see *SVS*, 1895–96, 168.

74. İlber Ortaylı asserts incorrectly that the journal "never mentions religion." This is not surprising considering that he also wrote that in the Dönme schools "great stress was laid on secular education." Ortaylı, "Ottoman Modernisation and Sabetaism," 101.

75. "Mekteb," , *Gonca-i Edeb*, no. 8 (June 15, 1883): 126–27.

76. *Gonca-i Edeb*, no. 2 (March 15, 1883): 45–46.

77. *Gonca-i Edeb*, no. 11 (March 15, 1884): 174.

78. Alkan, *Terakki Vakfı ve Terakki Okulları*, 50.

79. Interview, summer 2006.

80. Eden and Stavroulakis, *Salonika: A Family Cookbook*, 36.

81. Yıldız Sertel, *Annem*, 18, 21.

82. Ibid., 31.

83. Şişman, "A Jewish Messiah in the Ottoman Court," 341–42.

84. *Gonca-i Edeb*, no. 10 (February 15, 1884): 145–46.

85. "Bir Allah var ikilik bin bir esma iktizasıdır / Du harf-ı kesret-i ağyarı kaldır zahir olsun yâr."

86. Scholem, "Sprouting of the Horn of the Son of David," 383.

87. *Gonca-i Edeb*, no. 10 (February 15, 1884): 159.

88. Yalman, *Turkey in My Time*, 17–18.

89. Ibid., 18.

90. Ibid., 15.

91. Ibid., 19. Terakki students, teachers, and graduates had written pieces for that journal as well as for *Çocuklara rehber* (Guide for Children), two of the best journals of the kind in the empire. Alkan, *Teraki Vakfı ve Terakki Okulları*, 63.

92. Sandalcı, *Feyz-i Sıbyân'dan Işık'a Feyziye Mektekpleri*, 87.

93. Ernest Ramsaur Jr., *The Young Turks: Prelude to the Revolution of 1908* (Princeton: Princeton University Press, 1957), 121.

94. *Journal de Salonique*, July 10, 1905, quoted in Sandalcı, *Feyz-i Sıbyân'dan Işık'a Feyziye Mektekpleri*, 87.

95. Scholem, "Crypto-Jewish Sect of the Dönmeh," 159.

96. Sandalcı, *Feyz-i Sıbyân'dan Işık'a Feyziye Mektekpleri*, 70–72.

97. Ibid., 97–98.

98. Alkan, *Terakki Vakfı ve Terakki Okulları*, 374n97; 48.

99. Ibid., 5, 7.

100. Yalman, *Turkey in My Time*, 16, 87.

101. Most representative of this approach is İlber Ortaylı's "Ottoman Modernisation and Sabetaism." For a discussion, see Reşat Kasaba, "Kemalist Certainties and Modern Ambiguities," in *Rethinking Modernity and National Identity in Turkey*, ed. Sibel Bozdoğan and Reşat Kasaba (Seattle: University of Washington Press, 1997), 15–36. See also Deringil, *Well-Protected Domains*, and Fortna, *Imperial Classroom*.

102. See Somel, *Modernization of Public Education in the Ottoman Empire*, which is an example of the continued application of the modernization and secularization thesis to the history of Ottoman education.

103. Yıldız Sertel, *Annem*, 59.

104. Aslı Yurddaş, "Meşru vatandaşlık, gayri meşru kimlik? Türkiye'de Sabetaycılık" (MA thesis, İstanbul Bilgi Üniversitesi, June 2004), 19. See "Tarihleri adetleri kendi ifadeleriyle Sabetaycılar: Üniversitede ilk kez tez konusu olan cemaatın gizemli öyküsü," *Nokta* 28 (August 30–September 6, 2004): 29–40.

105. Volkan and Itzkowitz, *Immortal Atatürk*, 30.

106. Mazower, *Salonica, City of Ghosts*, 221. But then he accurately describes how the Dönme schools promoted a modernizing Islam.

107. Fazlı Necip defines which morals and religious customs are acceptable and which should be despised, since they are not "modern," in *Gonca-i Edeb*, no. 6 (May 15, 1883:) 91, and see also Şişman, "*Gonca-i Edeb*'ten iki 'söz,'" 11.

108. Şerif Mardin, *Religion and Social Change in Modern Turkey: The Case of Bediüzzaman Said Nursi* (New York: State University of New York Press, 1989). One offshoot of the Nurcu, the Gülen movement, behaves more like the Dönme. For an account of their international educational ventures based upon Islamic morality and ethics, see Berna Turam, *Between Islam and the State: The Politics of Engagement* (Stanford: Stanford University Press, 2007).

109. Van der Veer, *Imperial Encounters,* 44–45; 53.

110. See ibid., 33, 41.

Chapter 3

1. *Istoria tēs epicheirēmatikotētas stē Thessalonikē,* ed. Roupa and Chekimoglou, 3: 280–83. Roupa and Chekimoglou say that the firm was established in 1872, but Yusuf would have been only fourteen years old at that time.

2. *SVS,* 1907–8, 582.

3. Hanssen, *Fin de siècle Beirut,* 9, 84–112.

4. See Yerolympos and Colonas, "Un urbanisme cosmopolite," and Anastassia-dou, *Salonique.*

5. The best study of this overall process is Anastassiadou, *Salonique.*

6. Donald Quataert, "Premières fumées d'usines," in *Salonique, 1850–1918,* ed. Veinstein, 177; and id., "The Age of Reforms, 1812–1914," in *An Economic and Social History of the Ottoman Empire,* vol. 2: *1600–1914,* ed. Halil Inalcik (New York: Cambridge University Press, 1994), 831.

7. May Seikaly, "Haifa at the Crossroads: An Outpost of the New World Order," in *Modernity and Culture: From the Mediterranean to the Indian Ocean,* ed. Leila Tarazi Fawaz and C. A. Bayly (New York: Columbia University Press, 2002), 96–97.

8. Anastassiadou, *Salonique,* 94–95.

9. Mazower, *Salonica, City of Ghosts,* 216. The first rail service to the rest of Greece was established in 1916, four years after Greek troops took the city.

10. Jacob, *Strangers Nowhere in the World,* 13.

11. Anastassiadou, *Salonique,* 356–59.

12. Ibid., 187–89.

13. Ibid., 192–95.

14. David Harvey, *Paris, Capital of Modernity* (New York: Routledge, 2002).

15. Anastassiadou, *Salonique,* 14; Yerolympos and Colonas, "Un urbanisme cosmopolite," 162.

16. On late Ottoman clock towers, see Hanssen, *Fin de siècle Beirut,* 243–47.

17. Yıldız Sertel, *Annem,* 15–16; photograph, 17.

18. Nathan Wachtel, *La foi du souvenir: Labyrinthes marranes* (Paris: Seuil, 2001), 14.

19. Ibid., 16.

20. Ibid., 19.

21. Ibid., 26.

22. Ibid., 20.

23. Yuri Slezkine, *The Jewish Century* (Princeton: Princeton University Press, 2004), 104, 121.

24. Achille Mbembe and Sarah Nuttall, "Writing the World from an African Metropolis," *Public Culture* 16 (Fall 2004): 360.

25. Cf. postmodern Miami: see Edward LiPuma and Thomas Koelble, "Cultures of Circulation and the Urban Imaginary: Miami as Example and Exemplar," *Public Culture* 17 (Winter 2005): 153–177.

26. E. A. Chekimoglou, *Thessalonikē: Tourkokratia kai mesopolemos* (Thessaloníki: University Studio Press, 1996), 67–68.

27. *Istoria tēs epicheirēmatikotētas stē Thessalonikē,* ed. Roupa and Chekimoglou, 3: 280–83.

28. *SVS,* 1902–3, 134; *SVS,* 1904–5, 76.

29. *SVS,* 1885–86, 104; *SVS,* 1894–95, 152; *SVS,* 1902–3, 134, 419–20; and *SVS,* 1904–5, 76. See also *Annuaire commercial & administratif du Vilayet de Salonique,* 144, which lists Mehmet Kapancı as a banker. Mehmet Alkan notes how Mehmet Kapancı headed the Chamber of Commerce in 1886. Alkan, *Terakki Vakfı ve Terakki Okulları,* 35. French and American commercial and diplomatic sources also noted the importance of this banker.

30. *Istoria tēs epicheirēmatikotētas stē Thessalonikē,* ed. Roupa and Chekimoglou, 3: 280–83.

31. Evangelos Chekimoglou, "The Jewish Bourgeoisie in Thessaloníki, 1906–1911: Assets and Bankruptcies," in *The Jewish Communities of Southeastern Europe from the Fifteenth Century to the End of World War II,* ed. Iōannēs K. Chasiōtēs (Thessaloníki: Institute of Balkan Studies, 1997), 178; Chekimoglou, *Thessalonikē: Tourkokratia kai mesopolemos,* 229; Dēmētriadēs, *Topografia tēs Thessalonikīs,* 189.

32. Dēmētriadēs, *Topografia tēs Thessalonikīs,* 192.

33. *SVS,* 1889–90, 257; *SVS,* 1902–3, 419–20.

34. *SVS,* 1889–90, 257; *SVS,* 1904–5, 95; *SVS,* 1907–8, 133. See also *Annuaire commercial & administratif du Vilayet de Salonique,* 172, which lists him as a dealer in manufactured goods.

35. *SVS,* 1907–8, 133.

36. Interviews, fall 2005, summer 2006, summer 2007.

37. *Annuaire commercial & administratif du Vilayet de Salonique,* 144, 150.

38. Interviews, summer 2003.

39. *SVS,* 1900–1901, 361; *SVS,* 1902–3, 432. See also *Annuaire commercial &*

administratif du Vilayet de Salonique, 181, which lists Hasan Akif and Hüsnü, the husband of his oldest daughter, Fatma, in the tobacco business.

40. Özferendeci, "Soyağacı: Tütüncü Hasan Akif ailesi," 100–109.

41. J.-D. Kieffer and T.-X. Bianchi, "Douhan tudjari thaifesi," in *Dictionnaire turc-français à l'usage des agents diplomatiques et consulaires* (Paris: Impr. royale, 1835–37).

42. Gordlevsky, "Zur Frage über die 'Dönme,'" 207–8.

43. Relli Shechter, "Selling Luxury: The Rise of the Egyptian Cigarette and the Transformation of the Egyptian Tobacco Market, 1850–1914," *International Journal of Middle East Studies* 35 (2003): 53.

44. Mazower, *Salonica, City of Ghosts*, 216.

45. *Faros tēs Makedonias* (Thessaloníki), October 14, 1892, 3.

46. MMKTT 34632, 34656.

47. MMKTT, A34634.

48. MMKTT, A34638.

49. MMKTT, A34637.

50. National Archives of the United States, microfilm MMA4/b/7, no. 102, December 21, 1908, Museum of the Macedonian Struggle, Thessaloníki.

51. National Archives of the United States, microfilm MMA4/b/7, no. 293, September 28, 1909, Museum of the Macedonian Struggle, Thessaloníki.

52. Mehmet Kapancı was noted as an important banker in a list of businesses and businessmen sent to the U.S. State Department the following year. See Horton to State Department, June 2, 1910 (cited Chapter 2, n. 58, above).

53. France, Archives du ministère des Affaires étrangères, vol. 60 (2B), microfilm MMA5/b/22, 1910.44b, Museum of the Macedonian Struggle, Thessaloníki.

54. G. Kofinas, *Ta oikonomika tēs Makedonias* (Athens: National Printing House, 1914), 225.

55. France, Archives du ministère des Affaires étrangères, vol. 60 (2B), microfilm MMA5/b/22, 1910.44a, Museum of the Macedonian Struggle, Thessaloníki, Greece.

56. France, Archives du ministère des Affaires étrangères, vol. 60 (2B), microfilm MMA5/b/22, 1910.44c, Museum of the Macedonian Struggle, Thessaloníki, Greece.

57. *Annuaire commercial & administratif du Vilayet de Salonique*, 178, and Horton to State Department, June 2, 1910 (cited Chapter 2, n. 58, above).

58. *Istoria tēs epicheirēmatikotētas stē Thessalonikē*, ed. Roupa and Chekimoglou, 3: 20.

59. Basilēs Kolonas and Olga Traganou-Delēgianni, *Oi arches tēs biomēhanias stē Thessalonikē, 1870–1912* (Thessaloníki: ETBA, 1987), 34.

60. Nikolaos G. Inglesis, *Odigos tēs Elladas . . .* , year 3, vol. A, 1910–1911,

pt. 2, Georgios Hadjikiriakou, *Makedonia meta tou parakeimenou tmēmatos tēs Thrakis* (Athens: n.p., 1911), 35, 39, 48, 49.

61. *Annuaire commercial & administratif du Vilayet de Salonique*, 144.

62. Julia Phillips Cohen, private collection.

63. Eden and Stavroulakis, *Salonika: A Family Cookbook*, 17.

64. Interview, summer 2002

65. For a discussion of the transformation of the meaning of food from the mystical to the nostalgic in the context of the secularization of Dönme culture, see Avram Elqayam, "Bishulim Shabtaim: Ochel, zikaron, ve-zehut nashit ba-tarbut ha-Shabta'it be-Turkia ha-modernit," *Pe'amim* 105–6 (Autumn–Winter 2005–6), 219-51.

66. Scholem, "Sprouting of the Horn of the Son of David," 99–138.

67. Ibid., 103.

68. Eden and Stavroulakis, *Salonika: A Family Cookbook*, 29–30.

69. Ibid., 203.

70. Yıldız Sertel, *Annem*, 48.

71. Danon, "Une secte judéo-musulmane," 272, 275; Scholem, "Sprouting of the Horn of the Son of David," 385.

72. Eden and Stavroulakis, *Salonika: A Family Cookbook*, 29–30.

73. By the early twentieth century, small branches had also appeared in New York and Boston.

74. Kevin H. O'Rourke and Jeffrey G. Williamson, *Globalization and History: The Evolution of a Nineteenth-Century Atlantic Economy* (Cambridge, MA: MIT Press, 1999).

75. Faruk Tabak, "Imperial Rivalry and Port-Cities: A World-Historical Approach" (paper presented at the Eighth Mediterranean Social and Political Research Meeting, Florence and Montecatini Terme, March 21–25, 2007, organized by the Mediterranean Programme of the Robert Schuman Centre for Advanced Studies at the European University Institute).

76. In the seventeenth century, when the Dönme established themselves, for example, the leading Jewish palace physician converted to Islam, and two descendants of his received the title of Sheikhulislam, that of the leading Muslim religious authority in the empire. See Baer, *Honored by the Glory of Islam*, 136.

77. Jacob, *Strangers Nowhere in the World*, 2.

Chapter 4

1. Galanté, *Nouveaux documents sur Sabbetaï Sevi*, 75–77.

2. *Haim Nahum: A Sephardic Chief Rabbi in Politics, 1892–1923*, ed. Esther Benbassa, trans. Miriam Kochan (Tuscaloosa: University of Alabama Press, 1995), 5–9.

3. Galanté, *Nouveaux documents sur Sabbetaï Sevi*, 76. The quotations that follow in the text are also from this source.

4. On the new class of bureaucrats and centralization, see İlber Ortaylı, *İmparatorluğun en uzun yüzyıl*, 3rd ed. (1983; repr., Istanbul: Hil Yayın, 1995), 77–150.

5. Hanssen, *Fin de siècle Beirut*, 43.

6. Mazower, *Salonica, City of Ghosts*, 225.

7. Anastassiadou, *Salonique*, 356–59.

8. Hanssen, *Fin de siècle Beirut*, 115–16.

9. Kemal Karpat, *The Politicization of Islam: Reconstructing Identity, State, Faith, and Community in the Late Ottoman State* (New York: Oxford University Press, 2001).

10. Anastassiadou, *Salonique*, 3, 12.

11. On Izmir's new municipality, see Vangelis Kechriotis, "Protecting the City's Interest: The Greek-Orthodox and the Conflict Between Municipal and Vilayet Authorities in Izmir in the Second Constitutional Period" (paper presented at the Eighth Mediterranean Social and Political Research Meeting, Florence and Montecatini Terme, March 21–25, 2007, organized by the Mediterranean Programme of the Robert Schuman Centre for Advanced Studies at the European University Institute).

12. Hanssen, *Fin de siècle Beirut*, 139, 145–49.

13. See Halil Sahillioğlu, "Yeniçeri çuhası ve II. Bayezid'in son yıllarında Yeniçeri çuha muhasebesi," *Güney-Doğu Avrupa araştırmaları dergisi* 2–3 (1973–74): 415–66; Benjamin Braude, "International Competition and Domestic Cloth in the Ottoman Empire, 1500–1650: A Study in Undevelopment," *Review of the Fernand Braudel Center* 2 (1979): 437–51; Bruce McGowan, *Economic Life in Ottoman Europe, Taxation, Trade, and the Struggle for Land, 1600–1800* (New York: Cambridge University Press, 1981); Immanuel Wallerstein and Reşat Kasaba, "Incorporation into the World-Economy: Change in the Structure of the Ottoman Empire, 1750–1839," in *Economie et sociétés dans l'Empire ottoman (fin du xviiie–début du xxe siècle)*, ed. Jean-Louis Bacqué-Grammont et al. (Paris: CNRS, 1983), 335–54; Shmuel Avitsur, "Le-toldot ta'asiyat arigei ha-tzemer be-Saloniki," *Sefunot* 12 (*Sefer Yavan* II, 1971–78): 145–68; and Minna Rozen, *Be-netivei ha-Yam ha-Tikhon: Ha-pzura ha-Yehudit-Sfaradit ba-me'ot ha-16–18* (Tel Aviv: Tel Aviv University Press, 1993).

14. I.-S. Emmanuel, *Histoire de l'industrie des tissus des Israélites de Salonique* (Paris: Lipschutz, 1935), 19.

15. Daniel Goffman, "Izmir: From Village to Colonial Port City," in *The Ottoman City Between East and West: Aleppo, Izmir, and Istanbul*, ed. Edhem Eldem, Daniel Goffman, and Bruce Masters (New York: Cambridge University Press, 1999), 99–100. Among those drawn to Izmir and then to Shabbatai

Tzevi's movement were Portuguese conversos. For more on this community, see Ya'kov Barnai, "Ha-Kahalim be-Izmir ba-me'a ha-shva-esre," *Pe'amim* 48 (1991): 66–84. For documents attesting to Jewish trading networks across the Ottoman Empire, see Haim Gerber, *Yehudei Ha-Imperiya Ha-'Otmanit ha-me'ot ha-16–17: Kalkala ve hevra* (Jerusalem: Zalman Shazar, 1982).

16. Minna Rozen, "Contest and Rivalry in Mediterranean Maritime Commerce in the First Half of the Eighteenth Century: The Jews of Salonika and the European Presence," *Revue des études juives* 147 (1988): 309–52.

17. Faroqhi, "Selānīk," 125.

18. *Faros tēs Makedonias*, February 26, 1886, 1.

19. François Georgeon, "Selanik musulmane et deunmè," in *Salonique, 1850–1918*, ed. Veinstein, 106.

20. Dēmētriadēs, *Topografia tēs Thessalonikēs*, 203.

21. *Arazi ve Emlaki Esasi Defteri*, 7: 108, 110.

22. *SVS*, 1902–3, 432.

23. Paul Rabinow, *French Modern: Norms and Forms of the Social Environment* (1989; repr., Chicago: University of Chicago Press, 1995), 12–13.

24. Aleka Karadimou-Yerolymbou, "Archaeology and Urban Planning Development in Thessaloniki (19th–20th c.)," in *Thessaloniki: Queen of the Worthy. History and Culture*, ed. Iōannēs K. Chasiōtēs (Thessaloníki: Paratiritis, 1997), 258.

25. Hanssen, *Fin de siècle Beirut*, 15.

26. Anastassiadou, *Salonique*, 6, 85, 89–90, 150, 154.

27. *Faros tēs Makedonias*, March 6, 1891, 1.

28. Mazower, *Salonica, City of Ghosts*, 160, 163. Mazower says that the Jewish, Greek, and Dönme bourgeoisie found a partner in the Muslim-led local government, but it would be more correct to say in the Dönme-led local government. Ibid., 224, 231.

29. Anastassiadou, *Salonique*, 90.

30. Yerolympos and Colonas, "Un urbanisme cosmopolite," 165–67; Anastassiadou, *Salonique*, 130, 133, 196; and N. C. Moutsopoulos, "Une ville entre deux siècles," in *Salonique, 1850–1918*, ed. Veinstein, 35.

31. Karadimou-Yerolymbou, "Archaeology and Urban Planning Development," 259; Anastassiadou, *Salonique*, 156.

32. İbrahim Alâettin Gövsa, *Sabatay Sevi: İzmirli meşhur sahte mesih hakkında tarihî ve içtimaî tetkik tecrübesi* (Istanbul: Lûtfi Kitabevi, 1939), 74–76.

33. *SVS*, 1893–94, 152–59.

34. Giannēs Megas, *ē epanastasē tōn Neotourkōn stē Thessalonikē* (Thessaloníki: University Studio Press, 2003), 63.

35. Fazlı Necip in *Gonca-i Edeb*, no. 8 (June 15, 1883): 118.

36. Paul Dumont, "Naissance d'un socialisme ottoman," in *Salonique, 1850–1918*, ed. Veinstein, 195–207; Anastassiadou, *Salonique*, 4.

37. M. Şükrü Hanioğlu, *The Young Turks in Opposition* (New York: Oxford University Press, 1995), 4.

38. Ernest Ramsaur refers to him as "Selânikli Nazım" and explains that this was because he was "a resident of Salonika." But the reason the organization's founder, İbrahim Temo (upon whose World War II–era memoir Ramsaur bases his history) called him Salonikan was because he was a Dönme. By World War II, "Salonikan" was equated with "Dönme." Ramsaur, *Young Turks*, 15; and İbrahim Temo, *İttihad ve Terakki Cemiyetinin teşekülü ve hidematı vataniye ve inkılâbı milliye dair hatıratım* (Medgidia, Romania: n.p., 1939), 16–18; and Mehmet Zeki Pakalın, "Dönme," *Osmanlı tarih deyimleri ve terimleri sözlüğü* (Istanbul: Milli Eğitim Basımevi, 1946), 474.

39. Ramsaur, *Young Turks*, 24.

40. Hanioğlu, *Young Turks in Opposition*, 200.

41. Ibid., 202–3; Ramsaur, *Young Turks*, 90–91.

42. M. Şükrü Hanioğlu, *Preparation for a Revolution: The Young Turks, 1902–1908* (New York: Oxford University Press, 2001), 306.

43. Hanioğlu, *Young Turks in Opposition*, 18–23, 71.

44. Ibid., 208–9. Demolins's work was entitled *A quoi tient la supériorité des Anglo-Saxons?* [To What Is Anglo-Saxon Superiority Due?] (Paris: Firmin-Didot, 1897) and claimed that the secret lay in British and American governmental decentralization and individualism, or private initiative. See also Ramsaur, *Young Turks*, 81–87.

45. Yusuf Akçura, "Üç Tarz-ı Siyaset," *Türk*, no. 24 (April 14, 1904): 1, quoted in Hanioğlu, *Preparation for a Revolution*, 67.

46. Hanioğlu, *Young Turks in Opposition*, 210; id., *Preparation for a Revolution*, 40–41. The Armenians, it was claimed, had "done nothing for the maintenance of the common fatherland" and had "not shed a drop of blood to this end." Sami Paşazade Sezai, "Ermeni mes'elesi," *Şûra-yı Ümmet*, no. 57 (August 13, 1904): 120, quoted in Hanioğlu, *Preparation for a Revolution*, 42. Moreover, "The fortunes that they have made, the arts that they have mastered all arise from the fact that they have lived at our expense." Uluğ, "Ermeniler," *Türk*, no. 110 (n.d. [1906?]): 2, quoted in Hanioğlu, *Preparation for a Revolution*, 69.

47. Hanioğlu, *Young Turks in Opposition*, 211, 216.

48. Ibid., 168.

49. Ibid., 53. See also Ramsaur, *Young Turks*, 109–113. He also mentions the Melami order's role.

50. Irène Melikoff, "L'ordre des Bektaşi après 1826," *Turcica* 15 (1983): 155–70.

51. Quoted in Ramsaur, *Young Turks*, 113.

52. Hanioğlu, *Young Turks in Opposition*, 54.

53. Ibid., 54–65.

54. Ibid., 34.

55. Ibid., 34–35.

56. Ibid. 38.

57. Ibid., 40.

58. Hanioğlu, *Preparation for a Revolution*, 212.

59. Hanioğlu, *Young Turks in Opposition*, 41.

60. Jacob, *Strangers Nowhere in the World*, 97–98.

61. Ibid., 8.

62. Hanioğlu, *The Young Turks in Opposition*, 35.

63. Robert Olson, "The Young Turks and the Jews: A Historiographical Revision," *Turcica* 18 (1986): 231; Paul Dumont, "La Franc-Maçonnerie d'obédience française à Salonique au début du XXe siècle," *Turcica* 16 (1984): 74.

64. Dumont, "Franc-Maçonnerie," 93.

65. Yıldız Sertel, *Annem*, 35.

66. Osman Adil, "Arz," *Gonca-i Edeb*, no. 2 (March 15, 1883): 23; "Bahçe," ibid., no. 4 (April 15, 1883); "Su," ibid., no. 5 (April 30, 1883): 77, continued in no. 6 (May 15, 1883): 94; "Ziya," ibid., no. 7 (June 1, 1883): 109; "Mısır," ibid., no. 8 (June 15, 1883): 124–25, continued in no. 9 (January 15, 1884): 138, and no. 10 (February 15, 1884): 150.

67. Dumont, "Franc-Maçonnerie," 73.

68. Ibid., 77.

69. Ibid., 71.

70. Ibid., 72–73.

71. Alkan, *Terakki Vakfı ve Terakki Okulları*, 46–47.

72. David Farhi, "Yehudei Saloniki be-mehafikat ha-Turkim ha-Tzeirim," *Sefunot* 15 (1981): 135–53.

73. Yıldız Sertel, *Annem*, 47.

74. Ibid., 36.

75. It also paralleled that of Jews. As Hanioğlu notes, "prominent figures of the Jewish community in Salonica, such as Emmanuel Carasso, Nesim Matzliach, Nesim Ruso, and Emmanuel Salem, became CPU members and worked closely with the CPU Internal Headquarters." Because these men were also influential Freemasons, they made their lodges available for secret meetings and the storage of their secret documents. Hanioğlu, *Preparation for a Revolution*, 260.

76. Hanioğlu, *Young Turks in Opposition*, 88.

77. Ibid.

78. Ibid., 89.

79. Ibid., 168.

80. M. Şükrü Hanioğlu, "Jews in the Young Turk Movement to the 1908 Revolution," in *The Jews of the Ottoman Empire*, ed. Avigdor Levy (Princeton: Darwin Press, 1994), 521.

81. Slousch, "Deunmeh," 483.

82. Megas, *ē Epanastasē tōn Neotourkōn stē Thessalonikē*, 189; Alexandros Dagas, *Sumbolē stēn ereuna gia tēn oikonomiki kai koinoniki exelixi tēs Thessalonikēs* (Thessaloníki, 1998), 131.

83. Yıldız Sertel, *Annem*, 41.

84. Georgeon, "Selanik musulmane et deunmè," 118.

85. Hanioğlu, "Jews in the Young Turk Movement to the 1908 Revolution," 522.

86. Slousch, "Deunmeh," 494.

87. The postcard is reproduced in Yıldız Sertel, *Annem*, 45.

88. Ibid., 46.

89. Dumont, "Franc-Maçonnerie," 72.

90. Yalman, *Turkey in My Time*, 23.

91. Ibid., 35.

92. Alkan, *Terakki Vakfı ve Terakki Okulları*, 94.

93. Ad. Beaune, "L'ecole Féizié: La jeune turquie," *Journal de Salonique*, December 21, 1909.

94. Ibid., 88.

95. Leskovikli Mehmet Rauf, *İttihad ve Terakki Cemiyeti ne idi?* (1911; repr., Istanbul: Arba, 1991), 85.

96. "Abdul Shed Tears as He Lost Throne," *New York Times*, May 2, 1909.

97. British Consul General Harry Lamb, Salonika, to Ambassador Sir Gerard Lowther, Istanbul, despatch 38, March 24, 1909, United Kingdom, National Archives, Foreign Office Papers, FO 195.2328, Museum of the Macedonian Struggle, Thessaloníki.

98. France, Archives du ministère des Affaires étrangères, vol. 60 (2B), microfilm MMA5/b/22, Microfilms, 1910.36a, 1910.36b, Museum of the Macedonian Struggle, Thessaloníki.

99. *SVS*, 1906–7, 254, 259; *SVS*, 1907–8, 487. Selim İlkin, "Câvid Bey, Mehmet," *İslâm Ansiklopedisi* (Istanbul: Türkiye Diyanet Vakfı, 1988–), 7 (1994): 175–76, refers to him as "the son of Receb Naim Efendi, a merchant from the Dönme community." See also Erik Zürcher, *Turkey: A Modern History* (London: I. B. Tauris, 1995), 351.

100. Ramsaur, *Young Turks*, 98.

101. Hanioğlu, *Preparation for a Revolution*, 211.

102. Sandalcı, *Feyz-i Sıbyân'dan Işık'a Feyziye Mektekpleri*, 100, 102.

103. Yıldız Sertel, *Annem*, 44.

104. Yalman, *Turkey in My Time*, 22.

105. Ibid., 4.

106. Yalman, *Yakın tarihte gördüklerim ve geçirdiklerim*, 1: 75–76.

107. For comparison with the Soviet case, in which it was claimed Jews played

too prominent a part in the Bolshevik Revolution, became the core of the Communist Party, and implemented the teachings of a Jew, Karl Marx, see Slezkine, *Jewish Century*, 181.

108. Jacob, *Strangers Nowhere in the World*, 104.

109. Ibid., 122.

110. Ibid., 2.

111. Ibid., 4.

112. Ibid., 2.

113. Kıbrıslı Derviş Vahdetî, "Millet selâmettedir," *Volkan*, no. 45 (February 14, 1909): 213–14.

114. Lewis, *Emergence of Modern Turkey*, 207–8n4. See the sentiments of several British writers quoted in Ramsaur, *Young Turks*, 106–9.

115. See Elie Kedourie, "Young Turks, Freemasons, and Jews," *Middle Eastern Studies* 7 (1971): 89–104.

116. See Stanford Shaw, *The Jews of the Ottoman Empire and the Turkish Republic* (New York: New York University Press, 1991), passim, which frequently contrasts the antisemitism of Armenians and Greeks, who he claims introduced antisemitism to the Ottoman Empire, with the tolerance of the Ottoman Muslims. Lewis, for his part, is more inclined to discuss antisemitism among Arabs, particularly Palestinians, than among Ottoman Muslims or Turks. See Bernard Lewis, *The Jews of Islam* (Princeton: Princeton University Press, 1984), passim.

117. See Sander Gilman, *The Jew's Body* (New York: Routledge, 1991), 60–103, 169–233; and Efron, *Defenders of the Race*, 13–57.

118. See Paul Bessemer, "Cavid Bey'e mektuplar," *Tarih ve Toplum* 38 (July 2002): 22–23.

119. *Volkan gazetesi, İkinci Meşrutiyetin ilk ayları ve 31 Mart olayı için bir yakın tarih belgesi: 11 Aralık 1908–20 Nisan 1909* [December 11, 1908–April 20, 1909], *tam ve aynen metin neşri, hazırlayan M. Ertuğrul Düzdağ* (Istanbul: İz Yayıncılık, 1992).

120. A. Şehâbeddin, "Din," *Volkan*, no. 27 (January 27, 1909): 123.

121. Kıbrıslı Derviş Vahdetî, "Mülk-vatan ve din muhabbeti," *Volkan*, no. 42 (February 11, 1909): 196–97.

122. Kıbrıslı Derviş Vahdetî, "Dindarlık-dinsizlik ve tarikatlar," *Volkan*, no. 36 (February 5, 1909): 166–68.

123. Kıbrıslı Derviş Vahdetî, "Ulemâ-yı kirâmın nazar-ı intibâhına," *Volkan*, no. 40 (February 11, 1909): 186–88.

124. Kıbrıslı Derviş Vahdetî, "İttihad," *Volkan*, no. 54 (February 23, 1909): 256–57.

125. This is also asserted in Yalman, *Yakın tarihte gördüklerim ve geçirdiklerim*, 1: 205.

126. Kıbrıslı Derviş Vahdetî, "Gazetelerde görülen telgrafnâme sûretidir," *Volkan*, no. 78 (March 19, 1909): 375–77.

127. Kıbrıslı Derviş Vahdetî, "Kuvve-i mâneviyyeyi kırmak, ne fenadır!" *Volkan*, no. 49 (February 18, 1909): 233.

128. Kıbrıslı Derviş Vahdetî, "Zaman! Asır!" *Volkan*, no. 73 (March 14, 1909): 351–32.

129. Sheikh Abdurrahim, "Aydın: Efkâr-ı milleti aydınlatıyor," *Volkan*, no. 84 (March 25, 1909): 408–9.

130. "Doktor Nâzım Bey'in konferansları," quoting *İkdam*, *Volkan*, no. 72 (March 13, 1909): 345–46.

131. İbrahim Hilmi, "Bursa'dan varaka," *Volkan*, no. 77 (March 18, 1909): 371–72.

132. Kıbrıslı Derviş Vahdetî, "İttihad ve Terakki Cemiyeti," *Volkan*, no. 81 (March 22, 1909): 390–91.

133. Farhi, "Yehudei Saloniki be-mehafikat ha-Turkim ha-Tzeirim."

134. Mazower, *Salonica, City of Ghosts*, 270.

135. Sciaky, *Farewell to Salonica*, 139.

136. Hanioğlu, "Jews in the Young Turk Movement to the 1908 Revolution," 519.

137. Later it was learned that, unlike Atatürk, Lenin was in fact partly of Jewish descent (on his mother's side). Slezkine, *Jewish Century*, 245–46.

138. See Slezkine, *Jewish Century*, 150–55.

139. Ibid., 173.

140. Ibid., 175–7.

141. Ibid., 169.

142. Ibid., 91.

143. Ibid., 154–55.

144. Feroz Ahmad, "Unionist Relations with the Greek, Armenian, and Jewish Communities of the Ottoman Empire, 1908–1914," in *Christians and Jews in the Ottoman Empire: The Functioning of a Plural Society*, ed. Benjamin Braude and Bernard Lewis (New York: Holmes & Meier, 1982), 1: 425; and id., "Vanguard of a Nascent Bourgeoisie: The Social and Economic Policy of the Young Turks, 1908–1918," in *Türkiye'nin sosyal ve ekonomik tarihi (1071–1920)*, ed. Osman Okyar and Halil Inalcik (Ankara: Meteksan, 1980), 332.

145. Hanioğlu, *Preparation for a Revolution*, 244.

146. Ibid., 244.

Chapter 5

1. www.thessalonikicity.gr/eikones/1800-1917-photosel-2/cityhist_1800-17-istgeg28.htm (accessed March 26, 2009).

2. Faroqhi, "Selānīk," 122–26.

3. Mazower, *Salonica, City of Ghosts*, 281.

4. K. E. Fleming, *Greece: A Jewish History* (Princeton: Princeton University Press, 2008), 68–69.

5. Benaroya became the architect of Greek socialism, founding the Greek Socialist Labor Party (SEKE) and the General Confederation of Greek Workers (GSEE). But he was exiled to Israel after the Greek Civil War. Mazower, *Salonica, City of Ghosts*, 271.

6. Carasso died in Trieste in 1934. Mazower, *Salonica, City of Ghosts*, 271.

7. Sciaky, *Farewell to Salonica*, 154.

8. Quoted in Mazower, *Salonica, City of Ghosts*, 284.

9. Alkan, *Terakki Vakfı ve Terakki Okulları*, 83.

10. *Eklogikos katalogos periferias Thessalonikēs* (Thessaloníki, 1914), 176, voter no. 13,144, Mehmet Kapancı; 183, voter no. 13,690, Namık Kapancı; 184, voter no. 13,740, Feyrouz Kapancı; and 222, voter no. 16,645, Mehmet, son of Ahmet Kapancı.

11. *Salonik: Topographisch-statistische Übersichten* (Vienna: Osterreichisches Handelsmuseum, 1915), 142, 152, 165, 169, 170, İpekçi; 150, 175, Karakaş; 147, 161, Kibar; and 161, 175, Şamlı.

12. *Ktēmatikos Sundesmos*, Thessaloníki, January 1915, Historical Archive of Macedonia, Thessaloníki.

13. *Istoria tēs epicheirēmatikotētas stē Thessalonikē*, ed. Roupa and Chekimoglou, 3: 20.

14. *Neotera Mnēmeia tēs Thessalonikēs* (Thessaloníki, 1986), 224.

15. MMKTT, A34634.

16. MMKTT, A34637.

17. Periklis Argiropoulos, *O Makedonikos Agōn: Apomnēmonevmata* (Thessaloníki: Etairia Makedonikōn Spoudōn, 1957; Athens, 1970), 141.

18. Archive of the Thessaloníki Chamber of Commerce and Industry.

19. Archive of the Thessaloníki Chamber of Commerce and Industry, May 20, 1915.

20. Alkan, *Terakki Vakfı ve Terakki Okulları*, 109.

21. Ibid., 115–16.

22. MMKTT, A37856.

23. Alkan, *Terakki Vakfı ve Terakki Okulları*, 110–11, 117; Sandalcı, *Feyz-i Sıbyân'dan Işık'a Feyziye Mektepleri*, 110.

24. MMKTT, 34619.

25. Sandalcı, *Feyz-i Sıbyân'dan Işık'a Feyziye Mektepleri*, 120.

26. MMKTT, A31337.

27. Sandalcı, *Feyz-i Sıbyân'dan Işık'a Feyziye Mektepleri*, 124–25, 128–29, 134.

28. Tesal, *Selânik'ten İstanbul'a*, 36, 40–44, 48, 63, 65.

29. Sandalcı, *Feyz-i Sıbyân'dan Işık'a Feyziye Mektekpleri*, 118.

30. See MMKTT, A37726, A37733, A37737, A37956.

31. On the role the fire played in the remaking of the city, see Alexandra Yerolympos, "La part de feu," in *Salonique, 1850–1918*, ed. Veinstein, 261–29.

32. *Neotera Mnēmeia tēs Thessalonikēs*, 230; Kolonas, "ē ektos tōn toichōn epektasi tēs Thessalonikēs," 152. See also the web site of the National Bank of Greece's Cultural Foundation, www.miet.gr/web/en/miet/thess_history.htm (accessed March 26, 2009).

33. Anastassiadou, *Salonique*, 131.

34. Mazower, *Salonica, City of Ghosts*, 283.

35. MMKTT, 32440, 32441, 32442.

36. MMKTT, 32440, 32441, 32442.

37. MMKTT, A34634.

38. MMKTT, A34637.

39. MMKTT, A34638, 34646, 34662.

40. MMKTT, A34664.

41. MMKTT, A34668.

42. MMKTT, A34655.

43. MMKTT, A34660.

44. MMKTT, 34632.

45. *Emboriko Enkolpio, 1921* (Thessaloníki: Avgi, 1921), 253.

46. *Emboriko Enkolpio, 1922* (Thessaloníki: Avgi, 1922), 322.

47. Mazower, *Salonica, City of Ghosts*, 282.

48. Interview, fall 2005.

49. Dumont, "Franc-Maçonnerie," 71.

50. Interview, summer 2006.

51. Yalman, *Turkey in My Time*, 35.

52. Ibid., 49.

53. Yıldız Sertel, *Annem*, 79.

54. Ibid., 69.

55. Ibid., 71.

56. Ibid., 72.

57. Ibid., 74.

58. *Dönmeler: Hunyos, Kavayeros, Sazan* (Istanbul, 1919); page numbers from this anonymous publication are given parenthetically in the text.

59. Sazaniko: *-iko* is the diminutive ending in Judeo-Spanish. Galanté, *Nouveaux documents sur Sabbetaï Sevi*, 72. The Dönme may have been called "carp" because Shabbatai Tzevi supposedly placed a fish in baby clothes in a crib, or because Dönme in Edirne lived near the fish market.

60. Atik nizâmiye kırkbirinci alayının üçüncü taburu binbaşılığından mütekaid Sâdık, *Dönmelerin Hakîkati* (Der Saadet: Karabet Matbaası, December 18,

1919), 4; further page numbers from this publication are given parenthetically in the text.

61. On Evrenos Ghazi, see Cemal Kafadar, *Between Two Worlds: The Construction of the Ottoman State* (Berkeley: University of California Press, 1995), 74, and Heath Lowry, *The Nature of the Early Ottoman State* (Albany, NY: State University of New York Press, 2003), 56–61.

62. Scholem, "Sprouting of the Horn of the Son of David," 384. That there were no beggars among them due to their practice of mutual assistance is also noted in Leskovikli Mehmet Rauf, *İttihad ve Terakki Cemiyeti ne idi?* 86–87.

63. Eyal Ginio, "Port Cities as an Imagined Battlefield: The Boycott of 1913" (paper presented at the Eighth Mediterranean Social and Political Research Meeting, Florence and Montecatini Terme, March, 21–25 2007, organized by the Mediterranean Programme of the Robert Schuman Centre for Advanced Studies at the European University Institute).

64. Mazower, *Salonica, City of Ghosts*, 254.

65. Ahmet Refik Altınay, *İki komite, iki kıtal* (Istanbul: n.p., 1919), 14, 19, 60.

Chapter 6

1. Kemal Arı, *Büyük mübadele: Türkiye'ye zorunlu göç, 1923–1925* (1995), 4th ed. (Istanbul: Tarih Vakfı, 2007), 165.

2. Rıza Nur, *Hayat ve hatıratım* (1929; Turkish transl., Istanbul: Altındağ Yayınevi, 1968), 3: 928. Nahum was one of the last Ottoman chief rabbis, serving between 1909 and 1920. Two years after the Lausanne Conference, Nahum left Turkey for Egypt, where he became the chief rabbi of Cairo and served in that position until his death in 1960.

3. Yalman, *Turkey in My Time*, 134–35.

4. Nur, *Hayat ve hatıratım*, 3: 1081.

5. Ibid.

6. Pakalın, "Dönme," 474.

7. Garnett, *Women of Turkey*, 108.

8. See Kader Konuk, "Eternal Guests, Mimics, and *Dönme*: The Place of German and Turkish Jews in Modern Turkey," *New Perspectives on Turkey* 37 (2007): 5–30. The Dönme threat is thus similar to that perceived of converts to Christianity in colonial India, or converts to Islam in independent India. Gauri Viswanathan *Outside the Fold: Conversion, Modernity, and Belief* (Princeton: Princeton University Press, 1998), 87.

9. Quoted in Mazower, *Salonica, City of Ghosts*, 327.

10. See Zürcher, *Turkey*, 167–70; and Lewis, *Emergence of Modern Turkey*, 254–56.

11. Faroqhi, "Selānīk," 125.

12. Hanioğlu, *Young Turks in Opposition*, 40.

13. Count Stanislas de Clermont-Tonnerre, addressing the French National Assembly in 1789, declared "to the individual Jew, everything, to the community, nothing." Cited in Deborah Hertz, *How Jews Became Germans: The History of Conversion and Assimilation in Berlin* (New Haven: Yale University Press, 2007), 107.

14. Rogers Brubaker, *Nationalism Reframed: Nationhood and the National Question in the New Europe* (New York: Cambridge University Press, 1996), 152; id., "Aftermath of Empire and the Unmixing of Peoples: Historical and Comparative Perspectives," *Ethnic and Racial Studies* 18 (1995): 189–218.

15. Hippocrates Papavasileiou quoted in Mazower, *Salonica, City of Ghosts*, 277.

16. Sami Zubaida, "Cosmopolitanism and the Middle East," in *Cosmopolitanism, Identity and Authenticity in the Middle East*, ed. Roel Meijer (Richmond, Surrey: Curzon, 1999), 26–27.

17. Roel Meijer, "Introduction," in *Cosmopolitanism, Identity and Authenticity in the Middle East*, ed. id., 2.

18. Fuat Dündar, *İttihat ve Terraki'nin Müslümanları iskan politikası* (Istanbul: İletişim, 2001), 63–64, and id., "The Settlement Policy of the Committee of Union and Progress, 1913–1918," in *Turkey Beyond Nationalism: Towards Post-Nationalist Identities*, ed. Hans-Lukas Kieser (London: I. B. Tauris, 2006), 38.

19. Arı, *Büyük mübadele*, 8.

20. Fuat Dündar, *İttihat ve Terraki'nin Müslümanları iskan politikası*, 64–65, and in id., "Settlement Policy," 38.

21. Viswanathan, *Outside the Fold*, xii.

22. Cited in Howard Eissenstat, "Metaphors of Race and Discourse of Nation: Racial Theory and State Nationalism in the First Decades of the Turkish Republic," in *Race and Nation: Ethnic Systems in the Modern World*, ed. Paul Spickard (New York: Routledge, 2005), 248.

23. Ella Shohat, "Rupture and Return: Zionist Discourse and the Study of Arab Jews," in id., *Taboo Memories, Diasporic Voices*, 340.

24. Ibid., 337, 340.

25. *Lozan Barış Konferansı, tutanaklar belgeler*, ed. Seha L. Meray (Ankara: Ankara Üniversitesi Yayınevi, 1967–69), vol. 2.

26. Renée Hirschon, "'Unmixing Peoples' in the Aegean Region," in *Crossing the Aegean: An Appraisal of the 1923 Compulsory Population Exchange Between Greece and Turkey*, ed. id., Studies in Forced Migration, 12 (New York: Berghahn Books, 2006), 8.

27. Lewis, *Emergence of Modern Turkey*, 355.

28. Arı, *Büyük mübadele*, 19.

29. TBMM (Türkiye Büyük Millet Meclisi / Turkish Grand National Assem-

bly) Gizli Celse Zabıtları, Devre: 1 Cilt: 4, March 2, 1923, 8 cited in Eissenstat, "Metaphors of Race and Discourse of Nation," 248; Arı, *Büyük mübadele*, 16.

30. Arı, *Büyük mübadele*, 88.

31. Stanford Shaw, "The Population of Istanbul in the Nineteenth Century," *International Journal of Middle East Studies* 10 (1979): 266.

32. For a comprehensive discussion of the efforts to "Turkify" the Turkish economy in the 1920s, see Ayhan Aktar, "Nüfusun homojenleştirilmesi ve ekonominin Türkleştirilmesi sürecinde bir aşama: Türk-Yunan nüfus mübadelesi, 1923–1924," in id., *Varlık Vergisi ve 'Türkleştirme' politikaları* (Istanbul: İletişim Yayınları, 2000), 17–69; Rifat N. Bali, *Cumhuriyet yıllarında Türkiye Yahudileri: Bir Türkleştirme serüveni, 1923–1945* (Istanbul: İletişim Yayınları, 1999), 196–240; and Alexis Alexandris, *The Greek Minority of Istanbul and Greek-Turkish Relations, 1918–1974* (Athens: Center for Asia Minor Studies, 1983), 105–12.

33. Hanioğlu, *Preparation for a Revolution*, 289–93.

34. Ibid., 173–81.

35. Ibid., 306, 308.

36. See Hans-Lukas Kieser, "Dr. Mehmet Reshid (1873–1919): A Political Doctor," in *Der Völkermord an den Armeniern und die Shoah/ The Armenian Genocide and the Shoah* ed. Hans-Lukas Kieser and Dominik J. Schaller (Zurich: Chronos, 2002), 245–79.

37. The figure of 800,000 for the Armenians comes from the 1919 announcement by Ottoman Interior Minister Cemal Bey, based on the findings of the 1918 commission of previous Interior Minister Arif Değmer. Atatürk accepted this figure, as did the General Staff of the Turkish Army, which repeated the figure in a 1928 book about World War I losses. All are quoted in Taner Akçam, *A Shameful Act: The Armenian Genocide and the Question of Turkish Responsibility* (New York: Holt, 2006), 183, 345–46.

38. Avner Levi, *Türkiye Cumhuriyeti'nde Yahudiler: Hukukî ve siyasî durumları*, ed. Rıfat N. Bali (Istanbul: İletişim Yayınları, 1992), 64.

39. Arı, *Büyük mübadele*, 128.

40. Zürcher, *Turkey*, 172; Çağlar Keyder, *State and Class in Turkey: A Study in Capitalist Development* (London: Verso, 1987), 79.

41. Caroline Finkel, *Osman's Dream: The History of the Ottoman Empire* (New York: Basic Books, 2006), 547.

42. Vlachs were divided: those who were Orthodox Christians were sent to Greece; those who were Muslim were accepted in Turkey.

43. Galanté, *Nouveaux documents sur Sabbetaï Sevi*, 79.

44. Rıfat Bali, "Bir diğer düşman: Dönmeler veya gizli Yahudiler," in id., *Musa'nın evlatları Cumhuriyet'in yurttaşları* (Istanbul: İletişim, 2001), 412.

45. Quoted in Ben-Tzevi, "Preface," 74n17.

46. Dündar, "Settlement Policy," 41–42.

47. Arı, *Büyük mübadele*, 89–90.

48. Ibid., 19–20.

49. Ibid., 27.

50. Ibid., 12–15.

51. Ibid., 58–59.

52. Ibid., 42.

53. Ibid., 53–54.

54. Ibid., 59.

55. Ibid., 87.

56. Ibid., 75–76.

57. Ibid., 81–82.

58. Ibid., 114–15.

59. Ibid., 106–8.

60. Ibid., 109–11.

61. Ibid., 76–77.

62. Ibid., 91–92.

63. Ibid., 81–82.

64. Ibid., 96.

65. Tesal, *Selânik'ten İstanbul'a*, 66–68.

66. Ibid., 101.

67. Ibid., 139.

68. MMKTT, A37731.

69. MMKTT, A31332.

70. MMKTT, 32440, 32441, 32442.

71. MMKTT, A37753.

72. MMKTT, A34664.

73. MMKTT, A34668, A34660.

74. MMKTT, A34660.

75. MMKTT, A37726.

76. For an account of Muslim refugees from Greece who were given inadequate or no compensation by the Turkish authorities, who apparently did not even look at the documents they provided, see Tolga Köker (in collaboration with Leylâ Keskiner), "Lessons in Refugeehood: The Experience of Forced Migrants in Turkey," in *Crossing the Aegean*, ed. Hirschon, 199–200.

Chapter 7

1. *Akbaba* (Istanbul), no. 114 (January 7, 1924): 3.

2. Arı, *Büyük mübadele*, 163.

3. Ibid., 166–72.

4. In 1908, he was listed as a merchant of socks, stockings, blankets, umbrellas,

and imported galoshes in Salonika; in 1915 he sold galoshes and owned a knitting factory in his native city. See *Annuaire commercial & administratif du Vilayet de Salonique*, 164; and *Salonik: Topographisch-statistische Übersichten*, 150, 175.

5. "Rüşdü Bey'in eski teşebbüsleri," *Vakit*, January 12, 1924.

6. Gordlevsky, "Zur Frage über die 'Dönme,'"202. In other interviews, Rüştü claimed to have been banished at the age of thirty.

7. Ibid., 202–3.

8. "Dönmeler hakkında arîza-asıl mesele Selânik Dönmelerinin mübâdeleye tâbi olunmasını rica etmektir," *Vakit* (January 4, 1924).

9. "Ankara'da Karakaşzâde Mehmet Rüşdü Bey'den bilumum Selânik Dönmelerine açık mektup," *Vakit* (January 7, 1924); *Sebîlürreşat* 23, no. 583 (January 10, 1924): 174. *Sebîlürreşat* (The Straight Course) was an Islamist weekly that reprinted articles of interest from other newspapers.

10. Quoted in Hanioğlu, *Preparation for a Revolution*, 89. This Turkish nationalist was a graduate of the Royal Medical Academy and private physician to the second in the line to the Ottoman throne. That a physician should make such a comment was typical for the age. Hanioğlu credits him with transforming the CUP into a well-organized revolutionary committee. Ibid., 130–31, 136. From 1906 to 1918, he and another medical doctor, Dr. Nâzım "established a firm, controlling grip over the organizational affairs of the committee." Ibid., 140.

11. Ahmet Cevat, *Haram yiyicilik: Felâketlerimizin esbabı* (Istanbul, 1912–13), quoted in Ginio, "Port Cities as an Imagined Battlefield."

12. Talat Paşa, *Talat Paşanın anıları* (Istanbul: Say Yayınları, 1986), 75. Talat Pasha, who had taught Turkish at an Alliance israélite universelle school in Edirne and worked in Salonika in the Post and Telegraph Department, was also a Freemason, joining Macedonia Risorta in 1903. He became an MP, minister of the interior, head of the CUP, and prime minister. His memoirs were published as part of an effort to counter the claims of mass murder by Armenians. He was assassinated by an Armenian in Berlin in 1921. In 1943 his remains were reburied in Şişli, Istanbul.

13. *Sebîlürreşat* 23, no. 583 (January 10, 1924): 174.

14. Ibid. 23, no. 585 (January 24, 1924): 205.

15. Ibid. 23, no. 583, 172–73.

16. Ibid., 173.

17. Ibid.

18. *Vakit* (January 7, 1924); *Sebîlürreşat* 23, no. 583 (January 24, 1924): 175.

19. Ibid., 172.

20. Ibid., 173.

21. Gordlevsky, "Zur Frage über die 'Dönme,'"201.

22. *Akşam*, January 12, 1924; *Sebîlürreşat* 23, no. 584 (January 24, 1924): 189–90. When Becerano was the chief rabbi of Edirne and Atatürk was a regimental

commander there, Atatürk often visited him. Chief rabbi during the crucial first years of the republic, from 1920 to 1930, Becerano did his best to keep alive a community suffering financial ruin and legal constraints on its institutions; the chief rabbinate itself was stripped of secular powers in 1926. Becerano died in 1931, and the lay leadership found it unnecessary to select a new chief rabbi. Turkish Jewry remained without a spiritual leader until 1960. See Bali, *Cumhuriyet yıllarında Türkiye Yahudileri,* 38, 91, 241.

23. *Sebîlürreşat* 23, no. 584 (January 24, 1924): 190.

24. Ibid., no. 583 (January 24, 1924): 172.

25. Ibid.: 174. Not all reports were negative. Köprülülü Şerif, writing in *Akşam* (Evening), says that because Dönme youth played a progressive and revolutionary role in Salonika and elsewhere in Macedonia and Kosovo, they should not be called "Dönme" (regarded as a derogatory term) but embraced as part of the Turkish community. Ibid.: 172. *Akşam* also reported how Dönme Receb Kaymak, who was the owner of the Islam Library in Karşıkaya in Izmir, responded to Rüştü's claims. *Sebîlürreşat* 23, no. 585 (January 24, 1924): 205. The immigrant Hacı Mehmet sent a telegram to *Akşam* from Rhodes asserting that everything said about the sect was incorrect; they were Turks and Muslims, not secret Jews. Gordlevsky, "Zur Frage über die 'Dönme,'" 201. According to *Sebîlürreşat, Tanin,* the CUP organ, and *Akşam* also defended the Dönme. Ibid., no. 583 (January 24, 1924): 175.

26. Robert Young, *Colonial Desire: Hybridity in Theory, Culture and Race* (New York: Routledge, 1995), 4.

27. Ibid., 1–28.

28. Ibid., 7–10.

29. Alexandris, *Greek Minority of Istanbul,* 106.

30. Bali, *Cumhuriyet yıllarında Türkiye Yahudileri,* 82.

31. Rıfat Bali, personal communication, spring 2006.

32. Sentiment and policy that promoted Muslim merchants and later Turks over traders from other ethno-religious groups was not new, but an inheritance of late Ottoman thinking and practice. See Hanioğlu, *Preparation for a Revolution,* 299; Erik Zürcher, "Young Turks, Ottoman Muslims, and Turkish Nationalists: Identity Politics, 1908–38," in *The Ottoman Past and Today's Turkey,* ed. Kemal Karpat (Brill: Boston, 2000), 150–79; Sciaky, *Farewell to Salonica,* 147; Zafer Toprak, "Osmanlı donanması, Averof zırhlısı ve ulusal kimlik," *Toplumsal Tarih* 113 (2003): 10–19; Ginio, "Port Cities as an Imagined Battlefield"; Toprak, *Türkiye'de "milli iktisat" (1908–1918)* (Ankara: Yurt Yayınları, 1982), 60–68, 98, 170–73; and Keyder, *State and Class in Turkey,* 61–62.

33. Gordlevsky, "Zur Frage über die 'Dönme,'" 201.

34. Jean Brunhes and Camille Vallaux, *La géographie de l'histoire: Géographie*

de la paix et de la guerre sur terre et sur mer (Paris: Alcan, 1921); *Mihrab*, January 15, 1924; *Sebîlürreşat* 23, no. 585 (January 24, 1924): 203.

35. Gövsa, *Sabatay Sevi*, 5.

36. *Sebîlürreşat* 23, no. 585 (January 24, 1924): 204–5; and ibid., no. 586: 220.

37. Robert Dankoff, "An Unpublished Account of *mum söndürmek* in the *Seyahatname* of Evliya Chelebi," in *Bektachiyya: Etudes sur l'ordre mystique des Bektachis et les groupes relevant de Hadji Bektach*, ed. A. Popovic and G. Veinstein (Istanbul: Isis, 1995), 69–73.

38. Garnett, *Women of Turkey*, 108.

39. *Resimli Dünya*, September 15, 1925, 4–6; October 15, 2–4; November 15, 3–4. Quoted in Paul Bessemer, "Who Is a Crypto-Jew? A Historical Survey of the Sabbatean Debate in Turkey," *Kabbalah* 9 (2003): 109-52. Bessemer adds: "the account fits a little too neatly with the journal's standard fare of passionate romances, true crime, and tales of degradation, heartbreak, and woe to render it completely above suspicion."

40. *Resimli Dünya*, November 15, 1925, translated into French in Galanté, *Nouveaux documents sur Sabbetaï Sevi*, 50.

41. *Akşam*, May 4, 1935, trans. into French in Galanté, *Nouveaux documents sur Sabbetaï Sevi*, 53.

42. For an example of the classic approach to this topic in the Islamic press, see Yesevizade, "Dönmelerin müm söndü," *Sebil*, June 18, 1976. He says that although it is rumored that Kızılbaş [Alevi] engage in the practice, no one from the group has ever publicly admitted it. On the other hand, Jews [Dönme] (who have a "perverted and exploiter mentality") have admitted to the practice. What frightened him was that the germs of these sick people, "pigs" who "spread sexually perverted propaganda" such as beauty contests and pornographic films, "would infect the entire society."

43. *Vakit*, January 18, 1924, 1–2.

44. "Dönme meselesi: Selânikli genç bir Dönme imzasıyla aldığımız son derece mühim ve şayan-i dikkat bir mektup!" *Resimli Dünya* 15, no. 3 (November 15, 1925): 3–4.

45. See Erol Şadi Erdinç, "Ahmet Emin Yalman: Bir yaşam hikayesi," and "Ahmet Emin Yalman'ın anlattığı dönemler," in Ahmet Emin Yalman, *Yakın tarihte gördüklerim ve geçirdiklerim*, ix–xxii.

46. *Vatan*, January 11, 1924, 1.

47. *Vatan*, January 15, 1924, 2.

48. *Vatan*, January 19, 1924, 2.

49. Interview, fall 2002.

50. *Vatan*, January 17, 1924, 2.

51. *Vatan*, January 22, 1924, 2.

52. *Vatan*, January 20, 1924, 2.

53. Ahmet Midhat Pasha served as grand vizier from July to October 1872, and again from December 1876 to February 1877. After playing a leading role in the coup of 1876 and authoring the Ottoman constitution, he was exiled to Arabia by Sultan Abdülhamid II in 1877; he died, in suspicious circumstances, at Ta'if, near Mecca, in 1884. See Zürcher, *Turkey*, 384–85.

54. Galanté, *Nouveaux documents sur Sabbetaï Sevi*, 62.

55. Apparently, the Karakaş shaved neither their heads nor their beards; the Kapancı did not shave their heads but shaved their faces. The importance of shaving for Dönme distinction led to the claim that all the barbers in Salonika were Dönme. Ben-Tzevi, "Preface," 74; Gordlevsky, "Zur Frage über die 'Dönme,'" 216.

56. Authors from Galanté to Ortaylı have repeated the false assertion. See Galanté, *Nouveaux documents sur Sabbetaï Sevi*, 63.

57. *Vatan*, January 20, 1924, 2.

58. *Vatan*, January 21, 1924, 2.

59. Ibid.

60. *Vatan*, January 22, 1924, 2.

61. David Hollinger, "Amalgamation and Hypodescent: The Question of Ethnoracial Mixture in the History of the United States," *American Historical Review* 108 (2003): 1366.

62. See Viswanathan, *Outside the Fold*, 75–82.

63. Gövsa, *Sabatay Sevi*, 6.

64. Gövsa was a well-known writer and teacher. Zeki Gürel, *İbrahim Alâettin Gövsa*, Türkiye Cumhuriyeti Kültür Bakanlığı, Türk büyükler dizisi (Ankara, 1995). See also Marc David Baer, "Osmanlı Yahudilerinin mesihi ve onun Türkiye Cumhuriyetindeki izleri," trans. Esra Özyürek, *Virgül* 11 (September 1998): 48–51. Gövsa authored nearly forty works of education and literature, popular encyclopaedias and dictionaries. He is especially famous for children's literature. He taught Turkish in a Jewish school in 1910–11 and was the director of the Karakaş Dönme Makriköy [Bakırköy] Girls' School at the beginning of the 1920s. For over a decade, beginning in 1929, he served in parliament, representing Rıza Nur's Sinop as well as Istanbul, and once held the office of chief inspector in the Department of Education. He died of a heart attack on Republic Day while writing his column for the daily *Hürriyet*.

65. Baer, "Osmanlı Yahudilerinin mesihi"; Gürel, *İbrahim Alâettin Gövsa*.

66. *Yedi Gün*, no. 212 (March 31, 1937): 14–6, 26; no. 213 (April 7, 1937): 11–2; no. 214 (April 14, 1937): 12–3; no. 215 (April 21, 1937): 12–3, and no. 216 (April 28, 1937): 12–3, 25. The series mainly concerned the life of Shabbatai Tzevi, with a short section on the Dönme at the end of the last section. The book, which was published two years later, is an expanded version of the series, bringing the

history up to date and discussing the Dönme at length. Page numbers given parenthetically in the text refer to the book, Gövsa, *Sabatay Sevi*.

67. Interview, summer 2006.

68. When Yitzhak Ben-Tzevi visited the descendants of Dönme in 1943 to assess their situation in the new republic, he found that some Dönme prayers were still in use. Ben-Tzevi, "Preface," trans. Lenowitz, 102.

69. Ibid., 72.

70. *Son Saat*, November 26, 1925.

71. *Son Saat*, November 27, 1925.

72. Todd Endelman, "Jewish Self-Hatred in Britain and Germany," in *Two Nations: British and German Jews in Comparative Perspective*, ed. Michael Brenner et al. (Tübingen: Mohr Siebeck, 1999), 344; 362–63.

73. Till Van Rahden, "'Germans of the Jewish Stamm': Visions of Community Between Nationalism and Particularism, 1850 to 1933," in *German History from the Margins, 1800 to the Present*, ed. Mark Roseman, Nils Roemer, and Neil Gregor (Bloomington: Indiana University Press, 2006), 38.

74. Interview in *Vakit* by İhsan Arif, January 17, 1924.

75. Aamir Mufti, "Secularism and Minority: Elements of a Critique," *Social Text* 45 (1995): 75–96.

76. Carlebach, "Ohne Messias: Dönmehs," 176.

77. Viswanathan, *Outside the Fold*, xi.

Chapter 8

1. Tesal, *Selânik'ten İstanbul'a*, 77, 95, 100, 101.

2. Interviews, summer 2003; Yıldız Sertel, *Annem*, 80–81. Perlmann, "Dönme" (cited in Introduction, n. 21, above), claims otherwise: "This change of domicile, the dispersal that followed, the loss of contact with the solid Jewish atmosphere of Salonika, the influence of the secular Turkish national school, all contributed to a growing loss of cohesion and indifference among the younger generation of the *Dönme* although group existence, especially in the area of social welfare, continued."

3. İlkin, "Câvid Bey, Mehmet."

4. Mustafa Rahmi, descendant of Major Sadık's hero Evrenos Ghazi, was an influential and early member of the CUP in Salonika, deputy in the Ottoman parliament in 1908 and 1912, and governor of Izmir in 1914–15, but was also forced into exile and sentenced in absentia for plotting against the president. Mazower, *Salonica, City of Ghosts*, 144–45.

5. Çağlar Keyder, "The Setting," in *Istanbul: Between the Global and the Local*, ed. id. (Lanham, MD: Rowman & Littlefield, 1999), 3.

6. Ibid.

7. Ibid., 6.

8. Ibid.

9. Çağlar Keyder, "The Consequences of the Exchange of Populations for Turkey," in *Crossing the Aegean*, ed. Hirschon, 49.

10. Ibid., 50.

11. Yalman, *Turkey in My Time*, 87, 110.

12. See the discussion of Gramsci in Amanda Anderson, "Cosmopolitanism, Universalism, and the Divided Legacies of Modernity," in *Cosmopolitics: Thinking and Feeling Beyond the Nation*, ed. Pheng Cheah and Bruce Robbins (Minneapolis: University of Minnesota Press, 1998), 270–71.

13. Bruce Robbins, "Comparative Cosmopolitanisms," ibid., 248.

14. Gazi Mustafa Kemal Atatürk, *Atatürk'ün söylev ve demeçleri* (Ankara: Atatürk Kültür Dil ve Tarih Yüksek Kurumu, 1997), 2: 130, cited in Rıfat Bali, "The Politics of Turkification During the Single Party Period," in *Turkey Beyond Nationalism*, ed. Kieser, 47.

15. Ibid., 202–44; Alexandris, *Greek Minority of Istanbul*, 104.

16. Keyder, "Setting," 10.

17. Interview, summer 2003.

18. An unnamed Karakaş interviewee of Aslı Yurddaş ("Mr. B")'s family moved to Teşvikiye in 1949. The Karakaş H. K's grandfather (1914–70) arrived in Eminönü, Istanbul, from Salonika after the population exchange in the 1930s. He settled his family in Nişantaşı in the following decade and had his son educated at the Terakki and Feyziye schools in the 1950s. Members of the family are all buried in the Karakaş section of Istanbul's Bülbüldere Cemetery. Yurddaş, "Meşru vatandaşlık, gayri meşru kimlik?" 25, 139.

19. Almost all of a Karakaş interviewee's male relatives, including his textile-factory-owning grandfather, born between the 1880s and World War I in Salonika, passed away in Istanbul from the 1930s on. Thus one concludes that they were subject to the population exchange, or at least moved to Turkey after Greece took Salonika. Yet one male relative was born in Thessaloníki in 1914 and died there a dozen years later, demonstrating that some Dönme, including children, managed to stay in the city a bit longer. Moreover, some of his female relatives were actually born in Istanbul between World War I and the population exchange. Thus his textile merchant family already had branches established in the Ottoman capital before the population exchange.

20. Yurddaş, "Meşru vatandaşlık, gayri meşru kimlik?" 30.

21. Interview, summer 2006.

22. Interview, summer 2002.

23. MMKTT, A31331. As of 1915, they specialized in forges, steam hammers, cigarette paper, iron cash boxes, and haberdashery in Thessaloníki. See *Salonik: Topographisch-statistische Übersichten*, 147, 161, and 183.

24. MMKTT, 32176.

25. MMKTT, 32176.

26. MMKTT, A31336.

27. Interview, fall 2005.

28. In 1945, Haldun Nüzhet buried his father at the Muslim cemetery in Feriköy, where many Yakubi Dönme lie.

29. Interview, summer 2006. Ahmet Tevfik Ehat's oldest son, Osman Ehat Tevfik, married Marie-Madeleine de Mokrzecka, formerly of St. Petersburg, Russia, in Beyoğlu in 1934. One of their sons, Tevfik Erhat, married a Belgian, Béatrice Bastin, and settled in Belgium; a younger son, Dr. Mustafa Fazıl Ehat, married a Frenchwoman, Yvette Ligeard, in 1954 and settled in France. Ahmet Tevfik Ehat's elder daughter, Fatma Akile Ehat, married the Turkish consul in Antwerp, the Dönme Osman Nuri Nusret, in 1930, but the marriage only lasted about six years. In the late 1940s, the second husband of his youngest daughter, Aisha Azra, a journalist and writer, was Hungarian.

30. Tesal, *Selânik'ten İstanbul'a*, 193.

31. Carlebach, "Ohne Messias: Dönmehs," 176. In Salonika, her family had owned a large home with a courtyard, but in the Turkish Republic, they lived in a hut; in Salonika, they had had the money and the wherewithal to have their youth exempted from military service and lawbreakers released from jail, but in Turkey, her only uncle was conscripted. Where once they had been able to solve their own problems, never having to ask for outside assistance, the Dönme lost their communal sense of responsibility and had to turn to others for help; none was forthcoming. Carlebach, "Ohne Messias: Dönmehs," 183.

32. Sandalcı, *Feyz-i Sıbyân'dan Işık'a Feyziye Mektekpleri*, 29.

33. Ibid., 139. Further page numbers for this source are given parenthetically in the text.

34. MMKTT, A37726.

35. The İpekçi Brothers business in Salonika dealt in crystal and porcelain in 1908, in haberdashery in 1910, and, finally, in blankets, glass and mirrors, furniture and furnishings, perfume, and pianos in 1915. See *Annuaire commercial & administratif du Vilayet de Salonique*, 155; Horton to State Department, June 2, 1910 (cited Chapter 2, n. 58, above); and *Salonik: Topographisch-statistische Übersichten*, 142, 152, 165, 169, and 170.

36. İsmail İpekçi, who had been active in the school since its foundation in Salonika. The *Journal de Salonique* informed its readers on July 13, 1903, that the Feyziye Girls School was looking for a Turkish-speaking administrator who would teach sewing; applicants were to apply to the owner of Bonmarché, İpekçi İsmail Efendi. Sandalcı, *Feyz-i Sıbyân'dan Işık'a Feyziye Mektepleri*, 333.

37. Alkan, *Terakki Vakfı ve Terakki Okulları*, 122.

38. Ibid., 126.

39. Ibid., 133.

40. Alkan, *Terakki Vakfı ve Terakki Okulları*, 135, 144.

41. Namık Kapancı would bequeath 500 lira to the school in his will. Alkan, *Terakki Vakfı ve Terakki Okulları*, 163, 199. On their Salonikan professions, see *Annuaire commercial & administratif du Vilayet de Salonique*, 144, 173, and 178; and *Salonik: Topographisch-statistische Übersichten*, 153, 186.

42. Mecdi Derviş, "Aile ile mektepte elbirliği için en güzel bir masal: Bir hususî mektebimizin 55inci yıldönümü, Şisli Terakki Lisesi, 1879–1934," *Resimli Şark* 38 (February 1934): 1.

43. Interview, summer 2002.

44. As late as 1962, a general board meeting included members of the Telci, Kapancı, and Akev (descendants of Duhani Hasan Akif) families. Alkan, *Terakki Vakfı ve Terakki Okulları*, 207.

45. On the Bülbüldere Cemetery, see www.uskudar-bld.gov.tr/portal/En_/11.jsp?PageName=guideAyr&ID=228 (accessed April 1, 2009).

46. See B. Serdar Savaş, Ömer Karahan, and R. Ömer Saka, "Delivery of Health Care Evaluation Studies, Financing, Health, Health Care Reform, Health System Plans Turkey," in *Health Care Systems in Transition*, ed. Sarah Thomson and Elias Mossialos, vol. 4, no. 4: *Turkey* (Copenhagen: European Observatory on Health Care Systems, 2002), www.euro.who.int/document/E79838.pdf (accessed April 1, 2009).

47. Alkan, *Terakki Vakfı ve Terakki Okulları*, 86.

48. Ibid., 83; *SVS*, 1904–5, 319.

49. *Faros tēs Makedonias*, February 6, 1891, 1.

50. Yılmaz Öztuna, "Selanikli Udi Ahmet Bey," *Türk besteciler ansiklopedisi* (Istanbul: Hayat Neşriyat Anonim Şirketi, 1969), 35.

51. Ho, *Graves of Tarim*, 3, 7.

52. Ibid., 3.

53. Ibid.

Chapter 9

1. Quoted in Ayhan Aktar, "Homogenising the Nation, Turkifying the Economy: The Turkish Experience of Population Exchange Reconsidered," in *Crossing the Aegean*, ed. Hirschon, 81.

2. Aktar, "Nüfusun homojenleştirilmesi ve ekonominin Türkleştirilmesi," 26.

3. Evangelos Hekimoglu, "Thessaloniki, 1912–1940: Economic Developments," in *Thessaloniki: Queen of the Worthy*, ed. Chasiōtēs, 142–54.

4. Arı, *Büyük mübadele*, 63.

5. Yıldız Sertel, *Annem*, 69.

6. An estimate of eighteen thousand is given in Sciaky, *Farewell to Salonica,* 90; that of twenty thousand in Yıldız Sertel, *Annem,* 24.

7. Iōannēs K. Chasiōtēs, "First After the First and Queen of the Worthy: In Search of Perennial Characteristics and Landmarks in the History of Thessaloniki," in *Thessaloniki: Queen of the Worthy,* ed. id., 28; Mazower, *Salonica, City of Ghosts,* 310.

8. Mazower, *Salonica, City of Ghosts,* 327.

9. Interview, summer 2007.

10. *Efēmeris tōn Balkaniōn,* March 21, 1923.

11. Kostas Tomanas, *Chroniko tēs Thessalonikēs, 1821–1944* (Skopelos, Greece: Nēsides, 1996), 39–40.

12. Mazower, *Salonica, City of Ghosts,* 323.

13. MMKTT, 33270.

14. MMKTT, 38629.

15. Mazower, *Salonica, City of Ghosts,* 340.

16. *Efēmeris tōn Balkaniōn,* June 10, 1925.

17. Ibid., June 14, 1925.

18. Ibid., June 15, 1925.

19. Ibid., June 17, 1925.

20. Ibid., October 30, 1927.

21. Tomanas, *Chroniko tēs Thessalonikēs,* 39.

22. Ioannis A. Skourtis, "Prospathies idrisis austriakou emborikou epimelitērēou kai austriakis trapezas stē Thessalonikē (1887–1894)," in Greek Historical Society, *XVI Panhellenic Historical Congress (May 26–28, 1995), Proceedings* (Thessaloníki), 315.

23. Stavroulakis, *Salonika: Jews and Dervishes,* 17.

24. Ibid., 17, 47.

25. Gordlevsky, "Zur Frage über die 'Dönme,'" 200–201.

26. Mazower, *Salonica, City of Ghosts,* 383; Fleming, *Greece: A Jewish History,* 94, 97.

27. Mazower, *Salonica, City of Ghosts,* 410–16.

28. Stavroulakis, *Salonika: Jews and Dervishes,* 383.

29. Ibid., 418.

30. Stavroulakis, *Salonika: Jews and Dervishes,* 18.

31. Interview, summer 2007.

32. Corry Guttstadt, *Die Türkei, die Juden, und der Holocaust* (Berlin: Assoziation A, 2008), 267.

33. Hıfzı Topuz, *100 soruda Türk basın tarihi,* 2nd ed. (Istanbul: Gerçek Yayınevi, 1996), 82–83.

34. Yalman, *Yakın tarihte geçirdiklerim ve gördüklerim,* 2: 1032, 1053.

35. Yıldız Sertel, *Annem,* 115.

36. Topuz, *100 soruda Türk basın tarihi*, 84.

37. Ibid., 97.

38. For a discussion of the dispute, see Emin Karaca, *Türk basınında kalem kavgaları* (Istanbul: Gendaş, 1998), 111–39.

39. Karaca, *Türk basınında kalem kavgaları*, 111.

40. Ibid., 120.

41. Ahmet Emin Yalman, "Yerlerde Türkçe," *Tan* 4 (March 1937). The article appears in Ayhan Aktar, "Cumhuriyetin ilk yıllarında uygulanan 'Türkleştirme' politikaları," in Aktar, *Varlık Vergisi ve 'Türkleştirme' politikaları*, 122–24.

42. Avram Galanti, *Vatandaş Türkçe konuş!* (Istanbul: Hüsn-i Tabiat Matbaası, 1928).

43. Karaca, *Türk basınında kalem kavgaları*, 127–28.

44. *Sebîlürreşat* 23, no. 583 (January 24, 1924): 175.

45. Ibid., 128–9.

46. Ibid., 130.

47. Ibid., 130.

48. Karaca, *Türk basınında kalem kavgaları*, 133.

49. Ibid., 137.

50. Topuz, *100 soruda Türk basın tarihi*, 97.

51. Interview, summer 2002.

52. Interview, summer 2004.

53. However, her grandfather was not a successful businessman, and was distracted by other interests, sports being chief among them. His son, the interviewee's father, first worked as an accountant in Istanbul, and then started a business with four other Dönme from Salonika putting labels on shirts, one of the oldest such businesses in the Turkish Republic.

54. "Turkish Tax Kills Foreign Business," *New York Times*, September 11, 1943, quoted in Rıfat Bali, *The "Varlık Vergisi" Affair: A Study on Its Legacy. Selected Documents* (Istanbul: Isis Press, 2005), 350.

55. Yalman, *Yakın tarihte gördüklerim ve geçirdiklerim*, 2: 1258.

56. Ibid., 2: 1251.

57. Yalman, *Turkey in My Time*, 204.

58. Yalman, *Yakın tarihte gördüklerim ve geçirdiklerim*, 2: 1161.

59. Ibid., 2: 1228.

60. Ibid., 2: 1163.

61. Ibid., 2: 1163–4.

62. Ibid., 2: 1259.

63. Bali, *"Varlık Vergisi" Affair*, 53.

64. Yalman, *Turkey in My Time*, 204.

65. Faik Ökte, *Varlık Vergisi faciası* (Istanbul: Nebioğlu Yayınevi, 1951), 81.

66. In Yılmaz Karakoyunlu's novel *Salkım Hanımın taneleri* [Mrs. Salkım's

Pearls] (Istanbul: Simavi Yayınları, 1990), which deals mainly with the wealth tax, and the film of the same title directed by Tomris Giritlioğlu in 1999, the Dönme category is incorrectly depicted as including, not the Dönme who are the subject of this book, but rather any former convert to Islam. See Ayhan Aktar, "Malın var, mı, derdin var!" *Radikal* 2, November 28, 1999.

67. United Kingdom, Public Record Office, FO 371/33376/R8573/810/44, December 12, 1942, quoted in Bali, *"Varlık Vergisi" Affair*, 408.

68. Leyla Neyzi, "Remembering to Forget: Sabbateanism, National Identity, and Subjectivity in Turkey," *Comparative Studies in Society and History* 44, no. 1 (2002): 145–46, 149.

69. Bali, *"Varlık Vergisi" Affair*, 246.

70. See Rıfat Bali, "Yirmi Kur'a İhtiyatlar olayı," *Tarih ve Toplum* 179 (November 1998): 4–18.

71. See Konuk, "Eternal Guests, Mimics, and *Dönme*," 24n61.

72. For a detailed account, see Douglas Frantz and Catherine Collins, *Death on the Black Sea: The Untold Story of the Struma and World War II's Holocaust at Sea* (New York: ecco, 2003).

73. Corinna Görgü Guttstadt, "Depriving Non-Muslims of Citizenship as Part of the Turkification Policy in the Early Years of the Turkish Republic: The Case of Turkish Jews and Its Consequences During the Holocaust," in *Turkey Beyond Nationalism*, ed. Kieser, 50–56. For a detailed account of the tragic fate of Jewish citizens of Turkey in Nazi-occupied Europe, see also id., *Die Türkei, die Juden und der Holocaust*, esp. 259–485. Guttstadt's work disproves most of the claims made in Stanford Shaw, *Turkey and the Holocaust: Turkey's Role in Rescuing Turkish and European Jewry from Nazi Persecution 1933–45* (New York: Macmillan, 1993).

74. Guttstadt, *Die Türkei, die Juden, und der Holocaust*, 365.

75. Bali, *Cumhuriyet yıllarında Türkiye Yahudileri*, 551.

76. Ertan Aydın, "Secular Conversion as a Turkish Revolutionary Project in the 1930s," in *Converting Cultures*, ed. Washburn and Reinhart, 161.

77. Bali, *Cumhuriyet yıllarında Türkiye Yahudileri*, 538–41.

78. U.S. diplomatic cable, spring 1943, quoted in Bali, *"Varlık Vergisi" Affair*, 95.

79. Bali, *"Varlık Vergisi" Affair*, 36.

80. Leyla Tavşanoğlu, interview with Cahit Kayra, *Cumhuriyet*, December 19, 1999, quoted in Neyzi, "Remembering to Forget," 146.

81. Bali, *"Varlık Vergisi" Affair*, 52.

82. Ibid., 40.

83. Cemil Koçak, *Türkiye'de millî şef dönemi (1938–1945)* (Istanbul: İletişim, 1996), 2: 508, quoted in Bali, *"Varlık Vergisi" Affair*, 55.

84. Bali, *"Varlık Vergisi" Affair*, 89.

85. Ibid., 120.

86. Interview, summer 2004.

87. As reported in "Turkish Tax Kills Foreign Business," *New York Times*, September 11, 1943, quoted in Bali, *"Varlık Vergisi" Affair*, 350.

88. Bali, *"Varlık Vergisi" Affair*, 11.

89. Şevket Süreyya Aydemir, *İkinci adam*, 7th ed. (Istanbul: Remzi, 1991), 2: 235–36, quoted in Bali, *"Varlık Vergisi" Affair*, 56–57.

90. Bali, *"Varlık Vergisi" Affair*, 46.

91. Ibid., 53.

92. Ibid., 85.

93. Ahmet E. Yalman, "Berbad bir rahatsızlık," *Vatan*, September 25, 1944.

94. Yalman, *Turkey in My Time*, 204.

95. Ibid., 203, 205.

96. Yalman, *Yakın tarihte gördüklerim ve geçirdiklerim*, 2: 1250–57. See also Rıdvan Akar, *Aşkale yolcuları: Varlık Vergisi ve çalışma kampları* (Istanbul: Belge Yayınları, 1999); Bali, *Cumhuriyet yıllarında Türkiye Yahudileri*, 424–95; Ayhan Aktar, "Varlık Vergisi nasıl uygulandı?" in id., *Varlık Vergisi*, 135–214; id., "Varlık Vergisi sırasında gayri menkul satışları ile servet transferi: Istanbul tapu kayıtlarının analizi," in ibid., 215–43; Ökte, *Varlık Vergisi faciası*; Lewis, *Emergence of Modern Turkey*, 297–302; and Alexandris, *Greek Minority of Istanbul*, 207–33.

97. Yalman, *Yakın tarihte gördüklerim ve geçirdiklerim*, 2: 1252.

98. "I saw firsthand the pure and robust mountainous surroundings so beneficial to the health and I learned from the locals of just how well the persons who had been sent there were treated, of the ease and comfort in which they lived and of the great facilities that they found there to regain their health." Yalman, *Yakın tarihte gördüklerim ve geçirdiklerim*, 2: 1252. This sentiment is contradicted by testimonies of those who actually did time there.

99. Alexandris, *Greek Minority of Istanbul*, 220.

100. Yalman, *Yakın tarihte gördüklerim ve geçirdiklerim*, 2:1259.

101. Ibid., 133.

102. Yalman, *Turkey in My Time*, 3.

103. Ibid., 279.

104. Yalman, *Yakın tarihte gördüklerim ve geçirdiklerim*, 1: 12–13.

105. Ibid., 11.

106. Ibid., 11, 15.

107. Ibid., 20.

108. Ibid., 701.

109. Ibid., 205.

110. Ibid., 124.

111. Ibid., 311–12.

112. Ibid., 2: 884.

113. Ibid., 897.

114. Ibid., 899.

115. Ibid., 952.

116. Yıldız Sertel, *Annem*, 175–76.

117. Ibid., 175.

118. Ibid., 188.

119. Ibid., 198.

120. Ibid., 311.

121. Ibid., 193–94.

122. Ibid., 212.

123. Ibid., 221.

124. Ibid., 214.

125. Ibid., 223.

126. Ibid., 290.

127. Ibid., 234. Ultimately, they settled in Azerbaijan in the USSR in the early 1960s. Sabiha Sertel was buried in Baku in 1968. Through the 1970s, in the mind of the public she remained the stereotypical anti-Muslim, atheist, disloyal, communist journalist Dönme. Ibid., 237, 240.

128. See Soner Çağaptay, *Islam, Secularism, and Nationalism in Modern Turkey: Who Is a Turk?* (New York: Routledge, 2006). Çağaptay argues that the ethnicization of religion—the collapsing of the categories Muslim and Turkish—explains why many Muslim groups were accepted as Turks in the early republic yet Christians were excluded from the body of the nation. Failing to concede the extent to which racism was prominent in the early republic, however, he argues, contrary to historical evidence, that Jews—separated from others mainly by their linguistic choices, he contends—were only marginalized, and not the victims of exclusion or government antisemitism.

129. See Viswanathan, *Outside the Fold*, 82–89.

130. TBMM, Zabit Ceridesi, Devre: 1 Cilt: 4, October 4, 1920, 478, cited in Eissenstat, "Metaphors of Race and Discourse of Nation," 246.

131. *Türk vatandaşlık hukuku: Metinler, mahkeme kararları*, ed. Ilhan Unut (Ankara: Sevinç Matbaası, 1966), 39–42, cited in Eissenstat, "Metaphors of Race and Discourse of Nation," 249.

132. Andrew Davison, *Secularism and Revivalism in Turkey: A Hermeneutic Reconsideration* (New Haven: Yale University Press, 1998), 2.

133. Aydın, "Secular Conversion as a Turkish Revolutionary Project."

134. Asad, *Genealogies of Religion*, 40–41.

135. Viswanathan, *Outside the Fold*, 97.

136. For a comparison with the experience of Karaite, communist, and bourgeois Jews in Egypt and a critique of nationalist histories denying that Jews can

be Egyptian, see Joel Beinin, *The Dispersion of Egyptian Jewry: Culture, Politics, and the Formation of a Modern Diaspora* (Berkeley: University of California Press, 1998).

Conclusion

1. Van der Veer, *Imperial Encounters*, 14.

2. Ibid., 19.

3. Ibid., 20.

4. It was not theocracy or the alleged militaristic and intolerant nature of Islam that impelled the forced migration and massacres of Armenians in 1915–17, but rather new, secular concepts of nation and race.

5. See, e.g., Zorlu, *Evet, ben Selânikliyim*; Baer, "Revealing a Hidden Community"; and Eden and Stavroulakis, *Salonica: A Family Cookbook*.

6. Esin Eden, *Annemin yemek defteri: Selanik, Münih, Brüksel, İstanbul* (Istanbul: Oğlak Yayınları, 2001).

7. See Elqayam, "Bishulim Shabtaim."

8. Dumont, "Franc-Maçonnerie," 92.

9. Macar, "Yeni Cami," 29. The Dönme mosque was closed in 1940 and re-opened only in 1953; in 1968, it became a storehouse for the new archaeological museum. In 1973, the Greek Orthodox Church sought to turn it into a church, but without success. More recently, it has been used as gallery for temporary exhibits.

10. Maria Lilimpaki of the Organization for the Master Plan Implementation and Environmental Protection of Thessaloníki (which then occupied the building), interview, Thessaloníki, summer 2003. *In memoriam: Hommage aux victimes juives des Nazis en Grèce*, 88, 93, calls Kapancı's house a Jewish villa; Mazower, *Salonica, City of Ghosts*, 400, refers to it as a suburban villa.

11. Chasiôtês, "First After the First and Queen of the Worthy," the lead article in an edited volume published in 1997 to celebrate the history of the city, ignores the Dönme role in investing their own resources and serving as the crucial intermediaries transforming the city and instead praises Belgian, British, and French interests (23).

12. These conceptions of time come from David Harvey, "Geographical Knowledges / Political Powers," in *The Promotion of Knowledge: Lectures to Mark the Centenary of the British Academy, 1902–2002*, ed. John Morrill (New York: Oxford University Press, 2004), 87–115.

13. Yurddaş, "Meşru vatandaşlık, gayri meşru kimlik?" 60, 30.

14. Interview, fall 2005.

15. Yurddaş, "Meşru vatandaşlık, gayri meşru kimlik?" 64, 78–84.

16. See Bali, "Bir diğer düşman: Dönmeler veya gizli Yahudiler"; Yurddaş,

"Meşru vatandaşlık, gayri meşru kimlik?" 21–22. For an example of anti-Dönme writing, where the author conflates "Jewish" with "Dönme" and employs antisemitic rhetoric throughout, see Mehmet Şevket Eygi, *İki kimlikli, gizli, esrarlı ve çok güçlü bir cemaat: Yahudi Türkler yahut Sabetaycılar* (Istanbul: Zvi-Geyik, 2000).

17. Ahmet Yıldız, *Ne mutlu Türküm diyebilene: Türk ulusal kimliğinin etnoseküler sınırları (1919–1938)* (Istanbul: İletişim, 2001), 16–18; Zürcher, *Turkey*, 198–99.

18. "About the 'Mohammedan Greeks'!" *Turkey*, no. 2, March 1921, 6, cited in Hans-Lukas Kieser, "An Ethno-Nationalist Revolutionary and Theorist of Kemalism: Dr. Mahmut Esat Bozkurt, 1892–1943" in *Turkey Beyond Nationalism*, ed. id., 23.

19. İsmet İnönü in *Vakit*, April 27, 1925, cited in Füsun Üstel, *İmparatorluk'tan ulus-devlete Türk milliyetçiliği Türk ocakları, 1912–31* (Istanbul: İletişim, 1997), 173, and in Bali, "Politics of Turkification," in *Turkey Beyond Nationalism*, ed. Kieser, 44.

20. Mahmut Esat in *Son Posta*, September 20, 1930, cited in Şaduman Halıcı, *Yeni Türkiye'de devletin yapılmasında Mahmut Esat Bozkurt (1892–1943)* (Ankara: Atatürk Araştırma Merkezi, 2004), 348, and in Kieser, "An Ethno-Nationalist Revolutionary and Theorist of Kemalism," 25.

21. "Masonluk meselesi, sabık adliye vekili Mahmut Esat Beyin Masonlara cevabı I," *Anadolu*, October 18, 1931, cited in Hakkı Uyar, *"Sol milliyetçi" bir Türk aydını Mahmut Esat Bozkurt (1892–1943)* (Ankara: Büke, 2000), 72, and in Kieser, "An Ethno-Nationalist Revolutionary and Theorist of Kemalism," 27.

22. See Ahmet Almaz and Pelin Batu, *Geçmişten günümüze Yahudilik tarihi* (İstanbul: Nokta, 2007); and Eygi, *Yahudi Türkler yahut Sabetaycılar*.

23. Van der Veer, *Imperial Encounters*, 21.

24. Valensi, "Conversion, intégration, exclusion," 180–81.

25. Derek R. Peterson and Darren R. Walhof, "Rethinking Religion," in *The Invention of Religion: Rethinking Belief in Politics and History*, ed. id. (New Brunswick, NJ: Rutgers University Press, 2002), 8.

26. See the presentation of this model in Richard Eaton, *The Rise of Islam and the Bengal Frontier, 1204–1760* (Berkeley: University of California Press, 1993), 269–90.

27. Reinkowski, "Hidden Believers, Hidden Apostates," 427.

28. Nissimi, *Crypto-Jewish Mashhadis*, 37.

29. Hertz, *How Jews Became Germans*, 193.

30. See Esra Özyürek, "Convert Alert: German Muslims and Turkish Christians as Threats to Security in the New Europe," *Comparative Studies in Society & History* 51, no. 1 (January 2009): 91–116.

31. Baskın Oran, "The Story of Those Who Stayed: Lessons from Articles 1 and 2 of the 1923 Convention," in *Crossing the Aegean*, ed. Hirschon, 110.

32. Alevis themselves in Germany and Turkey are today debating whether Alevism is simply the true interpretation of Islam, a sect of Shi'ism, or a separate religion.

33. Yalman, *Yakın tarihte gördüklerim ve geçirdiklerim*, 2: 1018.

34. Faur, *In the Shadow of History*, 3.

35. There were, however, massacres of Alevi following uprisings (Sheikh Said in 1925, Dersim in 1937).

36. Distrust of Alevi has led to periodic outbursts of sectarian violence against the group, such as the burning of the Madımak Hotel in Sivas in east-central Turkey in 1993 by radical Islamists, which killed thirty-seven writers and musicians gathered for an Alevi cultural conference. On the Alevi, see Esra Özyürek, "Beyond Integration and Recognition: Diasporic Constructions of Alevi Muslim Identity Between Germany and Turkey," in *Transnational Transcendance: Essays on Religion and Globalization*, ed. Thomas J. Csordas (Berkeley: University of California Press, forthcoming, 2009); David Shankland, *The Alevis in Turkey: The Emergence of a Secular Islamic Tradition* (London: Routledge Curzon, 2003); *Turkey's Alevi Enigma: A Comprehensive Overview*, ed. Paul J. White and Joost Jongerden (Leiden: Brill, 2003); Hülya Küçük, *The Role of the Bektāshīs in Turkey's National Struggle* (Leiden: Brill, 2002); Harald Schüler, *Türkiye'de sosyal demokrasi: particilik, hemşehrilik, Alevilik* (Istanbul: İletişim, 1999); Irene Melikoff, *Hacı Bektaş: Efsaneden gerçeğe* (Istanbul: Cumhuriyet Kitapları, 2004; 1998); and *Alevi Identity: Cultural, Religious and Social Perspectives. Papers Read at a Conference Held at the Swedish Research Institute in Istanbul, November 25–27, 1996*, ed. Tord Olsson et al. (Istanbul: Swedish Research Institute in Istanbul, 1998).

37. Slezkine, *Jewish Century*, 36–37.

38. Ibid., 41, 43.

39. Jacobs, *Hidden Heritage*, 28.

40. Ibid., 29.

41. Ibid., 30.

42. Gilman, *Jew's Body*, 169–93.

43. Levi, *Türkiye Cumhuriyeti'nde Yahudiler*, 110.

44. Günay Göksu Özdoğan, *"Turan"dan "Bozkurt"a: Tek parti döneminde Türkçülük, 1931–1946* (Istanbul: İletişim Yayınları, 2001), 197.

45. Renée Levine Melammed, *Heretics or Daughters of Israel? The Crypto-Jewish Women of Castile* (New York: Oxford University Press, 2002), 7.

46. This concept of the stranger or outsider comes from Georg Simmel, quoted in Wolff, *Sociology of Georg Simmel*, 402–8, cited in Jacobs, *Hidden Heritage*, 127.

47. Tomas Atencio, "Crypto-Jewish Remnants in Manito Society and Culture," *Jewish Folklore and Ethnology Review* 18 (1996): 59–68.

48. Brian Pullan, "'A Ship with Two Rudders': 'Righetto Marrano' and the Inquisition in Venice," *Historical Journal* 20 (1977): 25–58.

49. Sartre, *Anti-Semite and Jew,* trans. Becker, 143, quoted in Shohat, "Post-Fanon and the Colonial," in id., *Taboo Memories, Diasporic Voices,* 253.

50. See Rıfat Bali, "II. Dünya Savaş yıllarında Türkiye'de azınlıklar: 'Balat Fırınları' söylentisi," *Tarih ve Toplum* 180 (December 1998): 11–17; and Laurent Mallet, "Karikatür dergisinde Yahudilerle ilgili karikatürler, 1936-1948," *Toplumsal Tarih* 34 (1996): 26-33.

51. Quoted in Mazower, *Salonica, City of Ghosts,* 395.

52. Mazower, *Salonica, City of Ghosts,* 410. For the text, see *Documents on the History of the Greek Jews: Records from the Historical Archives of the Ministry of Foreign Affairs,* ed. Photini Constantopoulou and Thanos Veremis, 2nd ed. (Athens: Kastaniotis Editions, 1999), 254–56. Archbishop Damaskinos and other eminent Athenians asked for "the suspension of the expulsion of the Jews."

53. Bessemer, "Who Is a Crypto-Jew?"

54. Interview, summer 2007.

55. Frantz Fanon writes of the stigma of race: seeing oneself as a despised outsider, internalizing the image of the detested one, seeing oneself through the racist eyes of the majority culture that hates one. Frantz Fanon, *Black Skin, White Masks,* trans. Constance Farrington (New York: Grove Press, 1967).

Postscript

1. Yalman, *Turkey in My Time,* 255.

2. Ibid., 258.

3. Ibid., 4, 251.

4. "Hicazdeki veba bir Yahudi oyunudur!" *Büyük Doğu,* July 17, 1952, 1; Slezkine, *Jewish Century,* 308.

5. Such as in *Büyük Doğu,* August 22, 1952, 1.

6. "Avdeti Ahmet Emin," *Büyük Doğu,* May 29, 1952, 1. The cartoon of Yalman as a spider appeared in the August 19 issue. Numerous articles in the same newspaper in June and July 1952 focused on the beauty contests and the paper reprinted a photograph of two American sailors kissing a Turkish contestant.

7. *Büyük Doğu,* August 30, 1952, 1. For the assassination attempt, see Yalman, *Yakın tarihte gördüklerim ve geçirdiklerim,* 2: 1589–1621.

8. *Ulus,* November 23–27, 1952. Üzmez later proudly described taking the gun from his accomplice's hand, when the latter became immobilized by panic, and firing six shots. He expressed no remorse and speaks of his great disappointment when he learned Yalman had not died. When Yalman's wife visited him in jail immediately after the attack, he told her he would finish the job as soon as he was released. Hüseyin Üzmez, *Çilenin böylesi* (1977), 6th ed. (Istanbul:

Timaş, 2002), 10. After serving part of his sentence, Üzmez eventually earned a law degree and worked for several government ministries in the 1970s and 1980s. He is currently a writer for the Islamist newspapers *Akit* and *Vakit*. On his book's jacket, the former prime minister Necmettin Erbakan praises him for being "like a stone crusher smashing into powder every stone appearing as an obstacle in the path of national and spiritual issues."

9. Yalman, *Turkey in My Time*, 252–23. Given this charge, it is ironic that Üzmez himself was arrested in December 2008 for paying a mother to have sexual relations with her fourteen-year-old daughter.

10. Ibid., 159, 252, 261.

11. Karaca, *Türk basınında kalem kavgaları*, 224–25.

12. See Jacob Landau, *Tekinalp: Turkish Patriot, 1883–1961* (Istanbul: Nederlands Historisch-Archaeologisch Instituut te Istanbul, 1984). Yalman passed away in 1973. The Yalman family tomb in the Muslim cemetery in Feriköy is plain, without ornamentation, or anything Islamic, a very tall and wide, book-shaped white marble block, with only "Yalman Family" and a dozen names of family members inscribed on it. Another prominent journalist of Dönme origin, Abdi İpekçi (b. 1929), was not so lucky. He was assassinated in 1979 by Mehmet Ali Ağca, who would later attempt to kill Pope John Paul II.

13. See Nissimi, *Crypto-Jewish Mashhadis*, 18–21.

14. Wachtel, *Foi du souvenir*, 330–31.

15. *Sakladım söylemedim/Derdim gizli uyuttum.*

16. Valensi, "Conversion, intégration, exclusion," 182.

Index

Italicized page numbers refer to illustrations.

Made in the USA
Columbia, SC
04 May 2020

95873463R00214